Me
and
Shakespeare

Adventures with the Bard

Me *and* Shakespeare

Herman Gollob

DOUBLEDAY
New York London Toronto
Sydney Auckland

PUBLISHED BY DOUBLEDAY

a division of Random House, Inc.

1540 Broadway, New York, New York 10036

DOUBLEDAY and the portrayal of an anchor with a dolphin are
trademarks of Doubleday, a division of Random House, Inc.

Book design by Deborah Kerner/Dancing Bears Design

Photo on title page: William Shakespeare,
attributed to John Taylor. By courtesy
of the National Portrait Gallery, London

Library of Congress Cataloging-in-Publication Data

Gollob, Herman.
    Me and Shakespeare: adventures with the Bard /
Herman Gollob.— 1st ed.
        p.   cm.
    1. Gollob, Herman.   2. Shakespeare, William, 1564–1616—
    Study and teaching—United States.   3. Shakespeare, William,
    1564–1616—Appreciation—United States.   4. English teachers—
    United States—Biography.   5. Oxford (England)—Description and
    travel.   I. Title.

PR2972.G65 A3 2002
822.3'3—dc21   2001053799

ISBN 0-385-49817-9

PRINTED IN THE UNITED STATES OF AMERICA

May 2002
First Edition
10   9   8   7   6   5   4   3   2   1

FOR BARBARA

Contents

Part One

Gladly Learn, Gladly Teach

*A*nd gladly would he learn,
And gladly teach.

—GEOFFREY CHAUCER,
The Canterbury Tales

1.

Somewhat past the middle of the journey, my life had taken an unexpected turn. On a golden day in October 1997, I found myself driving to Caldwell College, a small Catholic school in New Jersey operated by Dominican nuns, where I would be teaching an eight-week, two-hours-per-week course on Shakespeare to adults over fifty.

This would be my first experience as a teacher. I was not a Shakespeare scholar. At the age of sixty-seven, I was embarking on what might turn out to be a new career, a reinvention of myself.

The thrills and chills accompanying a journey into the unpredictable were escalating into the queasiness and near-panic of that primal terror, stage fright. I felt I had to bedazzle the audience that awaited me; I needed to prove myself as someone capable of bringing the work of Shakespeare dramatically alive for mature students, filling his plays with an immediacy that would make them resonate in the hearts and minds of the class as it had in mine during a recent period of obsessive self-instruction. Moreover, I wanted these people to adore me.

I'd been rehearsing the introductory lecture for two weeks, day and night, to the point where I knew much of it from memory, and I began reciting it aloud as I drove west on Bloomfield Avenue, through the town of Verona, no less, toward another beginning: "I'm Herman Gollob, and I'll be your guide for the next two months on a magical mystery tour of what Ralph Waldo Emerson described as the Planet Shakespeare."

The noted and notably idiosyncratic twentieth-century man of letters Ford Madox Ford once referred to himself as an old man made mad by a love of writing. I'd become an old man made mad by a love of Shakespeare.

How had it happened?

Early in the spring of 1995, I decided to retire in July, when I turned sixty-five. For more than thirty-five years I'd been editing books for a variety of publishers in various capacities, some of them managerial, and I'd ultimately maneuvered myself into the executive hierarchy as a senior vice-president.

A certain weariness had begun to overtake me. In fact, I'd begun to resemble my briefcase: outside, battered and worn; inside, musty and cluttered. In a short story by the singularly gifted and, alas, recently deceased American writer Andre Dubus, an editor is haunted by the idea that he carries around an author's dreams in his briefcase. But in reality he also carries, all too often, evidence of an author's unfulfilled promise, unrealized expectations, and irremediable incompetence. T. S. Eliot, in one of his *Four Quartets,* "East Coker," described writing as "a raid on the inarticulate / With shabby equipment always deteriorating," and I discovered that in my case Eliot could just as well have been describing the editorial process.

For some time the fun had gone out of publishing. My competitive fires were banked; the hunger to acquire new books, the thrill at discovering new authors and championing them inside the company and in the Darwinian world of commerce, had subsided. Worse, I'd begun to greet submissions from agents not with a sense of expectancy but with resentment: why was I being asked to consider yet another lame and halt manuscript that would have been better served had it been placed into the hands of a faith healer? My career was no longer an adventure in the exciting and political New York literary scene, crackling with suspense, but a recurring cycle of the predictable and familiar. Again, T. S. Eliot seemed to be speaking to me, in yet another of his quartets, "Little Gidding":

> *Let me disclose the gifts reserved for age*
> *To set a crown upon your lifetime's effort.*
> *First, the cold friction of expiring sense*
> *Without enchantment, offering no promise*
> *But bitter tastelessness of shadow fruit. . . .*
> *And last, the rending pain of re-enactment*
> *Of all that you have done. . . .*

In compensation, I'd entered what Erik Erikson terms "the stage of generativity," the concern for guiding the next generation. I'd become the tribal elder, fifteen years older than the next oldest colleague and old enough to be the father of many of the rest. I'd evolved into something of a mentor, and this I did relish. But it wasn't enough to fill the day, or the spirit, and I didn't want to find myself changing from Jethro, Moses' sage counselor and father-in-law, into Falstaff, an old reprobate roistering with young bloods and recalling the chimes at midnight.

Publishing was no longer a country for old men? Was it ever?

It was time to retire.

My decision coincided with Passover. At our Seder, my wife, Barbara, asked our guests to describe how they were released from some form of bondage during the past year. I said I'd been delivered from bondage to a career, and someone at the table quipped, "Yes, and now it's time for those forty years in the desert."

But I didn't envision retirement as a sojourn, lonely and afraid, in a sterile and forbidden realm. It would be my very own Messianic Age, a time of peace and contentment and goodwill to all, my career not extinct but resurrected in a Higher Form. I would avoid the grind of indiscriminate freelancing and hire out as a samurai editor exclusively for manuscripts I thought worth the effort, some of which I'd acquired on the basis of prospectuses while still on the job and which had yet to be completed. I would spend more time as a hospice volunteer, a community service I'd undertaken three years previously, hoping to give the kind of comfort to those in the final stages of cancer that I'd been unable to devote to my proud and stubborn old father, who, when stricken with prostate cancer at the age of eighty-one, remained by his own choice in Houston, Texas, where he'd lived most of his life, too far for any regular hands-on care and comfort from me.

Mainly, though, I would loaf and invite my soul. I would read that library of books, watch that hoard of videotapes, listen to that cache of CDs I'd amassed for this paradisiacal era.

It would be a time of self-enlightenment, self-enlargement. "A lot of 'selfs' in there," Barbara noted when I described this Grand Design to her. "Yes," I replied, "I'm going to think only of myself." Her answer: a raised eyebrow, implying, "So what's new?" She had once observed that I was at once the most self-absorbed and least introspective person she'd ever known. In truth, I constantly thought about myself: what I was doing, where I was going, who was with me, who was against me, how did I look, how did I feel, etc., etc. But rarely did I give a thought to the *who* of me, the *why* of me. Years ago, in my forties, a friend of mine who'd been in analysis for decades asked me why I'd never been curious about taking a guided tour of my psyche. "A therapist named Karen Horney wrote a book titled *The Neurotic Personality of Our Time*. She could have had you in mind, Herm." He suggested I make an appointment with his therapist, a woman whom he described as pragmatic and hard-nosed. Suspending my profound skepticism about psychoanalysis, which too often, it seemed to me, kept self-indulgent narcissists locked in perpetual and fruitless treatment, I decided at least to test the waters.

At my first session, the doctor, middle-aged, with short brown hair cut in bangs, and a faint Teutonic accent (perfect!), asked me to tell her about my mother and father. "That's personal," I said.

"I beg your pardon?" she replied, with a slight smile; surely I jested.

But I was deadly serious, irked that someone I'd just met, psychiatrist or no, expected me to open up with guns blazing at my parents. "I said that's personal. Private. I don't talk to strangers about my mama and daddy."

"But psychiatry is all about the personal and private. It's about reaching those areas you've kept personal and private all too long. If you resist doing this, we're wasting our time, and your money. And I won't be a stranger to you for long."

That's where you're wrong, lady, I thought. You'll always be a stranger to me. But I said, "Thanks, but I'm not ready for this." So ended my brief interlude on the couch.

And here I was, sixty-five, self-absorbed and nonintrospective. Was it too late to reverse this trait? Appropriately enough, the process had begun when I encountered, a few weeks before retiring, that enduringly fascinating and enigmatic soul-searcher Prince Hamlet of Denmark, portrayed on the New York stage by Ralph Fiennes in a production that had become all the rage in London and now on Broadway. Swept up in the excitement generated by the press, I actually stood in line for over an hour to buy tickets at the box office a few days after the play opened. Waiting for my turn at the window, I realized with a certain shock that I'd never seen a stage performance of *Hamlet,* not even Richard Burton's in the mid-sixties. Why had I missed that one? I couldn't recall. Of course there were the film Hamlets: Laurence Olivier, Nicol Williamson, Mel Gibson. Gibson's I'd avoided—perhaps out of snobbery (I mean, after all, he's not a classic actor) or just plain indifference. Williamson's mercurial prince I'd seen in the 1970s, in the gripping production directed by Tony Richardson, with Anthony Hopkins as an energetic, youthful, and not unlikable Claudius. And Olivier's, the first of the movie Hamlets, was one of the monumental artistic and commercial triumphs of the 1940s, creating a sensation which exceeded that enjoyed by the recent *Shakespeare in Love,* and catapulted Olivier onto the cover of *Time.*

So pervasive had been the success of Olivier's *Hamlet,* which he also directed, that it even managed to infiltrate the rural precincts of College Station, home of Texas A&M, in those days a military college, where I was a sophomore. It drew long lines at the campus theatre, called the Campus Theatre (no-nonsense nomenclature prevailing in a military environment).

The night I saw *Hamlet,* I returned to my quarters to find my roommate at the time, Sam Tom Stackhouse, swilling a Coke (he consumed about a dozen a day) and poring over an encyclopedia published in 1879, a gift from his grandmother, a family heirloom, I imagined, which he used largely to the exclusion of his textbooks and which may have contributed to his failing several of his courses. Sam Tom hailed from a small town in central Texas. Sam Tom was six feet two inches tall and athletic. He'd rejected a basketball scholarship to Texas A&M because he no longer enjoyed the discipline and demand of organized sports. He wanted to play games just for the fun of it all, much to the displeasure of his daddy, who'd been a guard on the Aggie football team back in the twenties, and of the coaches, who constantly pressured him to change his mind. He was inherently smart but essentially uneducated: the academic standards at his high school were not taxing, however, and he'd graduated as class valedictorian. When I entered our room, he looked up from his book of wisdom and asked where I'd been. I replied that I'd just seen *Hamlet.* "What's that?" he said, not a question you might anticipate from a class valedictorian in most schools. I explained that it was the story of a young guy whose uncle had murdered his father, prompting the guy to seek revenge. Also, the uncle had married the guy's mother and had probably been fucking her before the murder. "Does the guy get killed in the end?" asked Sam Tom.

This was not an idle question. Sam Tom avoided any movie in which the hero was slain; he could not endure the deaths of good guys—it was not the way the world was supposed to be.

I thought for a moment before answering Sam Tom. Then I said no, Hamlet does not get killed. It was a white lie: I didn't want to deprive him of a significant cultural experience. I only hoped he wouldn't search for a reference to *Hamlet* in his trusty encyclopedia, but then again, the editors of that volume might have considered *Hamlet* too esoteric for their readership.

So off went Sam Tom to the Campus Theatre, returning in a few hours in a tearful rage. "Goddamn you, roommate, you told me the fucking guy didn't get killed!" He had experienced pure catharsis. Unlike those of us who have read the play long before seeing it for the first time, Sam Tom had been the naive spectator, unaware of what was going to happen next, held in suspense until those final heartrending moments, expecting that any second a doctor would rush in with an antidote for the poison: "Here, son, take a swig of this and you'll feel better in no time." More to the point, he had a better reason to identify with Hamlet than most adolescents.

When I'd first met Sam Tom, he'd told me that his father was the mailman in town, and I concluded that despite his Aggie education, or perhaps because of it, Daddy was some dog-ass sharecropper who needed to earn the extra pennies by toting Sears catalogs to his equally dog-ass neighbors. Then I discovered that he was a prosperous farmer who simply dropped off the mail as a favor to his tenants, who constituted most of the town's population. Sam Tom very likely saw in Hamlet an image of himself, a teenager enduring the rites of passage, pressured by his powerful father and the macho ethos of the state to do something against his nature—play college sports.

Standing in line at a New York theatre, recalling that episode at Aggieland almost fifty years in the past, I considered myself not that far removed from old Sam Tom in my innocence about things Shakespearean.

An English major, I'd taken the obligatory Shakespeare course, but it was only a semester, and there was much we'd neglected, especially the so-called romances—*Cymbeline, Pericles,* and *The Winter's Tale,* which I'd yet to read. Ditto *Troilus and Cressida, All's Well That Ends Well,* and *Coriolanus.* I could count on the fingers of one hand the Shakespeare dramas I'd seen onstage: *Antony and Cleopatra* with Laurence Olivier and Vivien Leigh in their acclaimed 1951 New York production; *Much Ado About Nothing* with John Gielgud and Margaret Leighton, in a tent theatre on the banks of the Charles River in Boston; *Romeo and Juliet,* starring John Barrymore, Jr., and of all people Margaret O'Brien (still pronouncing *r* as *w:* Womeo, Womeo) at the Pasadena Playhouse; *Macbeth,* directed by and starring Nicol Williamson at Circle in the Square, New York, a fiasco of almost farcical proportions; and *Othello,* starring James Earl Jones and Christopher Plummer at the American Festival Shakespeare Theatre in Stratford, Connecticut. Not once had I ventured to the New York Shakespeare Festival, indoors or in Central Park, which means I'd missed among other treats George C. Scott's Richard III, an exuberant *Much Ado* set in late-nineteenth-century America and starring Sam Waterston, and a production of *Hamlet* also starring Mr. Waterston. I scored higher when it came to Shakespeare on film: the Olivier productions, *Hamlet, Henry V, Othello, The Merchant of Venice, King Lear;* Franco Zefferelli's peerless *Romeo and Juliet;* Joseph Mankiewicz's *Julius Caesar,* with matchless performances by John Gielgud as Cassius and a much-underrated Marlon Brando as Mark Antony; Trevor Nunn's made-for-TV *Antony and Cleopatra,* surely the most perfect rendition attainable, with Richard Johnson, Janet Suzman, Patrick Stewart, and Corin Redgrave. And oh yes, years ago I'd seen the Hallmark Hall of Fame's televised *Macbeth,* starring Maurice Evans and Judith Anderson.

Th-th-th-that's all, folks. My grasp of Shakespeare was tenuous, my reading of the plays shallow and incomplete. Over the years I suppose I'd smugly fancied myself quite knowledgeable about the life and works of the Immortal Bard, when all along I had only what the wit and pianist Oscar Levant once termed "a smattering of ignorance." What I felt for Shakespeare was hardly more than the knee-jerk reverence that's prevailed for more than two centuries in Western culture. It should have been otherwise. Not only had I majored in English, but when I was ten years old, my father, who relished only Shakespeare's tragedies and histories ("I can't stand those goddamned comedies with women dressing up like men"), had me memorize long speeches and soliloquies of Iago, Cassius, Edmund, Richard III. "Son," he'd said, "when you grow up, you're going to discover that the world is filled with mean selfish bastards like these vicious hombres in Shakespeare, so you might as well learn what they're like right now." And at one time, as a theatre student, I'd actually played Richard III. What, then, accounted for the monumental indifference to Shakespeare that had afflicted me for lo these many years? Not the distracting burdens of a career: no matter that I spent most of my days and many of my nights reading and editing manuscripts, I always found time, occasionally on weekends but usually during my bus commute from the Jersey suburbs, to read and reread the nineteenth-century literary masters, and modern works destined to endure, and literary biographies. But at no time was I possessed by the urge to reacquaint myself with the Man from Stratford. Why? Had Shakespeare's language simply been too demanding for me to grapple with during my autodidactic intervals? It's one thing for a tired businessman on his way home to struggle with the rhetoric and syntax of *The Ambassadors* or *Absalom, Absalom,* quite another for him to absorb the imagery and dazzling paradoxes of *Love's Labour's Lost.*

It was a puzzlement—at least to the Duke of Nonintrospection. But definitely unbaffling was the reason for the stir created by Ralph Fiennes's scalding rendition of Prince Hamlet. He was a man possessed—dark, violent, agonized, sardonic, he could have been mistaken for one of the Karamazov boys. The swift pace of the production, the speed and precision with which the cast delivered the lines, the continuity of action, were galvanizing. One moment in particular I would never forget: Fiennes, in a frenzy of excitement, bursting into the room from upstage center and exclaiming, triumphantly, "To be or not to be, that *is* the question!" Fiennes's (and/or the director, Jonathan Kent's) surprising decision not to depart from the standard iambic pentameter stress on "is" implied that Hamlet had been wrestling with an existential question for God knows how long, at last had found an answer, and was desperately eager to share his thought processes with us. And Fiennes himself had found the solution to a problem that must vex any actor playing this role: how to make this almost tiresomely famous speech seem alive, dynamic, freshly minted.

The next day in the office, I found myself speaking about the production more or less in these same thrilled terms to a colleague. She listened patiently to my effusion, and to my laments about how little I really knew about Shakespeare, on and off the page, and then she said, "I assume from what you're telling me that you didn't manage to catch that incredible program on Channel 13 a few years ago—*Playing Shakespeare.*" No, I hadn't been aware of it. "What a shame. It's a series of master classes, or workshops, conducted by this bearded lovable bear of a man, John Barton, a big-deal director at the Royal Shakespearean Company. And the class isn't exactly a bunch of schleppers: you've got actors the likes of Judi Dench, Ian McKellen, Patrick Stewart, Peggy Ashcroft, Ben Kingsley, David Suchet, doing scenes from the plays. They listen to critiques from Barton, discuss them with him, then do the scenes again. If seeing Ralph Fiennes got you this pumped up, Barton and his bunch would have had you crawling the walls." I bet; simply hearing this description released a trickle of adrenaline. I wondered if Channel 13 planned to repeat the series anytime soon, or at least might know where I could locate videotapes. "Phone them," my colleague urged. "And if they draw a blank, check with the Drama Book Shop—it's just a few blocks from here on Seventh Avenue."

The person I reached at Channel 13 seemed annoyed by my inquiry; he couldn't recall the program at all—perhaps it had been on cable?—and hadn't the slightest idea if videotapes were available. From his tone, I gathered that he felt his position at one of the nation's citadels of quality television didn't require him to be a Customer Service flunky.

But the man who answered the phone at the Drama Book Shop knew immediately what I was talking about and exactly where to find the tapes: Films for the Humanities & Sciences, an educational mail-order firm in Princeton. A week later I owned *Playing Shakespeare,* a set of eleven fifty-minute videotapes, at a cost exceeding my four-year tuition at Texas A&M. Expensive perhaps. But something of a bargain, too, considering that it was to change my life.

The first two parts, with John Barton and Trevor Nunn conducting the workshops, were produced in 1980; the remaining nine, with Barton alone at the helm, appeared in 1983. Both men seemed appropriately Elizabethan in mien. Nunn, very dashing with his mustache and short black beard, could have been a courtier. Barton, every bit as ursine as my colleague had described him, with a mass of crinkled brown hair and a thick beard, and heavy pouches under his eyes, appeared a trusted member of the Privy Council, wise and world-worn and infinitely resourceful and pragmatic.

In un-Elizabethan brown cardigan, brown trousers, and knit tie, Barton dominated and gave coherence to the proceedings, which took place on a studio soundstage. The actors, dressed in jeans, khakis, sport shirts, sneakers, and reading from scripts, performed segments from the plays, observed by Barton, who sat on the floor or knelt nearby. After each demonstration Barton would engage in a discussion with the actors about their interpretation, suggesting different approaches, and the actors would do the scene again, incorporating Barton's ideas. Before and after each of these demonstrations, Barton, often looking directly into the camera, would make what he called expositions and explanations clarifying the ways in which Shakespeare's text actually works, and how actors should come to terms with it. Among his key points:

- Shakespeare's text is full of hidden hints to the actors about how to act a given speech or scene. It's stage direction in shorthand. When an actor becomes aware of them, he will find that Shakespeare himself starts to direct him. For example, when Shakespeare gives a short verse line, a line that has fewer than the ten syllables of iambic pentameter, he is indicating a pause of some sort.
- Shakespeare's words are not to be thought of as something that preexists in a printed text. They must be found or coined at the moment an actor utters them. They must find their life for the first time at the moment the actor speaks them. Because he needs them to express his intention, his situation, his character.
- Shakespeare uses irony over and over again, and an actor who cannot handle it will overlook a vital element in the character he is building. And irony always involves ambiguity—the double meaning in a single word or phrase. So the speaker has to be at once outside and inside the situation, to show emotions and at the same time stand outside those emotions.

- It's almost always right to share a soliloquy with the audience. And it must rise out of a situation, it must have a story, and it must be spontaneous. And it must be real.

I watched the tapes compulsively in one day, a euphoric marathon, swept up in the irresistible current of intellectual and emotional excitement, the inspired give-and-take between Barton and the actors, and swept away by the sheer joy apparent in these supremely gifted, articulate professionals collaborating on a labor of love. Immersion in this world was nothing less than an epiphany for me: I began to recognize what acting, the theatre, and Shakespeare really were.

Take just a few representative samples of the riches cramming this video cornucopia:

Here were David Suchet and Patrick Stewart, each of whom had played Shylock in productions of *The Merchant of Venice* directed by Barton (though neither of them saw the other in the part), discussing and illustrating through performance the ways in which their interpretations differed. Stewart saw Shylock as an outsider who happens to be a Jew; Suchet, himself a Jew, said that Shylock was an outsider *because* he was a Jew. Stewart, to free himself from the traditional appearance and behavior attached to the role, avoided the ringlets, the gown, the nose. And because he thought that an outsider's survival depended on assimilation into the culture, he adopted an accent more cultured and refined than the natives. Suchet did just the opposite. He played a Shylock who definitely was foreign, complete with slight accent, a man who never wanted anybody to forget he was an outsider, a Jew who was proud of his Jewishness. In the final scene, when Shylock gets his comeuppance, Stewart, playing a Shylock who wants to get away with as much as he can, humiliated himself, groveling, bowing, and scraping as he exited. Suchet played a Shylock defeated but grimly proud, almost defiant in loss, leaving the stage with perceptible dignity, unwilling to show humiliation. And there was Barton, stressing that Shylock could not be played as a goodie or a baddie, that actors must look for the deliberate ambiguities and inconsistencies that Shakespeare delights in.

Here was Ian McKellen, starkly pale, with close-cropped hair, and thin almost to the point of emaciation, dressed in khakis and a pale sport shirt, taking a seat alone in the center of the soundstage and describing how he went about interpreting Macbeth's "Tomorrow and tomorrow and tomorrow" soliloquy. In the background I could make out some of his fellow actors—Stewart and Suchet—and Trevor Nunn, all of them rapt, relishing the moment.

Two of the most striking particulars of McKellen's interpretative tour de force were his emphasis on time ("We've had tomorrow, we've had Today, now we've got Yesterday, we've got the whole complex of Time"), which, earlier, Barton had identified as the most important word in Shakespeare, and even more original, his gloss on the soliloquy's theatrical references: "Fools," he said, is a pun, meaning village idiot and a Shakespearean character such as Lear's Fool or Feste in *Twelfth Night;* and for "Walking Shadow" he cites "Walking Gentleman," a phrase, he said, that is still used in the theatre to describe someone in any company who plays a small part. "But life is not even a Walking Gentleman, he's a 'walking shadow,' less than even the meanest player . . . 'a poor player, that struts and frets his hour upon the stage. . . .' And although Macbeth is talking about time, about life, Shakespeare is making those vasty concepts very concrete . . . not just to Macbeth himself but to the actor who is playing Macbeth. . . ."

And next, here was Patrick Stewart, at the time playing Enobarbus in a Royal Shakespeare Company (RSC) production of *Antony and Cleopatra,* contrasting his current interpretation of Enobarbus's speech to Agrippa and Mecenas describing Cleopatra on her barge during their first meeting on the river of Cydnus with his earlier rendering of the speech in his first RSC Enobarbus in 1972. The first time, he dwelled on each image, each adjective,

> *because we were showing an old military man, an old sweat, returning to a Rome which he felt was sterile and intellectual, and wanting to impress Mecenas and Agrippa with an experience which, because they hadn't had it, would somehow leave them poorer in life. But there was also the sense that perhaps none of it was true . . . it was a traveler's tale. But it was of course also a reaction to that particular kind of Rome. This year, in this production, we have a very different Rome, a Rome which is alive . . .*

*very passionate, a volatile Rome. What's different . . . now is that I feel
a need to tell this story about Egypt, a need which comes from a man who
has shared in some kind of mystery . . . and that there is about Egypt as
compared to Rome a spiritual quality, an indefinable something which he
tries to reach out and touch. There was a transformation on that river
which lifted him and all the observers and obviously Antony too out of the
real life into something very much deeper, much more profound. . . .*

It struck me that Patrick Stewart was describing exactly what had
been happening to me as I lost myself in Barton & Company's exploration
of the Shakespearean universe. I felt I was sharing some kind of mystery,
that I was being drawn in by a spiritual quality, that I was being transformed and lifted out of reality into something deeper and more profound. The passion I'd begun to develop for Shakespeare was a mystical
experience, a religious experience. And I realized that it was not unlike
my return to Judaism seven years previously, a spiritual reawakening that
had also been engendered by a dramatic occasion, a ritual, and during
which I began to form ideas about the human condition, the nature of
man, of good and evil, of faith and despair, that were to influence the way
I understood Shakespeare.

2.

My turning back to Judaism in effect was a conversion, given that for most of my life I'd been a nonobservant Jew.

My father, a lawyer, had no patience with organized religion. He worshiped Voltaire, Twain, Mencken, and a freethinking gun-toting Texas journalist, W. C. Brann, whose orotund invective filled the pages of his biweekly tabloid, the *Iconoclast,* during the latter part of the nineteenth century and early into the 1900s. My father was not a godless man, but neither was he Torah-intoxicated. He read the Bible for the poetry of the Psalms, the skeptical wisdom of Ecclesiastes, the commonsense reflections of Proverbs, the narrative richness of Kings and Chronicles, and especially the moral and ethical power of the Prophets. A framed quote from Micah—"Do Justly, Love Mercy, and Walk Humbly with Thy God"—dominated one of the walls of his law office. He considered it the perfect credo for a lawyer.

My father liked to think of the Bible as the world's first great western saga. He observed to me when I was a boy that it contains all the elements of the classic western: pioneers braving hardships, entering a land filled with barbarians whom they ultimately conquer, cattle barons building empires. "Son," he would say, "remember that the pioneers to Texas were led by *Moses* Austin. Imagine those first settlers as Hebrews, the Mexicans as Canaanites, Texas as Israel. Abraham was a cattleman who drove his stock from Mesopotamia to Canaan, then he had to split up with Lot because their cowhands didn't get along, and they divided up the herd and carved out hunks of land for themselves. Laban was a cattle baron who tried to cheat Jacob out of his cowboy's wages, so Jacob cut out a few steers for himself in a shrewd piece of cattle-rustling. Esau was a cattle baron, too, who brought his four hundred cowpokes to a meeting with Jacob." And of course the Bible was filled with good-bad heroes, paramount among them King David: "David had a lot in common with Sam

16

Houston, son. Both were great warriors, great sinners, great leaders. Sam was a drunk who once lived with the Cherokees. David was once a bandit chief who for a time went over to the goddamned Philistines. David became King of Judah, Sam became President of Texas."

Of such Texan analogies was his theological tutelage. Although he'd been born on the Lower East Side of Manhattan and lived for a time in Brooklyn, he'd migrated to Waco, Texas, with his Russian-born parents when he was eight, and he was Texan to the core. His father, who'd worked in New York's garment industry before striking out West to join relatives in operating a dry-goods store, was an Orthodox Jew unable to instill his rigorous piety in his five children.

My father believed in Jewishness, not Judaism. We weren't assimilated Jews who denied our heritage; we were secular Jews who joined Jewish community centers, not temples. We did not have Christmas trees, we didn't go on Easter egg hunts; but neither did we keep kosher or celebrate Hanukkah, and we ignored Succoth. We never had a Seder: during Passover we simply abstained from bread for the prescribed time and ate matzos. On Yom Kippur, my father stayed home for the day and fasted; with the Gollobs, it was the High Holiday, not the High Holy Days.

Although ritualism was virtually nonexistent in our home, Jewish pride was rampant. My father's Jewish pantheon consisted of overachievers in the arts, sciences, music, literature, sports. In my father's theology, Paul Muni was God, Edward G. Robinson was Moses, John Garfield was Joshua. I remember how elated he was when he discovered that Kirk Douglas was a Jew whose real name was Issur Danielovich. I think Kirk was his King David.

A voracious reader, my father especially admired the Jewish proletarian authors, the scribes, from New York. Highest in his estimation was Clifford Odets, whom he looked upon as the Jeremiah of dramatists. For my eleventh birthday, he gave me *Six Plays by Clifford Odets,* a Modern Library collection. My father was anything but a radical or a revolutionary. He was a law-and-order man. His idea of the class war was Democrats versus Republicans, Roosevelt versus the Rich Mamzers.

When I was fourteen, one of my mother's uncles expressed dismay that his niece's son had not been bar mitzvahed. After all, I bore the name of one of his late brothers. He and his Cohen siblings had come to America from Germany, peddling their way across the South and Southwest and winding up in Texas, eventually opening up ladies' ready-to-wear stores in Brenham, Del Rio, and Houston, where my mother was born. Urged on by her uncle, my mother somehow convinced my father at least to join a Reform temple so that I could attend Sunday School for a couple of years and be confirmed, which was essentially a graduation ceremony. My father even suggested the topic for my confirmation speech: the Jew in sports. We managed to squeeze in the boxing champions Barney Ross and Benny Leonard, pro quarterback Sid Luckman, and baseball immortal Hank Greenberg. Omitted was the former heavyweight champion Max Baer; my father discovered Baer was a phony Jew who wore the Star of David on his trunks merely to lure hordes of Jews and anti-Semites into the arena to watch a holy war.

Seventeen years passed before I entered a Jewish house of worship again, this time Temple Sinai, a Reform congregation in Brookline, Massachusetts, where on a Sunday afternoon Barbara and I were married. My parents could scarcely believe they'd been lucky enough to see their son wed to a woman beautiful inside and out and, to cap it off, Jewish. Nonobservant though they were, a gentile daughter-in-law would not have gladdened their hearts. And although I'd never felt obligated to pick a Jewish mate, standing under the chuppah—the canopy—with Barbara, exchanging vows, then smashing a glass under my foot as a reminder that we live in an unredeemed world, celebrating one of the holiest of the life cycles in a traditional ceremony, I felt for the first time in my life a shiver of ecstasy that was as much tribal as spiritual but, as it turned out, too fleeting to sustain itself beyond that mystical instant and transform me into a keeper of the faith.

That change, almost as radical as a conversion, would not come until twenty years later when, for the first time since my wedding, I found myself back in a Jewish sanctuary for another life-cycle event, the bar mitzvah of close friends and neighbors. It turned out to be as crucial an occasion in my religious life as it was in that of the boy who was coming of age.

I'd never seen a bar mitzvah, and the pageantry overwhelmed me. Among other things, it was terrific theatre, reminding me that drama evolved from religious festivals in ancient Greece, and it evoked an almost terrifying sense of mystery and awe, the *mysterium tremendum* (as Rudolph Otto calls it in *The Idea of the Holy*) common to religious experience and to profound drama as well—drama such as the works of Shakespeare.

Wearing a tallith—the prayer shawl—for the first time, draped over my shoulders, I felt embraced by God. Years before, as a theatre student, I'd read in Konstantin Stanislavsky's *Building a Character* that simply wearing a costume can help an actor develop a characterization and in particular capture the true emotions of a character as much as any psychological analyzing of motivations. So here I sat in a Conservative synagogue, in full costume—yarmulke (or in Hebrew, *kipah,* the skullcap) and tallith, Reb Herman the Pious. When the Torah was removed from the Ark and brought down the aisle in procession, congregants sitting on and near the aisle kissed the fringes of their prayer shawls and pressed them against the Torah as it passed. Caught up in the ecstasy of the moment, I followed suit. Not yet aware of the term, I was an incipient *ba'al teshuva,* a nonreligious Jew who becomes religious.

At the reception following the ceremony, I cornered the father of the honoree and rhapsodized about the power and glory of the bar mitzvah service. He seemed nonplussed. "What do you mean, bar mitzvah service? That was a regular Shabbat morning service. The only thing that made it a bar mitzvah was that my son is now obligated to fulfill the commandments and can be called to the Torah. So he did what bar mitzvah boys always do: after the reading of the weekly portion of the Torah he chanted a haftarah, a section from the Prophets. Didn't they do that back in Houston?"

This incident unsettled me. For one thing, it made me embarrassed by my profound ignorance of Judaism—its practices, its history, its theology, its philosophy. For another, it brought to the surface a particular sense of inadequacy which I'd buried since early adolescence: a sense that I'd missed out on something vital by not being bar mitzvahed, that I'd been denied one of life's essential rites of passage. True, the physical and mental rigors of my freshman year at a military college were potent initiatory factors in the coming-of-age process, but the benefits were psychological, not spiritual.

Determined to educate myself in the faith of my fathers as quickly as possible, I began by concentrating on the observances of Shabbat; after all,

19

the Fourth Commandment was "Remember the Sabbath day and keep it holy." Secular though Barbara and I were, we maintained in our home (as did our otherwise nonobservant parents) two of the basic Jewish practices, durable and enduring filaments of tradition which kept us ever so slightly connected to that old-time religion: on Friday night, Shabbat eve, Barbara lighted candles and said the prayer in Hebrew and English; and when we moved into our apartment and then our home, we immediately posted on our doorjambs a mezuzah, the small box containing a scroll on which is written the first and second paragraphs of the Shema, the most famous prayer in Judaism. But I moved beyond this.

At a store in Manhattan's West Forties specializing in Judaica, I bought several items: *The Pentateuch and Haftorahs,* edited by J. H. Hertz, which contained the five books of Moses, each chapter followed by an excerpt from the Prophets, in Hebrew and English (Conservative and Orthodox synagogues read through the entire Torah during Shabbat services over the course of a year); a *kipah;* a paperback edition of *Prayerbook Hebrew the Easy Way,* a title more than slightly misleading; and a Richard Tucker tape, *Welcoming the Sabbath.* Equipped with these basic tools, I began to study, and to observe an idiosyncratic version of Shabbat in my den, Temple Beth Herm.

It was now evident to me that my newfound enchantment with Judaism was the result of an increasing dissatisfaction with the professional side of my life, the competitiveness, anxieties, and self-absorption of careerism, the editorial function itself, the emotional sterility of operating for the most part in a critical, analytical mode, in the thrall of the intellect, my life dominated by what Carl Jung bleakly observes in *Man and His Symbols* as "the goddess Reason, who is our greatest and most tragic illusion."

Searching out books of Jewish philosophy and theology, I found several that spoke directly to my spiritual crisis:

* *The Sabbath* and *God in Search of Man,* by Rabbi Abraham Joshua Heschel. A renowned Jewish thinker, leader, and religious activist who once walked arm in arm with Martin Luther King, Jr., during the 1965 civil rights march in Selma, Alabama, Heschel was deeply influenced by the Prophets and indeed wrote like a man whose soul was

on fire. In *The Sabbath,* Dr. Heschel notes that the word "holy" is used for the first time in the Book of Genesis, at the end of the story of creation, when it is applied to time: "God blessed the seventh day and made it holy." The Sabbath separates time from the world of space: "Six days a week we live under the tyranny of things of space; on the Sabbath we try to become attuned to holiness in time. . . . He who wants to enter the holiness of the day must first lay down the profanity of clattering commerce, of being yoked to toil. . . . He must go away from . . . the nervousness and fury of acquisitiveness and the betrayal in embezzling his own life." In *God in Search of Man,* Heschel writes, "To the modern man, everything seems calculable. . . . He has supreme faith in statistics and abhors the idea of a mystery. . . . The awareness of grandeur and the sublime is all but gone from the modern mind. . . . What we need to cultivate is the sense of wonder, of radical amazement. Awareness of the divine begins with wonder."

- *The Essence of Judaism,* by Leo Baeck, a leader of the Jewish Community of Germany during the Hitler period who survived the Theresienstadt concentration camp and went on to become an internationally acclaimed Jewish philosopher. In a vein similar to Heschel's, Baeck suggests that "the approach to the best in the Bible lies not in sharp intellect or through reading or precise formula but only through reverence and love."

- *Judaism and Modern Man,* by Will Herberg, a former communist who had undertaken a journey of return to Judaism which resulted in his writing this work of Jewish philosophy. Herberg defines *teshuva,* the turning, the return, as the abandonment of delusive self-sufficiency, so as to turn to God. Sin, he asserts, is self-centeredness, self-absorption, the very same qualities that my father had marked in Shakespeare's villains.

And in rereading the Book of Genesis, I found the stories of Adam and Eve and of the Tower of Babel parables of man's ultimate hubris, not lust of the body but lust of the mind, the hunger to be as God, omniscient.

My studies and my eccentric version of observing Shabbat soon began to have an effect on Barbara. She suggested that there might be something rather solipsistic, if not downright creepy and perhaps highly improper, about the solitary Saturday ritual I'd devised. Moreover, she, too, having been reared in a nonobservant family, was being drawn by the example of my new obsession toward the idea of redefining her Jewish identity, of experiencing at last a deeper sense of God and, most of all, connecting with the Jewish community. We'd lived in Montclair, New Jersey, for twenty years completely detached from this community, and we decided now to take the plunge and join a synagogue. We chose a Conservative synagogue because its ritual practices struck a balance between the strict traditionalism of the Orthodox and the too-rational modernity of the Reform. And for me it was imperative to hear the Torah and haftarah chanted in Hebrew; I was struggling to achieve a basic comprehension of the language, but even when I couldn't grasp its meaning, the sounds cast a mystical spell.

Soon after joining I began to study for my bar mitzvah, ready after all these years to become a man, a man of faith. I knew that I couldn't turn again to Judaism without undergoing a ceremony so integral a part of Jewish heritage, a ceremony that I'd denied to my own son through non-involvement with the Jewish community. "How but in custom and in ceremony / Are innocence and beauty born?" asked William Butler Yeats in my favorite poem, "A Prayer for My Daughter." It seemed to me that the way toward regaining a sense of God's glory and wonders, the holiness of the Divine Creator, was through participating wholeheartedly in the customs and ceremonies of my indestructible tribe, the people of the Covenant.

Our rabbi at the time was Joshua Chasan, a fiery and intense ex–social worker who, like Heschel, had a prophet's fiercely uncompromising passion for social justice. He insisted that I not merely chant a haftarah, as was customary, but also assume the role of cantor, or chazan, and conduct the entire service, much of it in Hebrew. I couldn't resist the challenge. And in truth, my motives were not entirely pure. Earlier in life, I'd envisioned a career in theatre, and I saw this an occasion to perform, to put on a hell of a show in a socko solo act, to be adored by an audience. I wanted this to be a bar mitzvah for the ages. Barbara had a different take on the situation: "You want to prove you can outdo a thirteen-year-old, right?"

I spent a year preparing for the occasion: studying Hebrew, listening to tapes, practicing, practicing, practicing—at home, at my office (early in the morning, with the door shut, before anyone arrived), in hotel rooms during business trips. Came the big day, I didn't feel like a performer; holding the Torah, I felt a sense of joy, a mystical sense of being at one with the Divine, and for the first time truly understood that God made his covenant not only with the Israelites but with all the future generations. I was standing at Sinai, with an aching humility and a feeling of innocence and beauty that brought me close to tears frequently during the service. And I felt the presence of my father and mother: I could hear my father, antisynagogue but always ready to applaud a good performance by his son, exclaiming, "Goddammit, you were better than Al Jolson in *The Jazz Singer!* You sounded like those old cantors on the Lower East Side!"; and my mother, awash in tears: "You may think you're a man, but you'll always be my baby."

During the reception that followed, Barbara took me aside and said, "You had me fooled for a while—there were times when I thought you actually *were* a thirteen-year-old. You looked like a kid, pure in heart and soul. Of course, no thirteen-year-old could have given that speech. Nor could many adults. It was swell. *Mazel tov.*"

Yes, like any bar mitzvah boy, I had to give a speech, telling the congregation what I'd been learning, and in my special case, why I'd waited forty-five years to undergo the process.

I aimed my words at two special people in the audience—my children, then in their twenties, Emily, a financial analyst at the Federal Reserve Bank of New York, and Jared, a medical student at Columbia. They'd been slightly nonplussed when Barbara and I suddenly joined a congregation, and more than a little astonished when they discovered I was immersed in bar mitzvah studies. They remembered that not all that long ago December had been a time when our living room had featured a menorah on the mantel and a Christmas tree in the corner. But from now on it would be known as the month of Dad's bar mitzvah. (Although I was born in July, Rabbi Chasan had allowed me to choose any date I wished, and I picked one with a haftarah that I found exceptionally dramatic—David's dying words to Solomon. The day was December 24. A friend told me, "Too bad it wasn't the twenty-fifth. Then you and Jesus

23

could have been bar mitzvah boys together.") In conversations with Emily and Jared over the past year, I'd treated the subject either lightly ("I'm officially now in my second childhood") or evasively ("Gosh, it's hard to talk about these spiritual changes"), but now it was time to make them understand exactly what had transformed me. Who knew—perhaps my example would eventually bring them into the fold. In truth, I felt more than a twinge of guilt: here I was, a parent, experiencing a rite-of-passage ceremony ahead of my kids, because I'd failed to give them the traditional Jewish education that I, too, had been denied as a child. The life cycle was out of whack. I had some explaining to do.

In the speech, I emphasized the ideas I'd gleaned from Heschel and Baeck and Herberg about the danger of worshiping pure reason, perhaps the most dangerous form of idolatry. And I also talked about *Abandonment to Divine Providence,* a spiritual work by Jean-Pierre de Caussade, an eighteenth-century Jesuit, which Rabbi Chasan had given me to supplement my studies. I must have been the first bar mitzvah boy in history to quote from this book. I was struck by how similar de Caussade's ideas were to those of the twentieth-century Jews I'd admired. In particular, he proclaimed, "Without God, all our theorizing and reading are useless— all they do is drain the heart and fill the mind. Why should we be astonished that our human reason is baffled by divine mysteries? When God speaks he uses mysterious words, and they are a death blow to all that we are as rational beings, for all the mysteries of God destroy our physical senses and our intellectuality—the darker the mystery, the more we are illumined by it."

I pointed out that John Keats, the Romantic poet I revered above all others, as much for his letters as for his poems, had sounded very much the same note when, in a letter to his brothers, George and Tom, he singled out as Shakespeare's singular quality what he termed "negative capability, the ability to be in uncertainties, mysteries, doubts, without any irritable reaching out after fact and reason."

Continuing in this vein, I cited Pascal's conviction that "the heart has its reasons, which reason can never explain," and a piercingly dramatic passage I'd memorized from *Moby-Dick* when rereading it in my late twenties, Ahab's agonized soliloquy as he stands on the deck of the *Pequod* late at night, gazing at an effulgent moon: "This lovely light, it lights not me. All loveliness is anguish to me, since I can ne'er enjoy. Gifted with the high perception, I lack the low enjoying power. Damned, most subtly and malignantly. Damned in the midst of paradise. Good night—Good night!" This, to me, is Ahab's defining moment, and represents the core idea of a novel markedly influenced by the Bible, not merely in the obvious ways—for example, the biblical names (Ahab, King of Israel, married to the Phoenician worshiper of Baal, Jezebel; Ishmael, the outcast, Abraham's disinherited son by Hagar, the Egyptian bondswoman); Father Mapple's thundering sermon on Jonah; a whaling captain named Bildad, the name of one of Job's comforters; the appearance of an old sailor who calls himself Elijah and utters prophecies—but in the warning it sounds from Genesis about the perilous results of intellectual pride. Ahab has developed his mind at the expense of the heart; his monomaniacal pursuit of a white whale is his attempt to rival God, to be God, not simply to imitate Him, by destroying the monster of the deep, the Leviathan that God describes in the Book of Job, a quote from which precedes the epilogue.

And the poetry, the imagery, the soliloquies of Ahab, Starbuck, Stubbs, reveal yet another influence in *Moby-Dick*—the works of Shakespeare. In 1848, at the age of twenty-nine, Herman Melville bought a seven-volume edition of Shakespeare's plays and began to read them for the first time, in a seizure of Bardomania perhaps not unlike the one that had me, at the age of sixty-five and approaching retirement, in its transcendent grip with the kind of intensity and obsessiveness that had characterized the Return and the bar mitzvah.

In his stimulating and illuminating *Shakespeare and the Bible,* Steven Marx, an English professor at Cal Poly University, speculates that Shakespeare might sometimes have "regarded his own role of playwright and performer as godlike, his own book as potent and capacious as 'The Book.'" I found that the autodidactic fervor that possessed me in the wake of viewing the *Playing Shakespeare* tapes led me to subject Shakespeare's plays to the kind of close reading I'd devoted to the Bible ten years earlier, as if they were indeed Holy Writ.

I began with the many plays I'd ignored all this time, such as *Troilus and Cressida, The Winter's Tale, Cymbeline, All's Well That Ends Well, Measure for Measure, Pericles, Timon of Athens, Henry VI (1, 2, 3), Henry VIII,*

King John, Love's Labour's Lost, then took up those I thought I understood, and discovered to my dismay not only how much about them I'd forgotten but how limited had been my grasp of their meaning.

For tutelage, I turned to some of the most illustrious scholars in the field, whose writing was so personal, warm, and human that I had the impression each was talking directly to me in my own private university.

My first discovery was Harold Goddard, whose two-volume *The Meaning of Shakespeare* brings to bear on all the plays the spaciousness of mind and soul their content requires and deserves. Goddard was head of the English department at Swarthmore College from 1909 to 1946. He died in 1951, just before this masterwork was published. Unique in his approach are frequent references to Fyodor Dostoyevsky, whose "insights into and outlook upon life" and depiction of the "high tension between the conscious and unconscious" are similar to Shakespeare's, a similarity he counts as "one of the most impressive phenomena in the history of the human imagination." I wondered if Ralph Fiennes owed his Dostoyevskian Hamlet to Goddard's reading, or if he sniffed out that quality on his own.

Then came Maynard Mack, Sterling Professor of English at Yale University, who in *Everybody's Shakespeare: Reflections Chiefly on Tragedy* endearingly addresses his wise and compelling essays on the tragedies to common readers disaffected by "the tribal wars and Byzantine pedantries that now balkanize professional students of literature into new-critics, new-historicists, neo-marxists, feminists, structuralists, and other cells of the elect, each claiming sole possession of the truth. . . ." Especially impressive is the final chapter, which elucidates some of Shakespeare's principles of construction distinctive to the tragedies, such as "umbrella speeches," which shelter more than one consciousness: Macbeth's "Cans't thou not minister to a mind diseased" speech applies as much to the griefs that haunt his mind as to those that are tormenting his wife, and Enobarbus's description of Cleopatra on her barge mirrors the power Cleopatra exerts over Antony.

Caroline Spurgeon, whose *Shakespeare's Imagery,* first published in 1935, remains one of the most significant and thrilling books on Shakespeare ever published, enthralled me at the outset with the expression of her belief that analogy "holds within itself the very secret of the universe. . . . Great metaphor in great poetry moves and stirs us in a way impossible to account for purely rationally and logically . . . it awakens something in us, which I think we must call spiritual, at the very roots of our being. For, as the poet well knows . . . it is only by means of these hidden analogies that the greatest truths, otherwise inexpressible, can be given a form or shape capable of being grasped by the human mind." She goes on to demonstrate how the imagery in the plays illuminates Shakespeare's personality, temperament, and thought, and how it reveals the themes and characters of the plays. And she also shows how Shakespeare's imagery differs from that of his Elizabethan contemporaries Christopher Marlowe and Francis Bacon.

And I admired the ingenuity with which Marvin Rosenberg, professor emeritus of dramatic art at the University of California Berkeley, combined theatre history, dramatic criticism, and personal experience in his extraordinarily innovative, exhaustively detailed, and radically comprehensive Mask series—*The Masks of King Lear, The Masks of Macbeth, The Masks of Hamlet, The Masks of Othello.* Analyzing each play, scene by scene, Rosenberg juxtaposes interpretations by critics and by directors and actors, ranging over the past two centuries and selected from hundreds of books, essays, periodical reports, memoirs, and acting versions, as well as from his notes on performances and rehearsals he attended and from his interviews with actors—all of this organized by his own interpretation. The series is a veritable Talmud of Shakespeare study in which scholars, reviewers, and theatre professionals from one era seem to be conducting arguments and discussions with those from another. On one of the forty-six pages devoted to act 1, scene 5 of *Hamlet,* in which Hamlet insists that Horatio and Marcellus swear an oath of silence concerning the appearance of the ghost, Rosenberg (1) describes how Mark Rylance as Horatio sank to his knees in one production, how Stacy Keach as Hamlet gnashed his teeth on the phrase "old mole" in another, how Edwin Booth made a slight mocking motion of his hand when uttering the word "philosophy" in his lines to Horatio in a nineteenth-century production; (2) probes Hamlet's subconscious motive for making jokes at the ghost's expense; (3) points out that Herbert Beerbohm Tree, following the Folio edition, said "dreamt of in *our* philosophy," whereas Edwin Booth, as per the quartos, said *"your."*

Years earlier I'd struggled through several chapters of Northrop Frye's complex *Anatomy of Criticism* before growing loutishly impatient with its theoretical subtleties, and was surprised to find his collection of nine essays, *On Shakespeare,* adapted from lectures given to an undergraduate class at Victoria College, delightfully accessible, lively, and conversational. I suppose I'll always be an undergraduate at heart; *Anatomy* was probably aimed at Ph.Ds. Frye, late professor of English at the University of Toronto, studies plays from each of the Shakespearean genres, and right at the start treats us to a provocative insight: "In every play Shakespeare wrote, the hero or central character is the theatre itself." And he offers an invaluable piece of advice to readers of the plays: "try to reconstruct the performance in your mind: assume you're directing the play. . . ." Commonsensical, and crucial to making it live in the mind.

I don't think it's possible to fully comprehend and savor the ten plays Shakespeare wrote on medieval history—eight on the later Plantagenets, one on the early Plantagenets, and one on the Tudors—without the clear, concise, charmingly erudite Professor Peter Saccio as a guide. In his definitive *Shakespeare's English Kings: History, Chronicle and Drama,* Saccio, the Leon D. Black Professor of Shakespearean Studies at Dartmouth College, points out that Shakespeare could rely on a measure of prior knowledge in his audience that we moderns lack and that make it difficult for us to firmly grasp anything about the historical plays except the central characterizations, thus depriving us of much of the theatrical experience and placing a formidable obstacle to intelligent criticism of the plays. Saccio intends his book as background reading and concentrates on the persons and issues Shakespeare dramatized. What I found especially valuable was Saccio's demonstrations of how Shakespeare, "taking historical liberties out of artistic necessity . . . changes the personalities of historical figures, invents characters, compresses the chronology, alters the geography, devises confrontations that never took place, commits anachronism . . . and above all, personalizes," translating into persons and passions all that we mean by "the times."

Saccio has extended his reach to an audience outside academia through a series of taped lectures (audio and video) on Shakespeare offered by the Teaching Company. I bought the audio version, which cast an irresistible spell over me equal to that exerted by *Playing Shakespeare.*

Charged with élan, bursting with a hyperrelishment of his subject, and animated with a considerable theatrical flair which includes a gift of laughter, Saccio gives the impression that he's just shared a few pints of ale with the Bard at the Mermaid Tavern and can't wait to tell us about his good friend Will and what he's been up to lately. I was hooked from the very beginning, when he took up the concept of Bardolatry, the worship of Shakespeare as a god, or, if you will, God, a direction in which I was leaning. It began with John Dryden's pronouncement of Shakespeare as "the largest and most comprehensive soul." Shakespeare consequently became a culture hero, a lawgiver, a prophet. According to Saccio, the most extreme form of Bardolatry is to say Shakespeare didn't exist, and this led the professor to a brief account of the anti-Stratfordians, that misguided band of heretics who believe that the plays were written not by Shakespeare the actor who was buried at Stratford-on-Avon but by the likes of Christopher Marlowe or Sir Francis Bacon or the Earl of Oxford. The main impulse behind this phenomenon is social snobbery: how could a middle-class boy without a college education write so gloriously and depict the nobility with such authority? Dismissing anti-Stratfordianism as utter nonsense, Saccio reminds us that the facts of Shakespeare's life are as well recorded as we could expect—domestic facts about his life in Stratford, tributes to his talent from his colleagues in the London theatre—and that there is not the slightest evidence that he did not write the plays. Provocative stuff, which made me hunger to know more about Shakespeare the man.

Three biographies got me started:

First, Marchette Chute's learned and engaging *Shakespeare of London,* based entirely on contemporary documents. Like Saccio, Ms. Chute emphasizes that more is known about Shakespeare than about any other playwright of the period with the exception of Ben Jonson, and that some parts of his life are better documented than Jonson's (she ought to know—she's also written a splendid biography of Jonson). She avoids discussing Shakespeare's plays as literature, and deals with them only as they concern the working conditions of the London stage. She writes with narrative flair and is adept at making the period come alive.

Unlike Ms. Chute, Russell A. Fraser, Austin Warren Professor Emeritus of English Literature and Language at the University of Michigan, searches for illuminations of Shakespeare's character in his plays, as did Caroline Spurgeon in her fashion, and his two-volume biography, *Young Shakespeare* and *Shakespeare: The Later Years,* combines a dramatic account of Shakespeare's life with an original consideration of his art.

Samuel Schoenbaum, an urbane and incisive scholar who taught at Midwest and East Coast universities and was a trustee of the Folger Library, in *William Shakespeare: A Compact Documentary Life,* takes the same approach as Marchette Chute, concentrating in narrative fashion on the major documents, from the entry in the parish register noting Shakespeare's christening to Shakespeare's will, bequeathing his second-best bed to his wife, Anne, and although he spends less time on life in Stratford and in the London theatre than Ms. Chute, he brings to our attention something that the latter neglects: the influence of religion on Shakespeare's upbringing. And what truly piqued my interest was the fact that Shakespeare was especially familiar with the Book of Genesis. I'd begun to detect an idea that seemed to run through the plays I was studying—the eternal conflict between head and heart that besets the human race, and the dark consequences of allowing the former to prevail. Could this outlook be traced to the influence of the stories of Adam and Eve and the Tower of Babel? Is this how Shakespeare interpreted God's creating mankind with the good impulse and the bad impulse, and the free will to choose between them?

I realized that I, a twentieth-century Texas Jew long transplanted to New Jersey/New York, was developing a kinship with a sixteenth-century Stratfordian Protestant transplanted to London. Both of us were of the middle class, bourgeois to the hilt: my father had once been assistant to the president of the Waco Electric Company and had then become a lawyer; Shakespeare's father had been a tradesman—a glover—and also the bailiff (the equivalent of mayor) of Stratford; and both had endured financial setbacks—my father as a result of the Depression, Shakespeare's father as a consequence of his sharp business practices and his penchant for overextending. Both of us were Young Men from the Provinces, who left home to seek fame and fortune in the Mythical Metropolis (in my case, two cities, Los Angeles and New York). So Shakespeare outdid me, so what? I'd had myself quite a time of it, too, starting way back in the 1950s.

During my senior year at Texas A&M, the college's drama club, the Aggie Players, challenged me to try out for a role in an upcoming production of *The Milky Way,* a shoddy farce that had played for a time on Broadway and had been adapted into one of Danny Kaye's least hilarious movies, *The Kid from Brooklyn.* As amusements editor for the *Battalion,* the college daily, I'd made snide remarks at the Players' expense on too many occasions, under the spell of George Jean Nathan, the debonair New York drama critic who'd coedited the *American Mercury* with H. L. Mencken, and whose collected reviews were published annually and given to me each birthday by my father, who venerated Nathan with the same ardor as he did Mencken. Sniffing at a production of Karel Capek's *RUR* (Rossum's Universal Robots), I accused the actor playing Rossum of being more robotic than his creations. Hah-hah. Now the Players were daring me to prove that I could do better. I auditioned, and what do you know, was cast in one of the leads—a brash, wisecracking fight manager named, of course, Gabby—and hailed as a thespian wonder.

This adulation, and the concentrated and exhilarating work of rehearsals, reawakened a yearning for the stage that had lain dormant in me since childhood, and that had been stimulated by my father, whose own theatrical bent served him well in his days as a trial lawyer and as a bedtime storyteller nonpareil. I still remember his tales of the West in which Jews always popped up in unlikely roles—Indian chiefs, frontier scouts, chuck wagon cooks specializing in latkes—and in which he assumed the voice of all the characters ("Hey, Mendel," said Tex, "why do these here pancakes taste like taters?"). And I have photographs of him performing in comic skits that he had written for the Masonic Lodge when he was a young attorney in Waco, before our move to Houston. His birthday gifts to me (always signed "Love, Mom and Dad," but I knew the true source) were usually anthologies of plays and screenplays, the Odets volume being only one example, and the George Jean Nathan annual. Coached by my father, I directed and acted in excerpts from *Ah, Wilderness!, Our Town,* and *How Green Was My Valley* (performed at grade school programs). I did Cassius's opening speech to Brutus from *Julius Caesar* garbed in a toga whipped up by my mother from an old sheet, and on occasion,

31

with heavy collaboration from my father, I wrote playlets, usually historical (e.g., Sam Houston trouncing Santa Ana at the battle of San Jacinto), which I directed and in which I usually cast myself in the lead.

My mother looked on all this approvingly. Always an observer, only an encourager. But if she'd had the will, the ambition, the opportunity, to pursue a career, she might have become one hell of an actress: self-dramatizing, unstable, temperamental, a wickedly funny mimic. And a raving beauty, with haunted expression that would have made for heartbreaking close-ups on-screen. I have the newspaper clipping of a photograph of my mother in her bridal gown; it's from the *Houston Chronicle,* which had chosen her the city's most beautiful June bride. But it could easily have been from a Sylvia Sidney movie.

Actually, my mother saw the hand of destiny reaching out again on my behalf, a hand once extended only to be repulsed several years earlier, in 1933, when I was three. My parents had driven in their Chevrolet to Los Angeles, quite a trek in those days. It was not a pleasure excursion for the Family Gollob. My father was on a desperate mission to scout out more-promising opportunities for a lawyer than existed in Depression-stricken Houston, where he and his partner, his older brother, Sol, were struggling to keep their practice viable. We weren't exactly the Joads, but times were hard. And it seemed we were constantly moving from apartment to apartment, each successively bleaker, a situation my mother found degrading. During her childhood and teens, she'd been raised in well-to-do circumstances, Rubye Cohen, Jewish southern belle, the daughter of a prosperous merchant, only to see her father lose his small fortune in the stock market: he'd invested heavily in commodities and was ruined when his margins were called. My mother and her siblings, three sisters and a brother, still felt the humiliation of being déclassé in Houston's aggressively materialistic social circles, and now she faced the prospect of worse days ahead. What I do remember from that period is her recriminations against my father for his failings as a provider, and the ferocious quarrels that ensued.

My father's search yielded a few vague possibilities in the legal departments of oil companies in the region, but our funds were running low and he couldn't afford to stay in town much longer to follow through on these flimsy leads.

One Sunday he took us to Santa Monica beach to relieve the pressure, if only for an afternoon. As I romped on the beach, charming the multitudes with my long golden curls (a not uncommon hairstyle for boys in that era) and my elfin exuberance, a photographer from the *Los Angeles Times* spotted me and snapped my picture. He asked my father for my name and the address of our motel, and promised to send a print of the photo, which he hoped would appear in the following morning's edition. It did, and that afternoon my father received a call from a talent scout with the studio that produced the Our Gang comedies. He'd obtained our address from the *Times* photographer and wondered if my parents could bring me to his office the next day. I appeared to be the type of kid who could fit in with Spanky and the bunch, but the producer wanted to check me out in person before arranging a screen test.

I wowed the fellow, it seems, at one point jumping in his lap and asking him why he was going bald. He found this enchanting. He would see about setting up a screen test as soon as possible and would call later in the week with a date. God works in strange and mysterious ways, apparently choosing me as the Messiah to lead my family into the Golden Age.

That night, however, came a more ominous phone call—from Houston. My uncle pleaded with my father to return at once if he wanted to save the practice. Relocating in California had never appealed to him. Uncertain that the talent scout would actually call, and figuring that even if he did, there was no assurance I'd be offered a contract after the test, my father decided to leave if he'd heard nothing in two days. During that time, he did try to reach the talent scout, who, he was told, was out of town and wasn't expected back until the following night. My father left a message that if we didn't hear from the studio by the end of the week, we'd have to return to Texas.

Time ran out, no call, and it was good-bye to Hollywood. Back in Houston, my father received a letter from the talent scout, to whom he'd given his business card, apologizing for the delay in responding to him and promising to have me tested at once if we could come back now. But that was not to be; my father couldn't afford another trip, and the practice couldn't survive another leave of absence by him.

This episode haunted my mother (in the years to come, no sooner would I introduce her to friends than she'd ask, "Did you know that Her-

man could have been a movie star?") and made it difficult for her to sympathize with my father's efforts to keep the practice afloat. Her reviling of
him intensified and frequently included insults about his Russian Jewish
lineage, the mark of social inferiority to German Jews such as my mother.
As she watched my flame burn bright as the Orson Welles of Oran M.
Roberts Elementary School, she was certain that I'd make it yet in showbiz, big-time. Through me would come her redemption.

But the flame dimmed when I entered the unadmiring universe of
junior high school, in which I found myself no longer an esteemed
prodigy but a stranger and afraid, anonymous and ignored, all but invisi-
ble. I turned away from playwriting and performing (well, I did play the
accordion—another of my father's enthusiasms—at school programs),
from the creative arts, and over time developed a knack and a zest for
criticism, which blossomed while I was on the editorial staff of the *Battalion,* only to fade with the resurgence of those starstruck dreams of glory.

An English major, I'd planned to join the drama desk of one of the
dailies in Houston or Dallas, someday becoming a cultural arbiter a la
Nathan and Mencken. But now I resolved to study acting and directing
when I graduated, but this pursuit was delayed for two years while I
served with the air force, part of that time in Korea; most of the Class of
1951 were called into active duty immediately or shortly after graduation.
Just as well, because the G.I. Bill footed the costs of three years of trial
and error at the Pasadena Playhouse, in Lee Strasberg's private classes, and
at the University of Houston.

While in Korea, I sent for a catalog from the Yale School of Drama,
alma mater of my idol, Elia Kazan, who'd directed *A Streetcar Named Desire* and *Death of a Salesman* on Broadway, and the movie *Viva Zapata!,*
starring Marlon Brando. Kazan first came to my attention as an actor,
when I was nine; my father took me to see *City for Conquest,* in which
James Cagney played a boxer and Kazan was featured as a sympathetic
gangster named Googi. "That goddamned little Kazan stole the picture,"
correctly raved my father. Kazan had been one of the original members
of the Group Theatre, founded by Harold Clurman, Lee Strasberg, and
Cheryl Crawford in an attempt to replicate in America what Stanislavsky
and the Moscow Art Theatre had accomplished in Russia: a theatre dedicated to creating psychological and social truth onstage.

But visions of Yale faded quickly from my mind when I returned to the States. On my way to Texas to be discharged from active duty, I stopped over in Los Angeles to visit an uncle and cousins; they thought I might want to investigate the Pasadena Playhouse, a professional theatre that also operated a drama school, before applying to Yale. I was seduced by the facilities, by the town, nestled against the San Gabriel Mountains, and by the swarms of head-turning all-American coeds, not an unappealing sight to someone who'd spent four years at an all-male military college and had just returned from Asia, where Madam Butterflys were scarcely in evidence.

My application to the Playhouse was quickly accepted, no audition necessary. Reveling in the heady social whirl of the school, I devoted far too much time to the private drama of ill-fated romantic flings and to bull sessions at the students' favorite haunt, Nardi's, a long dark bar across the street from the Playhouse, arguing whether Brando was better than Montgomery Clift, and far too little time to studying the crafts of acting and directing. But I did muster the discipline to achieve a considerable success in our senior class project and graduate on a high note. The faculty adviser, Jack Woodford, the best teacher at the Playhouse, who had a powerful intellect and the build of a middleweight boxer, and moved with the graceful intensity and controlled ferocity of a panther, suggested that we transform a little-known novella by Dostoyevsky, "The Friend of the Family," into a long one-act play. He asked me to do the adaptation, which I completed in a week, and then cast me in the lead role, Foma Fomitch, a pious fraud akin to Molière's Tartuffe. We gave five performances, each to a standing ovation. In the dressing room after opening night, the stage manager brought me a business card handed to him by one of the audience who'd appeared in the wings shortly after the final curtain and then hastily departed. Printed on the front of the card was "Milton Lewis" and the address—Paramount Pictures, 5451 Marathon, Hollywood, California—and scrawled in scarcely decipherable script on the back was a message: "Call me for an appointment." Lewis was a renowned talent scout for the studio. By some bizarre coincidence could he be the one who spotted me on the Santa Monica beach twenty years ago? Perhaps at last the destiny my mother had foreseen would be realized; kismet had directed me to Pasadena rather than Yale. At last I'd get my screen test. But forget about those inane Our Gang comedies; and move over, Brando, Gazzara, Clift.

Such were my thoughts as I was ushered into Milton Lewis's office. Short, slender, balding, in his fifties, I guessed, Mr. Lewis came right to the point: "Kid, you were damned good. A few years' more training and maybe you could be another Morris Carnovsky. Terrific potential for character roles. Especially old men. Morris was playing old men when he was in his early thirties. But you're still raw. Do some community theatre somewhere—here, New York, wherever. Take acting classes. Stay with it. A hard road—only the strong survive. Try to be strong. And tough. Someday we'll meet again. Thanks for coming by. And remember: there's always work for a good character actor."

From a missed opportunity at becoming a screen playmate of Spanky and the gang to a possible career shuffling around stage and screen sets in a cardigan sweater as beloved old Gramps or Papa. Could this be progress? One had to be realistic—and, of course, strong and tough. No leading man, I. So what? Paul Muni, the reigning deity in my father's pantheon, had built his legendary career as a character actor. But Lewis had singled out Carnovsky: was this merely another coincidence, or had he been delivering a subtle hint? Carnovsky had been one of the Group Theatre's stalwarts, a colleague of Lee Strasberg's. It so happened that under the influence of Harold Clurman's extraordinary memoir about his experiences with the Group, *The Fervent Years: The Group Theatre and the Thirties,* which I'd read a few months previously and in which Lee Strasberg figures prominently, along with the Group's resident playwright, Clifford Odets (another omen?), I'd been mulling a move to New York, where I could study with the master, Strasberg. After the demise of the Group in 1941, Strasberg, Kazan, and Crawford went on to create the workshops and master classes known as the Actors Studio, for those who had established careers for themselves but wanted to continue working on their craft. Strasberg, in addition, conducted private classes for a mix of professionals and hopefuls.

The interview with Lewis was the impetus that put me on the Greyhound to New York. To join Strasberg's class, you had to phone him at home to arrange an interview, which he granted only if there was an opening in a particular group. He was listed in the Manhattan directory.

A humble and democratic touch, this accessibility, I thought. His phone must ring constantly. How could he endure it? Actually, it was a test of the student's endurance and determination: I phoned him at least twice a week for a month. "No, nothing yet," he'd say, and hang up. Finally, I broke through: "Yes, there's a slot on Thursdays, two o'clock," he said brusquely. "Come to my apartment tomorrow night, seven sharp, and we'll talk."

Sitting in Strasberg's living room, I found his presence intimidating. He was as Clurman had described him: "very short, intense-looking, with skin drawn tightly over a wide brow. He spoke with a faint foreign accent. . . . [and] had a face that expressed keen intelligence, suffering, ascetic control, with something . . . withdrawn and lofty about it." His once "full head of curly hair" had thinned considerably by the time I met him. I imagined him as one of the leaders of a revolutionary party (the Group had been, in fact, revolutionary in its approach to the American theatre), one of those fanatical theorists out of Dostoyevsky's *Demons,* with cold piercing eyes behind steel-rimmed spectacles. Years later, in Coppola's *Godfather II,* he emanated much the same quality in his role as the visionary mob boss based on Meyer Lansky. Our conversation lasted all of ten minutes. He asked me why I wanted to act, where I'd studied, what actors and directors and playwrights I admired, and why. And, as if in passing, my favorite poem. Yeats's "A Prayer for My Daughter," I said. He nodded, and that was it. On a bus back to my room at International House, a student residence in Morningside Heights, I wondered if Strasberg was familiar with that Yeats poem, especially the line "An intellectual hatred is the worst." I hadn't chosen it deliberately, as a subtle insult. Just another of life's little coincidences.

The initiation ritual in a Strasberg class was the Sense Memory Exercise: a student was required to mime an activity he or she performed each morning, concentrating intensely on each step so as to recall precisely the physicality of the process and convey it to an audience. The class would then try to identify what the student had done. I mimed cleaning my electric razor: removing it from its soft leather case, opening the top, removing the blade, wiping it with a small brush, reinserting it, returning the razor to the case. The class was mystified and impressed. So was Strasberg.

But I never felt I belonged to the tribe. In fact, there was no tribe, just a bunch of individuals who scarcely knew each other, united only by their ambition and their reverence for the Master. I found myself deficient in both cases. To me, Strasberg was an intolerant dogmatist, warping the concepts of Stanislavsky, whose "Method" was an approach to achieving emotional truth in acting, the way so many psychiatrists misconstrue the teachings of Freud, who encouraged us to discover the hidden truths about ourselves. In fact, Strasberg managed to warp both Stanislavsky and Freud—I felt he was practicing psychiatry without a license. "You must pay the price," he would intone portentously when criticizing a scene I'd performed without digging deep enough into my psyche: "you're too cold, too artificial." But that wasn't really the problem: the problem, I realized after four grim months, was that I lacked not only the unswerving will and determination to succeed as an actor, the desire, for example, to take essential separate classes in voice and movement, but also the talent to compete against the best. I was no worse than the least talented members of the class. How encouraging.

If this Young Man from the Provinces was to make a name in the theatre, it would not be as another Muni, another Carnovsky. It would be as another—Kazan! Shazam! Herm the Director. The signs had been there all along: hey, I was the kid who directed those playlets at Roberts Elementary, and in a directing course taught by Jack Woodford at Pasadena I'd staged scenes from Odets's *Golden Boy* and Herman Wouk's *The Caine Mutiny Court Martial* that had earned plaudits from Woodford and my classmates. At Woodford's suggestion, I'd bought *Fundamentals of Play Directing,* by Alexander Dean, who'd been head of the Yale School of Drama when Kazan was a student there, but except for that particular class, I'd read it principally from an actor's perspective, for a total awareness of what a director would have in mind as he shaped a production in which I was performing.

Once again I contemplated applying to Yale, and once again I decided to go elsewhere. This Young Man would return to the Provinces, to Texas, and establish a foundation in my craft before assailing the walls of Broadway. I'd pursue a master's in directing, at the University of Houston, and at the same time if possible work in a backstage capacity at Houston's nationally renowned Alley Theatre, an in-the-round facility cofounded and operated by the handsome, formidably gifted Nina Vance. Then? Well, one step at a time. But it turned out I was taking a misstep.

"Fiasco" was a word invented to describe my semester at dear old U of H. The year I entered, the Drama School was under the leadership of a diminutive mediocrity who had a doctorate in makeup from the University of Idaho and who'd brought with him to Houston two of his lackeys, one who taught scene design, the other directing. I spent most of my time in a graduate carrel in the library, reading drama reviews by Robert Benchley and Dorothy Parker in back issues of the *New Yorker.* At the Alley, Ms. Vance took me on as an assistant stage manager on a production of *The Glass Menagerie;* I was responsible for seeing that the props were on hand and in place for each performance. For recreation, I drank beer with U of H cronies at Stubby's Lounge, a windowless concrete blockhouse with the best jukebox in town. Something had gone terribly wrong. I'd lost my bearings, my sense of vocation. What was my true calling? In one of John Osborne's early plays, *Epitaph for George Dillon,* the eponymous antihero, a would-be playwright who's begun to doubt his talent, laments his plight thusly: "What if I have the symptoms of the disease, without the disease itself?" That seemed to apply to me. Perhaps I had the sensibility of a director, but neither the exceptional skill nor the consuming dedication to become a professional. Someone with a true calling would not be daunted by the Three Stooges of the U of H drama department. He would plug ahead, fight the good fight, make the best of the situation, get the goddamned degree, move up the ladder rung by rung.

3.

One night at Stubby's someone punched up on the jukebox the theme from *The Bad and the Beautiful,* that wonderfully hard-boiled softhearted movie about Hollywood written by Charles Schnee and directed by Vincente Minnelli, starring Kirk Douglas as the good/bad producer and Lana Turner as the alcoholic actress he redeems, then abandons. The music was a siren song, enticing me back to the Land of the Lotus-Eaters, where I'd once beguiled a producer and a talent scout. This time, though, I wouldn't be burdened with fantasies of becoming another Muni, another Kazan. I had a more realizable Grand Illusion: I'd become a movie producer, like old Kirk, perhaps head of a studio. With my aptitude as a critic, coupled with my knowledge of literature—novels, short stories, plays—I'd aim for a job as reader with the story department of a studio, assessing the movie potential of novels and stories and plays, intending to rise to story editor and proceed from there to producing. If necessary, I'd start at the very bottom, moving up the ladder rung by rung.

It was necessary. With no relatives in the business, I wasn't a candidate for nepotism, a well-trod path to Hollywood executive suites. But I had the next best thing to a relative: a connection. The wife of a good friend of mine during the Playhouse days happened to be one of Cecil B. De-Mille's private secretaries, who used her pull to get me hired on right away at Paramount Studios as a messenger in the mail room, one of the most coveted entry-level positions in the business. Ten messengers, thousands of applicants. Tough luck, fellas. The mail room was not a training program: messengers were not promoted to other departments when openings arose; they had to use wit and wiles to unhook themselves from the oars and join the crew on deck. I delivered my résumé to the head of the story department, who glanced at it cursorily and told me that nothing was likely to develop in the near future. He was prophetic: after two months in the mail room, I was laid off as part of an economy drive that lopped three $60-per-week messengers and two $150-per-week accountants off the payroll.

What next? At Paramount I'd learned that training programs were to be found at talent agencies such as MCA, the colossus in the realm, and its chief rival, the William Morris Agency. Agencies were traditional launching pads for producers and for studio executives in other capacities, including story editor. I opted for MCA, with an eye on becoming an agent in the literary department, which would allow me to promote myself with studio story departments. Move over, Sammy Glick.

MCA's training department, called the traffic department, was a glorified mail room. In addition to sorting and delivering mail, trainees—who were required to wear dark suits and ties—operated the Teletype machine and the Xerox machine (a cumbersome piece of equipment in those days, which required the user to run the paper through a redolent chemical solution before inserting it into the slot), stocked the office bars each morning, picked up clients from and delivered them to the airport, arranged screenings in the swanky projection room suite in the building—in short, did a lot of trafficking back and forth.

To be hired, an applicant first had to be interviewed by the head of the department who decided if he was traffic material. Surviving that test, the applicant was told to phone from time to time to determine if there was an opening to fill. Luck and timing and persistence were in play. The Strasberg Method again, of all things. Adept at this by now, I phoned every day for a month. Finally, the department head said, "I almost fired someone just to get you off my damned back. But that wasn't necessary. One of the guys was promoted yesterday. Come in tomorrow."

MCA's offices were in a Beverly Hills building that resembled Monticello. The office furniture was colonial, the books in the waiting room were leather-bound editions of the classics. The impression conveyed was that MCA was a grand old American institution that had been in business since the days of the Continental Congress. Belying this aura of staid conservatism was the manner and method of the agents themselves, an almost uniformly ruthless, mercenary, and saturnine lot who would have looked at home at a board meeting of Murder, Inc.

Soon after I became a trainee, I arranged an interview with Ned

Brown, the head of the literary department, a small, bald, dapper, glowering bundle of tightly controlled rage. Looking at my résumé and hearing me talk of my desire to become a literary agent, he gave me a thin, faintly contemptuous smile and said, "Most of you guys want to be agents for the movie stars. What's the matter with you?" Flustered, I struggled for a snappy answer, but he dismissed me with a curt "You may have a long wait, chum. I'm full up right now."

Several weeks later, as low man on the traffic totem pole, I was assigned the ignominious chore of chauffeuring the boss's daughter, Jean Stein, whose father, Jules, had founded the agency, to the family's gothic mansion in Beverly Hills, which reportedly had been Rudolph Valentino's legendary domicile, Falcon's Lair. The engine in her car had malfunctioned, and why should she pay for a cab when she could use a company vehicle and not be required to tip the driver.

She turned out not to be a snobbish, haughty bitch but an agreeable, attractive young woman who insisted democratically on sitting up front. We exchanged small talk for a few minutes, then she asked, "Do I detect a Southern accent?" "Texas," I said. "Do you like Faulkner?" she responded. Did I ever. I went into my English-major spiel about how Faulkner's true strength was as a regional realist and folk humorist, and that the Snopes novels and the Jason Compson section in *The Sound and the Fury* were in my humble opinion his triumphs. She argued for *Absalom, Absalom* and *Light in August,* and then there we were, at Falcon's Lair. "Tell me," she said, opening the car door, "what's a guy who loves Faulkner doing at a place like MCA?" I revealed my ambitious plan; she smiled and wished me luck.

A week later Ned Brown called me into his office. "Chum, I've been keeping my eye on you since our little talk, and I like what I see. I'm bringing you on board. You'll be my personal assistant for a while, then I'll let you get your feet wet covering some of the secondary producers and independents and checking in with the studio story departments. One piece of advice: keep your bowels open and your mouth shut."

Naively, I didn't connect this unexpected piece of luck to my encounter with Jean Stein. Years later, at a party in New York, she came over and upbraided me: "I'm very mad at you. You never thanked me for getting you that job with Ned Brown. That was very rude of you." I stared at her uncomprehendingly, and she laughed. "Good Lord, did you think Ned took you into his department because he took another look at your résumé? I told him you struck me as a bright young man and he ought to get you out of that mail room and let you show your stuff."

It was all very Horatio Alger. Or Theodore Dreiser, Lite: *An American Comedy.* Capping it off was my subsequently discovering that Jean at one time had been an intimate friend of Faulkner's, which is how she came to write the "Writers at Work" interview with him for *Paris Review.* What if I'd said I hated Faulkner, found him an incoherent bombastic pretentious bore? Our fate hinges on the convergence of dirty spark plugs, a Texas accent, literary taste, and a menial chore.

And an unexpected visitor. A few months into my job I was getting restless. I'd yet to make a deal for any of the books and screenwriters that Ned had dropped on my plate, and small wonder: predominantly they were the hopeless cases, the lepers on the list, and I was Damien of Molokai. Furthermore, my on-the-job training—the only way to learn the ropes, akin to those aspirant attorneys in days of yore reading law in an attorney's office as their legal education—suffered from Ned's quaint notion of mentoring. His answer to a query about the suspiciously convoluted language in a studio contract was, "Listen, chum, in this business, the less you know the better off you are." One day, when I was driving him to the airport, I took the opportunity to relate a concern about the future of one of the screenwriters we represented, and in the middle of my monologue he interrupted me: "Chum, can you do me a favor?" "Sure, Ned." "Will you for Christ's sake shut the fuck up." Compounding the frustration was the lack of an escape valve: none of my contacts in the story departments I was calling on seemed encouraging about openings on their staffs in the near future.

Then one fine day a novelist came calling. A shy, polite Mississippian, Thomas Hal Phillips, tall, lanky, with Scotch-Irish sharp features. His recent novel, *The Loved and the Unloved,* dramatized the coming-of-age of a Mississippi farm boy; less influenced by Faulkner than by Dickens, it had been praised by reviewers and ignored by the reading public. The publisher, Harper & Brothers (now HarperCollins), controlled the film rights and had asked us to represent them, sharing the commission. I'd schlepped it around to the bottom-feeding producers and independents I'd been assigned, but of course there'd been no takers.

Hal, however, was not all that concerned about the movie sale of his novel. He'd come to Hollywood to be a screenwriter. Even more of a naif than I, he could have stepped out of a Frank Capra movie—the unspoiled country boy in a land of con men and ganefs. As I tried to explain the futility of his aspirations (I was getting to be an expert on futile aspirations), focusing on his lack of experience, the brutal competition, and so on, the phone rang. Sol Lesser on the line, in a bind. A producer specializing in Tarzan adventure pics, Lesser agitatedly reported that the screenwriter on the next Tarzan epic had walked off the job and had to be replaced immediately. Did I have anyone available?

I looked across my desk into those innocent blue Mississippi eyes, and inspiration struck. "Well, Mr. Lesser, you may be in luck. It just happens that a distinguished southern novelist is in town to talk to the major studios about writing the screenplay of his new novel. In fact, Ned's with him at Metro this afternoon. He's already met with the people at Paramount and Fox, and they're keen on him. Even though he's never written a script, the dialogue in his novels is terrific, the structure cinematic. He's a natural. I'm not certain he'll have the time or inclination to take on a Tarzan assignment, but I could ask. What kind of money did you have in mind?" Desperate now to sign this hot young writer, Lesser came up with a high figure for an unknown. I said thanks, but it was inappropriate for a man of Phillips's stature. We haggled for a few minutes, he upped the offer substantially, and I told him I'd have to discuss this with Ned.

During this conversation, Hal stared at me, wide-eyed with disbelief and shock, and when I hung up he said, "You lied to that fella, didn't you?" "No, Hal, I didn't lie. This is Hollywood, land of fantasy, illusions, fairy tales. The proverbial dream factory. You know that line from *Death of a Salesman,* 'A salesman has got to dream, boy. It comes with the territory.' In this territory, no one expects you to tell the unvarnished truth. That's not the game. The truth is that you're able to make someone believe. It's not lying, it's storytelling. It's what you do as a novelist. Out here, we're simply living our stories as we go along."

He got the job, and one of the distinctive moments in his script was Jane reading to Tarzan a love poem she'd just written for him. Not quite a Sonnet from the Portuguese, but it brought a touch of literacy as rare in Ape Man flicks as an unfunny chimp.

While he was working on the script, we developed a friendship. A pair of Young Men from the Southern Provinces, at play in the fields of the Mayers and the Zanucks and the Goldwyns and the Selznicks. Eight years my senior, the son of a farmer and a schoolteacher, Hal had served with the navy during World War II and been involved in the invasion of Anzio. After the war he got an M.A. in creative writing from the University of Alabama, and just before coming to Hollywood had taught at Southern Methodist University in Dallas. I'd served with the air force in Korea during the war as public information officer and base labor officer at a jet fighter-bomber base near Taegu, in the South. "You must have felt right at home fighting for the South," he told me at lunch one day in a coffee shop near the studio, one of the lesser factories which lacked a commissary. "Yes," I said, "that also was a Civil War in which the North was the villain." Naturally, we talked about his fellow Mississippian Faulkner, or Mr. Bill as Hal called him, whom Hal had met on several occasions. And we discovered we shared a passion for Scott Fitzgerald and his greatest creation, Jay Gatsby, that American romantic, that ultimate Young Man from the Provinces, reinventing himself as he made a shady fortune in Gotham.

And finally, Hal asked me for a favor. To do so embarrassed him; he blushed and stammered, and for a second I thought he was going to paw his big toe in the dust and say, "Aw shuckins." Then, apologizing profusely for imposing on me, he said that he'd brought to California the first draft of his next novel, which he was planning to revise as soon as he said farewell to Jane and Tarzan, and he wondered if I'd have the time to read it and give him a candid opinion. I told him I was flattered, and would consider it a privilege, thus provoking another seizure of blushing and stammering.

The new novel was a major departure from *The Loved and the Unloved*. A six-hundred-page saga about a Mississippi political dynasty official in the state, it teemed with vivid characters, intrigue, betrayals, passion—and a slew of narrative problems. Making notes as I read, I found myself propelled by the kind of nervous energy and exhilaration that had seized me at Texas A&M when writing an essay for English 202 or a devastating analysis of a movie or a book for my column in the *Battalion.* But now, instead of merely detecting flaws, pronouncing judgments, and making jokes at the creator's expense, I was suggesting how to strengthen characters, enrich the narrative, dramatize exposition, create suspense and tension by reorganizing the plot, and pointing out where cuts would be helpful.

I incorporated these notes in a twenty-five-page memorandum and sent them by messenger the next morning to Hal at the studio. Late that afternoon he phoned me: "I've read your memorandum," he said evenly. "We have to talk about this. Why don't you come over for sandwiches tonight?" That was it. No bashful splutter of gratitude, not even a simple "thanks a whole bunch." I'd overstepped myself. Who did I think I was— Bunny Wilson lavishing my wisdom on F. Scott?

Hal's drab furnished apartment was in a grungy Spanish-style building on Yucca, near Hollywood Boulevard, an area that brought to mind the novels of Raymond Chandler. On this particular night, I felt exactly like Philip Marlowe, about to confront a client whose case I'd botched. Hal opened the door and stood there silently for a moment, holding in his hand the infamous memo, staring at me fixedly. Then he said firmly, as if talking to one of his SMU students, "You must quit your job as soon as possible. You must go to New York. You, my friend, are a book editor. Not an agent. Not a story editor. A book editor." Brandishing the memo in my face, he continued: "What makes this remarkable is that you aren't asking me to write the novel you'd have written if you could. You've somehow jumped into my doggone brain, into my soul, and you've seen the book I was trying to write but didn't have the perspective to bring off. Now, you could be a creative writing teacher like I was, if you wanted to go off and get a master's. But I think I know you. You're after something bigger. Both of us are. We're southern boys, we're the last of the romantics."

Now it was my time to splutter and stammer. But I didn't argue with the man. He'd held up a mirror, showing me who I really was. What I really could become if I had the will and dedication. By God, I'd quit MCA tomorrow, I promised. Hal and I spent the rest of the evening scarfing up the only kind of sandwiches he considered edible—peanut butter and bananas on white bread—and going over the memo point by point.

Forget about Raymond Chandler and Philip Marlowe. This had been a night straight out of Dickens or Balzac or Thackeray—I was Pip or Copperfield or Lucien Chardon or Pendennis, once again girding myself for a run at fame and fortune. With this difference: by chance—kismet again—I'd stumbled on my true vocation. Erik Erikson says that identity confusion comes from a disturbance in the sense of workmanship; I'd been in the throes of a prolonged identity crisis because I'd lost that sense of workmanship. Because of Hal, I'd regained it. Young Men from the Provinces flock to the fabled Metropolis not to invent themselves but to *discover* themselves, to realize their true selves. New York, here I come again, this time in pursuit not of a fantasy but of a career based on skills I actually possessed.

When I told Ned I was leaving, he said, "Good decision. You'd never have made a good movie agent. You like movies, not the movie business. I'd have fired you by the end of the year. Good timing, chum." He offered to write letters of recommendation for me to the publishing moguls of his acquaintance. On my own I took the Manhattan address and phone number of one of Ned's prized clients, the novelist James Jones, whose *From Here to Eternity* had been published just before I graduated from A&M, and whose about-to-be-published novel *Some Came Running* Ned had sold to Metro a few months previously. *Eternity*, a novel about soldiers on duty at Schofield Barracks in Honolulu just before and after Pearl Harbor, had torn me up. And *Some Came Running*, a gargantuan thousand-plus pages in hardcover, if not the Great American Novel as Jones surely intended it, struck me nevertheless as the definitive novel about middle-class Middle West American life. Maybe I'd give him a call when I hit town. Me and James Jones, buddies.

Just before I left California, Elliot Kastner, the agent who was replacing me, an affable savvy operator who'd been an agent in the New York office of MCA's formidable rival, William Morris, warned me that editorial jobs were scarce, and that Ned's letters notwithstanding, I'd likely find myself starting out in low-paying editorial flunkydom. "In New York," he said with a genial smile, "you won't be living in a modern apartment with a lot of stewardesses splashing around in the courtyard swimming pool. You'll be lucky to afford a single room with a naked lightbulb hanging from a link chain in the ceiling." He advised me to write Helen Strauss, head of William Morris's literary department. "Who knows, she may be looking for someone. Once you're an agent, you can make your own contacts with editors, learn the business, wait for a promising opportunity to come along. Forget about Ned's chums. They'll shake your hand and pass you off to the personnel department, and you know where that'll get you." I protested that I wanted nothing more to do with the agency business, that I was temperamentally unsuited for it. He smiled ungenially: "Don't be a fucking schmuck! Sit down at the goddamned typewriter and pour out your little heart to Helen Strauss—now!" Grudgingly, I obeyed.

Sure enough, Elliot's gloomy vision proved to be twenty-twenty. Waiting for me in Gotham were measly-salaried editorial assistantships, in which I'd be primarily a secretary who in my spare time would read whatever unpublishable scraps the boss would toss me and report on their unpublishability. Out of desperation, I phoned Helen Strauss. "Come right over," she ordered in a husky voice which somehow combined force with congeniality. "I need someone to replace a young man who's going into the army." Timing, luck, connections. When would this magic string desert me?

When I arrived in her waiting room, Miss Strauss was on the phone, but her secretary had been told to bring me into her office as soon as I showed up. Behind a desk piled with folders, papers, a manuscript or two, and smoking a cigarette sat a small, not quite dumpy woman probably in her late forties, with short wavy red-brown hair, thickish features, slightly protuberant eyes. Exhaling a thick plume of smoke in exasperation, she snapped at the party on the other end of the line, "Don't be a complete horse's ass, Bennett. Miss Janeway will not change the title of her novel, and that's final." Bang went the phone into its cradle. Here was a woman powerful enough to call Bennett Cerf a horse's ass and hang up in his face. She crushed out her cigarette in an ashtray and immediately lighted another. "I want to hear a lot of awful things about that mean little bastard Ned Brown" were her opening words. "Only if you promise to hire me," I replied. "Well, aren't you the brazen negotiator," she said. And after short pro forma introductions to Nat Lefkowitz, the diminutive head of William Morris, and Abe Lastfogel, the diminutive president of William Morris, I joined Helen Strauss's duchy within the Morris empire.

Actually, she was more queen than duchess, the monarch of her realm, the Elizabeth the Great of the agency business. A charismatic presence, she radiated a sense of authority, a fierce indomitability, and a merciless no-crap-permitted intelligence. Despite her plainness and her unprepossessing figure, she was impeccably stylish; she may not have been glamorous, but she did project a feminine allure. She was every inch a Lady, a Class Act. She did not suffer gladly loutish behavior, especially profanity.

I started with a bang, selling television rights to Robert Penn Warren's *All the King's Men* to the self-described distinguished producer David Susskind. Warren had been a client of Helen's for years. So had James Baldwin and Edwin O'Connor. And James Michener, who credited Helen with shaping his career as a novelist. Michener had been a textbook editor at Macmillan when Helen urged him to make a book out of his tales of the South Pacific; subsequently, she sold the theatrical rights to Rodgers and Hammerstein. Helen was one of the few agents who had the instincts of a publisher, making her valuable not only in negotiating lucrative terms for authors but in advising them on the direction their work should take and placing them with editors and publishers under whose guidance they'd be most likely to flourish.

I served my monarch diligently, hustling manuscripts and making deals, scouring magazines and writers' conferences and writing programs at Columbia, NYU, and the New School for prospective clients. Inadvertently, I almost reeled in none other than my hero among living authors, James Jones (in those days, major authors were heroic figures in the great romance of literature).

Not long after I arrived in New York, *Some Came Running* had been published to gleefully vicious reviews which rejoiced in declaring that *From Here to Eternity* had been a fluke and implied that nothing more of value would be written by this uneducated boor. I remembered how the critic for *Blackwoods Magazine* had reviled John Keats, that uppity Cockney, and how Lord Byron had risen savagely to his defense in his polemic "English Bards and Scotch Reviewers." But no Byron rose up on Jones's behalf. Up to then I'd been unable to muster the courage to phone Mr.

Jones, fearing that I'd come across like a sappy idolizer. But now that he'd been wounded—perhaps fatally, as far as his career went—I felt compelled to tell him how outraged I was by the goddamned eunuchoid critics, who didn't have the cojones to recognize an American titan. I dialed the number, and he answered on the second ring, his voice a raspy growl that matched the pugnacious bulldog face and barrel-chested torso on the dust jackets of his books. I identified myself, revealed that I'd read the novel in installments at MCA and that as far as I was concerned it put him in the ranks of the great American social realists. "Come on over and have a drink with me and Mossy," he said. Mossy was his wife, the former Gloria Mossolino.

I hit it off right away with Jim and the comely, earthy Mossy, a blunt wisecracking truth-talker, and began to see them frequently. Could this be happening? Boswell and Johnson, Gollob and Jones. And it got better: one night as we were getting sloshed in the crowded little bar at Rattazi's, an Italian restaurant around the corner from Scribner's on East Forty-eighth, Jim said, "Gloria and I like you. We trust you. I'm leaving Ned Brown and MCA, they give me a pain in the ass. We want you to be my agent. But I won't sign a contract with William Morris. As long as you're there, they can handle my stuff. If you leave, I leave."

When I reported this jubilantly to Helen, she looked at me ironically over her horn-rimmed half-glasses, took a puff of what must have been her umpteenth Parliament of the morning, put aside the letter she was reading, and said, "Mr. Gollob"—"Mr. Gollob" always prefaced a chastisement—"as you well know, it is a policy of this agency not to represent anyone who refuses to sign a contract. Why don't you ask Mr. Jones to have a drink with us and I'll explain this to him? I'll be charming. He'll understand."

Jones agreed to have drinks, warning me: "I'll listen to the woman, but I ain't changing my mind." He suggested we meet at Toots Shor's, his preferred watering place. Helen and I arrived to find Jim and Gloria ensconced in a booth, drinking martinis and laughing raucously. I could sense the very proper Miss Strauss bristle. Coarse jocosity was not her thing. Her severe expression did not herald an intent to charm. Jim and Gloria sized her up quickly: a prim disapproving spinster who put on airs.

After I'd made the introductions, Jim turned to Helen and said, "I was just telling Glo that I thought Ethel Merman was a dumb cunt. What do you think, Helen?" That set the tone for the evening's revelry. And a short evening it was: Helen excused herself after a half an hour, insisting that I remain. "I guess you ain't going to be my agent, Herm," Jim laughed. Right. "I wouldn't represent that bum if he signed a contract in blood," Helen told me the next day.

Over the months I'd cultivated editors roughly my age: Bob Gottlieb, Simon & Schuster's brash wunderkind; Henry Robbins, Knopf's charming, strong-minded executive editor; Jim Silberman, Dial Press's judicious editor in chief; Robert Lescher, Henry Holt's thoughtful, articulate executive editor; Harvey Ginsberg, Doubleday's incisive, opinionated senior editor; and above all, the polymath of polymaths, Alan Williams, the phenomenally erudite, slyly funny, large-souled New York editor of J. B. Lippincott, a Philadelphia-based house. Alan was not simply a simpatico professional acquaintance: he was a kindred spirit. How could I not warm to a man who, like me, had been stationed for a time at an air force base in San Antonio, who—wonder of wonders—knew that freshmen at Texas A&M were called "fish," and who was so adept at movie trivia that he could identify the croupier in *Casablanca* as a French actor named Marcel Dalio. Moreover, born into a middle-class family in St. Paul, Minnesota, Alan was yet another provincial who'd gone East to make good, graduating from Exeter and Yale—he looked the part, blond, regular-featured, handsome—and eventually becoming an editor.

A year passed, enough time, I thought, to begin capitalizing on my publishing relationships and to start dropping discreet hints about my ambition to become an editor. Given the knowledge I'd acquired about the economics of publishing, and the editorial judgment I'd managed to convey as I discussed the manuscripts I represented and the revisions that might be necessary, I felt it was unlikely I'd be given the brush-off.

Before I could put this process in motion, Alan Williams called to share a piece of good news. He'd just been hired away from Lippincott to be the New York editor of a Boston firm, Little, Brown & Company. I treated him to a very wet celebratory lunch at the Old Absinthe House, then a treasured publishing hangout, now long defunct. Braced with a few doses of Scotch, flushed with the warmth of camaraderie that overrode discretion, I confessed that when I grew up, I wanted to be an editor. Alan seemed startled, and I assumed I'd overreached. Not at all.

"Your timing couldn't be better," he said. Timing, luck, connections. My holy trinity at work again. It so happened that Little, Brown was interviewing candidates for an associate editorship in the home office. If I didn't mind the prospect of relocating to Boston, he'd recommend me for the job and arrange an interview with John Cushman, the managing editor. "Fish Gollob in Beantown. I'd pay to see that movie. It would be more fun than *A Yank at Oxford.*" "Which starred Robert Taylor," I added.

I returned to the office and told Helen I was leaving the agency to become an editor. "And where will you be editing, Mr. Gollob?" "I have an interview with someone from Little, Brown next week." Resigning before I'd been hired elsewhere struck Miss Strauss as a mite rash. Perhaps it was the alcohol speaking (it didn't take Bambi to detect the aroma I was exuding). I should go home, sleep it off, and make a decision when my faculties were intact. No, I insisted, I'm through. No matter what. "I'm not certain that Little, Brown is especially fond of hiring Jews," she observed. "In fact, I doubt they've ever had a Jewish editor. Maybe it's time they should. And you're not exactly Orthodox, are you? Next to me, you may be the most un-Jewish Jew in the agency. Sit down while I make a call." She phoned Arthur Thornhill, Sr., the crusty president of Little, Brown, who'd worked his way up from the mail room. "Arthur, a young man in my office, Herman Gollob, is foolish enough to want to leave the agency business and become an editor. He'd be a brilliant one." Hanging up after a minute or so of small talk, she glared at me and lighted a Parliament. "You didn't deserve that. Now, if you're sober enough, go do something useful. You're still on salary."

A month later, after a battery of interviews in Boston and New York with John Cushman, editor in chief Ned Bradford, executive vice president Arthur Thornhill, Jr., and vice president and publisher J. Randall Williams, I was on a train north.

Over the next three and a half decades I'd move on and move up, building a solid editorial reputation and ultimately becoming editor in chief at Atheneum and Harper's Magazine Press (which my old southern comrade Willie Morris asked me to establish in conjunction with the magazine, a la the Atlantic Monthly Press) and Doubleday, with stop-offs at Simon & Schuster and the Literary Guild along the way. I'd be the first to edit Donald Barthelme, James Clavell, Dan Jenkins, Bill Moyers. But nothing would generate the unalloyed near-manic joy that swarmed over Fish Gollob as he headed for his adventures in Beantown, staring out the train window as dusk fell on the wintry Connecticut landscape, eager and impatient to prove himself in his newfound profession, charged with what Scott Fitzgerald in *The Great Gatsby* had called a "heightened sensitivity to the promises of life." I recalled the cross-country trips by bus and train I'd made in pursuit of what turned out to be the wrong dream. And I must have realized I was kidding myself, because unlike the surging confidence I found difficult to control at the moment, on those treks back and forth from California to New York I often woke up in the middle of the night in some desolate stretch of southern farmland, seized with unnamed apprehensions difficult to shake off, as if I were a hobo riding the rails during hard times, down-and-out, no prospects at all.

Jay Gatsby, that archetypal romantic, had followed the wrong dream, not realizing it was leading him not into the future but into the past. And so had I, once upon a time not long before. Now, in wild anticipation rolling through the dark fields of the Republic, I thought of a real life Young Man from the Provinces, an Ohioan named William Dean Howells, who at the age of twenty-nine after sojourning in Europe and New York City, had come to Boston to join the editorial staff of the *Atlantic Monthly* and had gone to a glorious literary career as editor, critic, novelist. I, too, was twenty-nine, about to arrive in Boston filled with exalted ambitions.

Me and William Dean Howells.

And lest we forget, me and that young man from Stratford, William Shakespeare.

4.

With Ralph Fiennes's performance still very much on my mind during my early days of retirement in the summer of 1995, I reread *Hamlet* as part of the Shakespeare studies that had begun to take over my life, and I saw that Hamlet's lines to Horatio in 5.2, "There's a divinity that shapes our ends, / Rough-hew them how we will—," his way of explaining the impulse that led him to the discovery on the voyage to England of the documents that called for his execution, could be applied to the crucial happenings that shaped and would continue to shape my life, and which I'd once attributed to luck, fate, timing, connections. We're on this earth to serve a purpose, however humble or exalted it may be, and discovering that purpose is what the sense of vocation, the calling, is all about.

Maynard Mack, in *Everybody's Shakespeare,* which continued to be a source of enlightenment for me, speaks of Shakespeare's use of journeys to indicate that a character, for example Hamlet, is undergoing psychological change. Returning from his journey, Hamlet appears, spiritually, a changed man. From the vantage point of my sixty-fifth year, I could track the changes in my own character following each of my journeys, as I groped to find my particular niche in the scheme of things.

And as I made my way through the Shakespeare canon, I continued to discern a moral principle, a psychological observation, common to the plays I was rereading or reading for the first time, which could be summed up in Ralph Waldo Emerson's declaration that "pure intellect is pure evil." Shakespeare seemed to be convinced that the evil in this world is perpetrated by those who develop the intellect at the expense of the heart or those whose crooked hearts, twisted by nature or nurture, have poisoned their minds. Julius Caesar sounds the note in his penetrating, on-the-mark analysis of Cassius: "He thinks too much. Such men are dangerous. / . . . . He reads much, / He is a great observer, and he looks / Quite through the deeds of men. . . . / Such men as he be never at heart's ease / Whiles they behold a greater than themselves, / And therefore are they very dangerous." Caesar could just as well be describing Iago, Richard III, Edmund the Bastard, Aaron the Moor. And, of course, himself.

I wondered if Melville had shared this take on Shakespeare's vision of evil, and if it might have been one of the Shakespearean influences at work in the creation of *Moby-Dick*. Checking biographies of Melville by Laurie Robinson-Lorant and Herchel Parker, and Jay Leyda's incomparable *The Melville Log: A Documentary Life,* a compendium of letters and journal entries by Melville and his family and friends and publishers, newspaper clippings, reviews, and so forth, I came up empty. But I did find a clue, a tenuous indirect connection, in his review of Hawthorne's *Mosses from an Old Manse,* in which Melville claimed that Hawthorne was an American Shakespeare, because of a "blackness in Hawthorne," a blackness, says Melville, "that furnishes the infinite obscure of his background,—that back-ground against which Shakespeare plays his grandest conceits, the things that have made for Shakespeare his loftiest but most circumscribed renown, as the profoundest of thinkers. . . . Through the mouths of the dark characters of Hamlet, Timon, Lear and Iago, he craftily says, or sometimes insinuates the things, which we feel to be so terrifically true, that it were all but madness for any good man, in his own proper character, to utter, or even hint of them. . . ." But Melville fails to define that "blackness"; he neglects to elaborate on the truths spoken by Shakespeare's characters which affect all of us so profoundly.

Searching through biographies of Hawthorne by Edwin Havilland Miller and James R. Mellow, I found no evidence that this "blackness" shared with Shakespeare might be a belief in man's dangerous capacity to exalt reason over the heart's affections. So I decided to turn to Hawthorne's work, and bingo! there it was, in many of Hawthorne's best-known parables, spelled out most clearly and emphatically in "Ethan Brand," one of Hawthorne's most popular and unforgettable stories.

Ethan Brand had committed the unpardonable sin: he had pursued a "vast intellectual development, which in its progress, disturbed the counterpoise between his mind and his heart," raising him from "the level of an unlettered laborer" to an eminence which made him the envy of the world's philosophers. "So much for the intellect! But where was the heart? That, indeed, had withered—had contracted—had hardened—had perished! It had ceased to partake of the universal throb. He had lost his hold of the magnetic chain of humanity. . . . he was now a cold observer, . . . converting man and woman to be his puppets, and pulling the wires that moved them to such degrees of crime as were demanded for his study. Thus Ethan Brand had become a fiend. . . . from the moment that his moral nature had ceased to keep pace of improvement with his intellect." Tormented with guilt, Brand hurls himself into a lime kiln filled with a mass of broken red-hot marble; the next morning the lime burner and his son find in the midst of the lime Brand's skeleton, the shape of the human heart still visible in the rib cage. "Was the fellow's heart made of marble?" cried the lime burner.

In "Rappaccini's Daughter," Rappaccini, a famous doctor and scientist, cares infinitely more for science than for mankind. His patients are interesting to him only as subjects for some new experiment. He "would sacrifice human life" in the interest of science. Rappaccini has cultivated a poison garden which ultimately is responsible for the death of his daughter, the victim of the ingenuity and perverted wisdom of a scientist who has lost touch with humanity.

In "Egotism; or Bosom Serpent," Roderick Elliston has an actual reptile inside his body, poisoning his heart. Elliston can think only of himself, afflicted with the disease of self-centeredness, which has destroyed his human feelings.

My deduction: Melville, influenced by Hawthorne, derived from his reading of Shakespeare a conviction that man's unpardonable sin was his dehumanizing cultivation of the rational. And in support of this conclusion, I felt, was the debt that all three men owed to Michel de Montaigne (1533–92); who invented the personal essay and whose collected essays were translated into English first by John Florio in 1603 and read by Shakespeare, thereby, according to Park Honan, a recent biographer, "enriching his outlook and even his vocabulary." Delving into the lives of Melville and Hawthorne, I was reminded that on the day that Melville bought his two-volume edition of Shakespeare, he also bought the essays of Montaigne, and later, in *Hamlet* 2.2., he underlined Hamlet's "Why, then 'tis none to you, for there is nothing either good or bad but thinking makes it so; to me it is a prison," and commented in the margin, "Here is forcibly shown the great Montaignism of Hamlet." And Hawthorne claimed to have read and reread Montaigne early in youth.

In 1993, after reading Joseph Epstein's sparkling appreciation of Montaigne in *Commentary,* I bought M. A. Screech's translation of the complete essays and devoted much of the next year to reading through it. Now I picked it up again, somewhat daunted by the prospect of searching out in its twelve hundred pages precisely those reflections that related to the conflict of the mind versus the heart, and I found tucked into the front of the book Mr. Epstein's essay, which I'd presciently extracted from the magazine for just such an occasion. Happily, I also discovered that Mr. Epstein had done my work for me.

"In logic," writes Mr. Epstein, "Montaigne found crippling, even laughable, limitations." In "Apology for Raymond Sebond," the longest essay in the book, Mr. Epstein relates, and "the only one with a polemical intent, Montaigne sets out after rationalism, whose chief internal danger he views as establishing the belief in men that they can achieve universal truth outside religion, through the sheer power of their reasoning." Montaigne was on his father's side a Roman Catholic; his mother's was a family of Spanish Jews who had outwardly accepted Christianity. "In the 'Apology,'" Epstein continues, "Montaigne writes 'There is a plague on man: his opinion that he knows something.' . . . Montaigne is concerned that men will make the horrendously arrogant mistake of believing that they are in control of their own destinies. . . . With theories, opinion, custom, knowledge, even our senses forever changing, Montaigne concludes that he 'would rather be guided by results than by reason—for [the two] are always clashing.'" And Epstein could be referring to Shakespeare himself when he observes that Montaigne's answer to the question "If we cannot trust either our knowledge or our senses . . . what guidance do we then turn to in the hope of living our lives with a modicum of decency, dignity and contentment?" is "to understand experience rightly, and to quest for understanding human nature." Given the complex, contradictory quality of the human soul, that quest would be unending.

I recalled a passage from Montaigne's "Of the Inconsistency of Our Actions" I'd come across in the prologue to Marvin Rosenberg's *The*

Masks of Hamlet, to illustrate his point that Shakespeare had set out to cram into a single character "as much as possible of the clashing multiplicity of human personality": "He who examines himself closely will seldom find himself twice in the same state. . . . All the contradictions are to be found in me, according as the wind turns, and changes. Bashful, insolent; chaste, lascivious; talkative, taciturn; clumsy, gentle; witty, dull; peevish, sweet-tempered; lying, truthful; knowing, ignorant; and liberal and avaricious and prodigal. . . ."

To me it seemed evident that Montaigne had passed on his view of the human condition to Shakespeare, and through him to Hawthorne and Melville. What a lark, the thrill of literary sleuthing! And with no purpose in mind at all, no academic goals to achieve, no paper to write, no forbidding prospect of peer review, only the private satisfaction of the autodidact.

Toward the end of the summer, as if timed specifically to boost along my newfound pursuit, came a catalog from Elderhostel Program International, the travel-study organization designed for people over fifty, announcing among its plethora of courses one perfectly tailored to my consuming enthusiasm: a series of seminars on Shakespearean acting, directing, costume, speech, movement, and makeup, conducted over a period of ten days in Stratford-on-Avon and London by the Royal Shakespeare Company, and tickets to RSC performances of *The Taming of the Shrew, Romeo and Juliet, Julius Caesar,* and *Measure for Measure.*

Barbara and I enrolled, and within a few days received a list of recommended reading in preparation for the seminars. I bought two of the books: *Playgoing in Shakespeare's London,* by Andrew Gurr, professor of English at the University of Reading, and of all things a book I hadn't known existed, John Barton's *Playing Shakespeare,* a transcription—edited, cut, expanded, and in some places reworded for clarity—of the televised workshops.

In his preface, Barton reveals that the workshops were partly scripted and that because more material was recorded than was screened, segments on "Using the Prose," "Using the Sonnets," and "Contemporary Shakespeare" appear in the book for the first time. Right away I turned to these chapters, excited at discovering a new hoard of riches from a group I'd watched so often that I'd begun to think of them as friends and colleagues, and found that in my mind I could actually hear the participants speaking, that it was all coming to life in front of me. For example, in "Using the Prose," there were Michael Pennington (Mercutio) and Roger Rees (Romeo) working on the scene in which Mercutio has just been mortally wounded, and Barton pointing out how the speeches alternate between verse and prose, prose when Mercutio is speaking of the grim reality of death, verse when Romeo laments Mercutio's fatal hurt as soon as Mercutio is taken out.

Gurr's account of Shakespearean playgoing studies the physical structures of the different types of playhouses (the amphitheatre playhouses, the hall playhouses) and performing conditions (auditorium behavior); analyzes the social structure and the social types who were playgoers during the period (from craft apprentices to court ladies and royalty) and the mental composition of different audiences or spectators; and traces the evolution of tastes.

Before leaving for England, I couldn't resist buying two books not on the RSC list but no less useful as preparation for the course and the pilgrimage to Stratford. The first was *The Actor and the Text,* by Cicely Berry, voice director of the RSC and guru to the likes of Trevor Nunn and John Barton. Addressed primarily to actors and directors, it seemed to me much more than a manual of vocal technique for practitioners; it showed the way to discovering the inner life of Shakespeare's characters by studying the verse and the language. I began to highlight as I read, and after a time realized that each page was a solid sheet of yellow—every line was a revelation. One of Ms. Berry's key points, made at the start, is the danger of an overeducated response to words. Because we see lines on the printed page first, "we make a judgement on them from a cultural and sense point of view, so that our initial response to them is a 'read' one and not an intuitive one . . . it makes it difficult for us to live through the words as they happen, because we begin to feel out of control of the sense . . . we have to find ways . . . to make [words] part of our physical self in order to release them from the tyranny of the mind." And Ms. Berry sees breath as more than a means of giving the voice power, resonance, and flexibility. Breath, she declares, "is the physical life of the thought . . . the breath and the thought are one," and she goes on to say, "how the character breathes is how the character thinks." And this, on

Shakespeare's energy: "There is in Shakespeare an energy which runs through the text which is not a naturalistic one, an energy which impels one word to the next, one line to the next, one thought to the next, one speech to the next, and one scene to the next. . . ." Cicely Berry's text is charged with the same energy. In his foreword, Trevor Nunn describes Ms. Berry as "a voice teacher with a mission." Unsurprisingly, the book is a perfect companion to *Playing Shakespeare.*

The other book I added to my pre-Elderhostel reading was *Shakespeare's Lives,* by Samuel Schoenbaum, author of *William Shakespeare: A Compact Documentary Life.* An account of the lives and personalities of Shakespeare's biographers over the past two centuries, and over five hundred pages long, its erudition and verve and extraordinary narrative force held me in its clutches for the better part of a week. I found two of Schoenbaum's portraits especially wonderful:

- William Henry Ireland, a conveyancer's clerk in London, a rascal of epic dimensions who forged documents purported to be written by Shakespeare, including a love letter to "Anna Hatherrewaye," accompanied by a lock of Shakespeare's hair, tied with thick woven silk. Ultimately, his roguery was exposed by Edmond Malone, an Irishman who had abandoned a career in the law, moved to London, and written a distinguished study of Shakespeare and the documentary evidence pertaining to his life.
- Delia Bacon, an anti-Stratfordian extraordinaire, perhaps the most grotesque among the species, an eccentric Connecticut spinster who had operated private schools and dabbled in fiction before embarking on her great work, *The Philosophy of the Plays of Shakspere Unfolded,* in which she insisted that an ignorant peasant such as Shakespeare couldn't possibly have been the author of these masterpieces. Her candidate for authorship: Francis Bacon. Thoroughly mad, she claimed that the hieroglyphics of Bacon's name supplied the key to the mystery: they contained instructions for locating a will and other relics secreted in a hollow space beneath Shakespeare's gravestone. Thomas Carlyle, whom she'd visited in London, indignantly shouted at her, "Do you mean to say that Ben Jonson [Shakespeare's friend and rival playwright], and Heminges and Condell [Shakespeare's fellow actors,

who after his death collected the plays in the First Folio], and all the Shakespeare scholars since, are wrong about the authorship, and you are going to set them right?" The definitive response, I think, to the lunacies of this odd breed. One literary figure was surprisingly sympathetic to Delia: Nathaniel Hawthorne, who was dubious about her theory but responsive to her passionate faith in her misbegotten ideas. He gave her money, helped her in efforts to get her work published, even wrote a tepid preface; but when he refused to let the author dedicate the book to him, the friendship ended. Perhaps what Hawthorne actually found appealing in Delia Bacon was that she could have been a character in one of his stories or novels, a creature unhinged by a monomaniacal intellectual pursuit.

Barbara did not share my zest for all this preparatory cramming. "I don't want my head chock full of stuff before I arrive," she said. "I'd rather be a tabula rasa, waiting to discover something entirely new and fresh to me. You have different needs. Just remember: it's not essential for you to be the smartest little guy in the group."

Small chance of that, as it turned out. Among the thirty Elderhostelers on the trip, at least half had been college professors, schoolteachers, corporate executives. We met them during an orientation session and get-acquainted dinner at the luxurious Heathrow Airport hotel where we'd been taken shortly after landing. I immediately connected with Arthur Kay, a retired English professor who had been one of Lionel Trilling's protégés at Columbia. Art was a humanist of the old school, only too happy, it seemed, to have left the faction-ridden politicized world of the contemporary American university and to be devoting his life to travel with his wife, Rita, an artist, to private study, and to his beloved hobby, cabinetmaking. Over roast beef and ale that night, I gushed about a poem I'd come across recently, Delmore Schwartz's "Gold Morning, Sweet Prince," a tribute to Shakespeare which for me captured the essence of the man and moved me to tears, especially the final lines: "Gold morning, prince of Avon, sovereign and king / Of reality, hope, and speech, may all the angels sing / With all the sweetness and all the truth with which you sang of any- / thing and everything." Art smiled at me, one of those kindly, amused (but not a bit patronizing) Wise Professor to Eager Naive

61

Student smiles. "Yes, it's nice, sentimental of course, not all that complicated. But it can't hold a candle to Edward Arlington Robinson's 'Ben Jonson Entertains a Man from Stratford.' Are you familiar with it?" Ah, yet another item to add to my reading list.

The next morning we were bused to our Stratford accommodations, the Falcon Hotel, built in the late sixteenth century. Seminars were held in conference rooms which were part of a semimodern annex to the original Falcon. By far the liveliest were the voice-work session conducted by Andrew Wade, one of Cicely Berry's younger colleagues at the RSC, and a question-and-answer meeting with Julian Glover, an RSC stalwart for many years and featured as Friar Laurence and Cassius in the productions of *Romeo and Juliet* and *Julius Caesar* we'd be seeing that week.

Wade, bubbly and commanding, instantly had us on our feet, urging us to conquer self-consciousness and shout out ensemble a speech from *Coriolanus* he'd handed out at the beginning of class and then putting us through a couple more exercises from the Berry program. Quite a sight: thirty seniors, ranging from the mid-fifties to the early eighties, gesturing wildly and screaming Shakespearean verse at the top of their lungs. It could have been a class in iambic pentameter aerobics at the recreation room of a retirees' village in Boca Raton.

Julian Glover, tall, aristocratically handsome, probably in his late fifties but very well preserved, and gracefully ironic, talked about his career at the RSC and how his progress in status had been measured by his ascent, floor by floor, to the dressing rooms for the elite. Asked about his current roles, he said one thing in particular that made an impact on me: playing Friar Laurence, he made a point of learning the exact qualities of the potions that the friar was mixing for Romeo, to make that moment convincing onstage.

The Falcon was ideally situated for literary pilgrims, directly across from the site of Shakespeare's "New Place," the second largest home in Stratford, which he had bought for himself and his family in 1597 in the midst of his flourishing career and which had been demolished in the eighteenth century, and catercorner to the Guild Chapel and its adjacent schoolhouse, where Shakespeare attended the tuition-free grammar school. Walking past it, I could imagine young Will in one of the classrooms, where he remained from six or seven in the morning until five or six, with a short break for lunch, toiling at his Latin, poring over Ovid, Virgil, and Horace, especially Ovid, whose *Metamorphoses* he especially relished. This was the sort of education Shakespeare enjoyed during his youth, far superior to that offered to most university students today, and enough to give the lie to the accusation that he was an ignorant peasant scarcely able to write his name much less a dramatic masterpiece.

A few blocks away from the Falcon is Shakespeare's Birthplace on Henley Street. I'd made the obligatory visit to this literary shrine during my first trip to England in 1960. I'd been to London at least a dozen times since on business, accompanied once by Barbara, who had a fine old time shopping and sight-seeing while I avidly searched for manuscripts to buy in the offices of publishers and agents, the main "sights" of interest to me on that visit, but only now had I returned to the Birthplace. Initially, I'd come to pay dutiful but unreverential homage to a cultural deity whom I comprehended superficially at best and whom I accepted as a matter of course, without passion, without a sense of awe. But having become a born-again true believer, on this occasion I found the premises evoking a feeling of transcendence, creating an even greater emotional impact than Mark Twain's bizarre home in Hartford, furnished exactly as it was in Twain's lifetime, so that I felt I could actually see him sitting in his rocking chair, reading to his daughters gathered at his feet; or Dickens's home in London, where I couldn't help sensing the man at work on *Oliver Twist,* perhaps pacing the study and acting out a scene he'd just completed; or Samuel Johnson's house on Gough Square, where in the garret, bare now except for display cases, I had a vision of Johnson's six amanuenses at their small tables and chairs, with Johnson sitting at "an old crazy deal table" and an elbow chair with only three legs, propped against the wall for support, working on the monumental *Dictionary;* or the small bedroom on the top floor of the house in Rome adjacent to the Spanish Steps where John Keats, scarcely five feet tall, had lain on a child's bed, dying agonizingly of tuberculosis, and where I could hear echoes of the terrible coughing that convulsed his tiny frail body.

The Birthplace, a two-storied wood-and-plaster building with dormer windows, a massive stone chimney stack, and a raftered roof, served two purposes: one part of the building was the family's home, the other a shop where Shakespeare's father, John, plied his trade as a glover and wool dealer. The rooms are furnished in the style of middle-class homes of Elizabethan and Jacobean times. Upstairs is the Birthroom, where tradition has it that Shakespeare was born. Almost all the timberwork is original, and the room, furnished with a joined bedstead and a seventeenth-century cradle, exudes an aura of sanctity appropriate to the manger in Bethlehem. Downstairs were the kitchen and the living room, the latter being the main apartment of the house in Shakespeare's time and the room that I found most evocative.

Timber-framed walls and raftered ceiling; brick and stone fireplace; old broken stone floor believed to be the original; an Elizabethan armchair, a joined stool and a coffer, a seventeenth-century dresser. The charming, cozy living room of a solid bourgeois family, a setting wherein I could visualize the scene of a wrenching domestic drama in which a fourteen-year-old Shakespeare possibly first learned what life really is all about.

His father, John, was every inch a self-made man, and yet another Young Man from the Provinces, whose own father had been a tenant farmer on land owned by wealthy Robert Arden. John, go-getting, upwardly mobile, status-seeking, a mover and shaker, migrated as a young man to the thriving market town of Stratford, set himself up as a glover and whittawer (curer and whitener of skins), began to prosper as a tradesman, and married none other than Mary Arden, Robert's daughter. Now his ambition kicked into high gear: he added wool dealing and money-lending to his business enterprises, and became a civic leader, rising in the town council hierarchy from alderman to ale taster (ah, there's the job for me) to justice of the peace to constable to chamberlain and finally to the highest elective office, high bailiff, the equivalent of mayor. Then he began to fall on hard times. Typical of many wheelers and dealers, and civic leaders, he did not always play by the rules: on one occasion he was accused of breaking the usury laws by charging interest, and was twice accused of illegal wool dealing. And financial misfortunes beset him; an overreacher, he extended himself beyond his means, and incurred debts he was unable to pay. Further, he had neglected his duties as alderman and had been removed from the Privy Council.

This brought him to a moment I could see played out for me as I stood in the Birthplace living room, a scene that Arthur Miller could have written: a teenage Shakespeare witnessing a heart-crushing scene in which his once proud and successful father, now a failure, is forced to tell his wife that the only way to avoid ruin was to mortgage the land and house that had been Mary's inheritance. Whether Mary was sympathetic or recriminatory doesn't really matter. What's significant is that Shakespeare has seen his father humiliated, not ruined but reduced; for a teenage boy, the sight of a powerful father brought low can't help being profoundly, traumatically disillusioning. Not that it affected Shakespeare's love or sympathy for John; in fact, I think it intensified both, and motivated him to succeed in a big way and to restore the family's status and prosperity. After all, when he was thirty-six, a renowned London playwright, he renewed in his father's name an application for a coat of arms that had been denied John, who was now in his sixties, in 1568. And Shakespeare ultimately returned home in triumph and bought the New Place.

Perhaps that particular psychic wound—a father enduring pecuniary misfortune—is the driving force behind the Young Men from the Provinces. Scott Fitzgerald's father was a failed salesman in St. Paul; Mark Twain's father had failed as a farmer, storekeeper, trader, and land speculator; William Dean Howells's father was a struggling Ohio printer and journalist; Charles Dickens's father was a financially irresponsible clerk in the navy pay office who was sent to debtor's prison for his improvident ways; Anton Chekhov's father avoided debtor's prison by escaping to Moscow when his grocery store in Taganrog went bankrupt; Samuel Johnson's father was an impecunious Lichfield bookseller who couldn't pay his taxes (but nonetheless was so respected by his fellow citizens that, like John Shakespeare, he was elected bailiff of the town—nice touch that one of Johnson's greatest achievements was to be his commentaries on Shakespeare). Melville's father was ruined in his import business— although he was far from being from a provincial family. Arthur Miller's father failed in the Depression. My own father had been a close-to-impoverished lawyer in Depression-stricken Houston, and the spectacle of watching him submit to my mother's spiteful indictments of him as a loser made me love him all the more; whether it sparked my yearning to be Something Terrific I can't say for certain (perhaps I should have opened up to that psychiatrist after all), but I do know that nothing I was to accomplish meant anything to me unless it pleased my father.

Of the trio of plays we saw in Stratford, two proved disappointing, one surprisingly powerful. *Romeo and Juliet,* staged by the RSC's artistic director, Adrian Noble, was bland and dull, marred by a gasping and gushing Romeo, bouncing around the stage as if he were appearing in Prokofiev's ballet. Only Julian Glover's Friar Laurence served the play well. *Julius Caesar,* directed by the eminent Sir Peter Hall, was brisk and pedestrian and bloodless—bloodless, that is, with the exception of an enormous bust of Caesar which dominated the stage and from which blood began to flow with increasing force as the play progressed, an obvious and intrusive symbol. To the production's credit, setting and costumes were of the period, although the togas were red and black, another unnecessary symbolic touch. Give me white togas, if you please. Performances were no more than serviceable; Julian Glover's Cassius, for instance, was forceful and urgent, but missed the character's seething envy and lacerated ego.

The surprise was *The Taming of the Shrew,* surprising first of all because I've never been entertained by this play, in performance or on the page, and second because ordinarily I deplore interpretations that impose "timely" sociopolitical meanings on Shakespeare's text. Gale Edwards, the female director of the play, took a radical-feminist approach, and if her distortions warped Shakespeare's intent, they made for exciting and hilarious theatre. In Ms. Edwards's version of the induction, Christopher Sly, the drunken tinker, is not the victim of a hoax perpetrated by a lord and his fellow noblemen, who wake him from a boozy slumber, make him believe he, too, is a lord and then have a troupe of players perform for his pleasure the story of Petruccio and Kate; instead, the induction is Sly's sodden dream, in which a lord as dream master summons up figures from a dreamworld to enact the Taming of the Shrew, in which, as we later discover, Petruccio is Sly and Kate is Sly's wife. The most glaring alteration is the finale, in which Kate submits to Petruccio, a disturbing, harrowing moment in which Petruccio realizes the human cost to him and Kate of her humiliating submission. Sly awakens, chastened by the dream's lesson: treat your wife like an equal (cut, of course, were the lines "Why, there's a wench! Come on, and kiss me, Kate"). This was made all the more effective by its contrast to Ms. Edwards's sure-handed, wildly inventive touch with burlesque in the taming scenes and in the courtship of Bianca by Gremio, Hortensio, and Lucentio, commedia dell'arte hijinks of a high order.

In London, we saw only one play, *Measure for Measure,* at the RSC's Barbican. I'd read it for the first time two months previously and had never seen it performed. It's been a difficult play for scholars to classify: is it a comedy, a romance, a romantic comedy, a tragicomedy? Perhaps only Polonius could concoct an appropriately inclusive portmanteau definition to do it justice. The plot centers on a self-righteous, coldly rational, inhumane judge, a moral absolutist, who becomes human only after he succumbs to temptation and becomes corrupt. Angelo, deputy to the Duke of Vienna, is appointed to administer a law making fornication a capital offense. His first case involves a young man, Claudio, who has gotten his bethrothed Julietta pregnant. Even though betrothal in front of witnesses was valid in the eyes of the church, it could not be consummated until a church service had been performed, and the lovers had not complied with this provision. So Claudio must die. His sister, the pure Isabella, who is about to become a novice in an order of nuns, pleads for his life with Angelo. Smitten by her beauty and purity, Angelo lusts for Isabella; his sexual passion overcomes his moral principles, and he offers Isabella a deal: if she agrees to sleep with him, he'll free Claudio. By the end of the play, Angelo has been tricked into thinking he's bedded Isabella (the old "bed trick" device, a well-known folktale theme borrowed by Shakespeare) when actually it was Mariana, an ex-fiancée he ruthlessly jilted after her dowry was lost in a shipwreck. Revealed as a sinner (somewhat like the Reverend Dimmesdale in Hawthorne's *The Scarlet Letter*), he's prepared to accept his fate and die on the gallows. But he's spared by the duke and ordered instead to marry Mariana. And to love her, as if a man could be commanded to love. Angelo in fact never expresses his feelings for Mariana. His last words in the play reveal only his penitence and his desire for the death he deserves by having broken the law. What are we to make of this? My sense of it is that Shakespeare would have us believe that Angelo, his feelings and emotions awakened for the first time, will be in a state of confusion for some time to come, but that the intellect at last has given way to the heart in all its complexity and that the process of becoming fully human is well under way.

In the RSC's scintillating production, Alex Jenkinson was every inch an Angelo, particularly effective in projecting the character's inner torment with controlled pathos, and Toby Stephens (son of Maggie Smith and Robert Stephens) brought exceptional warmth and vigor to Claudio, most memorably in his rendition of the speech in 3.1 expressing the horrors of death. The scenes with the madam and her whores and the pimp (this Vienna was awash in licentiousness, hence the severe antifornication law) were enlivened by Brechtian costuming and atmospherics, with the madam doing a perfect imitation of Lotte Lenya.

On our last day in London, Barbara and I took a boat from Parliament to the Tower of London. On the way I glanced to my right and there, on a bluff overlooking the river, was the Globe. We'd learned during our lectures at Stratford that it was being reconstructed, that the interiors were yet to be completed, and that Mark Rylance, one of the RSC's most gifted young actors, had been made artistic director, but this had made only a faint impact. However, actually seeing the Globe as it must have appeared to sixteenth-century Londoners was a jarring time-travel experience.

I looked at the opposite side of the Thames toward the area where the first important purpose-built playhouse in London, the Theatre, had been built in 1576 by James Burbage, a carpenter who'd become a player and proprietor. His son Richard was a leading actor with the Theatre's resident company, the Lord Chamberlain's Men, in which Shakespeare was actor, playwright, and shareholder. In April 1597, the lease on the land on which the Theatre was built would expire, so James Burbage bought a piece of property which included an old building that had once been used by the monks of Blackfriars and set about converting it into a playhouse. But in November 1596, the residents of Blackfriars, fearing that such an enterprise would draw riffraff to the area, successfully petitioned the Privy Council to suppress the Theatre. James died three months later. Burbage's troupe moved to the Curtain playhouse but it proved inadequate and business slumped. Finally, Richard and his brother Cuthbert came up with an ingenious scheme, taking advantage of a clause in the original lease on the Theatre's land authorizing the tenant to dismantle and remove the building. On the night of December 28, 1598, the timbers of the Theatre were transported probably over London Bridge across the Thames to a site where the first Globe, a polygonal structure, was built, very close to where the reconstructed Globe now stands.

Gazing at the New Globe from the deck of a boat on the Thames, I was reminded of Mircea Eliade's observation in *The Sacred and the Profane* that the temples men build "are held to be at the Center of the World and, on the microcosmic scale, to reproduce the universe. . . . It follows that every construction or fabrication has the cosmogony as paradigmatic model." Given its circular shape, symbolizing the theatre as the world ("All the world's a stage"), the Globe was appropriately named. The stage covering of the first Globe was decorated with painted stars, planets, and other astrological emblems, further bearing out Eliade's conclusion that when man occupies an unknown space, "he symbolically transforms it into a cosmos through a ritual repetition of the cosmogony."

I recalled that Elizabethan theatre evolved from mystery and miracle and morality plays, and as I reflected on the first and the New Globes, it seemed to me that the construction of the former, with its unique form, represented a realization of the sacred nature of drama, of its allegorical power, just as the obsessive need to rebuild the Globe and re-create its manner of performance was akin to the ecstatic dream of rebuilding the Temple in Jerusalem and reinstating the ritual of animal sacrifice that possesses a segment of Orthodox Jewry even today.

Those who have re-created the Globe, and the audiences who will throng to it, reflect what Eliade calls the nostalgia for origins, which he says is equivalent to religious nostalgia: "Man desires to live in the world as it came from the Creator's hands, fresh, pure, and strong. . . . Such a nostalgia inevitably leads to the continual repetition of a limited number of gestures and patterns of behavior." We—I hope one day to be among the crowds—shall go to the New Globe to observe the reenactment of sacred myths and to worship Shakespeare the Creator in the manner of those who were there in the beginning.

At last arriving at the Tower of London, we were struck by the quarters in which Sir Walter Raleigh had been imprisoned for thirteen years on bogus charges of abetting Catholic conspiracies against King James. Raleigh's handsomely appointed suite of rooms—the Raleigh Condo as it were—did not exactly constitute cruel and unusual punishment. While in prison he pursued alchemical experiments and wrote a monumental multivolume history of the world. He was also, of course, a soldier and courtier, an explorer and adventurer. Ah, these Renaissance men, these dashing Elizabethans, I thought. And then I remembered: I once knew an Elizabethan who was confined for five years in a jail far more hellish than the Raleigh Condo, and used that ordeal for an exceptional literary work.

He was James Clavell, who as a British officer during World War II had been captured by the Japanese after the fall of Malaysia and condemned to Changi, the notorious prisoner-of-war camp near Singapore.

Born in the twentieth century, Clavell was temperamentally an Elizabethan, especially in his lusty, enterprising spirit, forged to a considerable degree by the war and the Changi years of danger and violence, a time when men had to be ready to meet blow with blow, and if necessary, to kill with steady nerves. I once asked him what he'd learned from the horrors of Changi, and without a pause he answered, "That all I would ever need to survive is a knife and a sack of rice." Also Elizabethan was Clavell's Machiavellian obsession with power, how it's attained and retained, how it's used and abused, how crucial it is to possess it, which is why he was always fascinated by the intrigues of the movie industry, where he worked for years as a screenwriter and director before and even during his career as a novelist.

Clavell had about him the air of a swashbuckler and the splendid bearing of an Elizabethan courtier. Tall, dark-haired, he walked with a slight limp, the result of a stiff leg incurred in a motorcycle accident just before his discharge from the service. He was a devout believer in kismet, and in fact it was a trick of fate that led him to write his first novel. For years he'd been mulling the notion of turning the experience of Changi into a novel, and when screenwriters went on strike in Hollywood, his wife challenged him to use this unexpected freedom to start work on what became the one-thousand-page first draft of *King Rat*. Sweet are the uses of adversity, and all that. His agent, a New York theatrical representative who'd once sold a play of his to a Canadian production company, submitted the *King Rat* manuscript to New York publishers, all of whom rejected it. Which is where I came into Clavell's life.

I'd been an editor at Little, Brown & Company for two years. Since I owed my publishing career in large part to luck and timing, I suppose Clavell would have considered my good fortune part of his kismet: he had an Elizabethan belief in the Great Chain of Being, the hierarchical order with God at the top, closely followed by King James, then, at some distance, the remaining mortals and beasts. And I imagine that even the fortuitous circumstances leading to my marriage would have struck him as crucial to his own destiny. As a matter of fact, they were.

Barbara and I had met at the home of a couple, the Birnbaums, who lived across the street from Barbara's parents in the Boston suburb of Newton Highlands, and were friends of a friend of mine, Murray Levin, a professor of political science at Boston University. Murray had taken Barbara to dinner recently and was smitten. "Herm," he'd rhapsodized to me one night over obscenely thick corned beef sandwiches at a deli in Coolidge Corner, "she's a miracle of beauty and brains. Graduated from Barnard, and those Barnard girls are whips. Majored in German, learned to speak it as a native during a couple of summers at Middlebury, got herself a scholarship to do graduate work in Germany, and came home last month with an M.A. I don't think the academic life appeals to her. She's working at the Brandeis bookstore, in inventory I think, while she figures out what to do next. Very, very classy. Her father's a doctor. Her mother didn't go to college until her late thirties and managed to pull off a junior Phi Bete at B.U. Barbara has a couple of younger brothers, but she's the prize. You can see for yourself in a little while. I told the Birnbaums I'd drop over later tonight. Come with me and when we get there I'll phone Barbara to join us."

When Barbara walked into the Birnbaums' living room, I knew that the enchanted evening Oscar Hammerstein had promised to all of us was coming to pass for me at that very moment. Here was the woman I'd marry. I could almost hear the Richard Rodgers music playing in the background. Or was that *Swan Lake*? Barbara entered with the elegance and graceful authority of a prima ballerina and bore a striking resemblance to Audrey Hepburn. Shoulder-length reddish brown hair worn in a French twist, blue eyes with a searching glint that bespoke an inquiring, undeceivable intelligence, and a smile that revealed a naturally joyful temperament and a boundless zest for life. Above all, here was a person who radiated integrity, a prodigious strength of character. I thought of the lines

71

from one of the greatest love poems in the English language, e. e. cummings's "somewhere i have never traveled": "nothing which we are to perceive in this world / equals the power of your intense fragility."

I phoned her the next day. At first she couldn't quite remember who I was. Apparently, the instant enchantment hadn't been mutual. And her tone was slightly cool. Did she find my attempt to move in on Murray a trifle insensitive, typical of a Texas yahoo? Undaunted, I asked her to go to the theatre with me that weekend, and she accepted. On our sixth date, I proposed and she accepted. "You owe me your firstborn," Murray responded when we told him we were engaged. Four months later, on April 9, 1961, we were married. Our wedding was, appropriately, Appomattox Day, the day when another southerner, Lee, surrendered to a Yankee. We decided to spend our honeymoon in New Orleans; it was Barbara's first trip west of the Mississippi. On our return we'd planned to stop in Washington for two days, but hadn't made reservations and discovered upon arriving that all the hotels were booked—it was spring vacation and the area was flooded with tourists. So we improvised a stop-over in New York City, and I brought Barbara to Little, Brown's New York offices to meet my good buddy Alan Williams, the New York editor.

In Alan's office, I noticed on a long table bearing manuscripts in the process of being rejected an imposing foot-high pile of yellow pages bound with rubber bands and towering majestically, almost insolently, over its doomed companions.

"What the hell is that?" I asked.

"Oh, that's a little number called *King Rat*." Yes, it definitely had a monarchical aspect. Alan continued: "It's a novel about a Japanese prisoner-of-war camp in Malaysia during the Second World War, written by a guy who survived the ordeal. I declined it a while back, but my letter was so polite that the author made a few cuts and sent it back to me. I'm afraid it needs more than a bit of trimming. It's got some raw power, but it's an awful mess—bad writing, sloppy plotting, the works. Reclaiming it would require a labor of love, and this beast is hard to love."

"Terrific title, though," I said. "And I'm a sucker for prisoner-of-war stories."

"You want to read it? I'll send it up to Boston and it'll be there to welcome you when you return, crying out, 'The honeymoon's over, Herm.' "

Sure enough, the manuscript was on my desk when I got back to Boston, and as Alan predicted, it heralded a jolting welcome back to the real world. In the two years I'd been an editor, I'd never read an agented novel as monstrous as *King Rat*. There was something practically defiant in its colossal ineptitude, especially the mangled grammar and syntax, the bizarre locutions ("He gasped his eyes open"). By comparison, the prose of Dreiser seemed graceful and supple. Could English really be this man's native tongue? He seemed to be inventing his own language, not a pretty thing. Maybe he'd been warped by reading *Finnegans Wake*. Whatever, struggling through those aggressively incoherent pages was driving me mad; time and again I pushed the manuscript aside, ready to phone Alan and tell him I was sending the body of *King Rat* back to New York for a decent burial. But something kept drawing me back to those infernal yellow pages, and I realized that *King Rat* was not dead at all. I remembered what Edmund Wilson had said about the first draft of Scott Fitzgerald's *This Side of Paradise:* it had every fault a novel could have except one—it did not fail to live. So it was with *King Rat*—it pulsed with life, with drama. This man Clavell was a natural storyteller. I could picture him sitting before a campfire, bardically chanting his tales of warriors and heroes, battles and intrigues, and in a lingo almost as indecipherable to me as Gaelic. But paraphrasing it as I went along, I could detect its formidable narrative power. Moreover, Clavell hadn't been content with telling a story; his soul had been tested in the furnace of affliction from which he acquired a Darwinian/Hobbesian vision of human existence. *King Rat* had a stunning metaphorical resonance; it was a naturalistic allegory.

By the time I'd finished reading the manuscript, I'd decided to plead its case with my colleagues; Alan gave his support ("Nice catch, Herm— you saved this one from premature embalming"), and that clinched it.

I spent six weeks editing the manuscript—a maximum effort, total immersion, seven days a week, twelve hours a day—and sent it to Clavell in Los Angeles. He devoted a month to responding to my suggestions. Only once during this process did we talk to each other on the phone. Our relationship was strictly postal. And we didn't meet until he came to New

York to publicize the novel, which had been enthusiastically reviewed (the leading salvo of praise came from Orville Prescott, then the influential daily critic for the *New York Times*), went on to become a best-seller for several weeks and enjoy a subsidiary rights bonanza—Book-of-the-Month Club, Fawcett paperback. Before publication, Columbia Pictures bought movie rights. Quite a success story for a first novel. And a huge boost for my career: it was the first best-seller I edited. All the result of kismet, Clavell insisted. If it hadn't been for the screenwriters' strike, and my unintended trip to New York during which I just happened to spot *King Rat* on the manuscript table, a few hours before it was to be shipped back to the author—well, it *was* kismet. And even Clavell didn't realize the extent of this mystical force until twelve years later.

He'd come to New York to promote his third novel, *Shōgun,* which was published in 1975. In 1964 I'd left Little, Brown to become an editor at Atheneum, a small but dynamic and thriving independent publishing house founded only five years previously by Simon Michael Bessie of Harper & Bros., Hiram Haydn of Random House, and Pat Knopf, an executive in the firm of his father, Alfred. Little, Brown had passed on its option on Clavell's next novel, which turned out to be *Tai-Pan* and which I brought to Atheneum. Published in 1966, *Tai-Pan* had been enormously popular, rising as high as number two on the *New York Times* best-seller list, topped only by Jacqueline Susann's *Valley of the Dolls.*

By the time *Shōgun* was published, Clavell had struck it rich in Hollywood too, on a vaster scale, with the modestly budgeted *To Sir, with Love,* which starred Sidney Poitier and which Clavell wrote, produced, and directed. What made it so profitable was that Columbia, reluctant to take on an apparently small, offbeat project about a black teacher in a working-class London school, finally consented only after Clavell and Poitier agreed to waive their salaries and work for expenses and a percentage of the profits. The movie turned out to be a sleeper, outgrossing *Lawrence of Arabia* for the studio.

On the first morning of his *Shōgun* week in New York, I had breakfast with Clavell in his hotel suite. He insisted on a champagne toast to bless the occasion, and as I raised my glass the sun happened to strike my Aggie ring, a large heavy piece of jewelry in the fashion of military-college rings. The gleam caught Clavell's eye. "What is that damned thing you wear?" he asked. We'd known each other for fifteen years, so he must have noticed this ring on my hand countless times, but only now, because it had been spotlighted by that vagrant beam of light, did he truly see it. "It's my college ring—Texas A&M."

Clavell paled instantly. Perhaps I should say he gasped his eyes open. He damned near dropped his glass. "You're an Aggie?"

"Yes," I said, "I thought you knew. Does this mean I can no longer be your editor? You thought because I was so brilliant I must be a Harvard man?"

"No, laddie. But, you see, ———— was an Aggie, too," he said, naming one of the major characters in the novel. "I changed his name to protect his identity."

So Clavell's first novel had been salvaged from the junk pile by an editor who by a fluke just happened to be in New York one morning and also just happened to be an alumnus of the college attended by the man who served as the basis for one of the novel's principal figures. Coincidence. Kismet. There is a divinity that shapes our ends, rough-hew them how we will.

I've called Clavell an Elizabethan, but I can be more specific: he was Shakespearean. Shakespearean in his movie career, working alone and in collaboration with others for profit in a popular entertainment medium. Shakespearean in his concern with the world of business, the joy he took in worldly affairs, in the realm of trade, interests reflected in all his novels. (Shakespeare invested in tithes, loaned money, hoarded grain.) Shakespearean in his passion for real estate: at one time he owned outright, no mortgages, five homes—one in Hollywood, one in West Vancouver, a town house in London's Buckingham Place, a mini–town house in Belgravia, and, appropriately, a sixteenth-century Tudor mansion in Dorset. (Shakespeare owned a house in London, the New Place in Stratford, a cottage and a quarter acre of land across from the New Place, and arable land and pasture in Old Stratford.) And finally, Shakespearean in his concern with politics, with how men handle power, how they rule, with the visions that motivate them, why they succeed or fail.

At a farewell party during our final night in London, Arthur Kay told me that if asked to sum up the "meaning of Shakespeare" in a line from

75

one of the plays, he'd choose "We are such stuff as dreams are made of." I opted for "What fools these mortals be." Fools because too often we think with our heads instead of our hearts, as did Enobarbus in *Antony and Cleopatra* when he followed his reason and abandoned Antony, only to die quite literally of a broken heart when the enormity of his betrayal overcame him. Fools because we are too prone to theorize about life, to search for perfection, to put that old debbil intellect to work weaving abstract utopian concepts in the manner of the King of Navarre and his nobles in *Love's Labour's Lost* who have vowed to retire from the world of power and devote themselves to asceticism and study and quickly learn how foolish it is to cut themselves off from life and love and beautiful women. Fools because far too often we neglect to use our common sense and our natural impulses; we fail to heed what God, in Exodus, referred to as "wisdom of heart," the quality that he detected in Bezalel and that led him to be chosen as the architect of the tabernacle.

Shakespeare may have been a rueful skeptic, but I did not believe he was, as some scholars claim, a cynic, revealing his misanthropy through such characters as Apemantus ("I wonder men dare trust themselves with men") and Timon ("I am sick of this false world") in *Timon of Athens* and Thersites ("Lechery, lechery, still wars and lechery, nothing else holds fashion") in *Troilus and Cressida*.

Nor was he the nihilist envisioned by Edward Arlington Robinson in "Ben Jonson Entertains a Man from Stratford." Shortly after returning home I bought a copy of Robinson's *Selected Poems* at a bookstore in Montclair and turned quickly to the portrait of Shakespeare limned by Jonson/Robinson. We're given a complicated, contradictory man, tormented by the knowledge that "King as he is, he can't be king *de facto, /* And that's just as well, because he wouldn't like it. . . . He can't be king, not even king of Stratford,— / Though half the world, if not the whole of it,— / May crown him with a crown that fits no king. . . ." And ultimately, Jonson/Robinson tells of coming upon a gloomy Shakespeare late one afternoon in Lambeth:

> *"What is it now," said I—"another woman?"*
>   *That made him sorry for me, and he smiled.*
> *"No, Ben," he mused, "it's Nothing. It's all Nothing.*

We come, we go; and when we're done, we're done. . . .
It's Nature, and it's Nothing. It's all Nothing.
It's all a world where bugs and emperors
    Go singularly back to the same dust.
Each in his time; and the old, ordered stars
        That sang together, Ben, will sing the same
        Old stave tomorrow."

The echoes here of *Macbeth* and *Hamlet* are unmistakable, the Hamlet of the graveyard scene and, of course, the Macbeth of "Tomorrow, and tomorrow, and tomorrow." But this is Hamlet and Macbeth speaking, not Shakespeare.

Shakespeare was a moralist, not a moralizer. He saw the human condition in terms of moral ambiguity, not moral certitude, the result, I imagine, of his own powers of observation (Robert Lowell tellingly referred to Shakespeare as "the poet of experience") coupled with the influence of Montaigne, whose awareness that contradiction is truth may have strengthened Shakespeare's own convictions about the paradoxical, ironical, contradictory quality of life.

5.

For a year after returning from England I maintained my hectic involvement in the Shakespearean universe and found myself in the same predicament as many autodidacts: I'd jumped on a horse and was going off in all directions at once. I was accumulating Shakespearean literature on a chain-reaction basis; a tantalizing bibliographical listing in a volume or a book referred to provocatively in its text or footnote was enough to prompt me to buy it. Random acquisition through browsing was also becoming a habit: rarely did I visit the Drama Book Shop or Barnes & Noble or Borders without finding a volume I deemed indispensable to furthering my grasp of Shakespeare's artistry and deepening my understanding of the plays. There was little method in my madness. A Jewish folktale tells of a young man who goes to a bookstore in Minsk and selects two formidable tomes; the proprietor, however, will allow him to buy only one: "When you finish the first, come back for the second." I should have heeded the parable's lesson. Haunted by the stacks of unread titles, I grew panicky, and like many involved in private studies, suffered the compulsion to read all the books simultaneously, a chapter in each book daily, until the mind reeled with fragmented overload.

I remembered what Orwell had said in his novel *Burmese Days:* "It is one of the tragedies of the half-educated that they develop late, when they are already committed to some wrong way of life." And an unforgettably elegiac line delivered by Charlton Heston as an aging over-the-hill cowboy in a neglected gem of a western, *Will Penny:* "Old too soon, smart too late." Had my late development as a Bardomaniac, without the proper scholarly underpinnings, doomed me, half-educated, if that, in Shakespeare, to scattershot dilettantism?

As a corrective, I felt that perhaps it was time to consider enrolling in a master's program at a nearby university and subjecting myself to rigorous academic discipline. But two things ultimately dissuaded me. First, the language requirement: I was daunted by the prospect of retooling my French, which had rusted away over the past forty-five years. Second, by chance I met at a party a Shakespeare professor at the university to which I was planning to apply; when I mentioned my esteem for Harold God-dard and Maynard Mack, this academic brushed them off as "old farts." Apparently, this was the type of "Byzantine pedant" Mack had in mind in his preface to *Everybody's Shakespeare.* I suppose the professor took it personally. Did I, an old fart pushing sixty-six, want to spend a year under the tutelage of this insufferable ageist? Not really.

Next I tried establishing for myself a College of One, as Scott Fitzgerald had termed the Great Books program he created for his mistress, Sheila Graham, the gorgeous, intelligent, but uneducated young London-born gossip columnist. I would systematize my reading, develop a curriculum and a schedule to be adhered to religiously each day. For example: Monday, Wednesday, Friday A.M., Shakespeare's Metrics, and in the P.M., Shakespeare's Stage Technique; Tuesday and Thursday A.M., Shakespearean Staging, and in the P.M., Shakespeare's Festive Comedies.

Within days, the regimen was honored more in the breach than the observance. For example, I came across a reference in Jean E. Howard's *Shakespeare's Art of Orchestration: Stage Technique and Audience Response* to A. C. Bradley, an ancient fart whose *Shakespearean Tragedy,* published in 1904 and based on his lectures at Oxford, has been one of the most influential and enduring works of Shakespearean criticism. I'd bought it a few weeks previously, intending to get to it in a month or two. But now I put down Howard, plucked Bradley off the shelf, and spent the rest of the day and much of the next reading the first lectures, "The Substance of Tragedy" and "Construction in Shakespeare's Tragedies." Among his most compelling ideas: "tragedy would not be tragedy if it were not a painful mystery. . . . We remain confronted with the inexplicable fact . . . of a world travailing for perfection, but bringing to birth, together with the glorious good, an evil which it is able to overcome only by self-torture and self-waste."

Then a mention of Henry James in C. L. Barber's *Shakespeare's Festive Comedy* reminded me of a section in Schoenbaum's *Shakespeare's Lives* describing Henry James's novella "The Birthplace," in which a couple become custodians of the birthplace of a revered author, never specifically named as Shakespeare but obviously intended as such, and eventually wind up doubting not only that the author had been born and raised there but that any such person had ever existed. I'd yet to read the novella—it was not part of my James collection—but now it occurred to me that James might have discussed it in his notebooks, which I did own. So I set aside Barber, and sure enough, found in the James notebooks a provocative entry for June 12, 1901. A story he heard about the case of a couple who had been in charge of Shakespeare's birthplace struck him as "possibly a little *donnée.* They . . . had embraced the situation with joy, thinking to find it . . . an appeal to all their culture and refinement, etc. But . . . at the end of six months they grew . . . desperate from finding it . . . full of humbug . . . and they ended by contracting a fierce intellectual and moral disgust for the way they had to *meet* the public . . . and after a while they . . . threw up the position. There may be something in it—something more than the mere facts. . . . Say they end by denying Shakespeare . . .—one day—in the presence of a big, gaping, admiring batch. *Then* they must go. . . ."

After that, in some weird trick of free association, George Wright's consideration of triple trochees in *Antony and Cleopatra* made me think of an essay in Anne Barton's *Essays, Mainly Shakespearean,* in which she discusses the diptych—the divided catastrophe—in the same play, and I couldn't resist abandoning Wright for Ms. Barton, rereading the piece on *Antony and Cleopatra* and reading for the first time her analysis of *Love's Labour's Lost* in which she points out that "it is obvious . . . from the very beginning of the play that the Academe [founded by the King of Navarre and his three friends] and the idea of immortality which it embodies must fail."

My own Academe, my College of One, was founded on vows somewhat less fantastic and contrived than those of the four young Frenchmen. But given the agitated, avid quality of the Bardism that possessed me (and "possessed" I seemed to be, like a Dostoyevskian character deranged by an idée fixe), Herm's Academe was nonetheless untenable. I closed up shop and returned to a pattern of study less programmed and more flexible, but in one significant aspect, quite focused. The lens through which I discerned a crucial Shakespearean motif happened to be my religion.

The process had started earlier, when I read Caroline Spurgeon's profile of Shakespeare in *Shakespeare's Imagery.* Unlike Schoenbaum, I didn't object to her psychobiographical methodology; what I took amiss was her summing up:

> *Shakespeare does not seem to have drawn any support from the forms and promises of conventional religion. . . . But he does show . . . a very strong belief in the importance of the way life is lived in relation to our fellows, so that we may gain the utmost from the ripening process of experience and love. . . . There is one thought . . . which we find recurring in his work in many forms all through his career, and it would seem, quite simply, to be this: that by, in and for ourselves we are nothing; we exist only in just so far as we touch our fellows, and receive back from them the warmth or light we have ourselves sent out. To befriend, to support, to help, to cheer and illuminate our fellow-men is the whole object of our being, and if we fail to do this, we have failed in that object, and are as empty husks, hollow and meaningless. Only thus can we fulfill ourselves and be in truth that which we are intended to be.*

What astonished me was that having concluded that Shakespeare was not conventionally religious, she demonstrates this proposition in a passage that defines the essence of the Torah, the five books of Moses: you must love your neighbor as yourself, the core tenet from Leviticus.

Some time later, at a Shabbat service the day after Shakespeare's birthday, I once again made the connection, because the Torah portion happened to be the section in Leviticus detailing what is now termed the Holiness Code. Listening to the chazan, the cantor, chant the Hebrew, and following the translation in my copy of the Chumash, the Pentateuch, I experienced again a sense of how powerfully the Bible influenced Shakespeare's vision of the world, of the human condition, and of the awesome divine force that rules the universe.

And over the next several days, I thought about the enormous impact the Holiness Code, which reinforces, extends, and elaborates on the commandments of Sinai, is likely to have had on a man such as Shakespeare, who feared the horrors of chaos (as we can see most emphatically in his history plays) and who, as an Elizabethan, had believed at least for a time in the Great Chain of Being, a condition in which the universe, created by God, is graded hierarchically from God and the angels through man, woman, and the lower animals to vegetation.

In Hebrew the word for holy is *kadosh,* literally "separate." According to J. H. Hertz, editor of *The Pentateuch and Haftorahs,* God's proclamation at the beginning of Leviticus 19, "Ye shall be holy, for I the Lord your God am holy," embraces three understandings of *kadosh.* The first is God as the exalted force that reduces man to feelings of unworthiness and creatureliness. Then the God of absolute perfection. And finally, holiness in its ethical sense. The Israelites made a covenant with the One Transcendent God, accepting the commandments, the divinely sanctioned laws and moral precepts that make possible a good society, a society in which altruism prevails over egotism, separate from the idol worshipers who among other abominations sacrificed children to Moloch.

In Leviticus 17–19, God commands the Israelites: "Ye shall fear every man his mother and his father"; "Turn ye not unto the idols"; "Ye shall not steal; neither shall ye deal falsely, nor lie to one another"; "Thou shalt not hate thy brother in thy heart"; "Thou shalt not take vengeance, not bear any grudge against the children of thy people, but shall love thy neighbor as thyself"; "The man that committeth adultery with another man's wife . . . shall surely be put to death"; "Thou shalt not uncover the nakedness of thy brother's wife"; "Thou shalt honor the face of the old man"; "And the soul that turneth unto ghosts, and unto the familiar spirits, to go astray after them, I will even set My face against that soul, and will cut him off from among his people." Additional commandments direct the Israelites to share their crops with the needy, protect the orphaned and widowed, be generous to strangers, remembering that we were once strangers and slaves in Egypt.

With this section in mind, I thought about *Hamlet.* We have Claudius uncovering the nakedness of his brother's wife. We have him not just committing murder but killing his brother, the primal biblical sin (as Schoenbaum points out, Genesis, too, affected Shakespeare profoundly), and guilty also of regicide, very close to deicide, considering the Great Chain of Being. Hamlet turns to the ghost of his father, a Levitical prohibition. Does Hamlet's struggle with the idea of revenge imply a recognition of God's edict? And does his line "The readiness is all" mean that he has abandoned the idea of revenge and that he is resigned to accepting whatever fate God intends for him? Hamlet did commit murder: he killed Polonius (earlier, by mocking him, he violated the commandment to honor the face of the old man—and compounded it by mocking Polonius even in death) and sent Rosencrantz and Guildenstern to certain death at the hands of the King of England. And there's Hamlet's sense of creatureliness, of being an insignificant speck in the universe: "What a piece of work is man! . . . and yet, to me, what is this quintessence of dust?"

I turned to *Macbeth*. When I think of Macbeth, I think of King Saul, and I wonder if Shakespeare did, too. Surely the man who read Holinshed's *Chronicles,* which modeled English history on the Bible's providential pattern, must have been enthralled by the Books of Kings and Chronicles, which relate the rebellion and ultimate secession of the ten northern tribes of Israel and the establishment of two kingdoms, Israel in the north and Judah in the south, followed by four decades of hostility—primarily border skirmishes—between the two kingdoms. Like Shakespeare, the compilers of Kings and Chronicles based their narratives on source material, "the Book of the Chronicles of the Kings of Israel" and "the Book of the Chronicles of the Kings of Judah." To the compilers, the safety and prosperity of the kingdoms depended upon the fidelity of the current king to the royal cult in Jerusalem. Thus the kings of Israel had done evil in the Lord by being unfaithful, and suffered the consequences—for example, conspiracies, palace coups, usurpation, assassination.

As Steven Marx relates in *Shakespeare and the Bible,* Holinshed arranged his accounts of history "to teach didactic lessons. . . . the succession of events demonstrated God's involvement on the side of legitimate authorities of State and Church. Rebellion was punished with civil strife, the weakening of the nation, and consequent human suffering. God also punished tyrannical or impious behavior on the part of leaders by causing their fall, but history taught that disobedience of any sort would bring down divine retribution." Saul, that fierce warrior king, consulted the Witch of Endor, and, to hold on to his power, was prepared to kill his beloved servant, David. Of course, unlike Macbeth, whose worst crime may have been his commissioning the murder of Macduff's wife and children, Saul's homicidal ferocity had its limits: his sin was that he disobeyed

God by not killing all the enemy. Macbeth, after an encounter with the occult, with soothsayers—the three sisters—a definite Levitical prohibition, kills an old man, who happens to be king; again, regicide bordering on deicide. And this unleashes a display of cosmic displeasure that generates in Lennox (and we must assume in Macbeth, too, notwithstanding his casual " 'Twas a rough night" aside) a sense of overwhelming mystery: "Lamentings heard i' th' air . . . / And prophesying with accents terrible / Of dire combustion and confused events. . . ." And there is Macbeth's horror of shedding blood. Caroline Spurgeon has pointed out Macbeth's description of himself wading in a river of blood, and she goes on to cite the picture of Macbeth "gazing, rigid with horror, at his own blood-stained hand and watching it dye the whole green ocean red." Lady Macbeth, driven mad with guilt, vainly attempts an act of purification by washing off the blood she imagines to be yet on her hands. In Leviticus, the Israelites are forbidden to eat the blood of animals because all blood is sacred, blood representing the vital principle of life: "the life of all flesh is the blood thereof." The Macbeths have violated this sacredness, hence the obsession with images of blood. They are truly an unholy couple.

And I had an unholy thought about a traditionally sainted Shakespearean character—Cordelia, whom we're supposed to admire for telling the truth to her daddy. Is that, I wondered, what's called honoring your father? Couldn't she have been just a wee bit less self-righteous and indulged the old man in his little whim and had a fine old time outdoing her sisters in professions of love? Think of the chaos that could have been avoided but for that act of pride, for which she paid dearly, as did Lear. And damned near everyone else except Edgar.

Not long after all this ruminating on Shakespeare and the Torah, I came across a section in another of the volumes I'd been hoarding, James Shapiro's invaluable *Shakespeare and the Jews,* which describes an attempt by yet another Herman, this one a Hermann Gollancz, a Hebrew professor living in London, to make a connection between Shakespeare and Judaism. What prompted it was, as with mine, Shakespeare's birthday, and it, too, occurred on Shabbat, the day before "Shakespeare Sunday," in which Christian churches paid homage to the Shakespeare tercentary. In a sermon delivered that Shabbat, Gollancz said that "the human side of life, in observation and delineation, is a feature common to the Rabbis of old and the Shakespeare of Elizabethan England." Shapiro then calls our attention to a pair of more recent and radical views of Shakespeare's relation to Judaism. Neil Hirschorn, in an article for *Midstream,* "The Jewish Key to Shakespeare's Most Enigmatic Creation," concludes from his reading of *The Merchant of Venice* that Shakespeare is "descended of forcibly converted Jews and brought up as a Christian resenting that condition. . . ." David Basch goes Hirschorn one better: in *The Hidden Shakespeare: A Rosetta Stone,* he argues that Shakespeare "was grounded in the particularity of a proud and committed Jew." I gave these theories the same credence as I do the lunacies of the anti-Stratfordians. But I found myself harboring an idea that could have landed me in a treatment center. No, Shakespeare was not a Jew. But who's to say he wasn't a prophet, touched by the hand of God? A prophet chosen by God to help us find the moral and spiritual strength in our struggle with good and evil in the world and within ourselves by creating works that, like scripture, sound the mysteries and riddles of existence and eternally challenge us to fathom their significance. Can this holy man be reconciled with the consummate man of the theatre, successful businessman, bourgeois property owner, and status seeker? As Montaigne wrote in his essay "Of the Inconsistency of Our Actions," "All contradictions are in me." And Gustave Flaubert, more than two centuries later, was to adopt as his credo "One should live like a bourgeois and think like a demigod."

Shakespeare may or may not have been a prophet. But that he was religious I think is incontestable. And as I reread *King Lear* later that year, I began to see it as Shakespeare's most religious play. Scholars consulting the text have concluded that to view it as a "Christian allegory" is inappropriate. They were correct. The dominant vision I was discovering in *Lear* was not Christian; it was Judaic.

The first clue is one of Shakespeare's sources, the usual suspect, Holinshed, who had derived his account of a pseudohistorical "King Leir" from Geoffrey of Monmouth's *Historia Regum Britanniae,* a fanciful mixture of history and legend which traces a supposed line of descent from a great-grandson of Aeneas of Troy to the historical kings of England. Leir is the tenth ruler in this genealogy. Holinshed significantly gives a biblical parallel to the time frame, as was his wont throughout the *Chronicles.* According to Holinshed, Leir had ruled over Britain the same time King

Joas had reigned in Judah (800–785 B.C.E.), and Cordelia, the youngest daughter of Leir, was admitted Queen and Supreme Governess of Britain when King Uzziah reigned in Judah and King Jeroboam II ruled over Israel (785–745 B.C.E.). The latter entry refers to the Holy Land divided in north and south after the rebellion described in the Books of Kings and Chronicles, and parallels the division of Britain by Cordelia's sisters.

And, most strikingly, there is the Genesis factor. Genesis is haunted by sibling rivalry: Cain murders Abel. Isaac's elder half-brother, Ishmael, Abraham's son by Hagar the Egyptian, is cast out by Abraham at the insistence of his wife, Sarah, and is destined to become someone "whose fist will be in every man's face." Jacob tricks his elder brother, Esau, into selling him his birthright for a bowl of stew, and urged on by his mother, Rebecca, disguises himself as Esau to acquire his father's blessing as his successor. Joseph, Jacob's favorite, spoiled son, is hated by his older brothers, who sell him to Ishmaelite traders and later report to Jacob that he has been slain by wild animals.

It's not difficult to see in these tales a strong resemblance to the stories of Lear and his daughters and Gloucester and his sons, in which a parent's favoring one child over another turns child against child with terrible results. "He always loved our sister most," Goneril observes to Regan. In the early moments of act 1, the Earl of Gloucester humiliates his bastard son, Edmund, in the presence of the Earl of Kent by referring to his illegitimacy and the randiness of his mother, then tells Kent that Edmund has been gone nine years and is preparing to leave again. In a footnote to the Arden edition, the editor, R. A. Foakes, speculates that Gloucester may have sought to distance himself from Edmund, an awkward reminder of his indiscretion.

As for Lear himself, not King Lear, but Lear, the unaccommodated man, Lear in rags, deranged by anguish—reading his speeches aloud to myself, I heard the voices of the Prophets, and occasionally the Psalmist, raging against injustice. Lear, no longer a pagan king but a Jeremiah, a Micah, a David the psalm singer, condemning the moral and ethical blindness of his own rule.

Here is Lear in the hovel during the storm: "And thou, all-shaking thunder, / Strike flat the thick rotundity o' the world, / Crack nature's moulds, all germens spill at once / That make ingrateful man!" "Poor

naked wretches, wheresoe'er you are, / That bide the pelting of this piti-
less storm, / How shall your houseless heads and unfed sides, / Your
looped and windowed raggedness, defend you / From seasons such as
these? O, I have ta'en / Too little care of this. Take physic, pomp, / Expose thyself to feel what wretches feel, / That thou mayst shake the su-
perflux to them / And show the heavens more just." And Lear, on the
heath, in his tirade to Gloucester about injustice to the poor: "Plate sin
with gold, / And the strong lance of justice hurtless breaks; / Arm it in
rags, a pygmy's straw does pierce it."

By comparison, in Micah I found this: "The Lord is coming forth out
of His place, / And will come down and tread upon the high places of the
earth. / The mountains will melt under Him / And the valleys will be
cleft, / . . . All this for the transgression of Jacob. / And for the sins of Israel." "I will go stripped and naked; / I will make lamentation like the
jackels, / And mourning like the ostriches. . . ."

And Jeremiah: "Woe is me because of my hurt! / . . . My tent is destroyed, / All my cords are broken; / My children have gone from me, /
They are not."

And Psalm 82:

> How long will you pervert justice?
> How long will you favor the wicked?
> Champion the weak and the orphan;
>   uphold the downtrodden and destitute.
> . . . But they neither know nor understand;
>   they wander about in darkness
>   while the earth's foundations are shaken.
> I thought you were Godlike, children of the Most High,
>   but you will die like mortals,
>   like any prince you fall.

That Psalm is among my favorites; I read it once a week during my
morning prayers. *King Lear* could have been written with it in mind. In
particular, I think of Lear and Gloucester, wandering about in darkness,
one figuratively, the other literally blind, both facing imminent death,
while around them the earth's foundations are shaken by the wrath of God.

87

And I'd detected a Judaic refrain in act 5, scene 3. Lear and Cordelia, defeated in battle, have been captured by Edmund, and Cordelia wants Lear to join her in appealing for clemency to "these daughters and these sisters"—apparently she can't bring herself to utter their names. But Lear responds:

> *"No, no, no, no. Come, let's away to prison;*
> *We two alone will sing like birds i' the cage.*
> *When thou dost ask me blessing I'll kneel down*
> > *And ask of thee forgiveness. So we'll live*
> > *And pray, and sing, and tell old tales, and laugh*
> > *At gilded butterflies, and hear poor rogues*
> > *Talk of court news; and we'll talk with them too—*
> *Who loses and who wins, who's in, who's out—*
> *And take upon's the mystery of things*
> > *As if we were God's spies. . . ."*

And I found the wisest and, for my purposes, most pertinent interpretation of these lines, especially the line about "God's spies," in *Old Age,* a slender, penetrating book by Helen M. Luke, a Jungian counselor living in Michigan, given me not in jest as a going-away present by my young assistant, Scott Moyers, who's now a highly esteemed senior editor at Random House. "Don't take this the wrong way, Herm," he'd said. "You're going to love it."

Turning to Ms. Luke's chapter on *King Lear,* I realized how indebted I really was to Scott when I read the lines about God's spies: "A spy is one who penetrates into a hidden mystery, and a spy of God is that one who sees at the heart of every manifestation of life, even behind the trivial talk of 'poor rogues,' the *mysterium tremendum* that is God. . . . the true mystery is the eternal paradox at the root of life itself—it is that which, instead of hiding truth, reveals the whole, not the part."

Moreover, what I found truly revealing was that for the first time in the play, God is singular with a capital G (in both the Quarto and the Folio, thus nullifying any skeptical conjecture about "printer's error"). Until now, we've had gods, and a goddess, nature. "Thou, Nature, art my goddess; to thy law / My services are bound," Edmund exults. Nature worship, a pagan concept. And at the end of the speech comes Edmund's diabolical exhortation, "Now gods"—using the plural this time, Edmund is now appealing to the entire barbaric pantheon—"stand up for bastards!"

Later there's the nihilistic observation by a desolate and hideously maimed Gloucester, whose eyes had been gouged out earlier by Regan's husband, the Duke of Cornwall, as punishment for abetting the cause of Lear: "As flies to wanton boys are we to the gods; / They kill us for their sport." Such are the ways of malignant pagan deities. Or so he thinks. But he's committed adultery, a sin the Torah decrees punishable by death, and I sensed a deliberate, ironic biblical inference in his plight. Even his son Edgar, confronting Edmund in 5.3, sees divine retribution in Gloucester's blindness; although not gifted with the exalted monotheistic vision of a redeemed Lear, one of God's spies, he attributes it to the "gods," who "are just and of our pleasant vices / Make instruments to plague us: / The dark and vicious place where thee he got / Cost him his eyes," thus foreshadowing the ultimate development of Torah-based morality decreed by a transcendent deity.

It seemed to me, then, that in one important respect, if not *the* most important, *King Lear* is an allegory of mankind's evolution from paganism to ethical monotheism. Perhaps it's Shakespeare's midrash on the Torah, a midrash being in some instances a rabbinic interpretation of Scripture in the form of a sermonizing tale. Could all the plays of Shakespeare be seen as midrashim on the entire Hebrew Bible, the Tanach?

Now, *there* was a concept for a master's dissertation, I thought. It might have been worth entering graduate school, as I'd once intended to do, just to have been able to propose that off-the-wall topic to the nemesis of Old Farts, who in all likelihood would have been my professor and thesis adviser, and watch the horrified reaction. Not that I felt there was anything preposterous about my basic idea, the Judaic nature of *King Lear.* After all, scholars have traditionally, and I think mistakenly, compared Lear to Job, as if that was the major biblical parallel. But they've failed to see that perhaps Shakespeare is turning the Book of Job on its head. The only point Lear and Job have in common is their suffering and their cries of pain. Job's ordeal is inflicted on him by God as a test, instigated by Satan, of his unconditional love. Lear's ordeal is self-inflicted, and while it, too, comes as the result of a love test, Lear is its instigator. Job never learns why God has afflicted him; God's justice is not to be questioned; man can never understand the working of Divine Wisdom. King Lear is only too aware that he's been guilty of neglecting the poor naked wretches of the world. Furthermore, in the manner of the Bad King in the Book of Kings, he has done an even greater evil in the sight of the Lord (and Shakespeare)—he has recklessly divided his kingdom and precipitated chaos and anarchy.

In the future, I'd be alert to anything in my Shakespearean and Jewish studies that could buttress or, heaven forfend, invalidate my concept. At least it deserved closer examination.

The image of King Lear as a Hebrew prophet prompted the recollection that Lear had once been played by that grand Jewish American actor Morris Carnovsky, whose career the talent scout at Paramount had suggested I use as a model for my own. I searched in Marvin Rosenberg's *The Masks of King Lear* to see if Carnovsky had found a biblical parallel in the role, but apparently he hadn't. His very presence, though, undoubtedly would have suggested a monarch out of the Book of Kings, and a Jeremiah.

Carnovsky was another favorite of my father's. Not quite on the level of Paul Muni but definitely a supporting actor whose film performances, in my father's opinion, frequently surpassed those of the stars. Leaving the theatre after seeing *Rhapsody in Blue,* the cheesy biopic about George Gershwin in which Carnovsky played the composer's impractical father, my father loudly announced, in his favorite critical mode, "That goddamn Carnovsky stole the show!" He was right, of course.

Too bad he didn't get to see Carnovsky's Lear. Actually, my father himself took on the role of Lear for real during the last month of his life, the Lear who cried out that he was bound upon a wheel of fire, his tears scalding like molten lead.

Two years earlier, when he was eighty-one, he'd been operated on for prostate cancer, which metastasized to his spine, generating pain in his legs so excruciating he could hardly walk. He'd been unperturbed by the diagnosis, the agony, and the surgery. Ever the stoic and the realist (not a Job—a Marcus Aurelius, whose meditations he dipped into frequently), he accepted his condition as yet another phase of "the way things are supposed to be." When he was being wheeled into surgery, he chatted it up merrily with the attendant, a young black man who roared with laughter when my father said, "I pulled all the goddamned cooling units out of my windows last year. All they did was pump stale air in the house, and that's unhealthy."

The prognosis was cheerless. The doctors told me he might last a few months, and that he would definitely need to be confined to a nursing home. But he beat the odds. As he loved to say, "I'm just an old son of a bitch." Meaning, they can't kill me, son. I'd arranged with social services at the hospital to have him moved to the nursing home I'd selected, a Catholic facility which accepted patients on a nondenominational basis. The Jewish home had infuriated me by demanding a substantial donation up front, in addition to exorbitant daily costs. My father had heatedly rejected the idea of coming to live with us in New Jersey. He was too proud and independent for that, too determined not to be a burden to anyone. And too much a Texan: "Goddammit, son, when I die I'm going to die in Harris County."

Three days after the operation I returned home. Over the next few weeks we talked on the phone daily. He sounded vigorous and cheerful, his only complaint being the kitchen's inability or unwillingness to make the toast dark enough. He preferred his toast semiburned, which, during the winter, he would cover with canned creamed corn as hearty breakfast fare. Then one night I picked up the phone and heard him jubilantly announce, "Son, I'm back home. And you did a hell of a goddamned job cleaning the house before you left. Miss Ruybe would have been proud." (My mother, whom he always referred to in the southern manner, had died in 1970.)

It seemed that my father had been ambulatory for some time. His legs no longer pained him. He couldn't abide the exclusive company of the aged, to say nothing of the sorry quality of the toast, and had told his doctors he was perfectly capable of tending to himself. They agreed, and it seemed miraculous. One of his neighbors, a middle-aged evangelist, had told me the day before I'd left that she'd cured her ovarian cancer by putting her hand on the radio when Oral Roberts was delivering a sermon, and that she'd be praying daily for my daddy because Jesus was known to heal good Jews like Mr. Abe. Yes, there are things in heaven and earth never dreamed of in our philosophy.

Over the ensuing months he went for periodic checkups and, more important to him, every month had his tiny 1972 Honda serviced by the dealer, even though the mileage was scarcely over one thousand, and visited his law office once a week to handle affairs for his devoted clients, who knew they couldn't find anyone else as honest, decent, and just plain goddamned wise. He was convinced he'd been healed. And so was I. All is for the best in this best of all implausible worlds. This man was immortal. As the jargonistas are fond of saying, we were in the wonderland of denial.

In the fall of 1981, the cancer reemerged with a crippling ferocity. He would have to be hospitalized and then sent back to the nursing home. My son, Jared, who was then a Columbia undergraduate and is now an oncologist, has told me that few things are more heartrending than the despair of a patient who learns that the cancer is no longer in remission. Standing by my father as he lay in his hospital bed in Houston, I heard him say weakly, "I want to cross to the other side."

He was to live for another two weeks, but those were the last words he spoke. He lay impassively, refusing to talk, rejecting food, sipping a minimum of liquids. With his long white hair, his white sideburn whiskers, his long flowing white mustache, he looked like a cross between his beloved Mark Twain and his beloved Micah the Prophet.

He wanted to die. I'm certain that if there'd been a Dr. Kevorkian handy, my father would have summoned him. He was long out of denial. But not I. Another little miracle must be just around the corner. I knew how Dylan Thomas must have felt when he urged his father to rage against the dying of the light. I wanted to grab the stubborn old son of a bitch and shake some fucking sense into him.

He looked at me, his eyes now repeating soundlessly, "I want to cross to the other side." I wouldn't have it. Get the goddamned nurses in here and force-feed him. He's going to pull out of this. Shit, I'd even brought him a copy of a book I'd edited, Margaret Brenman-Gibson's biography of Clifford Odets, the Odets whose plays he'd given me for my twelfth birthday, the Odets whom he once thought I might emulate. Gibson had included in her biography a reference to a letter I'd written to Odets when he was working in Hollywood in the 1960s and I was an editor at Little, Brown, inquiring if he'd consider writing a memoir. Odets had scrawled a note on my letter indicating he intended to get in touch with me to discuss the idea, but not long after, he was stricken with stomach cancer and died before he could respond. I read this section aloud to my father; surely it would perk him up. He simply closed his eyes. Before leaving to fly back to New Jersey, I placed the book on his bed—perhaps it would act as a restorative talisman—and made arrangements once again for my father's return to the nursing home. The hospital's work was done.

Days later, the call came. "Your father choked on a feeding tube. He has pneumonia and congestive heart failure. We're sending him back to the hospital. You'd better come as quickly as possible." He died before I arrived. Two days before his eighty-fourth birthday. He died in Harris County, yes indeed. Not in his home, as he'd planned. In a hospital room. Alone.

In the funeral parlor his casket was open. He was dressed in a white shroud, according to Jewish tradition. In the end he was back with the fathers, since he'd been named after the first of them, Abraham, and since he was born on February 12, after that other country lawyer named Abe, whose portrait hung in my father's office. I closed my eyes and remembered not this frail white patriarch but a fast-striding red-haired orange-mustached man in his forties getting off the Bellaire bus at 6:00 P.M. every day, carrying a beat-up old briefcase (I know that unlike me, he didn't think of it as a metaphor for his condition—he loved the law) and waving his arm and whistling his special greeting as I ran to the corner to meet him. The man was my best friend. And he died alone.

I thought of Kent's words near the end of *King Lear:* "He hates him much / That would upon the rack of this tough world / Stretch him out longer." In the hospital I'd been unable to look upon my father as a man racked by pain and fear and despair, aware that there would be no more miracles.

The night I returned from the funeral home, I dreamed that I'd come back and had been motioned by an attendant to a room at the rear of the building. There, on a rather high platform, lay my father, his white locks and mustache now neatly trimmed. Suddenly, he rose up, and smilingly turned to me. "Goddammit, son, didn't I tell you I was going to be all right? I'm just an old son of a bitch. Let's go get some barbecue."

My father died alone in Houston. But he was buried in Waco, in the Hebrew Rest Cemetery, next to my mother. And to Waco I traveled in March 1997, before going on to Houston for a periodic inspection of the family home, which I'd made a rental property soon after my father's death, unable to relinquish to strangers ownership of the house that had marked my parents' redemption from residential hell and unwilling to sever the bond to my homeland.

In Waco, a close friend, Theron Palmer, who lived in Salado, a small community halfway between Austin and Waco, met me at the airport. I'd known him since 1969, when he was the Texas sales representative for Harper & Row and I was editor in chief of that company's newly formed co-venture, Harper's Magazine Press. Tall and strapping, with a black handlebar mustache, Theron could have been one of the original Texas Rangers (as had been an ancestor of his) or the marshal of Tombstone. His appearance belied his gentleness, his wisdom, his erudition. The descendant of sharecroppers, he'd been the first person in his family to go to college. An avid book collector, he had to build a separate wing on his house to accommodate the thirty thousand volumes that he owned, many of them signed first editions of American novels.

Theron drove me to the Hebrew Rest Cemetery, located on one of Waco's main thoroughfares, adjacent to the Texas Ranger Hall of Fame and Museum, where Theron's Ranger forebear is buried. Not far away, Brann the Iconoclast, that fiery polemicist whom my father so esteemed, had been fatally shot in the back by a revered trustee of Baylor University, a Baptist institution, whom he had mercilessly assailed for hypocrisy; before succumbing, however, Brann had whipped out his pistol and killed his assailant, metaphorically having the last word.

My parents are buried on the same plot as my paternal grandparents, Channa and Jacob, who'd met on the voyage across the Atlantic. They ultimately came to Texas and opened a combination dry goods and grocery store in Mart, just a few miles from Waco. When my grandfather died at the age of forty-six in a flu epidemic fifteen years before I was born, my grandmother sold the store in Mart and bought another in Waco, where my father, his three brothers, and a sister helped out. Later my father attended Toby Business College, got a job with the Waco Electric Company, studied law at the Lafayette Extension College, and in his spare time was the boxing reporter for the *Waco Times Herald* (I still have clippings of his blow-by-blow accounts of the local fights). Boxing was a special passion of his, and later in life he became addicted to A. J. Liebling's *The Sweet Science:* "That goddamned fat boy is a writing fool" was his ringing endorsement of the indeed obese Mr. Liebling.

Standing at the graveside, I wasn't exactly Hamlet in act 5, brooding on the brevity of existence, the futility of achievement, the dark fate that awaits us in the end. No, I am not Prince Hamlet, nor was meant to be. All I could manage was a short conversation with the dead, beginning with a word in Hebrew: *Hineni,* Here I am. It's been a while, folks. Nine years in fact. I don't even get to Houston all that often, and as for going on to Waco, well, it's sort of out of the way, don't you know? Anyway, big doings back at home since our last little get-together. I've retired. Don't worry, Dad, I won't let my mind rot; in fact I've found a pastime to while away the hours—I'm studying Shakespeare on my own. Yes, Mom, I remember the toga you made for me when I recited the part of Cassius in that sixth-grade program. And yes, Mom, I'll remember to tell Theron that I once had a chance to be a member of Our Gang. Barbara's teaching Latin and health education at a local private school. Emily's a senior analyst with the Federal Reserve Bank of New York, Jared's an oncologist living in Brookline. Yes, that's right, they're truly mensches. No, neither is married yet, but they have terrific careers and Barbara and I aren't all that impatient to have grandchildren. Like hell we ain't.

On the way back to the airport for my flight to Houston, I mentioned my current obsession with Shakespeare. "That doesn't surprise me," Theron said. "I remember that at your daddy's funeral, you read those lines from *Julius Caesar* and *Hamlet*."

Theron had been among the handful of people at the grave site that February 12, 1982, my daddy's birthday, Lincoln's birthday, my daddy's burial day. A few old friends, and the children of friends, and one of my Houston cousins who'd married a Wacoan. In addition to reciting the Kaddish, the traditional mourner's prayer, I'd read the segment from Marc

Antony's tribute to Brutus: "His life was gentle, and the elements / So mixed in him that Nature might stand up / And say to all the world, 'This was a man.' " And Hamlet's praise of his father: "He was a man. Take him for all and all, / I shall not look upon his like again."

I hadn't visited the house in Houston—a two-storied, two-bedroom, one-and-a-half-bathroom ranch-style dwelling with a long narrow front porch, its cover supported by four brown cedar columns—since 1988, when I'd arranged for renovations to make it more enticing to potential tenants: for example, having a central air-conditioning unit installed and repairing the damage done by the most recent occupants, two brothers who'd skipped town owing a month's rent and leaving behind the kind of squalor and disrepair characteristic of a shooting parlor for addicts. The current occupants were a divorced nurse and her two teenage children, whose upkeep of the premises was exemplary, but not in the same league as that of my mother, who was given to scouring the place daily in an obsessive-compulsive hygienic frenzy.

As the nurse walked me through the place on an inspection tour, I remembered how my parents had been able to build the home in the summer of 1939 with the help of an FHA loan; how exciting it had been to drive to the building site at twilight on those warm summer nights to check the progress of the construction and listen to my father chat it up with the contractor, a tubby, jovial, gap-toothed middle-aged woman who wore a battered fedora and matched my father goddamn for goddamn; how, finally, released from the tiny drab one-story duplex, we'd roamed through paradise, marveling at the metal kitchen cabinets, the magical Sears Coldspot refrigerator (the duplex featured a dilapidated ice-box, in the literal sense—the iceman cameth daily to deposit a huge frozen block in the top compartment), and the modern pink-and-blue-tiled bathroom with, of all things, a shower.

I finally took my leave, thanking the nurse for taking such good care of the place, and as I was walking out the front door I noticed a familiar object tacked inside the jamb: a small mezuzah, which had been painted over so many times that its shape was barely discernible and had probably been ignored by all the tenants thus far, including the nurse. My father had posted it the day we moved in, more than fifty years ago, and there it had remained. For a moment I considered asking the nurse if I could detach it, to prevent anyone from removing it in the future and depriving me of a treasured family memento. But I decided to let it remain as a symbol of my parents' continuing presence in the home, which in a way still belonged to them.

6.

I spent the night before leaving Texas with one
of my old Aggie buddies, Tom Fontaine, a cherished friend for fifty years,
who'd retired not long ago from a career as a mechanical engineer and built
with his own hands a fishing cabin in Cold Springs, a small community
eighty miles from Houston where he and his wife, Jackie, spend their time
when they're not roaming the USA in their RV, which I call a Joadmobile.
An East Texas country boy who speaks slowly and deliberately in a raspy
high-pitched voice, he struck me when I first met him at A&M as a genial
rube, but I quickly discovered that his appearance belied his agile, penetrating, and skeptical mind, his uncanny common sense, his shrewd wit.
He's another of life's truth-tellers, a Lear's Fool with an exceptionally fine-
tuned shit detector which he's turned in my direction all too often over the
decades, shaking his head and prefacing a bluntly critical observation with
a squinty-eyed ironic grin or gleefully wheezing mocking laughter.

In Cold Springs that night, Tom and I had picked up a heap of Tex-
Mex victuals—tamales wrapped in corn shucks, supremely delicate en-
chiladas, tomato-free chili heavily flavored with cumin powder—at a
local take-out joint and he and Jackie and I feasted and drank Pearl beer,
the only quaffable Texas brew, and, in the regional vernacular, shot the
shit for hours. The pragmatic Tom was not enthralled by my voyage into
the Shakespearean expanse, which he judged to be a pedantic whim.
"What on earth are you going to do with all that special knowledge? You
sure as hell won't be able to teach it anywhere, not even Aggieland, without a Ph.-fucking-D. So what're you going to do? Get on a quiz show?
Be the king of Trivial Pursuit?" He chastised me for wasting my true skill,
editing manuscripts. If I didn't want to be a freelance editor, then I had
an obligation to teach writing to upcoming generations of authors. With
my experience, surely one of the universities in the area would welcome
me as a creative writing professor.

I argued that teaching writing was not a mission I felt obliged or eager to undertake. As an editor, I'd in effect been grading papers for too many years, and I couldn't abide the prospect of plunging once again into the swamps of semiliteracy, muddled thinking, and poor technique. Nor did I consider teaching a course in editing at one of those publishing programs offered at several universities. To me, editing was not a teachable skill; it could best be learned by on-the-job training as an editorial assistant, a rarely available entry-level position I'd been able to bypass because of related experience and well-developed connections.

Mulling this Pearl-saturated bull session on the flight home the next day, however, I did find myself enticed by the prospect of becoming a teacher. But what would I teach? I briefly indulged the fantasy of standing in front of a classroom waxing eloquently about Shakespeare and his world, but as Tom had recognized, that was out of the question. No university, no public or private school, would think of hiring someone without the proper academic credentials. Perhaps I could obtain a forged accreditation from Señor Ugarte, that unsavory habitué of Rick's American Cafe in *Casablanca*.

Not long after returning to New Jersey I came upon two passages in the Pirke Avot (Sayings of the Fathers) section of the Talmud during my Shabbat afternoon studies that spoke directly to my situation: Hillel's "Do not separate yourself from the community" and Rabbi Yishmael's "He who studies so that he may teach, is given the opportunity both to study and to teach."

I had to admit that contrary to Hillel's advice, I'd withdrawn from the community, studying Shakespeare in solitary confinement, similar to the way I'd conducted my private Shabbats before joining a congregation, and I was growing slightly barmy without anyone to share the excitement I was deriving from my close reading of the plays and my absorption with the critical literature on Shakespeare. As to Rabbi Ishmael's adage, similar to Tom's candid assessment, it was true that I hadn't been studying Shakespearean drama in order to teach it—no graduate school for me—so I could hardly describe myself as faculty bait.

Then it occurred to me: why not volunteer as a tutor for students who might be struggling with their papers on Shakespeare? That would satisfy Hillel and Ishmael, and possibly even Tom: I'd be serving the community by tutoring young minds, not only in ways to perceive the significance of Shakespeare but also in how to express their ideas clearly and concisely. Perhaps a social services organization might point me in the right direction, and I decided to try the RSVP, Retired Seniors Volunteer Program, which offered to people fifty-five and over service activities in areas such as outreach programs and community education.

I wasn't new to volunteerism. Four years previously I'd become a hospice aide. All that talk in the Torah about loving your neighbor and helping the needy and ministering to the ill had gotten through to me. The Talmud declares that whoever visits a sick person removes one-sixtieth of his illness, while he who ignores a sick person hastens his death. And Judaism teaches that performing good deeds long enough will transform one into a better person. In *Love's Labour's Lost,* one of the vain young lords in the Academe, Berowne, notorious for dazzling verbal pyrotechnics and cruel slashing wit, is challenged by the woman he loves to visit the "speechless sick" and "groaning wretches" for a year and see if his "gibing spirit," which she finds appallingly inhuman, amuses them. If they don't, he is to "throw away that spirit, / And I shall find you empty of that fault, / Right joyful of your reformation." Neither a Mother Teresa nor an Albert Schweitzer, I nonetheless found that giving care and comfort to the suffering, forgetting for a time my own vexations and anxieties, putting on hold my impulse to indulge in cynical belligerent smart-ass japery, did wonders for my feelings of self-worth.

My peak hospice experience lasted for almost two years, when I was assigned to a ninety-two-year-old Polish Jew, Morris, stricken with prostate cancer. He hadn't been expected to survive more than a few months after the diagnosis, but like my father, he was beating the odds. That had always been his style—beating the odds. As a young man he'd moved from Poland to Paris, worked as a waiter, and then, with his wife, opened a kosher restaurant. When the Nazis arrived, he lived by his wits, courage, and humor to safeguard his family and himself during the Holocaust. At the beginning of the war, he'd joined the French army and been captured by the Germans, who somehow were unaware he was a Jew. One day he approached the officer in charge of the POW camp and told him he suffered from asthma and needed to go to the infirmary. Instead, the officer, who'd taken a liking to him, discharged him from the camp and sent him home. Subsequently, he moved his family to the country-side and managed to send his son and daughter to Switzerland. At the war's end, he and his wife went to Switzerland, found the children, and returned to Paris. They reopened the restaurant, which became enormously popular with visiting American Jews, including the famous entertainer Eddie Cantor. Soon after his daughter married a G.I. and moved to America, Morris and his wife followed.

Morris was a small, wiry man with an unruly shock of white hair and huge, powerful hands, symbols of his strength of body and mind and spirit. He spoke Polish, Yiddish, and French, but even after all his years in America, he managed only broken English. An impish old bastard, he always found a way to make me laugh, uttering Yiddish obscenities that I didn't understand and that he'd immediately translate for me, pretending to be shocked by my ignorance of the language, and gossiping about his neighbors in the apartment complex: "That mamzer Levine. On Yom Kippur he didn't go to shul. He sat on a chair in the front yard and read a newspaper, so we could all see he didn't give a futz about the Torah!" Sometimes his humor was unintentional: he once referred to the legendary Yankee outfielder as Mickey Mendel. Who knows—perhaps Shakespeare's Berowne would have found in Morris a patient who'd have roared at his "gibing spirit." I saw him every weekend until he died, in bed, in his one-bedroom second-story apartment, and I sat shiva with his family. He was the grandfather I never knew. And he was my surrogate father. Through Morris, I discharged my filial obligations to the father who'd died far away, alone, without benefit of hospice, with no son at his side.

In the RSVP offices, I introduced myself to the program director, Pam Palladino, a pretty, dark-haired young woman with a winning disposition. Just as I was about to take up the subject of tutoring, I noticed on her desk a catalog from the Lifelong Learning Institute at Caldwell College. An affiliate of the Elderhostel International Network—my old alma mater!—it was part of Caldwell College's Center for Continuing Education, offering noncredit courses and seminars designed "to educate, entertain, and enlarge the world of seniors 50 and 'better.' " Moreover, it encouraged prospective members who were experts in their fields or qualified in their particular topic to volunteer as teachers.

I asked Ms. Palladino if the LLI came under the aegis of the RSVP. It did.

I was struck once again by those occasions in the past when I happened to be in the right place at the right time. Fortuitous? Or providential, the hand of God, the Divinity that shapes our end? I'd come here to offer my services to kids who might need help in mining the riches of Shakespeare. But now I saw the perfect opportunity to satisfy my newborn vocational fantasy of becoming a lecturer on the subject, in a milieu hospitable to a nonacademic, to an amateur scholar.

The LLI required that a teacher be either an expert in the field or someone qualified in a specific topic. While not an expert, I did feel qualified by my consuming passion for Shakespeare and the scope and intensity of my studies. The zeal to pass along what I was learning to my peers, fifty years and "better," whose intellectual curiosity remained undiminished, outweighed any desire to coach teenagers overwhelmed and intimidated by the Stratford Immortal. Motivated seniors, those Lifelong Learners, would bring to an appreciation of Shakespeare their own life experiences, the wisdom they'd acquired from being parents, from serving in the armed forces, from learning a skill and earning a livelihood. They had survived three wars and a Depression, heart attacks and chemotherapy; they'd been to their share of weddings and funerals, baptisms and bar mitzvahs; they'd been hired and fired, passed over and pensioned. They would know what Hamlet meant when he spoke of the whips and scorns of time, the oppressor's wrong, the proud man's contumely, the pangs of dispriz'd love, the law's delay, the insolence of office; when Hector, looking down at the gates of Troy in *Troilus and Cressida*, poignantly speculates that Time, that old common arbitrator, will one day end it, and when the King of Navarre, in *Love's Labour's Lost*, vows to outwit cormorant, devouring Time.

Sorry, all you young folk trying to sort out the imagery in Macbeth's "If 'twere done when 'tis done" soliloquy, you're on your own. I would be offering my services to my fellow grown-ups.

"I'd like to volunteer as a teacher at LLI," I announced to Ms. Palladino.

"What would you teach?"

"Shakespeare." I described how feverishly I'd been immersing myself in the plays and the criticism since retiring, and how eager I was to engender in others my own high-octane enthusiasm. "I'm not a Shakespeare scholar," I added, "I'm a lifelong learner myself. And they say the best way to learn a subject is to teach it. It focuses your efforts. Gives them structure and a purpose. So I guess I have a selfish motive."

"That's swell. Really. You should suggest this to Rose Gainey, the program coordinator at LLI, right away," Ms. Palladino said, writing down the phone number. "If this pans out, let me know, and I'll mail you our monthly report forms—we need a record of the hours you work."

Before calling Rose Gainey, I thought it advisable to decide on exactly which plays I planned to cover in the course. The LLI classes ran from four to eight weeks, one to one and a half hours a class. Using the maximum number of weeks and stretching the class time to two hours, I could accommodate six plays, allowing for an introductory lecture on Shakespeare and his world and for video excerpts if VCRs were available in the classrooms. I'd try to keep student participation at a minimum—this would not be a seminar. There was simply too much ground to cover and too little available time to permit discursive freewheeling free-associative interruptions.

Now to a specific description of the course. Would I let genre be my guide: the histories? the tragedies? the comedies? the romances? Or should I opt for a potpourri? A little bit of this, a little bit of that? What would be most enticing to prospective enrollees thumbing through a catalog? The more I pondered, the clearer it became to me that three of the plays that had made the greatest impact on me over the past year were those I'd read for the first time: *Titus Andronicus, Coriolanus, Troilus and Cressida.* The first two were tragedies; the third, as David Bevington points out in his introduction, is difficult to classify according to conventional definitions of tragedy, comedy, and history, but is "nominally tragic in that it presents the fall of great Hector and adumbrates the fall of Troy." Add to these *Julius Caesar* and *Antony and Cleopatra* and *Timon of Athens,* another play that had escaped my attention until recently, and what did you have? Tragedies featuring a bunch of Romans, Greeks, and Trojans. At least four of them would probably be unfamiliar to the LLI audience and therefore likely to provoke their curiosity; uniting them with the two popular tragedies, I had my organizing theme and a title for the course: "Shakespeare's Romans, Greeks, and Trojans: the dark and darkly comic vision of war and politics, pride and power, ambition and passion, idealism and opportunism in . . ." And I would also stress an equally important refrain that seemed to run through this sextet: the clash between the head and the heart, between love of one's self and love for one's neighbors (egotism and altruism), and the misfortunes that ensue when the former prevails.

I spelled out my ideas for the course in a phone conversation with Rose Gainey. "It sounds fine to me," she said. "Would you mind putting all this in a letter and include a résumé I can show to our advisory board?"

Done. A week later, Rose phoned me back. "Congratulations, you're all set. The board is very keen on the course."

"Don't they want to meet me before giving the final okay?"

"No, they're satisfied that with your background you'll do just fine. But there is one thing they've asked me to tell you: they want you to reduce the length of the class to one hour. Two hours might be too long for our seniors."

"I can't do that. I couldn't possibly do justice to six plays in seven weeks. Remember, the first lecture will be a general introduction. And I want to augment the course with video excerpts. Condensing the course would be ruinous. Also, don't you think it's a wee bit patronizing to assume that elders might doze and drool if forced to remain in a room for more than an hour? I can tell you that seniors in the two-and-a-half-hour Elderhostel seminars I took in England had no problem remaining alert. My challenge will be to hold their attention, to excite their interest. I'm confident I can do that. If the board doesn't share my confidence, I can understand that—they don't know me. And I'd be happy to meet with them and try to persuade them in person. But please tell them I won't teach the course if I have to compromise its integrity."

I was eager to report this conversation to Barbara, who, as a teacher, would surely appreciate the stand I'd taken. For six years, Barbara had been teaching health education and Latin at the middle school of Montclair Kimberley Academy, a private school less than a mile from our home. During the first fifteen years of our marriage, she had concentrated mainly on being a wife and mother, occasionally putting her language skill to use by reading German manuscripts for publishers and translating a few books for young readers. Once our children were in high school, she embarked on her own search for a vocation, and since she is happiest when learning something new, exploring the untried and unknown, and is a quick study no matter what the subject, her endeavors ranged from nursing in New Jersey hospitals (after two years of study) to administering student exchange programs to directing community and staff development at a resident center in New York City for international graduate students and trainees. Then a friend in our synagogue who knew of Barbara's nursing background and her desire to work closer to home told her of a job opening at the school where she herself taught. And lo and behold, Barbara found her métier, her true calling. She was a born teacher. She actually liked her students, and she never patronized them; she treated them as she treated our children when they were growing up, fairly but firmly, with honesty and humor and respect.

When she returned from school the afternoon of my chat with Rose Gainey, I lost no time in recounting the position I'd taken with the LLI board.

"You have a goddamned nerve," she sympathized. "Compromise the integrity of the course? They'll wonder what kind of pompous ass they're dealing with. Who the hell do you think you are? You've never taught a day in your life. And don't tell me about all the times you lectured at writers' conferences and publishing courses—that's not the same as facing a class week after week, trying to devise fresh techniques to get through to them, to make the material come to life. Those people on the board don't know you, they're accepting you on faith, and you in effect are telling them to go to hell—do it my way or else. What chutzpah! You've just blown a chance to do something useful and earn some terrific experience, Herr Professor Doktor Gollob!"

The morning after my conversation with Rose, she phoned to tell me the board had green-lighted the two hours. Herr Professor Doktor Gollob indeed, Mrs. Gollob!

The course was scheduled for fall 1997, five months off. I've never been one of those last-minute types who live on the edge, writing a term paper the night before it's due, scribbling notes for a speech on the back of an envelope while waiting for a previous speaker to finish (no, I am not Abe Lincoln, nor was meant to be), arriving at an air terminal moments before the gate for my flight is closed. I'm a planner, a plodder, a grind, desperate to succeed, to get there on time, terrified of failing, of missing the plane. Control is my game: leave as little to chance as possible.

Right away I began to prepare my lectures, drawing on what I'd been learning from the professors in my College of One—Goddard, Mack, Frye, Spurgeon, Saccio, Barton, Berry, et al.—and from my own closer study of the plays, aware that I'd be revising each lecture probably up to the day I had to present it, allowing for insights and observations gleaned from future reading and from further meditations on the material.

Late in the summer I wrote the introductory lecture to the course, and a month before the fall semester began I decided it was time to visit the Caldwell College campus and inspect the classroom I'd been assigned, the theatre in which I'd be performing. I took Barbara along to help me test the acoustics, and I also brought a videotape so that I could master the operation of the classroom VCR.

The college is a few miles from my home in Montclair, a fifteen-minute drive at most. Founded by the Sisters of Saint Dominic in 1939 as a Catholic liberal arts college for women, it became coed in the fall of 1986 and has an enrollment of 2,100. The seventy-acre campus in the midst of a residential homeowner community comprises six building complexes which include classrooms, administrative offices, student residences, a student center, an art center, a science building, and a library, which expanded in 1993 to include the Center for Continuing Education and a theatre.

Rose Gainey was sweet and accommodating, and gave us a tour of the campus, which seemed as serene and graceful as a retreat. I felt an immediate sense of belonging, of security. This was no high-powered intimidating educational factory. The premises exuded an aura of seclusion, of acceptance, of humility. My classroom was on the first floor of one of the older buildings. Standing at the lectern, with Barbara seated in the rear, I rattled off a few lines from Antony's "Friends, Romans, countrymen" oration, and Barbara counseled me to lower my voice a few decibels—the acoustics enabled me to speak in an almost conversational tone. A surge of confidence and excitement possessed me: I was in control, in character, the beloved Herr Professor Doktor itching to do my stuff. Even the VCR proved user-friendly.

But driving to the college on the first day of class, I suffered a near-terminal case of performance anxiety, exacerbated by Rose telling me when I arrived that the enrollment for my course was extraordinarily high for the Lifelong Learning Institute: twenty-two (sixteen women, six men—just about the standard male/female ratio in many adult education classes). Given my theatrical training, I was a skillful public speaker, adept at combining entertainment and illumination, with a history of rousing presentations at biannual sales conferences. For example, I once introduced as a prop a rubber chicken which I christened Bubba and which for some baffling reason so captivated the sales force that I was compelled by popular demand to find ingenious ways to use it during every conference.

But this was a new role for me, one that I'd have to sustain for eight lectures. Moreover, I felt I had to win the class over on the first day. I didn't want to walk into the room on the second week and discover that only a handful had returned. One of the main challenges was how to cover in two hours all the material I'd jam-packed into the lecture. I found that I could do it by speaking rapidly, but clearly, of course, and con brio. And allowing for no toilet breaks.

I arrived at the classroom a half hour early. A few minutes later people began to trickle in and take their seats. Elderhostel revisited. I smiled and helloed, and the panic crescendoed. I left the room and walked down the hall to the lavatory. Returning, I was surprised to find among the enrollees two of my fellow congregants at Shomrei Emunah, Gilda and Rose. An exchange of pleasantries, and then it was time. I took my place at the lectern. The room was full. Expectancy was in the air. I took in the faces: expressions ranging from curiosity to geniality to the downright challenging.

The instant I began to speak, the jitters vanished, as always, and I was swept up in an ecstasy bordering on the evangelical as I warmed to the subject, aware that I was taking the class with me into an enchanted realm that had begun to enrapture them with an intensity that matched my own. Gilda and Rose were beaming. Two women who looked enough alike to be twins and had to be sisters turned and nodded to each other. A man about my size, five eight, compact build, short white beard and a fringe of white hair, arrived a few minutes late and as soon as he sat down pulled out a pad and began taking notes assiduously. A slender woman wearing a neck brace smiled approvingly during the period, closing her eyes occasionally and swaying slightly, as if in a trance. Good grief, had I mesmerized her? An older woman, probably in her late seventies, short sandy hair and a genially skeptical mien, was in the first row, directly in front of me, and also scribbling notes. Even a sour-looking fellow who had in the beginning glowered at me beneath a preposterous toupee, which gave him the appearance of Shemp of Three Stooges fame, seemed shocked to discover that he was actually enjoying himself. I scarcely looked at my notes as I worked up a head of steam, moving away from the lectern, pacing in front of the class, taking care to make eye contact at all times, eager to give the impression that I was talking to each student personally.

I described Shakespeare's life and times: the family background, the years in Stratford, the thought of the Elizabethan age, the theatrical conventions and practices of the Elizabethan stage, the theatre companies, the difference between good quartos and bad quartos and the Folio.

I made a special point of quoting from the American poets who had original and moving and funny things to say about Shakespeare—Robert Lowell and Delmore Schwartz and Edward Arlington Robinson and W. H. Auden and Don Marquis. In addition to his "Gold Morning, Sweet Prince," Schwartz had written an interpretation of *Coriolanus* in the form of a dramatic account of the play given by a spectator at a performance, who in the course of his narrative remarks, "Let us judge all things according to the measure of our hearts, otherwise we cannot live," which reminded me of Auden's "We must love one another or die," both poets expressing what I take to be Shakespeare's essential meaning. Auden, too, wrote a meditation on a Shakespearean play, "The Sea and the Mirror," which he called "a commentary" on *The Tempest,* and which contains the provocative line "Magic is the enchantment that comes from disillusion," spoken by Prospero, reinforcing, I felt, the concept of Shakespeare's skepticism, which Robinson, in "Ben Jonson Entertains a Man from Stratford," saw as nihilism.

Don Marquis's "Pete the Parrot and Shakespeare" depicts the Bard as a frustrated poet forced to grind out hack melodramas for money. It's hilarious, but I indicated that the notion of Shakespeare as an artist who thinks he's prostituting his talent would probably be better applied to the so-called University Wits—the Cambridge grads such as Christopher Marlowe, Thomas Nash, and Robert Greene who thought of themselves primarily as literary men. It's likely that Shakespeare saw himself as simply another professional man of the theatre who moved almost casually from playacting (he was an accomplished actor) to playwriting. He was very much a man of his time, who learned to exploit brilliantly the stagecraft, the acting, and the public taste of his day. The theatre—that is, the performance of plays on a daily basis at a specific time in structures created for that purpose, and to which admission was charged—was a relatively new phenomenon. The public appetite for drama was insatiable, theatre was a craze, and since there was no established repertoire of plays on which to draw, the demand for fresh material was insistent, the pressure to create product intense. Audiences didn't want to see the same material repeated constantly. Which is why many if not most of the plays were based on stories readily available in other forms: histories (e.g., Holinshed's *Chronicles),* biographies (e.g., Plutarch's *Lives),* literature from other countries and other times—Roman drama, Spanish, Italian, and French drama and novels and novellas.

I compared the situation to Hollywood in the early days of the movies and actually up to the end of the studio system—a new form of popular entertainment seized on rapturously by the public, engendering the construction of theatres across the country which required new material on a weekly basis. Consequently, novelists, short-story writers, playwrights, were lured to Hollywood to create new scripts or adapt their own plays or novels or those of others; sometimes a screenwriter would collaborate with a colleague; sometimes the draft of a script would be given to another writer to revise (or "polish" in movie parlance) closer to the producer's or director's vision. Many of these writers had contempt for the medium. I speculated that some of these conditions may have prevailed in the Elizabethan theatre. How much control did Shakespeare exert over his script? As one of the owners of the company, at least after a time, probably extensive, so perhaps he was spared the ordeal of having his work altered by another writer. But that's not to say he was free of the collaborative nature of theatrical enterprise—suggestions for lines or scenes by a fellow actor or writer during rehearsals, or after a performance that revealed weaknesses. Shakespeare, I stressed, was not writing to be studied and interpreted in universities, he was not concerned with critical exegeses, he did not yearn to be a darling of the literati. He was writing popular entertainment to be performed onstage for an audience not unlike ourselves, a mix of educated and uneducated, high- and middle- and lowbrow, eager for an emotional experience. And in conclusion, I urged, "As you read these plays, be your own director and cast, act out the scenes in your mind or walk through them in your living rooms, reading the lines aloud, taking every role or enlisting the help of your family. Make your home the Globe."

I was done. "Thank you," I said, and as I started to gather up my notes there was an ovation, a salvo of "bravos." How could I top that? Gilda, wry and generous, a retired kindergarten teacher, and Rose, silver-haired and gracious, a former secretary, came over to hug me. Neither had read Shakespeare since high school. The note-taker with the short white beard grinned and shook my hand. He was Bob, and asked me if I'd mind repeating the names of the works by Schwartz and Marquis and Auden. The two women who looked alike and indeed were sisters, Madelyn and Marie, said they hadn't expected the course to be this exciting. The wry sandy-haired lady said, "Welcome to the club. I'm Midge, and I teach an LLI class in opera." It turned out she was also a member of the LLI advisory board and had been one of the strongest supporters of the two-hour class. A tall, rangy, bespectacled man, Chuck, who was probably close to my age, patted me on the shoulder and said, "That's just about the best-planned, most informative, most entertaining speech I've ever heard. It alone was well worth the price of tuition." But just as I was closing my briefcase, I received a cold dash of criticism: "I liked what I heard, but I only heard about a third of what you were saying. You talk too fast, and I had a hard time with your Southern accent." The speaker was a woman probably in her seventies, undoubtedly known in her circle as one who always spoke her mind, devil take the hindmost. Her complaints caught me off guard, coming as they did after that barrage of adulation. In fact, they annoyed me, and put me on the defensive. Smiling insincerely, I replied, "Then I suppose you'll just have to listen faster. And I'm afraid I was born with that accent, and I never want to lose it—it's part of my heritage. I go to Berlitz every month for a refresher course in the Texas drawl."

I left the tree-filled campus, which was glowing with the red-gold flush of a sunny late afternoon in autumn, and headed home, buoyed by the almost unanimous acclaim from the class. And I was terribly pleased with myself for the way I'd put my faultfinder in her place. I'd certainly taught her a lesson, yes indeed.

But that's not how Barbara saw it when I reported the incident to her that night at dinner. "You owe that person an apology, if she ever comes back to class, and she probably won't. When she enrolled for that course, she was taking you on blind faith, hoping you were someone who could tell her things about Shakespeare she hadn't known before, who could help her find meanings in the plays she hadn't been aware of. And someone who had enough respect for her eagerness to learn that he wouldn't sneer at her suggestion that he speak distinctly and clearly enough for her to understand him. You're not there to have your ego massaged. You're there to set their souls on fire with the passion for Shakespeare that's inflamed you since you retired. You don't give tests. You don't assign papers. The only way you can measure how effectively you've reached your students is to listen to what they say before and during and after class. Maybe you'll learn something—like a little humility. Remember that line from *The King and I*—'by your pupils you'll be taught.' Yes, you owe that woman an apology. If she comes back."

She came back the next week, and I didn't apologize for my Berowneish quip at her expense. But I did make a point of speaking less rapidly and modifying the drawl, and when class was over she came up to me and said, "Either you're speaking slower or I'm listening faster. I heard every word. Thank you." Her name was Erma. She and her slender, amusing husband, Ed, who had been a supervisor of a color testing lab at Du Pont before retiring, turned out to be two of the liveliest members of the group, and didn't miss a single class.

7.

Early on in the course, five people dropped
out—not an unusual attrition rate in adult education classes, I was told,
but significant enough to prick my thin skin and induce a flutter of self-
doubt. But my confidence returned when three others enrolled during
the second and third weeks on the recommendation of friends enthusi-
astic about my approach and undeterred by my No Lavatory Break policy. I rehearsed each lecture for hours so that I could continue to glance
up frequently from my notes and maintain eye contact with the class,
often moving away from the lectern to create a feeling of intimacy as I
looked into individual faces and spoke as conversationally as possible,
sometimes pretending to grope for words I actually knew so as to give
the impression of spontaneity, using the Barton/Berry technique of "discovering the thought." I often read aloud from the plays, especially long
speeches and soliloquies, noting up front, with a knowing look at Erma,
that according to the RSC guru, John Barton, American southern and
southwestern speech closely approximated that of the Elizabethans. I relished the opportunity to perform, or I should say perform roles from
Shakespeare, since the very act of teaching, if it's to be effective, has the
elements of performance. A teacher must dramatize his material, and
that's what I was attempting to do. But in my case, I was almost inadvertently creating a persona, the Shakespeare Maven, and at times I felt
like an impostor. I was in control of the material, but it was to a considerable extent a synthesis of the ideas of the scholars and critics I admired, shaped to convey what I thought to be the central concerns of
Shakespearean drama. True enough, I announced from the beginning
that I was an amateur, not an expert but an enthusiast, and I frequently
quoted my sources, even urging the class to buy the books I was so
avidly pillaging for ideas and insights. Nonetheless, the aura of spon-

taneity and immediacy I was able to project couldn't help implying that here was a man who really knew his stuff.

"I hope none of you proper citizens were too shocked by the sex and violence of this play," was my opener for our consideration of *Titus Andronicus* the following week.

"Was this an Elizabethan version of *Pulp Fiction*?" Gilda shot back.

"You bet. And Quentin Tarantino would be the perfect director for a movie version." (Alas, Julie Taymor got there first. Her grotesquely stylized, self-importantly "innovative," and radically incoherent film adaptation was released in 2000. The only offensive violence in the production was the violence done to Shakespeare's text.)

I explained that although for a century critics had undervalued *Titus* as a sleazy sentimental revenge melodrama in which Shakespeare, a fledgling playwright, was pandering to the bloodlust of the Elizabethans, whose idea of entertainment was public hangings and bull-baiting, it's now recognized that his signature qualities of irony, ambiguity, paradox, and antithesis were already in evidence in this work. Furthermore, *Titus* lays out themes that will mark Shakespeare's major classic dramas: power struggles over dynastic issues, mainly the right to the crown; the consequences of dangerous ambition; the conflict between love and duty, heart and head.

Titus, a great general, comes home in triumph after subduing the Goths, and brings with him as prisoners Tamora, Queen of the Goths, three of her sons and her lover, Aaron the Moor. The Romans, sworn to uphold the ideals of honor, dignity, and virtue, describe the Goths as barbarians. And therein lies the irony. Right away, one of Tamora's sons is sacrificed to the gods by the "civilized" Romans, hewn limb from limb. In a political clash between the two sons of the late emperor, Titus turns away from the youngest brother, who is good, and instead supports the eldest, a sadistic crazy boy in the Caligula mold; Titus is being faithful to the Roman concept of *pietas,* which demands that natural feeling be subordinated to public good. Soon thereafter he considers it an honor when the crazy boy, Saturninus, takes Titus's virginal daughter, Lavinia, as his wife, and later kills his own son, whom he wrongheadedly calls a traitor aiding in the attempted rescue of Lavinia from Saturninus's clutches.

113

Shakespeare is showing us Roman honor and virtue and duty at their most perverse extremes, the fruit of Roman idealism gone haywire. Honor, dishonor: apparently Shakespeare, like Stephen Dedalus in Joyce's *Ulysses,* fears "those big words which make us so unhappy."

Ironically, the good father in *Titus* is the demonic, diabolic Aaron the Moor, a consummate psychopath, the most vital, engrossing character in the play, a do-badder who prefigures Shakespeare's monumentally nihilistic villains, Iago in particular. Aaron has fathered a son by Tamora, and paternity ignites in him a spark of humanity. On the run from a rebellious horde led by another of Titus's sons, Aaron, holding his infant son, hides out in ruins and is discovered when the baby cries. Rather than save himself by killing the child when it began to wail, Aaron allows his paternal instinct, his heart, to prevail. Quite the opposite with Titus, who slew one son and banished another as a matter of "honor," of "virtue," both of them grand delusions.

"Aaron is a much nobler Moor than Othello, isn't he?" asked Midge. "Othello let that snake Iago trick him into thinking Desdemona was unfaithful, and then he strangled her. But Aaron refused to kill the thing he loved."

And on the subject of the noble Aaron, I referred Midge and the class to the scene in which Tamora comes upon Aaron plotting awful things to do to Lavinia. (Eventually, he incites Tamora's sons to rape Lavinia, then cut out her tongue and chop off her hands, resulting in one of the funniest stage directions in theatrical history: "Enter . . . Lavinia, her hands cut off, and her tongue cut out, and ravished.") Tamora immediately launches into a lyrically seductive twenty-line speech, melding the romantic and the erotic, at times so rhapsodic it could have been spoken by Juliet. The speech, filled with pastoral raptures, is all foreplay until the midway point—"We may, each wreathed in the other's arms, / Our pastimes done, possess a golden slumber, / Whiles hounds and horns and sweet melodious birds / Be unto us as is a nurse's song / Of lullaby to bring her babe asleep." But Aaron impatiently resists her overtures.

I decided to call on volunteers to suggest how they'd direct this scene. I had my own ideas, of course. Tamora is mocking the sentiments of a love song as she utters them, all the while lewdly caressing Aaron, trying to strip his clothes from him; he, in turn, finds himself aroused, respond-

ing violently at first, then pushing Tamora aside. An illustration in the
Bantam Classic edition seemed to confirm my interpretation: a photograph taken of the New York Shakespeare Festival production directed by
Gerald Freedman in 1967 shows Olympia Dukakis on the ground, strad-
dled by Moses Gunn, who seems about to have his way with her. I decided to ask one of the principals to verify this. Ms. Dukakis and I happen
to live in the same town, so I phoned her and popped the question: did
Freedman block the scene as I envisioned it? The voice on the line was
warm, humorous, direct, with a suggestion of no-bullshit-will-I-give-or-
take, and also a sense of the grand, the generous, the—what else?—
theatrical. "Yes, you're right, we made that scene an off-the-wall
seduction. Oh God, what a fabulous experience. Moses was wonderful.
We wore masks, wigs, helmets. And I had a dress that weighed fifty
pounds. Can you imagine tripping around the stage seductively in that? I
loved the outrageousness of that part—the whole play permitted such ex-
cess. It was a license for theatricality. And we made the most of it."

The consensus of the class, however, was that Tamora and Aaron
would stand facing each other onstage—Tamora gushing passionately,
Aaron remaining impassive and at last turning away. "Do you really think
that's the way to seduce a man?" I asked. "With words only? And do you
think Aaron could totally resist a temptress as sexy as Tamora?" Then I
offered my own conception and related my conversation with Olympia
Dukakis. "Don't be a name-dropper," Gilda chided me.

I'd decided to end each lecture with video excerpts from the play
we'd studied to drive home the fact that Shakespeare was primarily
meant to be seen and heard, and to allow students to compare these interpretations with their own. Today I screened a segment from *Playing
Shakespeare* with Patrick Stewart as Titus and Lisa Harrow as the muti-
lated Lavinia. It was Harrow, with her controlled pathos, who truly
moved the class. Huddled on the floor next to her father, who is be-
moaning his hideous situation, she whimpers softly, her eyes mirroring
the horror of the atrocity she's suffered. "She looked like a wounded
deer. The pain and shock in her face was so real," said Midge, drawing
murmurs of agreement from the rest.

The next week, as I was coaxing a cup of coffee from the eccentric
dispenser in the first-floor lounge before the *Julius Caesar* session, Bob

approached me, bringing in tow a ruddy elf of a man, vital and athletic-looking, probably in his mid-sixties. "This is my friend Lou," he said. "I've been raving about your course and he'd like to join us." "Bob's enthusiasms are irresistible," said Lou. "He'd be great at P.R. But I haven't registered yet. Can I do this after class?" Sure. They joined me for coffee and I discovered that Bob was supervisor in physical education and adjunct professor at a New Jersey college. Lou, who turned out to be in his eighties, was a World War II vet who'd been assistant to the CEO and president of a major corporation before retiring. He'd been passionate about Shakespeare since childhood.

I opened my lecture on *Julius Caesar* with a trick question: identify the character in this play who delivers the soliloquy "This lovely light, it lights not me," which I recited from memory. When no one answered correctly (Lou's choice was Cassius, but most chose Brutus), I revealed Captain Ahab as the speaker. "Oh, you're a sly one," Lou piped up. "There's madness in my method," I responded, and then explained my theory about Shakespeare's influence on Melville's vision of the perils of developing the reason at the expense of the heart. And I added that Melville was especially impressed by the timelessness of Shakespeare's political attitudes: in the margin of Melville's copy of Shakespeare's works, beside Casca's description of "the rabblement" hooting and clapping for Caesar with their sweaty hands, he jotted "Tammany Hall."

Then I asked for the identity of the character who spoke these lines: "He thinks too much. . . . / He is a great observer, and he looks / Quite through the deeds of men. . . . / Such men as he be never at heart's ease / Whiles they behold a greater than themselves." Lou held up his hand: "That's Ishmael describing Ahab." Much laughter. Ah, the class jester had arrived—and someone familiar with *Moby-Dick*.

It was, of course, Caesar's deadly accurate (no pun intended) description of Cassius, and might be an unconscious description of himself, and reflect a glint of Shakespearean irony. Cassius is Rational Man, a scorner of astrology and mysticism, an egotist, a cynic and manipulator, in love with his own mind, desperately envious, and selfish. Selfishness and envy, I stressed—the causes of much of the evil in the world. Cassius reminds me of the radicals, nihilists, theorists, and idealists in the novels of Dostoyevski, who, like Shakespeare, was deeply suspicious of intellectuals.

I continued: in Shakespeare's villains, from the start the head has prevailed over the heart. In the tragic heroes, such as Brutus, we witness the struggle between the two. Brutus says he's at war with himself, but we actually hear only the rational side of the argument, the case for assassinating a tyrant, or as it seems, a potential tyrant. Look carefully at his soliloquy in act 2, scene 1, I told the class. He knows "no personal cause" to bring Caesar down, only the "general." Nothing personal, folks. I'm just doing this for the people, the common good. An abstraction, impersonal. He says nothing of his affection for Caesar, he shares with us no warm remembrance of Caesar. Brutus is not *certain* that Caesar would be transformed into a monster if he becomes emperor. "That's the question," he muses. Chuck, who'd been silent up to now, said, "So he's a Hamlet figure, right?" "Absolutely. In fact, critics think of him as a prefiguration of Hamlet."

I pointed out that if we look closely at the text, we find that Brutus never tells us what Caesar has done to motivate these baleful conjectures—for example, that crowning Caesar would put a sting in him. And I spotlighted the most ironic lines in the soliloquy: "The abuse of greatness is when it disjoins / Remorse from power; and to speak truth of Caesar, / I have not known when his affections swayed / More than his reason." Brutus gives not a single example of Caesar's reason overcoming his affections, which may be a tad disingenuous. If he thought a little harder, I insisted, he could come up with several instances in which Caesar's affection swayed more than his reason: for example, he forgave Brutus for siding with Pompey, he made Brutus praetor over Cassius although the latter deserved it (like Othello earning Iago's hatred by promoting Cassio over him). We know this from reading Plutarch's *Lives*. Is this a weakness in Shakespeare's characterization? Only those familiar with Plutarch might suppose that Brutus is repressing any fond memories of Caesar, whom many thought to be his father. Ordinarily, I went on, when Shakespeare makes changes in his sources, it's to enrich the complexity of characters and to heighten the drama of the story. That's why reading the sources increases our appreciation of his genius as a playwright. Here, though, I'm puzzled: how many people in Shakespeare's audience would have been conversant enough with Plutarch to appreciate the psychological subtlety behind Brutus's repressing those memories?

This time Ed spoke up: "So you think we're missing something important in these Greek and Roman plays if we don't read Plutarch?"

"First of all, you'd be missing the rich experience of reading Plutarch for his own sake. And, yes, his *Lives* would give you a valuable perspective on these plays. Most of the editions have excerpts from Plutarch and other sources. But I'd urge you to buy the Modern Library version of the *Lives.*"

Then back to examining the irony of the lines I'd quoted: Brutus is unknowingly characterizing himself, he is letting his reason, his rationality, overwhelm his feelings. A further irony here: we see a Julius Caesar in the making. As Harold Goddard has observed, Brutus overrules Cassius at critical moments—for example, refusing to assassinate Antony and allowing Antony to deliver a funeral oration. "Brutus," says Goddard, "has become like Caesar!" Shakespeare is showing us the harm in the world that can be promoted by political idealists and ideologues, weaving utopian theories based on the notion that humans are rational creatures.

I showed scenes from the video of Joseph Mankiewicz's film version of *Julius Caesar:* the first scene between Cassius and Brutus, with John Gielgud feverishly resentful and menacingly cunning as the former and James Mason possibly a bit too remote in conventional interpretation of the reflective Brutus; and Mark Antony's funeral oration, in a definitive rendition by Marlon Brando bringing to the role the full force and intensity and acuity of his once formidable talent (the class applauded at the end of the scene). And I selected a moment from *Playing Shakespeare* in which Ben Kingsley, coached by Barton in Brutus's "It must be by his death" soliloquy, offers that here Brutus is rational, exploratory, feeling his way, deliberately pushing down his feelings for Caesar. "Hey, Herman, I guess Kingsley read Plutarch, too," said Chuck. "Yeah," chimed in Lou, "now we know where Herman stole his idea." Honest, fellas, I came up with it on my own. Jeers and catcalls.

When we came to *Antony and Cleopatra,* I had to admit to a strong bias: as a graduate of a military college and a former officer in the United States Air Force who served for a year in Korea, I often found myself impatient with Antony's inability to resist the charms of Cleopatra and his failure to do his duty to Rome, and sympathetic to Octavius Caesar's plea from afar, "Antony, leave thy lascivious wassails." In this instance, I said,

Shakespeare, ever aware of the contradictoriness of the human comedy, the paradoxes and ambiguities of existence, seems to be showing us that there are occasions in a person's life when the mind must prevail over the heart, when civic good must outweigh private pleasure. Antony is well aware of this when he exclaims, "I must from this enchanting queen break off. / Ten thousand harms more than the ills I know / My idleness doth hatch." Earlier, Cleopatra contemptuously remarks that Antony has had a "Roman thought," as if a sense of duty to one's country, a code of honor, were fit subjects for mockery. I singled out Antony's lament after the battle of Actium, "I have lost command," as one with special poignance to those of us with military backgrounds: Antony has lost command of his troops, has lost command of himself; he has been disgraced, has in effect lost his manhood. Remember: his most cutting insult to Caesar was to call him a boy.

I reminisced about a superior officer of mine, a major in the air force, who reminded me of Antony. I was a recently graduated second lieutenant—shavetail in service parlance—stationed at Kelly Air Force Base in San Antonio. Major Bailey, as I'll call him, had won the Distinguished Flying Cross as a bomber pilot in World War II. The son of a dirt-poor farmer, he'd boxed professionally for several years before joining the air force. Of medium build and height, he had red-brown hair and blue eyes which glistened with humor and challenge. He played hard, he drank hard. The junior officers and enlisted men loved him. Unfortunately, he was not a favorite of the higher-ups. Married to an insurance agent's daughter, a pretty and very proper brunet, and the father of two little girls, he'd flouted the puritan morality that prevailed among the conservative officer caste: he openly kept a mistress, and to compound the transgression, she was a Mexican American who worked in the post exchange at nearby Randolph Field. The major and his wife were Catholics; divorce was out of the question. But his scandalous behavior—his lascivious wassails—doomed him to minor assignments and no hope of promotion. Soon he'd have no choice but to resign from the service. He took a liking to me because I was an Aggie and a boxing fan and, as a basic training officer for reservists who somehow had missed that formative experience, a fiercely demanding son of a bitch. He insisted that I spar with him in the base gym two mornings a week, and though he toyed with

119

me, by the time we'd finished I'd be woozy from the lightning-swift left jabs with which he snapped my head back repeatedly. One day I marveled that for a man who'd once boxed professionally, his face was amazingly unmarked, his ears uncauliflowered. He then proceeded to take his thumb and forefinger and fold each ear into a tiny blob—they were paper-thin. "Great plastic surgery," he explained.

Not long before I left for overseas, I actually had the opportunity to meet Consuela, the infamous Other Woman. After one of our morning workouts, he put his hand on my shoulder and said, "Listen, Lieutenant, I have a favor to ask. This may sound like a shit detail, and you can say no without pissing me off. But Connie's fucking little poodle bitch needs to be taken to the vet today for a bath and trim, and her car is on the fritz. I can't break away, so can you be a pal and chauffeur the mutt just this once?"

Connie met me at the door of her apartment, holding a cage bearing the white poodle, Chi-Chi. I was expecting the typical Lupe Velez Mexican spitfire. Instead, Connie was short and dumpy with dyed-blond hair and a pockmarked face. But her incandescent black eyes, her quick affectionate smile, her husky voice, and her flamboyant gestures suggested a Cleopatra who was all "fire and air." This was the exotic paramour for the love of whom Major Bailey had lost command. Fifty years later I can almost hear him saying to her, as Antony said to Cleopatra, "There's not a minute of our lives should stretch / Without some pleasure now . . . / Tonight we'll wander through the streets and note / The qualities of people."

Then I turned to the play's scene stealer, Enobarbus. Rereading this play for the course, I realized for the first time that Enobarbus is in some respects one of Shakespeare's Fools, or one of those loyal right-hand men, those truth-tellers, total realists—the Duke of Kent in *Lear* is another example. And Sancho Panza. They speak their minds to their commanders, in fact to everyone, bluntly, sardonically. Men of common sense and earthy humor. Ironically, Enobarbus's reasonableness leads to his tragic downfall. This occurs after Antony's humiliation during the battle of Actium, in which Cleopatra, at the moment of crisis, orders her ships to flee and Antony abjectly follows suit. But soon thereafter, Antony's martial spirit revives and he is eager to take on Octavius Caesar once again. But

Enobarbus is wary. He contrasts the courage of Caesar, guided by a cool head, with the courage of Antony, which is headstrong and rash, "frighted out of fear," as he says, so that in a sense, as Northrop Frye notes, Antony's reason has been taken prisoner by Caesar. Enobarbus then draws the inference that the rational thing to do would be to desert to Caesar. But his reason has betrayed him. He's really betrayed not Antony but himself, his true feelings, his heartfelt loyalties. He finds himself, says Frye, in the deep cold hell of a deserter, no longer trusted by those he left, never to be trusted by those he is trying to join. Then comes the news that Antony, aware of his desertion, has sent on all his possessions and his treasures. He is totally shamed, mortified, despairing. He has done the rational, reasonable thing—but he is not greathearted. Heartbroken, he dies. His death is literal and symbolic. He has truly experienced what the great novelist Elizabeth Bowen has called "the Death of the Heart," of his essential self.

I showed in its entirety Trevor Nunn's unsurpassable 1973 television production starring Richard Johnson, a perfect blend of the dissipated and the heroic, as Antony, and Janet Suzman, the sultriest, sexiest, most volatile prima donna imaginable. "The gal playing Cleo made me understand why Antony made such a damned fool of himself over her, to put it mildly," said Lou. Marie commented that Suzman reminded her of Bette Davis as the lovably temperamental Margo Channing in *All About Eve;* Rose agreed, adding that it was amazing that Shakespeare had been so on the mark in creating a prima donna at a time when female roles were played by men. Erma said that in reading the play, she'd missed much of the humor revealed in the televised adaptation.

Almost an entire period was devoted to the film, and we spent the remaining time contemplating the complex and contradictory heroine. Was she a cunning manipulator or loving mistress? Opportunistic monarch who uses sex as a weapon in the political wars or helpless lovestruck female "commanded by such passion as the maid that milks and does the meanest chores"? Madelyn and Marie said in unison—a sister act no less—"She's both." And Marie added, "Remember, Enobarbus said she was a woman of 'infinite variety.' Isn't that what 'complex and contradictory' means?" General agreement.

"Okay. Let me frame the question differently. If Cleopatra had been convinced that Caesar would allow her to remain in Egypt and reign as queen after Antony's suicide, would she have taken her own life and joined Antony in that great bedroom in the sky?"

The class answered along gender lines. The women said of course she would have followed her heart and killed herself—she couldn't live without Antony. The men, including me, said of course she wouldn't have reached for the asp; she ended her life only because she was too vain and imperious to endure public humiliation and debasement; she wanted power above all, political and sexual, and would have followed her head and found another mighty ruler to seduce.

After class Bob and Lou joined me for coffee in the lounge, and Bob came up with a unique casting suggestion: "I think Lee Marvin would make a hell of an Enobarbus. He looks the part, he's got the right moxie, he's an ex–combat marine."

I had to agree. It was offbeat, but Marvin had talent; people tend to forget that he starred as Hickey in a movie version of Eugene O'Neill's *The Iceman Cometh* twenty years ago. This led me to relate the tale of my brief but memorably unnerving encounter with Mr. Marvin when I was an MCA trainee in Hollywood. Late one Friday afternoon I drew the chore of delivering a contract to Marvin at his home in the San Fernando Valley and returning it, signed, to the office. The traffic was hellish, and when I finally reached the Valley, I made a wrong turn and found myself hopelessly lost. The streets in that area were a maze, and my map was of no help at all. Somehow I managed to blunder onto the right street, and, almost an hour late, pulled up in front of Casa Marvin, or so it appeared to me, a formidable hacienda set far back from the road and distinguished by a huge veranda running the width of the house. My shirt soaked with sweat from the heat and from nervous agitation, I made my way across the vast lawn, and as I drew near the house, I could see Marvin sitting on the veranda railing, dressed in khaki pants and shirt, sleeves rolled back to just below the elbow, lighted cigarette in his hand. Every inch the marine top sergeant, he stared at me stonily, eyes narrowed to slits, occasionally shifting his basilisk's gaze to his enormous watch. When I reached the veranda, from down below I blurted out an apology for being late, in a voice that sounded decidedly unmarine in my ears, and, I was certain, in his. His eyes fixed on me, Marvin drew deeply from the cigarette, let the smoke linger for what seemed at least a minute in his lungs, exhaled at length in my direction, looked again at his watch, then back at me, and said, "If this was Tarawa, we'd all be dead, wouldn't we, Herman?" Enobarbus couldn't have said it better, as Bob put it.

By this time I'd developed a camaraderie with a group that included Bob and Lou, Ed and Erma, Marie and Madelyn, Chuck and Midge (I'd known Gilda and Rose before the course began). And I learned more about their backgrounds and interests.

Bob was a feisty dynamo galvanized by a voracious curiosity and hunger for experience. He'd played semipro baseball, he was a zealous golfer, a Civil War buff who toured battlefields around the country. He'd skydived, and on a trip to Israel he swam across the Sea of Galilee. He spoke rapidly, animatedly, with a sense of urgency no matter how casual the subject. But he rarely spoke up in class. And I never questioned him about his reticence—I didn't want to make him self-conscious. I figured that his feverish dead-serious note-taking indicated he was there to absorb the content of the lecture and didn't particularly welcome interruptions.

Lou, for all his eighty years, was a combative smash-'em whack-'em tennis player, and he spent the winter weekends skiing in Vermont. He unfailingly brought to class newspaper clippings about things Shakespearean, or brochures of coming events, or programs of shows he'd seen, many of them with Bob, who had a ravenous appetite for the theatre and movies.

Midge had been an executive secretary and administrative assistant at a sales engineering firm. She'd started college in her fifties, not aiming for a degree, and over a period of ten years took only the courses that interested her.

Chuck, like me a Korean War veteran, was a retired civil engineer, blunt, pragmatic, a no-nonsense guy, incisively intelligent and keenly focused, determined to fill in what he considered the yawning gaps in his knowledge of the liberal arts.

Madelyn was a retired school librarian, and Marie, a retired book-keeper/office manager. Lively and articulate, they'd taken several semesters of a Shakespeare course at a distant community college before moving from the area. Madelyn, who'd been a media specialist at her school li-

123

brary, acted as my "technical adviser," coming to my rescue when I pushed the wrong buttons on the VCR.

This group usually arrived early, attentive to my declaration at the beginning of the semester that I would start promptly and not squander precious minutes waiting for stragglers to wander in. We had a lot to cover, and comorant, devouring Time was our enemy. Rarely did our preclass conversation touch on what we were studying. General schmoozing prevailed—talk of children, grandchildren, travel plans, new movies, lousy television shows, health. Real-life stuff. Occasionally, students on their way to and from classes glanced in the room, slight frowns of puzzlement on their faces, as if annoyed by this intrusion of a different species into the kingdom of the young. Caught up in their sensual music, they had no use for us, the monuments of unaging intellect.

By now we were into the sixth week and ready to take on Coriolanus, fierce warrior, proud aristocrat, mama's boy. Before I could utter a word, Lou gave me the perfect intro by imitating James Cagney as the psychotic killer Cody Jarrett, screaming his immortal final words in the classic gangster movie *White Heat:* "Top of the world, Ma!" He's standing atop a blazing fuel tank, where he's been cornered by the cops, and is about to go up in flames rather than be captured, exulting in what he knows will be the approval of the ghost of his dead mother, herself even more wicked in life than Cody. No one else in the class understood Lou's ingenious if oblique reference, so I explained that Cody and Coriolanus were tough guys molded and dominated by ruthless mothers. And even more to the point, Cody suffers from migraine headaches, an indication that perhaps his violent life goes against his basic nature, and he might have turned out differently if it hadn't been for Mom.

Coriolanus, too, is a man converted to a doctrine of blood by his mother, Volumnia. His real self has been stifled by the martial indoctrination imposed by her during childhood in keeping with the Roman ideal of *virtus,* the Roman term for valor. Coriolanus's dilemma, I stressed, seems to be further proof of my notion that one of Shakespeare's principal convictions was that much of the pain and mischief in the world is the result of forcing an unnatural mode of behavior on another or on one's self in compliance with utopian ideals and theories. In the last act comes a moment of devastating irony. Banished by the demagogic tribunes for his refusal to truckle to the "citizens," Coriolanus has joined Rome's implacable enemy, Tullus Aufidius, general of the Volscians, and has returned at the head of a Volscian army prepared to raze the city and slaughter the populace. Now Volumnia finds herself appealing to Coriolanus to follow his heart, to let his love of family prevail over his coldly calculating campaign of revenge. He relents, thereby sealing his death warrant. Aufidius will use this act of charity to condemn Coriolanus to death as a traitor. "Perfidious Aufidius," Ed said in what he'd intended to be sotto voce but was made audible by the room's acoustics, greatly amusing the class.

In the remaining half hour, I again emphasized the timelessness and universality of Shakespeare by drawing a parallel to Coriolanus a bit closer to the mark than Cody Jarrett. Over the centuries, the essentials never change: we can observe the power struggles between the patricians and plebeians and say to ourselves, this is like bankers versus proletarians, without benefit of actors dressed in contemporary clothes. Isn't it patronizing to assume that audiences can't make these connections unaided by directorial inventiveness in updating time and place? In rereading this play, it occurred to me, without benefit of characters garbed in tunics, Sam Browne belts, riding britches, and boots, that Coriolanus has much in common with one of America's military titans of the twentieth century: General Douglas MacArthur. Brave, arrogant, wellborn, imperious, hungry for glory. Dominated by an aristocratic mother who drove him to be mercilessly ambitious. One particular episode in MacArthur's career is uncannily Coriolanean: his brutal treatment of the Bonus Marchers in 1932. Hard hit by the Depression, hungry and close to starvation—much the same as the plebeians in *Coriolanus* who revolt because of a grain shortage; they, too, are starving—almost twenty thousand World War I vets and their families descended on the Washington Monument, petitioning the government to pay them a cash "bonus." At the time, MacArthur was a general and also army chief of staff. He was convinced the marchers were communists and he sensed that revolution was in the air. He decided to take personal command of the eviction of the Bonus Marchers and led an assault that put the encampment to the torch. Two babies died from tear gas exposure.

Timon of Athens, the penultimate drama in the course, is one of my least favorite Shakespearean plays. I included it because it connects to *Antony and Cleopatra* and *Coriolanus,* and it also does illustrate, albeit heavy-handedly, Shakespeare's vision of the grim consequences that result when man, in this instance Timon, a wealthy benefactor and patron, violates the principle of the golden mean and develops mind at the expense of feeling, and vice versa.

Shakespeare tells us that Timon was once a great general, but he never reveals the why and how of Timon's alleged greatness; for example, there's nary a mention in the play of Timon's military career, his triumphs, his courage, his leadership. What we see at first is, I told the class, a wealthy schmuck idiotically lavishing presents and cash and fancy dinners on a bunch of hangers-on, flatterers and fawners. Eventually, he's forced to borrow heavily in order to finance his largesse; when the well runs dry and he asks his creditors for lenience, they refuse. Reduced to poverty, he's deserted by the parasites he nourished, and becomes virulently misanthropic. "Poor honest lord," laments Timon's steward, "brought low by his own heart, / Undone by goodness!" This sounds like the subtitle in a D. W. Griffith silent movie melodrama. You can almost see the actor miming the lines with stereotyped gestures. Timon's friend, the cynic Apemantus, observes more discerningly, "The middle of humanity thou never knewest, but the / Extremity of both ends." And that's the problem with this play. It's impossible to be moved by Timon's plight, as Ed observed. Hard to believe, but some critics have actually compared Timon to Lear. Nonsense. His ruination leads not to self-awareness but self-pity. After all, what could he say—"How sharper than a serpent's tooth is the ingratitude of hangers-on"? He's been a fool, but he blames others, not himself. Rose spoke up, for the first time in weeks: "Isn't he a complete materialist? He hasn't been a philanthropist, after all." Correct. He wasn't exactly doling out contributions to the poor naked wretches of the world. His "goodness" consisted of buying friendship. And his bitterness quickly grows wearisome.

Plutarch, in what is essentially a brief digression in his life of Antony, reported that after Antony was defeated at Actium, he withdrew to the Egyptian island where Timon is buried, and learned that Timon, embittered by ingratitude and hypocrisy, shunned all company except that of Alcibiades, whom he knows someday will do great harm to the Athenians. Plutarch also wrote a life of Alcibiades, but strangely, Shakespeare ignored it, and his portrait of Alcibiades in *Timon* resembles the historical figure only in his turning, a la Coriolanus, against his own country. Even odder, Shakespeare gives Alcibiades a different motive for going over to the Persian enemy. In real life, Alcibiades, handsome, wealthy, a brilliant commander on land and sea, had been falsely accused of destroying sacred images of the god Hermes and ordered back to Athens for a hearing; instead, he allied himself with the Persians. In *Timon,* Alcibiades is banished by the Senate for coming to the defense of a friend who had been condemned to die for a crime that Shakespeare only hints at but that we are to assume was murder in self-defense. Determined to avenge the injuries done him, he returns to Athens with an army, but in a burst of magnanimity relents when the Athenians express their regrets at the wrongs they've committed, and spares all the citizenry except "those enemies of Timon's and mine own."

It turned out that Ed brought with him to class a library copy of Plutarch. He was perplexed by Shakespeare's choosing to write a play about Timon and to make Alcibiades, whom he found much more enthralling and complicated, only a minor figure. Moreover, he argued, Shakespeare's Alcibiades pales in comparison to the man Plutarch describes. And he cited passages from Plutarch illustrating his point. "I have to care about a character if I'm going to enjoy a story and learn something from it. I didn't care a hoot for Timon. Alcibiades is my kind of hero." Midge answered for me: "I guess Mr. Shakespeare didn't want to repeat himself. He'd been down this road with *Coriolanus.* Why do *Son of Coriolanus?*"

I went on to say that *Timon* is really a morality play, with characters who are essentially abstractions: the Cynic, the Toady, the Hero, etc. Ed was right: Timon fails to involve our sympathies.

As with *Coriolanus,* I was unable to unearth any *Timon* video segments; instead, Ed and I alternated in reading aloud additional passages about Alcibiades from Ed's copy of Plutarch. And the class disagreed with Midge and me: *Alcibiades* would have been a hell of a play, *Coriolanus* or no *Coriolanus.*

At the end of the session, Gilda asked if I planned to continue the course in the spring. "Matter of fact, I do," I answered. "I'll take up the history plays."

The same question had been put to me the previous week by Roxanne Knott-Kuczborski, a handsome, sturdy go-getter aglow with élan, brimming with ideas and gifted with unearthly patience, who had succeeded Rose Gainey as LLI program coordinator. Given the success of the initial offering, and the general popularity of the subject, she anticipated an even larger enrollment than before.

I needed no persuading. I'd found an exhilarating new purpose in life. I hadn't actually reinvented myself, but I'd redefined myself and my aims, redirecting my aptitudes and interests to a different arena. I'd involved myself—as Barbara had reminded me—in an endeavor where I'd be required not only to teach but to learn. So I was a volunteer teacher, not a bona fide Herr Professor Doktor, so what? This did not minimize the significance of what I was accomplishing—namely, stimulating the minds and stirring the emotions of people whose craving for knowledge and wisdom hadn't diminished over the years, and charting for myself a route toward what might turn out to be one of those second careers often heralded in the pages of *Modern Maturity,* the journal of the AARP. And if, as I walked across campus carrying my old companion, the battered briefcase, crammed now with lecture notes, videotapes, and editions of Shakespeare's plays, and sat alone in the faculty lounge, adding last-minute thoughts to the lesson I'd prepared for the day or staring wistfully out the window at the surrounding hills, I couldn't help fantasizing a la Walter Mitty that I was one of the college's revered scholars, a veritable Peter Saccio, lionized for my dazzling pedagogy, where was the harm?

The course as I'd described it for the catalog was "Uneasy Lies the Head: Shakespeare's Unmerry Monarchs from Richard II to Richard III (via Henrys IV, V, VI)—a consideration of Shakespeare's vision of power and ambition, patriotism and treason, heroism and cowardice, love and hate, in the seven historical plays concerning the Wars of the Roses and their origin."

But it remained for me, in the last lecture of the fall semester, to deal with how Shakespeare approached these loaded matters in *Troilus and Cressida,* his scaldingly ironic masterpiece about a more ancient conflict, the Trojan War. Using as his principal sources Chapman's translation of Homer and Chaucer's *Troilus and Criseyde,* Shakespeare gives full throttle to his matchless command of irony and ambiguity, his pained skepticism about accepted values on the nature of love, war, honor, fame, beauty, truth, heroism.

In *Shakespeare in Perspective,* volume 2, a collection of essays taken from radio and television commentaries on the BBC TV productions of the complete Shakespeare canon, Norman Rodway, who played Thersites, described by Shakespeare as "a deformed and scurrilous Greek," describes this play as "two stories of love and war, each illustrating and reflecting the other; the star-crossed passion of Troilus and Cressida, framed in the larger context of the siege of Troy."

Troilus, son of Troy's King Priam and brother of the noble warrior Hector, is in love with Cressida, the daughter of a Trojan priest, and confesses this to Pandarus, Cressida's uncle, who brings the two of them together at his house, where Cressida promptly falls in love with him. They spend just one night together: on the following day, Cressida is handed over to the Greeks in return for a Trojan prisoner and immediately betrays Troilus with a Greek general, Diomed.

From time to time, Shakespeare brings Thersites onstage as a sort of cynical, nihilistic chorus and commentator on the action. "Lechery, lechery; still, wars and lechery; nothing else holds fashion," he cries. And, "All the argument is a whore and cuckold [Helen and Menelaus]—a good quarrel to draw emulous factions and bleed to death upon. . . ."

Reversing my standard format, I began with a video segment from *Playing Shakespeare:* Jane Lapotaire's interpretation of Cressida's fourteen-line soliloquy in act I, not technically a sonnet, I suppose, because of its rhyming couplets, but to me a sonnet nonetheless. In the soliloquy, spoken just before her first meeting with Troilus, Cressida proclaims what the critic Muriel Braddock, quoted in Talbot Donaldson's useful *The Swan at the Well: Shakespeare Reading Chaucer,* defines as the "simple creed, the art of the coquette raised to a Rule of Life, based on the assumption that what is to be looked for in Man is simply 'lust in action.' " "Men prize the thing ungain'd more than it is," Cressida asserts. Is she merely a flirtatious slut, worldly and witty, or an ingenuous, confused girl? Both, says Harold Goddard, pointing to what he feels is Shakespeare's belief in the divided nature of the soul, the inner struggle between the spiritual and the sensual.

I focused on Cressida at the outset in accordance with Donaldson's

129

declaration that there couldn't be a more appropriate heroine for a play one of whose major themes is human inconstancy and inconsistency. "The play is full of passionate statements of ideals which are then ignored by the very characters who stated them," Donaldson explains. "Every man in the play, except Pandarus and Thersites, who are unburdened by ideals, is inconsistent: Troilus, at first rendered by love too weak to fight, fighting a moment later. . . . in council arguing that the Trojans should keep Helen because one must at all costs hold on to the things one values, and then making no effort to prevent Cressida's transfer to the Greek camp; Hector, splendidly arguing that Helen must be returned to the Greeks and then abruptly turning his back on his own argument; . . . Achilles, a great martial hero, playing silly games in his tent with Patroclus, refusing to fight even after he has undertaken to, and when he finally fights, fighting like a coward; and Ulysses . . . who discourses magnificently on human behavior and behaves himself like a second-rate, incompetent Machiavel."

I turned in the latter part of the lecture to this Machiavel, Ulysses, in my estimation not quite the second-rate figure described by Donaldson. I go along with Harold Goddard, I told the class, who says that Ulysses might have been created by Shakespeare expressly to bring home the truth of Montaigne's maxim "All other knowledge is hurtful to him who has not the science of goodness." Ulysses is all mind, no heart. Politics is his meat. We first catch this theme, says Goddard, in the scene before Agamemnon's tent, when Ulysses complains that "the physical champion and their cohorts do not appreciate the part that the brain, or as he calls it, wisdom, plays in war." In Ulysses's words, "The still and mental parts / That do contrive how many hands shall strike / When fitness calls them on and know by measure / Of their observant toil the enemies' weights— / Why, this hath not a finger's dignity. They call this bed work, mappery, closet war. . . ." According to Goddard—and I agree—Shakespeare seems to be saying that pure intellect, mind divorced from virtue, always lends itself to envy and destruction. Ulysses also extols the virtues of law and order— "degree, priority, and place"—and his analogy for social and political order is the solar system with everybody in his proper orbit from the center out. The Great Chain of Being. And he warns that "when degree is shaked," the order of the world degenerates from, in Goddard's words, "its centripetal perfection to a centrifugal fever of envy, where every inferior is jealous of his superior until the whole body politic is infected." You can't help agreeing with Ulysses's unblinkable wisdom: law and order are sine qua nons of civilization. But the speech turns out to be a prime example of Shakespearean irony: shortly after delivering it, proving that any violation of degree involves the danger of anarchy, and deprecating envy and disdain, Ulysses hatches a plot to pull the proud Achilles out of his place by scheming to have Ajax chosen by lottery, instead of Achilles, to fight Hector, the valiant Trojan hero. A believer in degree resorting to a lottery. "Is that what's called keeping everybody in his place?" asks Goddard.

Perhaps the most poignant experience for the class, one with direct application to their own condition, came at the conclusion with my reading of Ulysses's "alms for oblivion" exhortation to Achilles, whom he is trying to lure back into battle against the Trojans. (Achilles has removed himself from combat because, in Shakespeare's twist on the *Iliad*, he's fallen in love with Priam's daughter, not, as in Homer, because Agamemnon has taken for himself one of Achilles's trophies, a Trojan beauty.) It's a shrewd, manipulative speech, with Ulysses pushing all the right buttons, playing to Achilles's pride and his craving for glory, but taken out of ironic context, and at face value, it's a powerful, moving statement about the pitfalls of resting on one's laurels, of retiring too radically from life's challenges and thereby risking physical and intellectual stagnation. The lines that struck home to the class, and to me, with the greatest force were these: "Perseverance, dear my lord, / Keeps honor bright; to have done is to hang / Quite out of fashion, like a rusty mail / In monumental mock'ry." I followed this by reading the final lines from Tennyson's *Ulysses,* in which Ulysses, here not a canny manipulator but an aging king with no cunning purpose but only an honest desire to inspire his fellow elders, urges:

> Old age hath yet his honour and his toil;
> Death closes all: but something ere the end,
> Some work of noble note, may yet be done. . . .
> 'Tis not too late to seek a newer world. . . .
> Tho' much is taken, much abides; and tho'
> We are not now that strength which in old days

131

> *Moved earth and heaven; that which we are, we are;*
> *One equal temper of heroic hearts,*
> *Made weak by time and fate, but strong in will*
> *To strive, to seek, to find, and not to yield.*

Early on in my recitation I began to choke up, and I had to struggle to keep from weeping as I continued. When I finished, there was scarcely a dry eye in the room.

And once again, applause, this time, in fact, nothing less than a standing ovation, led by Lou and Bob, and a barrage of "Thank you's." They began to flock around me, these dear new friends, these heroic hearts, these monuments to unaging intellect, hugging me and promising to be back for the next series.

Midge, unabashedly dabbing with a Kleenex at the tears in her eyes, said, "When Troilus and Ulysses eavesdropped on Diomedes making love to Cressida, I thought, 'What a great operatic quartet Verdi or Mozart could have made out of this.' "

"So why don't you dash one off yourself between semesters?" I responded.

"You mean I should play Strive and Seek?"

"Don't you always?"

After everyone had gone, I sat in the classroom for a few minutes, savoring the realization that evidently over the past eight weeks I'd accomplished what I'd set out to do. I'd made reading Shakespeare as lively an intellectual and emotional experience for a group of my peers as it was for me. And chances were I could keep at it for some time to come. I felt that if I'd been put on earth to do nothing else but this, it would have been no mean achievement.

8.

Buoyed by the success of the first semester and
the rapport I'd established with the class through forceful lectures and a
disciplined approach to student participation, I prepared for the next term
not only free of misgiving but with a zest enhanced by the exceptional
vigor and humanity of the plays themselves.

The histories teem with what Erich Auerbach, in *Mimesis: The Representation of Reality in Western Literature*, referring to the complete works,
describes as an inexhaustibly abundant mixture of the sublime and the
low, the tragic and the comic, "a delight in rendering the most varied
phenomena of life . . . inspired by the concept that the cosmos is everywhere interdependent, so that every chord of human destiny arouses a
multitude of voices to parallel or contrary motion."

Twenty-four students enrolled for the new course. Two among them
seemed particularly simpatico: Marjorie, a red-haired freckle-faced retired
postmistress, and Ted, a retired, easygoing high school math teacher.

At the outset, I urged the class to keep in mind that one of Shakespeare's besetting concerns dominated this cycle of historical dramas (and
underlay *Julius Caesar, Hamlet, King Lear,* and *The Tempest):* the chaos engendered in a monarchy when the legitimacy of a king supposedly ruling
by divine right is challenged by strong men motivated by belief in his un-
fitness or ruthless ambition. A monarchial government poses a problem
not easily dealt with: notwithstanding the follies and vices and weakness
of a particular king, since he's God's appointed ruler, how, short of divine
intervention, can he be removed from office? To acknowledge that subjects have a right to judge or remove their king threatens the stability of
the realm—any subject, dissatisfied for any reason and determined to
usurp the throne, might incite a revolt, leading to that devastating form
of chaos, civil war.

Shakespeare realizes, it appears, that the very least we might expect from a king is an awareness of the terrible burden of power, the awesome responsibility, on which Henry IV, formerly Henry Bolingbroke, usurper of Richard II's crown, and his son and successor, Henry V, soliloquize, revealing, I believe, Shakespeare's admiration of both men and his conviction of their fitness to rule: Henry IV bemoans the fact that while his poorest subjects slumber peacefully, he, the king, is denied this repose: "Uneasy lies the head that wears a crown." Henry V, too, just before the battle of Agincourt, laments, "What infinite heart's ease / Must kings neglect that private men enjoy!" And Shakespeare demonstrates his affection for the gentle, pious Henry VI, better equipped to be a priest than a king, when, sitting pensively on a molehill while the battle of Towton rages without him, he echoes his grandfather and father in a soliloquy in which he longs for the simplicity of a pastoral life, observing that a shepherd's "wonted sleep under a fresh tree's shade . . . / Is far beyond a prince's delicates."

Richard II, I made clear, is untroubled by the obligations of power. And I voiced my contempt for his weakness, vanity, corruption, self-indulgence, self-pity, and incompetence. A tragic figure? Not in my estimation, and I wonder if Shakespeare viewed him as such. And how many of you, I asked the class, would define Richard as tragic? Marjorie started to raise her hand but stopped when she realized she was alone in her estimation. "It's okay to disagree with me," I encouraged her. "But only once a semester."

Critics, though, I went on, have always preferred Richard to his nemesis, Henry Bolingbroke. Richard, they say, is a poet, Henry merely a pragmatist, an opportunist, a blunt man of action, as if being a poet somehow conferred upon Richard a moral excellence, a virtue extraordinaire. Harold Goddard reminds us that Richard was only ten when he inherited the crown and that it was only natural that while others governed in his name he played at being a king and went on conceiving life as a brilliant spectacle at which he was the center. To me, then, he's not a poet, he's an actor—a ham actor—every action a posture. He's constantly posturing, striking attitudes, playing at king until he's deposed. His conception of divine right is perverse and sentimental: never does he imagine that he must earn the respect of the people he governs, or balance his budget, or follow laws. He's surrounded himself with decadent cronies on whom he lavishes riches and titles. And he's banished Bolingbroke and stolen his inheritance. Most grievously, when he learns that Bolingbroke's father, John of Gaunt, is gravely ill, he prays to God to let a physician hasten his death so that Richard can confiscate his property to finance the war in Ireland. To me, that odious prayer itself was sufficient to cancel any claim to divine right of rulership. What deity would sanction the rule of such a contemptible fop?

I've been a Bolingbroke man unwaveringly since first reading the play in college, I declared. No self-respecting Aggie could be otherwise. When he defies Richard's edict of banishment and returns with powerful forces to claim his inheritance that has been stolen from him, he never soliloquizes about his motives or conduct, or discusses these matters with others, except to say that he merely wants his rights, the return of the Lancaster estates. He finds a demoralized nation and steps into the vacuum created by a disastrously weak and unqualified king, whom he deposes.

I referred the class to Peter Saccio's *Shakespeare's English Kings*, which shows us that this wasn't the first time Bolingbroke had been responsible for removing Richard from the throne. In the years before his exile, he had joined a group of the established nobility that called themselves the Lords Appellant, charged the king's favorites with treason, organized an army, and defeated the king's army in battle. In what was termed the Merciless Parliament, they won their case against the favorites, some of whom were executed, others dying in exile. The Lords Appellant ruled for a year, during which time the king was kept in the background and remained quiet until he came of age and announced his intention to rule on his own. Thereafter the coalition of Lords Appellant broke up. Unable to wield power effectively, Richard has paved the way for a succession of rivalries, jealousies, treacheries, battles, crime, rebellion, and treason, a state of civil war, of chaos, which ends only with Richard III's defeat by Henry, Earl of Richmond, who becomes Henry VII, Henry Tudor.

Bolingbroke as Henry IV is a ruler of insight and intelligence, endowed with a sense of justice, with nothing of the tyrant in his makeup. But he's also apprehensive about those who helped him usurp the throne, especially the Percy family, and as proof of the potency of the divine right concept no matter how justifiable the usurpation, guilty because of his leading role in bringing it about. The play's title is misleading: although the king appears in some key scenes, for long stretches the action focuses on other characters.

The first is his son, Prince Hal, who faces the hard truth that the inevitability and assumed legitimacy of inherited kingship have been called into question. He must make himself king through a sophisticated manipulation of power, and he proves himself a consummate politician, no more so than in his use of other people to serve his own ends. In an early soliloquy he tells us that his escapades with his raffish companions in an Eastcheap tavern are a political experiment—he's putting on a show designed for maximum effect, in which a reputation for being profligate will be suddenly reversed when he enters on his responsibilities. Also, as Northrop Frye tells us, in Eastcheap Hal will acquire skills he'll need when he ascends his father's troubled throne—learning the language of others, rehearsing their tongues, one of the arts of power. As a madcap prince, he has soaked himself in every social aspect of the kingdom he is going to rule—he is becoming his entire nation in an individual form, which is symbolically what a king is.

Hal's rival for preeminence in the kingdom is Harry Percy, Hotspur, son of the Earl of Northumberland, leader of the rebels against the king. An embodiment of medieval chivalry, Hotspur is eager above all not for power but for honor and the glory to be won in battle. What he's truly devoted to is fighting—it's the one thing that doesn't bore him. He divides people into men who fight and the snuff-sniffing popinjays such as the king's representative who accosted Hotspur after the battle of Holmden against the Scots and in the king's name demanded all of his prisoners, all the while berating Hotspur's soldiers as "unmannerly" for bearing the "slovenly unhandsome" corpses of fallen comrades "betwixt the wind and his nobility." He's dashing, mercurial, fearless, quick-witted, irreverent, charming. I admitted to the class that he was my favorite character in the play, and wasn't surprised to discover that the males in the class felt the same. Bob, as ardent a Civil War buff as I, laughed when I compared Hotspur to such dashing Southern cavaliers as Generals Jeb Stuart and George Pickett. I remembered that the professor who taught my Shakespeare class at A&M gave an A-plus to a paper on *Henry IV, Part 1* written by a World War II vet who had fought at the battle of the Bulge and was attending college on the G.I. Bill. In his essay, the vet had described Hotspur as a tragic figure who'd gone into battle against tremendous odds, abandoned by his father (who'd claimed to be ill and failed to bring his troops to battle), certain he was doomed but facing his destiny with insouciance ("Doomsday is near; die all, die merrily") and convinced his cause is right ("Now, for our consciences, the arms are fair / When the intent of bearing them is just"). For my part, I can't read the play or see it without being devastated by Hotspur's death. I singled out for the class a section from John Keegan's introduction in his erudite and engrossing *A History of Warfare* that struck me as pertinent to our understanding of the Hotspurs and Antonys and Coriolanuses of the world. Discussing the ethos of an army regiment, he observes that as an instructor at the Royal Military Academy Sandhurst his colleagues on the academic side were veterans of World War II, Korea, Malaya, Kenya, Palestine, Cyprus, or "any one of another dozen colonial campaigns. . . . Regimental loyalty was the touchstone of their lives. . . . A slur on the regiment would never be forgotten . . . so deeply would such a thing touch the values of the tribe. Tribalism—that was what I had encountered. . . . Soldiers are not as other men—that is the lesson I have learned from a life cast among warriors. . . . [War] must be fought by men whose values and skills are . . . those of a world apart, a very ancient world, which exists in parallel with the everyday world but does not belong to it."

Definitely not a warrior is Hotspur's polar opposite, his antithesis, Sir John Falstaff. I reminded the class of Shakespeare's frequent use of antithesis, his dramatic genius at setting word against word, image against image, scene against scene, character against character. And I took issue with Harold Goddard's romanticized vision of Falstaff. Admitting that Falstaff is a glutton, drunkard, coward, liar, lecher, boaster, cheat, thief, rogue, ruffian, he goes on to celebrate him as "the incarnation of charm . . . much of his charm resides in the fact that he is what we long to be and are not—free. . . . He realizes the dream of all of us—to awaken in the morning and know that no master, no employer . . . stands in his way—only a fresh welcoming day that is wholly ours." Those of us who have retired have realized this dream, too, haven't we, I asked the class. Does that make us Falstaffs? Only if we share what Goddard goes on to celebrate as Falstaff's immaturity: "he has never grown up—he turns everything into play. . . ." This is the description of a child, a self-indulgent selfish child. I noticed Bob reach over and pat Lou understandingly on the shoulder, much to the amusement of Ted, seated near them.

But there's more, I continued: Goddard hails him as a realist with a contempt for force. On the field of Shrewsbury he dismisses "honor" as a "word. . . . air. A trim reckoning." But he's a knight, involved in war whether he wants to be or not, and he's been empowered to recruit soldiers for the war against the Percys and their rebellious allies. He responds by becoming a profiteer, taking bribes to let the good recruits off and conscript only the worthless, whom he cynically describes as "food for powder." Loathsome enough, but Shakespeare dramatizes the true baseness of this reprobate's character in the scene in which Falstaff discovers the corpse of Hotspur, who's been slain in hand-to-hand combat with Hal, and congratulates himself that he's still alive: "The better part of valor is discretion, in the which better part I have saved my life," he declares over the body of the valiant warrior, in effect profaning it. Even more odious, fearing that Hotspur might be counterfeiting death, he stabs him in the thigh to make sure, and plans to take credit for killing him. Carrying Hotspur on his back, he exits, to me despicable beyond redemption. Here we see the true Falstaff, the man whom Hal earlier reviled, only partly in jest, as "Wherein cunning but in craft? Wherein crafty but in villainy? Wherein villainous but in all things." At times Shakespeare might look with skepticism upon lofty ideals such as honor and virtue and valor, but the man who shows us Falstaff lugging offstage the bloody corpse of Hotspur is showing us the difference between one who follows the selfish dictates of his head and one who heeds the heart's call to glory.

Admittedly, Falstaff, in his affection for Hal, is allowing his heart to rule, and ironically Hal, as king, in *Henry IV, Part 2,* breaks Falstaff's heart by rejecting him. We can't help pitying this shattered old rogue. But the most poignant moments for me, an opinion shared by the class, unsurprisingly come in two earlier scenes. First, Falstaff's exchange with Doll Tearsheet in the Boar's Head Tavern, when at last he recognizes that time has overtaken him. He begins by expressing his envy of Hal's friendship with the young and athletic Poins. Then, most touchingly, he asks Doll to kiss him; she obliges, and he gently accuses her of giving him "flattering busses." She remonstrates that she kisses him with "a most constant heart," and he responds, simply and honestly, without a trace of self-pity, "I am old, I am old," which seems to mirror Richard II's line in prison just before his murder, "I wasted time, and now doth time waste me."

"So you don't hate him that much, after all," said Marie.

"He has his moments," I admitted. "But I didn't shed a tear at his death."

The theme of time's remorselessness is sounded again in the next scene, when Shakespeare lets the senile old bore Justice Shallow, in a conversation with the dim-witted Justice Silence, reminisce, with an uncanny mixture of pathos and comedy, "Jesu, Jesu, the mad days that I have spent! And to see so many of my old acquaintance are dead!" (I noticed Gilda nodding ruefully; a good friend and fellow congregant of ours had recently died after a yearlong battle with cancer.) Shortly thereafter Falstaff enters, and Shallow continues his trip down memory lane, recalling the times he and Falstaff spent carousing and whoring, and prompting from Falstaff a line that resonates with those of us who have closed many a bar in our day: "We have heard the chimes at midnight, Justice Shallow."

Falstaff, like Enobarbus, dies of a broken heart. "The King has killed his heart," says Hostess Quickly in *Henry V,* 2.1, and in the next scene, one of the most hauntingly powerful in Shakespeare, gives an account of his death. Shakespeare could easily have shown the death of Falstaff, his friends gathering around him while he "babbled of green fields," as Hostess Quickly describes it, unaware that Falstaff is trying to pray, to utter the words of the Twenty-third Psalm, "He maketh me to lie down in green pastures." But Shakespeare's genius was to realize that the true power of the scene would come not by showing but by telling, and telling it tragicomically through his own Mrs. Malaprop, Hostess Quickly.

"Couldn't he have been thinking of the days when he was an innocent kid, playing in the countryside?" Ed asked from his seat in the rear.

"Excellent point. And that kind of memory might build more sympathy for this old reprobate than a deathbed return to the faith."

One of the videos I screened during this segment of the course, a production of *Henry IV, Part 1* directed by Michael Bogdanov and filmed live for the English Shakespeare Company at the Grand Theatre in Chelsea, contains a startling interpretation of the Falstaff-Hal relationship. In

Shakespeare's play, Hal and his brother, Prince John, stumble on Falstaff with the corpse of Hotspur on his back. When Falstaff asserts he killed Hotspur, and calls Hal a liar for saying otherwise, Hal graciously allows him to take credit for the deed: ". . . if a lie may do thee grace, / I'll gild it with the happiest terms I have."

In the Bogdanov version, Hal is accompanied not by Prince John alone but by his father, Henry IV, and a few retainers. When Falstaff accused Hal of lying about the circumstances of Hotspur's death, Henry IV glares contemptuously at his son: he actually believes Falstaff's version! Hal starts to protest to his father, but Henry turns away and exits, obviously convinced his son is a liar and coward. Stunned for a moment, Hal glowers hatefully at Falstaff, his very expression a condemnation. Abashed, and aware of the magnitude of the mischief he's created, Falstaff averts his gaze, then tries to regain his aplomb and feigns indifference as Hal stalks off. But we can see that he knows his fate is sealed. By adding the motive of retaliation for a personal grievance to that of political opportunism, Bogdanov mitigates the cold-bloodedness of Hal's ultimate renunciation of Falstaff. Ordinarily, I reminded the class, this sort of directorial tampering with Shakespeare's intentions makes me cranky, but in this instance I applauded its ingenuity.

As Henry V, a king at last, Hal shows himself an apt student of Machiavelli's *The Prince,* that manual of practical statecraft that taught rulers how to maintain their power through a mixture of guile, alliance, warfare, and personal force of character. And I can't agree with critics such as Goddard who claim that by rejecting Falstaff he's rejected the human side of his nature, as if being human, living life to the fullest, is to be equated with getting drunk and roistering with your companions. Hal never saw it that way. From the start, he intended to renounce Falstaff and his crowd; remember his response to Falstaff's admonition that to banish him is to banish life: "I do. I will." As we noted, all his moves are calculating, even his revels in Eastcheap. That doesn't make him lovable, but neither does it render him inhuman.

The first of Shakespeare's three plays on King Henry VI deals with the childhood and youth of the king, and the origins of those ruinous civil wars between aristocratic factions, the Yorks and Lancastrians, which are known as the Wars of the Roses. Part 2 dramatizes Henry's sad and inept involvement in the world of grown-ups, climaxing in the outbreak of the wars. Part 3 concerns the worst fighting of the wars, the final collapse of Henry's government, his increasing detachment from the world, and his final deposition and death.

What the class found most engrossing in the *Henry VI* trilogy were the Jack Cade rebellion and the emergence of Richard, Duke of Glouces-ter, the future Richard III, realizing that neither would have been possi-ble had not Henry VI been such an ineffective monarch, unready, unwilling, unable to rule. Lacking a strong king to rein them in, his feudal nobles contend with one another. In the struggle against the Lancastrians to seize the crown, the Duke of York, Richard's father, uses the Kentish Jack Cade as his stalking-horse.

Cade, a lower-class rebel, a demagogue with enormous spirit and physical strength, marches toward London, mobilizing artisan anger in a reign of terror against the privilege of gentlemen, whether these be con-ferred by literacy or inherited wealth. Much of his violence is directed against those who can read and write. It's class warfare. "You could com-pare this to the Russian Revolution and the Cultural Revolution in China," Tom offered. "Or the Khmer Rouge atrocities in Cambodia," Chuck added. I asked the group if they felt Shakespeare, in Cade, is dis-crediting popular rebellion or using Cade to articulate legitimate griev-ances of the common people. We compared Cade's rebellion to the uprising of the people, led by the tribunes, in *Coriolanus*. Cade is a vicious loutish rabble-rouser, but that doesn't wipe away the real social injustices of the time. As always, in Shakespeare we look not for absolutes but for ambiguity and irony.

Richard, in a bravura speech at the end of act 3, scene 2, that fore-shadows his opening soliloquy in *Richard III,* reveals his frustrations and desires—his deformity, his dream of the crown—and hard-heartedly maps a future course: he will "hew my way out with a bloody ax. / Why, I can smile, and murder whiles I smile." Determined to throw himself against impossible barriers, he's almost heroic in his relentlessness and cunning, a strange blend of courage, wit, adroit dissembling, and inexhaustible mal-ice. Shakespeare had actually begun to provide inner motives for Richard's violent ambition and compulsive shape-changing—he's a matchless role player. Deprived of nurturing and kindness—his mother loathed him—he tries to find compensatory satisfaction in cruelty and dissembling of his own. He suppresses the love instinct in favor of the power instinct. Midge, front row center as usual, declared, "Mind over heart." Right.

I recollected for the group a time when, as a student at the Pasadena Playhouse, I was rehearsing *Richard III,* which would be performed before the entire student body and in which I had been cast in the lead. The director, a faculty member whom I'll call Ronnie Atwood, was a pudgy, fair-haired, rather precious Englishman who'd attended the Royal Academy of Dramatic Art and had, as he put it, "puttered around" the London stage before coming to America. His forte was comedy, and he especially relished the sardonic, viciously humorous moments of the play, such as Richard's scene with the two young princes in which, as an aside in response to a precocious mot delivered by one of the princes, he observes, "So wise, so young, they say, 'Do never live long.' " But he seemed almost indifferent to Richard's more violent moods and outbursts, and he welcomed one of my suggested line interpretations in particular. In Richard's exhortation to his troops just before the battle of Bosworth, I cut the last line, "Amaze the welkin with your broken staves!," which struck me as a near-ludicrous anticlimax (take *that,* Mr. Shakespeare!), and finished with "Spur your proud horses hard, and ride in blood," shouting the last word not only in the sense of "get your blood up, boys," but especially as a terrifying call to butchery. "Cutting and/or transposing Shakespeare is not a criminal act," I said, "so long as you don't distort the meaning."

During our last meeting, I summed up the course: Shakespeare has shown us a once-civil world spiraling toward civil war, chaos. I wondered if Shakespeare's dread of chaos could be traced to the influence of Genesis, which begins with that revolutionary theological concept, one God, the Cause of all things, Who called matter into being and reduced chaos to order. The disruption of order could be seen as the ultimate sacrilege. And I speculated that Shakespeare's reading of Kings and Chronicles might have conditioned his dramatization of English history. We know that Holinshed, his source, laid out his chronicles in a pattern that established parallels between English and Hebrew monarchies. And Shakespeare would have seen in the power struggle between the proponents of Yahwism and Baalism under the Omrides in 1 and 2 Kings a similarity to the York/Lancastrian factional strife in the Wars of the Roses. I was struck by a passage in *A History of Ancient Israel and Judah,* by J. Maxwell Miller and John H. Hayes: ". . . the emphasis on Jezebel as the aggressive champion of Baalism represents a tendency noticeable elsewhere in the Scriptures—namely, to see the queen, the queen mother, or foreign wives as the source of royal apostasy." Think then of Shakespeare's portrait of Queen Margaret, the French wife of Henry VI, a woman who could teach Lady Macbeth a few lessons in cunning and malevolence and the use of sexual manipulation to achieve power.

After the final class, I had coffee with Bob and Lou in the Student Center.

"You really have a bug up the ass about old Falstaff, don't you, Herm?" Bob asked.

"Let me put it this way: I don't romanticize him," I replied. "And maybe I feel the portrait hits a bit too close to home. In my book-publishing years I squandered a lot of time at long wet lunches with authors and agents, and wasn't reluctant to toss back a few Scotches with cronies after work. Once I reached my sixties, I was this old guy drinking beer with my young colleagues, regaling them with accounts of my adventures in the trade. And remember—I'm the product of a military education. Duty, honor, country—hallelujah. All of us in the A&M cadet corps were indoctrinated with the Aggie spirit, that sense of belonging to a band of brothers, comrades-in-arms. Warriors. A tribe. We were the Twelfth Man who stood during an entire football game, in case one of us was needed on the field. Anyway, what am I getting at here, guys? Suppose you're standing at the Vietnam Memorial wall in Washington, and as you reach out to touch the names of those men who died in combat, you're aware of a fat drunken slob nearby, laughing sardonically as he shouts, 'The better part of valor is discretion.' Would that amuse you?"

"But wasn't Shakespeare antiwar?" Lou asked.

"He may have been antiwar, but he wasn't antihero, antivalor, anticourage, pro-coward. He hated the politicians who caused the wars, not the men who fought them. One of the best scenes in *Henry V* is the conversation between the three soldiers and Henry, who's incognito—'a little touch of Harry in the night,' as Shakespeare puts it. The soldiers talk freely and irreverently, and they sound a hell of a lot like the G.I.'s in the World War II dispatches of Ernie Pyle, and the Willie and Joe cartoons of Bill Mauldin—nonprofessional soldiers from the boondocks who may be afraid of what lies in store but are prepared to do their duty. In this country, a whole bunch of Americans not only opposed the Vietnam War, they called the men who fought it 'war criminals.' Not a pretty spectacle. Shakespeare must have had a hell of a good time creating Falstaff, but you can't tell me his heart wasn't with Hotspur. And who do you think he preferred in *Troilus and Cressida,* the Greeks or the Trojans? Easy—the heroic Trojans, not the wily Greeks. Thersites is a Greek, a truth-teller, but his cynical truth—'Lechery, lechery; still, wars and lechery; nothing else holds fashion'—ain't the whole truth. Another truth is the courage and nobility of Hector. And remember how he dies: Achilles, the celebrated Greek warrior, finding Hector unarmed on the battlefield, commands the Myrmidons to slay him, and then, in the Falstaffian mode, orders them to spread the word that Achilles hath the mighty Hector slain. Shakespeare is having it on with Homer and the Greeks—in the *Iliad,* Achilles himself kills Hector. Shakespeare's definitely in the Trojan camp."

"And so am I," said Lou. "How about you, Bob?"

"Oh yes. I was rooting for Hector all the way. And I was sort of hoping that someone would ram a spear into Thersites before the play ended and shut him up for good. He was the kind of guy who'd have been laughing it up with Falstaff at the Vietnam Memorial."

Now it was time to say our good-byes, and the three of us headed for the parking lot. The campus was in full bloom with spring flora, and the air had an April tang.

I wouldn't be back to the college until the leaves had turned their autumnal gold and red. Roxanne and I had agreed to press on with the Shakespeare series, and I'd decided to devote the entire eight-week fall semester to the four great tragedies—*Hamlet, Othello, King Lear, Macbeth.*

9.

For the present, I was about to edit, as a free-lancer, *Rude Behavior,* a new novel by Dan Jenkins, an old friend and treasured author. We met for the first time in the fall of 1971, shortly after I'd become editor in chief at Atheneum, to discuss revisions of his first novel, *Semi-Tough,* a bawdy comic novel about pro football, written in a distinctive good/bad-old-boy Texas vernacular.

Jenkins, at the time a senior writer at *Sports Illustrated* who'd been a reporter, sports editor, and columnist in Fort Worth before coming to New York, was a tall, white-haired Texan, a few inches over six feet, dressed in what turned out to be his standard costume—windbreaker, khaki pants, loafers. In his hand was a filtered cigarette, the first of several that he smoked during our conversation. His manner was cordial enough but slightly guarded, with just a trace of challenge: here's a fucking pointy-headed editorial wuss who wants to change everything I've written and convert all my slangy prose into proper English, so fuck him.

After a few ice-breaking pleasantries about our shared Texas origins, I handed him a memo from my desk and said, "These are some suggestions that I think might strengthen what's already a really original and wildly funny book."

He took a long puff from his cigarette, leaned back in his chair, exhaled, fixed me with a chilling "Are you talking to *me?*" squint, and after a moment said, too-deliberately nonchalant, "How many suggestions do you have?"

"Twenty-five," I said, waiting for the explosion.

But all he did was whip out from an inside pocket of his windbreaker a two-page, single-spaced document, which he handed to me, saying, "I thought you'd have more. Here are forty-two suggestions of my own. Maybe some of them match up with yours."

That was the essential Jenkins: competitive, ultraprofessional, ready to dig in and get the job done. Or at least part of the essential Jenkins: thinking about him now, I see him as a combination of Hotspur and Prince Hal. Hotspur in his volatility, his impatience with sham and pretense, his exuberant irreverence, hotheaded combativeness, and his black-and-white, good-guys-versus-bad-guys, I love/I hate take on life, the hate focused not infrequently on the villains in his universe, the "suits," the advertising and managerial execs who cared only for number crunching and bean counting, and the editors who tried to leach the originality and wit from his stories. Prince Hal in his keen relishment of tavern life, the companionship of the high and low in his preferred Manhattan watering places—P. J. Clarke's, Mike Manuche's, Elaine's, and the Ho-Ho, the bar in a Chinese restaurant near the Time-Life Building and a gathering place for the *Sports Illustrated* crowd—where, in the manner of Prince Hal, he would learn the language of others, rehearsing their tongues, and with his unerring ear and journalist's gift of observation transform what he'd heard and seen into a gallery of unforgettable characters speaking the kind of dialogue that would have made John O'Hara and Ring Lardner and Mark Twain burn with envy.

If Dan seemed a combination of Hotspur and Prince Hal, Willie Morris, several years our junior and, like us, a Semi-Young Man from the Southern/Southwestern Provinces who had made his mark in fabled Gotham, was Hotspur and Falstaff rolled into one. A native of Yazoo City, Mississippi, a graduate of the University of Texas, where he'd edited the *Daily Texan,* a Rhodes Scholar who'd earned a first in history at Oxford, a former editor of the liberal weekly *Texas Observer,* Willie had become in 1967, at the age of thirty-two, the youngest editor in chief in the 117-year history of *Harper's.*

Mercurial, dashing, quick-tempered, charming, he was a Hotspur always spoiling for a fight with the enemy, whom, like Dan, he perceived as the executives on the business side of the magazine, in Willie's case those concerned about the effects of Willie's bold and brilliant editorial ideas (e.g., Norman Mailer's controversial article decrying homosexuality) on circulation and advertising revenue. Willie also seemed to embody the Falstaff depicted by Harold Goddard as a man who has never grown up, the man who turns everything into play. He was irresistibly, incorrigibly boyish, boyishly handsome, with a hint of pudginess, and mischievously

funny. Perhaps his most striking Falstaffian trait was his herculean booz-
ing, and he favored two of the places frequented by Dan—Elaine's and
P. J. Clarke's. Oddly, like Dan he also found especially congenial the bar
at a humdrum Chinese restaurant, the Empire, a few blocks from the
Harper offices on East Thirty-third, where he ate lunch almost daily.

I first met Willie in 1965 when he was one of the editors at *Harper's,*
the editor-in-chiefship still two years away. I knew he was writing a
memoir, and I took him to lunch hoping to persuade him to sign a contract with Atheneum, where I was a senior editor. When I arrived, he was
already at the table, working on his first martini. On the phone the week
before, I'd confessed that I was an Aggie. A&M and the University of
Texas were fierce rivals: we called them teasippers, they referred to us as
shitkickers. "Goddamn, you must be the only Aggie editor in the history
of book publishing," Willie exclaimed. "I guess that means you can read
and write. But do you wear matching socks?"

During lunch, Willie proved to be an incomparable raconteur, spin-
ning tales of his boyhood in Yazoo City, his newspaper days in Austin, his
political advocacy, his time at Oxford. Obviously his memoir would be a
treasure.

Taking a sip of his second postprandial martini, Willie said, "I ought
to tell you that I'm probably going to make a deal for my book with
Houghton Mifflin. They've been after me for a long time, and I think I
have a chance to win the Houghton Mifflin Literary Fellowship. I didn't
want to tell you up front because I had to see for myself what kind of an
Aggie had infiltrated the sacred New York literary domain." And outside,
as we were parting, he said, "One of these days I'm going to write a novel
about my days at Oxford. I'm going to call it *Chimes at Midnight*—
that's from old Falstaff's line to Shallow in *Henry IV,* 'We have heard the
chimes at midnight.' "

Willie did sign with Houghton Mifflin, who granted him the Literary
Fellowship. And his book, *North Toward Home,* published in 1967, was a
phenomenal achievement—lyrical, funny, honest, dazzlingly intelligent,
and rich in narrative power.

Then, in 1969, it was Willie's turn to court me. A fiery competitor,
he was obsessed by his continuing battle for prestige and circulation with
Harper's century-old rival, the *Atlantic Monthly,* then edited by Robert

Manning. He was particularly frustrated by the fact that the *Atlantic Monthly* had a book publishing division, the Atlantic Monthly Press (AMP), a copublishing venture with Little, Brown & Company, which allowed but did not compel the two entities to commission books jointly, guaranteeing the printing of excerpts (or occasionally the complete manuscript, if important—and short—enough) in the magazine prior to book publication. Willie convinced John Cowles, whose family owned the Minneapolis Star Tribune Co., Harper & Row, and *Harper's*, that a symbiotic relationship between *Harper's* and Harper & Row, modeled along the *Atlantic*/AMP lines, would benefit both parties, and he gave me the chance to jump-start a new imprint as editor in chief of Harper's Magazine Press, presiding over a staff of two, me and an assistant. But who needed to rule an empire? I was content with the freedom to operate almost as I pleased, in the company of Willie and his editors nonpareil, Bob Kotlowitz and Midge Decter, and stellar contributors to the magazine such as David Halberstam, John Corry, and Marshall Frady.

In the course of two years, Willie and I commissioned several memorable books: *Listening to America,* by Bill Moyers; *The City Game,* by Pete Axthelm; and *Yazoo: Integration in a Deep Southern Town,* by that former Yazooite, Willie himself.

One of the most promising books we commissioned, and one not without Falstaffian reverberations, provoked a wave of excitement in the press and in publishing circles when we announced that it was under contract: *This Is Orson Welles,* by Orson Welles and Peter Bogdanovich. Although Bogdanovich had written and directed a much-admired low-budget movie thriller, *Targets,* he was known primarily as a journalist who specialized in feature articles on movies and in interviews with celebrated directors, such as Orson Welles. He was, I suppose, an American version of French auteurs/critics such as François Truffaut and Jean-Luc Godard. I broached with him the idea of publishing a collection of his interviews with directors. "Why not do just a book-length interview with Orson, like the one Truffaut did with Hitchcock?" he countered. "He and I have become close friends. He trusts me completely. We have terrific illustrations. I mean, just recently we discovered the scenes that had been chopped from *The Magnificent Ambersons* when the studio refused to let Orson make the final cut." I thought it was a dandy idea, but insisted that to ensure Welles's commitment to the book, he must be a party to the contract along with Bogdanovich. The deal was made, with a two-year delivery date, and we convinced ourselves that despite Welles's reputation for either abandoning projects or finishing them years behind schedule, with Bogdanovich in control, he'd come through on time.

One afternoon a few weeks later I answered the phone and heard a rich, familiar voice say, "Is this Mr. Gollob?"

"Yes."

"This is Orson Welles."

Before he could continue, I cut him off with "Goddammit, Willie, I'm not in the mood for one of your fucking jokes. I'm trying to finish editing a manuscript." Willie happened to be an accomplished mimic and was addicted to telephone pranks in which he posed as celebrities. I had to admit his Welles imitation was quite good.

"I beg your pardon," the mellifluous voice continued, "perhaps we have a bad connection. This is Orson Welles."

Uh-oh. I'd given Willie too much credit for mimicry. This was the man himself. "Oh yes, Mr. Welles, we've been having a problem with the lines. Sorry about the confusion."

"Well, so much for that. I'm in town for a day or so, and I know this is short notice, but since you'll be editing the book, I'd love to meet you and I wonder if you could come by the Plaza this afternoon and have a drink with me?"

An hour later I was sitting across from this imposing huge bellied, swollen-faced, majestically courteous hulk of a man, listening to him place an order to room service: "Hello, this is Orson Welles. May I have two double Scotches and soda, please, as quickly as possible. I'm so grateful." I wondered if the room service attendant thought it was a prank, too.

During our conversation, I mentioned that when I was ten my father had taken me to see *Citizen Kane* three times during its run in Houston. "Goddammit, son," he'd raved, "that boy could give Paul Muni a run for his money."

Welles roared, and the walls seemed to shake. "If only I'd been as fine an actor as Paul Muni. We all learned a few tricks from him. I remember him as the old music professor in that dreadful movie with Cornel Wilde as Chopin and Merle Oberon as George Sand. He of course was wonderful, and I recall one masterful piece of business, in which he kept taking his white gloves on and off to express agitation while talking to Wilde and Oberon. It was hilarious, and it was moving."

I told him that I still remembered vividly the Sunday night when my parents and I heard his Mercury Theatre's *The War of the Worlds* broadcast on the radio, and how even my father had bought into it for a few minutes.

"Radio was my favorite medium," Welles said. "You had to be much more inventive when you did a radio show. You had to rely on your audience's imagination, you had to stir their imaginative powers."

Several months later Bogdanovich phoned to say he and Welles were in town, and invited me for champagne cocktails that evening in their suite at the Plaza. "Orson's written some scenes for the book and he wants to read them to you. Bring along Willie Morris, too. I read *North Toward Home* a while ago and it's terrific."

After I'd introduced Willie, Bogdanovich repeated his praise for the memoir and asked Willie if he planned a sequel. "Yeah, but first I've got a lot more living to do, and there's a novel I want to write."

When Willie mentioned the title, Bogdanovich turned to Welles, who smiled knowingly and shrugged his shoulders. "You mean you aren't familiar with Orson's movie *Chimes at Midnight*?" Bogdanovich asked.

Embarrassed, we said no.

Welles chuckled. "Not surprising. It didn't make much of a stir when it was released three years ago. In fact, the distribution was a mess."

Bogdanovich continued: "Orson adapted the movie from the plays in which Falstaff appeared and the one, *Henry V,* in which his death is described. He directed, and he played—guess who?"

"Yes, I was Falstaff," Welles said, and, patting his stomach, "I didn't need much padding for the part. I made Falstaff the central character. I saw him as a tragic figure. He was a knight who'd once performed admirably in the service of John of Gaunt, but he wasted his life in drink and had become a buffoon."

I wondered if Welles was aware that his life was imitating Shakespeare's art. Surely he identified with more than Falstaff's girth. Falstaff's decline and fall was a metaphor for his own self-destructive career, marked by dissipation, gluttony, irresponsibility, reckless abuse of talent (genius, many would say), and, most grievously, self-caricature. To heighten the irony, the selection he read to us was a reminiscence of his friendship with another self-destructive artist reduced, in the end, to the role of self-parodist: John Barrymore, whose stage performance as Hamlet had been a milestone in American theatrical history, and whose alcoholism destroyed his career and his life.

The Falstaffian motif of the evening was prophetic in another way, closer to home: it augured the fate of my friend Willie Morris. Willie's heavy drinking had caused him to neglect his managerial responsibilities and had led to several intemperately defiant encounters with the owners of *Harper's* culminating, in the summer of 1971, with his forced resignation. Colleagues such as Kotlowitz, Decter, and Halberstam left soon thereafter, and the party—and a hell of a party it had been—was over. Two months later when Pat Knopf, chairman of the board at Atheneum, invited me to come back to the company in the role of editor in chief, I accepted without hesitation. Harper's Magazine Press closed up shop in 1974, and *This Is Orson Welles* was ultimately published in 1992 by Harper Collins. Bogdanovich went on to direct a film adaptation of Larry McMurtry's *The Last Picture Show*, which sent his career into orbit, earned an Academy Award for Ben Johnson (O rare Ben Johnson!), and introduced Cybil Shepherd and Jeff Bridges.

Eventually, Willie returned to his homeland and became a writer in residence at the University of Mississippi. He wrote over a dozen books, including the popular memoir of his youth, *My Dog Skip*, but he never got around to *Chimes at Midnight*. And nothing ever matched the beauty and power of *North Toward Home*. He died in 1999.

By the time I'd finished editing Jenkins's *Rude Behavior*, summer had arrived, and I began to plan for the fall course in Shakespeare's four major tragedies. A two-hour lecture on a play, followed the next week by a complete movie or television production of it on video, or perhaps large segments from two or more videos of the same play—for example, Kenneth Branagh and Nicol Williamson's *Hamlet*, and Olivier and Ian Holm's *King Lear*. Or a match-up of Trevor Nunn's superlative television adaptations of *Othello* and *Macbeth*, the former starring Ian McKellen as Iago, Willard White, a Jamaican operatic basso, as Othello, and Imogen Stubbs as Desdemona, and the latter starring McKellen as Macbeth and Judi Dench as Lady Macbeth. And as I'd done all along, I used three editions of each play I was teaching—Bantam, Arden, and Oxford—less for the editors' detailed analyses of the various texts (Quartos and Folio) in the attempt to construct an "authoritative" edition than for their interpretations of the meaning of the plays, their insights into Shakespeare's powers of characterization and his prodigious dramaturgical skills.

I decided to begin the course by discussing Maynard Mack's chapter "What Happens in Shakespearean Tragedy" from *Everybody's Shakespeare.* First, he asserts, the hero is an overstater, given to hyperbole. Besides the hyperbolist, there is the opposing voice, the hero's foil: Hamlet and Horatio, Lear and the Fool (and Kent), Othello and Iago, Macbeth and Lady Macbeth. According to Mack, by using foils, "Shakespeare lays open to us the central dialogue of tragic experience . . . the seventeenth-century dialogue of soul with body, the twentieth-century dialogue of self with soul. . . ." To which I would add, the dialogue of heart with intellect. And there are mirror scenes—for example, the witches of Macbeth, "whose 'foul is fair' and battle that is 'won *and* lost' anticipate so much to come." To Mack, the most important thing that happens in a Shakespearean tragedy is that the hero follows a cycle of change—in one phase of which he "tends to become his own antithesis" (e.g., Lear goes from powerful monarch to helpless crazed old man)—before he undergoes a process of illumination, some sort of regeneration.

I also wanted to discuss what I saw as an underlying motif in the four tragedies: the threat to the community posed by those consumed with envy. What led me indirectly to this notion was a passage in Martin Buber's *Moses.* The intention of the Decalogue, Buber insists, is "the constituting of a community by means of common regulation." The commandments that apply only to actions, he says, "are not enough to protect the Community from disorganization. . . . they do not involve attitudes which have not passed into action. There is one attitude . . . which destroys the inner connection of the Community even when it does not transform itself into actual action . . . and which may become a consuming disease of a special kind in the body politic. This is the attitude of envy. The prohibition of 'covetousness' . . . is to be understood as a prohibition of envy." Given the impact of the Bible on Shakespeare's sensibility, and the fear of chaos that pervades his work, I could envision him grasping in the prohibition of covetousness the same crucial significance to the preservation of society that Buber apprehended.

Iago picks up this theme in his ironic and all-too-knowing admonition to Othello: "O, beware, my lord, of jealousy! / It is the green-eyed monster which doth mock / The meat it feeds on." His jealousy of Cassio, who was promoted over him by Othello and whose handsomeness and decency make him feel inadequate ("He hath a daily beauty in his life / That makes me ugly"), and his rage at Othello for supposedly cuckolding him as well as elevating Cassio, make him very dangerous to Othello and Othello's wife, Desdemona, both of whom are destroyed as a result of Iago's envious hatred. Macbeth and Lady Macbeth, envious of Duncan and greedy for power, commit regicide. Claudius, who covets the throne and Gertrude, the wife of his brother, commits fratricide, regicide, and adultery in one fell swoop. Edmund, Goneril, and Regan, all jealous of a sibling, all lusting for power, threaten the stability of the body politic.

Sexual jealousy is a component of the covetousness that drives all but two of these possessed creatures. In one of his soliloquies, Iago says, almost offhandedly, that he loves Desdemona ("Now, I do love her too; / Not out of absolute lust"); in the sixteenth-century short story by Giraldi Cinthio that serves as Shakespeare's source, Iago's love for Desdemona is the actual motivation for his jealousy, and though critics such as Coleridge refer to Iago's "motiveless malignity," the more I read the play, the stronger I feel that Iago indeed is smitten by Desdemona, and that his feelings, while not exclusively physical, are anything but platonic. Claudius most definitely has succumbed to Gertrude's erotic allure. Goneril and Regan compete for the sexual favors of Edmund, who opportunistically services them both, waiting to see who prevails in the civil war. Although sexual envy is not a factor in the Macbeths' consuming ambition to seize the crown, Lady Macbeth uses sexuality as a weapon to goad Macbeth into action, questioning his virility, scorning him for what she calls his unmanliness, when he wavers at the prospect of murdering King Duncan.

I planned to consider as well other issues raised by these plays.

I would test out in class my theory about the Judaic quality of *King Lear.*

I would cite from G. Wilson Knight's essay "The Othello Music," in his collection of Shakespearean pieces, *The Wheel of Fire,* the ingenious observation that the changes in Othello's characters are illustrated in the changes we see in Othello's language before and after. In the beginning, there is something grand and romantic in Othello's speech. Once the poison of Iago enters his system, he indulges in ugly and idiot ravings. Also, I would use Iago's sly boast to Roderigo, "I am not what I am," to launch into a discussion of appearance versus reality in Shakespeare. And I'd call attention to how Iago matches the Israelites' description of "the satan," as cited in Elaine Pagels's *The Origin of Satan:* "a being of superior intelligence . . . the intimate enemy—one's trusted colleague, close associate . . ."

Macbeth, I needed to make clear, more than any other of Shakespeare's villains, has a clear-eyed grasp of the difference between good and evil. Macbeth is a noble and gifted man who chooses treachery and crime, knowing them precisely for what they are. He is a hero who becomes a villain.

Concerning *Hamlet,* I wanted to concentrate on what Maynard Mack refers to as "its almost mythic status as a paradigm of the process of 'growing up.' " Because of Hamlet's conversation with the gravedigger in act 5, we are led to believe that Hamlet is thirty, which begs the question, isn't thirty a trifle late to be growing up? And to answer a question with a question, why should there be a time limit on growing up, especially when it comes to the discovery of unpleasant truths about our families? Hamlet, at thirty, has suffered a terrible shock, not his father's death but the shock of a sudden disclosure of his mother's nature. I could relate to that. Although I didn't intend to bring this to the class's attention, I couldn't help thinking about another young man jolted only three months before he reached thirty by the discovery of a shocking truth about his mother. But unlike the noble Dane, I'd had a troubled relationship with my mother for as long as I could remember.

My earliest recollection of her goes back to the time I was three, in 1933. We had just moved from Waco to Houston, where, as I've related, my father was struggling to make a go of it as an independent lawyer. We were living in tiny adjoining rooms in the Auditorium Hotel in down-town Houston, across the street from the sports arena, the City Audito-rium. The hotel, drab and dingy and musty-smelling (even now I dream frequently of finding myself a resident in such establishments), catered mostly to traveling salesmen and to the occasional boxer or wrestler in town for a match.

To this day, the earliest remembrance of Mom still has the power to disturb. There I am, three years old, in that bleak, threadbare little room, watching a Gulf storm lash at the grimy window, sitting next to my mother as she chain-smokes cigarettes and drinks one of her countless cups of coffee while she listens to me read one of those Dick and Jane books. I'm not doing all that badly, but mystifyingly I constantly fumble the word "slide." I can't seem to pronounce it, and that's not good, be-cause each fumble produces an awful rage in my mother. She was, as I've said, a beautiful woman, but that day in the hotel her face is twisted with hate for inept little me, and she whacks me across the cheek every time I blunder, accompanying each blow with a curse. In the art of raising a child, she was way ahead of Joan Crawford. And perhaps she was onto something: far from traumatizing me, her technique produced a kid who loved to read—but not one, alas, who adored his mother.

What truly alienated me was her constant vilifying of my father, whom I worshiped. We were buddies, me and the old man, like Jackie Cooper and Wallace Beery in *The Champ,* like Jackie Coogan and Char-lie Chaplin in *The Kid.* But to my mother he was a man who turned out to be a lousy provider, and the sorry state of our finances humiliated this Jewish southern belle. Although we moved out of the Auditorium after several months, my father's law practice was a shaky proposition for years, and we lived in an ugly duplex bungalow until the FHA loan allowed us to build a home.

In more attractive surroundings, the strife between my parents began to subside, and the two of them seemed more companionable. Around this time, as I remember, my father began to call my mother "Miss Rubye." (Not long ago my son, Jared, remarked, "It's strange how Grandpa and Lincoln were born on the same day, and they both had neurotic materialistic southern wives who came from prosperous back-grounds.") And essentially, she was the same chain-smoking, coffee-guzzling neurotic, a frantically possessive mom, smothering me with affection one moment, screaming at me spitefully the next, hysterically anxious about my safety, fearful that death by accident waited for me around every corner, possibly because she subconsciously wished it. Without my father's intervention, she'd undoubtedly have turned me into a grotesque little wimp.

But he was always there for the male bonding, teaching me how to box and to play ball and to ride a bike and drive a car, taking me to the fights and the movies, and in my teens showing up for the Jewish Community Center boxing tournaments and softball games and sandlot tackle football games in which I participated, allowing me (against my mother's objections) to use our old '38 Chevy (we couldn't afford a new model) on dates.

So I had a relatively normal adolescence: I did well in school; my friends were street-smart and funny and daring, and forced me to be the same (e.g., sneaking into Rice University football games, stealing watermelons from roadside stands); and I suffered through a couple of pathetic romances.

And I found myself an adolescent rebel, constantly at war with my mother, exploding at her whenever she irritated me, which was whenever she opened her mouth, storming off to my room when my father would order me to treat Miss Rubye with respect. Too late for that. I couldn't bear to be around her.

And yet, and yet . . . she had that wonderfully offbeat sense of humor, she was a splendid cook whose potato latkes and kugel and meatballs and fudge and chocolate squares were matchless, she was the kind of obsessive-compulsive housekeeper who every day scrubbed and waxed the kitchen floor and scoured the bathrooms and washed clothes. But I couldn't wait to get out of that goddamned house.

College was the first step in my escape. I chose Texas A&M because I'd succumbed to the Cadet Corps mystique when the Aggies were in town for football games and parades. Then service with the air force in Korea. My father asked me to participate in a conspiracy: "Tell Miss Rubye you'll be stationed in Honolulu. If she thinks you're being sent to Korea, she'll go to pieces." So for a year I penned occasional fantasies to her about frolicking on Waikiki Beach, while actually I was standing hip-deep in snow in Taegu, seeing to it that Korean workers on our base were doled out sacks of rice as a bonus for their special labors.

In the spring of 1960, I went to Europe for the first time, a three-week lark in London and Paris, and returned to find a letter from my father. Seemed that Miss Rubye was recovering nicely from a lobotomy she'd had just before I left the country. She and my father decided not to tell me about it because they didn't want to spoil my vacation. Why a lobotomy? Well, for quite a spell my mother had been in psychoanalysis, diagnosed as a schizophrenic. She'd begun to hear voices, evil voices with murderous thoughts, and at times the voices sounded like her own, willing violence on loved ones. She underwent shock treatments, but the voices persisted. And finally, the lobotomy, ministering to a mind diseased, trying to pluck from the brain a rooted sorrow.

What stunned me more than the appalling news was the fact that my parents had kept me ignorant of the entire ordeal, not simply the operation but the shock treatments and psychotherapy she'd been undergoing long before my sojourn abroad. They didn't want to disturb me. They didn't think I should be bothered. Or was it they thought I couldn't care less? I'd made myself scarce for a long time, had little to say in letters and phone conversations, and was testy and impatient whenever they visited. It was apparent to them that my past, Mom in particular, was a nightmare from which I was trying to awaken. And they were careful to tread warily, from a distance or up close, never questioning or second-guessing my choice to study drama or the apparently erratic pattern of my career, always supportive, no conditions attached. Yes, what I'd been taking all along was unconditional love, and taking it quite literally—I'd been giving nothing back in return. That's what being a spoiled only child is all about.

I wondered what finally prompted my father to seek psychiatric counseling for my mother. Had she attempted suicide? A childhood remembrance flared up. Late one afternoon I was in the kitchen, drinking a glass of milk, when my mother, who'd just finished an agitated phone conversation with one of her sisters, rushed in, grabbed a butcher knife, and screamed, "My life isn't worth a goddamn! I'm going to cut my throat!" This wasn't the first time I'd heard her make the threat—it was her typical response to a crisis, and it remained so for years to come—but until now the histrionics had been considerably less vivid. I jumped up from the table, started to cry, and ran to her: "Don't hurt yourself, Mom." She threw the knife in the sink, pushed me away, went to the bedroom, and slammed the door. I could hear her sobbing for a long time. She was still in there when my father came home. I told him what had happened. His face reddened, quite a sight on a man with red hair and an orange mustache. "Goddamn her, goddamn her," he said. Then, hugging me, he said, "Don't worry, fat boy"—I'd been a plump baby, and he still called me by that nickname—"everything's going to be all right." He went into the bedroom. I could hear them talking but couldn't distinguish what they were saying. He emerged alone, closing the door behind him. "I'm going to make us some salami sandwiches. Your mother needs to rest. It was those goddamned Cohens again."

The Cohens, to my father, were the Little Foxes, that grasping, perniciously materialistic New Orleans clan etched in acid in the play of that title by Lillian Hellman. My father held the Cohens' worship of Mammon responsible for much of my mother's anguish and frustration, and that day in Boston, when I phoned him after reading his letter, I heard this theory again.

"Dad, why did you wait so long to tell me? That wasn't fair. Didn't you think I'd give a damn? Didn't you think I was strong enough to deal with it? Have they turned Mom into some kind of zombie?"

"No, hell no. Her memory's okay, she still talks to everyone she bumps into in the lines at the supermarket or the bus, she still gives me hell when she feels like it, she still drives the car. But those goddamned voices seem to be gone. She doesn't look tormented anymore. She's always been lovely, but now she's even prettier. And I get to thinking about those days in Waco when we were first married and you were born. We were so happy. She fixed up our little apartment just beautifully. She's always had such terrific taste in clothes and decorating. And the best thing was, there were no Cohens around. Her goddamned parents, those German Jews, didn't think I was good enough because I was one of the inferior Russian Jews, and I loved books and didn't worship the goddamned dollar. They couldn't believe your mother was happy. And then her goddamned mean son of a bitch of a father lost his money and died and the Depression hit Waco hard and your mother thought we ought to go back to Houston. Maybe things would be better there, and she missed her family. And I listened to her. And as soon as we got back, those Cohens started in on her: your husband's a fool, he'll never earn a dime as a lawyer, you're throwing yourself away. And she started to feel trapped, and guilty about feeling trapped, and—well, look, you can figure it out, you can guess what happens to a person pulled in all sorts of directions, how it can make a goddamned wreck out of you. And there are things you don't need to know, things you don't want to know. Listen, she's upstairs sleeping now, let me wake her up. She'll want to talk to you."

As I waited, mulling my father's angry, pained, and perhaps partially self-absolving explanation of my mother's illness, what did I feel? Well, how about pity and terror for starters? Until now I'd never thought of my mother's life as a tragedy of unfulfilled promise. But here was a woman of no mean intelligence—she'd excelled in high school, but never went to college (I don't know why—neither did her sisters or her brother). Is this something to pin on the Cohens, enemies of higher learning? And in the 1930s and '40s, housewives weren't exactly encouraged to enter university degree programs; even if they had been, going to college was not uppermost in my mother's mind. She had a flair for decor and design, and exquisite taste in clothes. Could she have turned these talents into a profession? And by God she could act. She had the emotional equipment, the instincts, the dramatic temperament, the powers of observation, that, along with her beauty, could have made her a star if she'd have single-mindedly pursued a career.

And there she was on the phone: "Well, baby, they opened up your mother's head and guess what they found inside—a brain. I bet you don't believe that." Her voice sounded slightly weary, but there was a note of bravery in that jest. My mother was a courageous woman. She'd been through the old mill, had Miss Rubye, demons had possessed her much of her life, she'd been electroshocked and lobotomized and as they say in showbiz, she was still here. I started to reply to her but instead found myself bursting into convulsive sobs, and I could hear her say, "Don't cry, baby, I'm fine," and I managed to blurt out, "I love you, Mom," and then my father was on the phone, "What's going on, son?" and, still all teary, I said, "I'm going to have to call you back later. Why don't I fly home this weekend?" He didn't think that was a great idea. "We're going to drive to Boston next month. No need for you to come now. Let your mother get her strength back and put on a couple of pounds and we'll come knocking on your door in May."

My mother spent the remaining ten years of her life relatively at peace with herself and with her lot. It was a serenity tinged with melancholy, but gone were the anger, the resentment, the voices. She lived to see me married to a woman who is beautiful, brilliant, and, above all, Jewish. She lived to see me ensconced in a lovely old house and established at last in a career. Most wonderful of all, she lived to see her grandchildren. Every autumn my parents would drive East, sometimes heading as far north as Canada before spending a week with us in New Jersey. My mother was the ideal grandma; perhaps it's true that being a grandparent gives us a chance to make up for the mistakes we made as parents. My mother relished being in the company of my kids, she was patient and amusing with them, she had plain old fun reading to them and asking them to read to her (gone were the good old days of slap-face instruction), she took Emily shopping for clothes and let her use her perfume and nail polish and try on her jewelry. Happy ending, nice and tidy: it can happen. Almost.

My mother died of a stroke a few days after her sixty-eighth birthday. She was buried in Waco: my father would not have her spend eternity in a Houston cemetery with the Cohens. In the funeral home, the coffin had been open. My mother seemed to be smiling, dreaming perhaps of a new dress she could buy for Emily. And most poignant of all, to me, were her beautiful small hands, fingernails painted bright red, her favorite polish, the shade she'd applied to Emily's nails. That touch of elegance, of glamour, about to be shut away in the ground.

My father outlived her by twelve years. The day after his death, as I was going through his safe-deposit box in Houston, I discovered a wallet. My mother's. I opened it and found the usual assortment of plastic cards, and her driver's license with a photograph of her smiling at the camera, her eyes revealing a survivor's sadness and bravery. Then, probing the little pockets, I found tucked away in one of them and folded in half a sheet of lined paper from a pocket memo pad. Opening it, I read a message printed in pencil obviously by a child: WE HATE TO SEE YOU LEAVE, WE LOVE YOU, EMILY. A farewell note which, judging from its worn condition, the paper beginning to tear apart at the folds, my mother had taken out and read countless times, cherishing the evidence of love untainted by guilt, unaffected by a family history of storm and strife. Alone in that bank vault, which seemed like a mausoleum, isolated from the living, sealed off from the present, I somehow could grieve as I'd never been able to, even at my mother's graveside. My father had just died, but at this moment it was the loss of my mother that tore at me, the regret that I hadn't seen her in the months before her death, I hadn't been able to say We Hate to See You Leave. I regretted, too, that I hadn't known about this note in time to read it at the burial ceremony as the most genuine of elegies, or to place it in my mother's casket as a light to lessen the awful darkness.

On the opening day of the fall semester, I was cheered to see among the twenty-plus in class the familiar presences of Bob, Lou, Midge, Madelyn, Marie, Gilda, Chuck, Ed (without Erma, who was ailing with a bad back and wouldn't be able to take the course). And I was disconcerted when halfway through the lecture one of the new students, a graying blonde whom I took to be in her sixties, accompanied by a frail, much older woman with thinning white hair and an expression of pain frozen on her lined face, interrupted me: "I just want to say you're doing a wonderful job. I taught Shakespeare in college for many years, but I'm learning many new things today. But you haven't introduced yourself. I have no idea who you are, I know nothing about you. And please—can't we have a ten-minute break?" With that cadre of Gollob regulars in front of me, I'd indeed neglected to identify myself to the newcomers, as I'd failed to do the previous semester, without drawing a protest. So I paused for a quick account of my background, and an explanation of my No Break policy. "But many of us do need to use the facilities," she persisted. I compromised on a five-minute break, knowing it would stretch to ten. During the break, Midge came up to me. "Those two are nuns," she said. "They'll keep you on your toes. No one else would have dared argue with you about bathroom privileges."

It's not often that contemporary events apply with startling immediacy to the action of Shakespearean drama, but on two occasions over this period I was able to draw parallels between headline news and the tragedies under scrutiny. Before the *Othello* lecture, I asked, "What's the first thing that springs to mind when you think of this play?" No answer.

"Okay," I said, "let me put it this way: when you first heard that O.J. had been charged with murdering his wife, how many of you said to yourselves, 'This is life imitating art, this is a real-life modern-day Othello'? A renowned, respected black man, a sports hero, totally at ease in the white world, driven to a murderous frenzy by we know not what." Again, and mystifyingly, no one raised a hand.

But no one had a problem recognizing a certain American political figure and his spouse when, in discussing *Macbeth,* I mentioned that the drunken Porter's reference to equivocators would have had a topical significance to Shakespeare's audience. It alluded to "A Treatise on Equivocation" by a Jesuit, Father Henry Garnet, who was involved in the Guy Fawkes Gunpowder Plot, intended to blow up Parliament while King James was in attendance. Garnet pleaded innocent, but government prosecutors made much of the fact that the treatise showed how to give misleading and ambiguous answers under oath. The class was quick to grasp how the treatise resonated in our own political climate, with a president lying under oath, and equally swift in drawing comparisons between the Macbeths and the Clintons. "They should play these roles on Broadway," Bob suggested. "I'd rather see Hillary as Goneril or Regan," Lou countered. At the time, Mrs. Clinton's aspirations to portray a United States senator had yet to be revealed. Many of us would have preferred that she follow the advice of Bob and Lou.

The wealth of Shakespearean productions and performances on videotape made the process of selectivity a challenge.

For *Hamlet,* I showed segments of Branagh's thrilling movie, to me the best of all film versions, a couple of scenes from Tony Richardson's excellent production, starring Nicol Williamson and Anthony Hopkins, and a segment from *Playing Shakespeare.* Branagh's direction was energetic, stirring, remarkably attuned to the shifting moods of tragedy and comedy, visually exciting. As an actor, he was every inch the Prince of Denmark, handsome, vital, brilliant, volatile, and one of his major accomplishments was conveying Hamlet's passion for the theatre, of acting and actors, and consequently reminding us implicitly that Shakespeare was celebrating his own love of his profession, his craft. Williamson was an older, scruffier Hamlet, most effective in the self-tormenting soliloquies—for example, "How all occasions do inform against me." From *Playing Shakespeare* I plucked Michael Pennington doing "To be or not to be" twice. At Barton's suggestion, he started by talking as if to himself. Barton responded: "I don't believe we go along with Hamlet's thoughts. Now try it the other way and share it with us." The second attempt drew praise: "Michael moved the speech forward and took us with him as if he were telling a story. . . . he didn't issue a statement about his state of mind . . . he made us think with him." During my lecture on *Hamlet*, I'd cited Pennington's acute analysis of this soliloquy in his vigorous and amusing book *Hamlet: A User's Guide:* "It is odd that the qualities we are most moved by in Hamlet—courage, wit, human optimism—are almost completely lacking in his most famous utterance. . . . it is utterly negative. . . . Perhaps that is the shocking point. . . . There is no personal pronoun in all its thirty-five lines, so it is in a sense drained of Hamlet himself."

The highlights of the Trevor Nunn RSC production of *Macbeth,* strikingly adapted for television, were Ian McKellen's interpretation of Macbeth's "Tomorrow and tomorrow and tomorrow" soliloquy, which he explained in such depth and detail in *Playing Shakespeare,* and Judi Dench as Lady Macbeth, her body convulsed as if possessed by the spirits she has summoned to unsex her, and later, in the sleepwalking scene, uttering a moan that builds excruciatingly to a hideous scream, as if she were exorcising at last these ghastly demons.

The video of *Othello* was yet another televised version of a Trevor Nunn RSC staging, with Ian McKellen again in a leading role, this time as Iago, in a production set in the late nineteenth century with the soldiery attired in uniforms oddly similar to those worn by the Army of the Potomac during the Civil War. Iago is a high-ranking enlisted man, probably a master sergeant, and we sense in McKellen's performance a hatred for the privileged class, the officer caste, his bitterness that he's not acceptable as officer material, his resentment of social privilege, his grievance at being undervalued. Even McKellen's rough manner of speaking indicates that Iago is of humble origins. And McKellen shows us an Iago aware of and excited by the risk he's taking as he provokes Othello's jealousy, at times even hesitant and almost fearful of the consequences of his recklessness as he concocts his sinister and ingenious plot and manipulates his victims. What's missing in his performance is Iago's deceptive charm and humor, which disarm those whom he is about to destroy.

Midge brought to class a video of Verdi's *Otello,* and I showed Justino Diaz singing Iago's aria "Credo," a soliloquy that the librettist Arrigo Boito created to motivate Iago's evil (Shakespeare, as he did with Hamlet, Lear, Macbeth, generated ambiguity by taking away the obvious motivation). "I believe in a cruel God," he exclaims, "who has created me in his image and whom, in hate, I name. . . . I am evil because I am a man; and I feel the primal slime in me. Yes! This is my creed! I believe . . . that whatever evil I think or do was decreed for me by fate . . . I believe that everything in [man] is a lie: tears, kisses, looks, sacrifices, honor. And I believe man to be the sport of an unjust fate from the germ of the cradle to the worm of the grave." Nihilism, existentialism, theatre of the absurd: man as a victim, toyed with by a God who enjoys our suffering, or like the gods who, as Gloucester suggests in *King Lear,* kill us for their sport. For me, the most haunting, wrenching moment in Nunn's production comes when Desdemona, played by the comely and vibrant Imogen Stubbs (Nunn's wife), frantically tries to escape Othello's murderous wrath and, leaping on a table, cries out, "Kill me tomorrow, let me live tonight!" Never before, in reading the play or seeing it staged, had I been so moved by the pathos of this scene.

I prefaced the screening of segments from a pair of television productions of *King Lear*—one starring Laurence Olivier, the other Ian Holm— with the comment "You'll note, with some chagrin I hope, that neither of these Lears seems particularly Hebraic." The class had lauded the Jewish perspective I brought to the play. Chuck had announced, "We're awarding you an LLI honorary master's degree," and Lou had chimed in, "Don't insult the man. Let's make it a Ph.D." Gilda, taking me aside after class, had suggested that I persuade the rabbi of our congregation to let me give a condensed version of the lecture at a Friday night or Saturday morning Shabbat service.

The Olivier and Holm portrayals were polar opposites. Olivier, with long white hair and flowing white beard, and painfully fragile (at the time, he was mortally ill), made it easy for us to believe that he was crawling toward death. Holm, with close-cropped gray hair, robust, vigorous, combative, was hardly a monarch who seemed ready to unburden himself of cares and business and hop into a grave.

At the end of the final class, I announced that although I was not,

Lear-like, relinquishing the throne, I'd decided to take a break from teaching, at least until the fall. "So you're going on a Royal Progress," said Sister Mary, the nun who'd brought about the Miracle of the Five-Minute Break. "No," Lou jumped in, "he's just going to recharge his batteries. We've worn him down."

In truth, I hardly considered myself a burned-out case, urgently requiring a restorative sabbatical, but try as I might, I wasn't moved to tackle the comedies or the romances (I hadn't considered *Troilus and Cressida* a romance, scholarly consensus notwithstanding). I didn't feel secure enough in my grasp of them. I needed to study them carefully and do more background reading. And I wasn't certain about how to structure future courses. I had to admit that the lecture/video format needed revamping, and that I would have to come up with techniques that would challenge the class to become more actively involved in grappling with the essence of Shakespeare and the essentials of his dramaturgy.

10.

In the early spring, I was alerted by an admiring
review in the *New York Times* to an off-Broadway production of *Macbeth*
by the Theatre for a New Audience (TFANA) at the American Place
Theatre on West Forty-sixth Street in New York. The director, Ron
Daniels, had staged productions of *Richard II* and *Richard III* the previous
fall, but for some reason I'd missed them, which was especially foolish
since at the time I was teaching the history plays, and in fact, a friend had
strongly recommended them to me.

I decided not to make the same mistake this time, and bought a ticket
for a Saturday matinee performance. Walking to the theatre from the Port
Authority Bus Terminal at Eighth Avenue and Forty-second Street, I jos-
tled my way through the weekend throngs in Times Square and tried to
imagine myself strolling in Southwark, on my way to the Globe. I
thought I could discern in the tumultuous crowd the successors to the
fetching disreputables of Elizabethan London—pimps, whores, pickpock-
ets, mountebanks.

At the American Place, I recalled the last time I was on the premises,
almost ten years before, at the memorial services for my old Houston
comrade, who, as it turned out, became an author of mine shortly after
I'd begun my career as a book editor. Donald Barthelme and I had met
while students in a course in Restoration drama at the University of
Houston. He had recently become the editor of the alumni magazine and
was taking a few courses in a leisurely, halfhearted progress toward a B.A.
degree. I was unhappily pursuing, but not for long, a master's in theatre
arts. He was also a Korean War veteran—Don had been an enlisted man
in the infantry, stationed in Korea and Japan, and had at one point been
on the staff of *Stars & Stripes,* the well-respected armed forces newspaper.
After his discharge, he'd joined the *Houston Post,* where he was a police
reporter and then a movie critic. I'd read his reviews during my brief in-

terludes at home in the midst of vision quests to the two coasts, and thought they were exceptionally trenchant and witty and graceful, and best of all, revealed a genuine affection for movies. He'd left the *Post* for his job at the university, and here we were, classmates. I introduced myself to him, told him I'd been a fan, and then proceeded to argue with what I recalled as his mocking assessment of *The Man from Laramie,* a western starring James Stewart. And that was the beginning of a beautiful friendship.

Don was as close to a Hamlet figure as anyone I've ever known. Hamlet's soliloquies and speeches could have sprung directly from Barthelme's soul, not just the pain, the bitterness, the scorn of "I have of late . . . lost all my mirth" (traceable, perhaps, to his being a lapsed Catholic and the son of a brilliant, eccentric architect), but the antic wit and humor of Hamlet the punster, the jiber—he had among his other talents a prodigious gift for laughter and a love of plays and players. Aristocratically handsome, with a touch of princely hauteur in his penetrating gaze, he was also very much the glass of fashion, very Ivy League in habiliment, the first person I'd known who wore button-down blue oxford shirts, rep ties, and tweed jackets. He drove an MG. And though he had a formidable intellect, his companions in those days were, like me, anything but professional intellectuals, which made life rather complicated for his wife Maggie, a French scholar and teaching assistant in the doctoral program at Rice University. He was addicted, as was I, to West Coast jazz and to Scotch, and we spent many an evening in his living room killing a fifth of Black and White, listening to Shelly Manne and Shorty Rogers and Bud Shanks and André Previn (a fantastic jazz pianist back then) and Dave Brubeck and Gerry Mulligan, descanting and descanting again on life and art (the latest Salinger story in the *New Yorker,* Robert Aldrich's scorching movie version of Odets's overheated Hollywood melodrama *The Big Knife),* while in the bedroom Maggie analyzed the genius of Mallarmé and Baudelaire, emerging occasionally to ask us, in a voice taut with controlled animosity, to turn down the music and lower our voices.

Miss Maggie was a sexy creature, but she suffered from a deadly case of intellectual snobbery. One night on a date at Stubby's Lounge with a Rice coed who happened to be one of Maggie's students, I allowed as how it must be awful to have such a snobbish bitch for a teacher. A few days later when I went by Don's office to pick him up for our almost daily lunch at a nearby barbecue joint, he looked up from his desk, stared at me balefully with those piercing blue eyes, and said, his voice all ice, "I understand you think my wife is a snobbish bitch." My date had ratted on me, possibly because I'd had the poor taste to take her to Stubby's, not one of Houston's chic watering spots. What could I do? Deny it? Try to explain it away as a little joke? I thought not. I'd insulted my friend's wife. Nothing to do but own up to my indiscreetness and face the music. "Yes," I said. "I do think she's a snobbish bitch." Rising, he patted me on the arm and said, "So do I. In fact, I'm getting a divorce. I'll have to look for an apartment right away. Why don't we share one?"

He was aware that I, too, was living with a woman from whom I wanted to separate. My mother. To save money, I was living with my parents, and I spent most of the days paralyzed with neurasthenia, not an uncommon affliction to children of any age who return even for short visits to the nest. I dreaded the times when I'd walk into the house and find my mother watching soap operas and screaming abuse at characters on-screen ("You little slut, leave him alone!").

Don and I, along with two of his cronies, both of whom were architects, rented a dilapidated Victorian monstrosity in the center of town, a gothic dwelling to gladden the heart of Charles Addams.

Don was working on a novel and told me that he'd already thrown away two complete drafts, without showing a single page to anyone. "Wasn't that sort of extreme?" I asked. "Maybe you're too harsh a critic of your own work. Maybe you could have benefited from someone else's perspective." He hit me with the kind of look that Hamlet must have given Claudius when the latter advised him to stop mourning because it was unmanly. "Thanks so much. I'll remember that when I'm throwing this third draft into the toilet. I can see that it's full of the same self-pitying shit that smelled up the others." I assumed it was autobiographical and rich in Maggie-inspired angst.

By the time I'd moved on and wound up editing books in Boston, Don, too, had carved out a new life. He'd left his job, and his studies, at the University of Houston and become director of the Contemporary Arts Museum. He'd married again: his new bride, Helen, was a public relations expert, warmhearted and down-to-earth. And he'd taken a radically different approach to fiction. Not only had he flushed the third draft of his novel down the toilet, he'd begun to write stories best described long ago by Roger Angell, who eventually became his editor at the *New Yorker:* "[These stories] share a hard and brilliant surface, a marvelous black humor, a half-delicate, half-ferocious emotion, mingling the grotesque with the matter-of-fact. . . . Testing the possibilities of parody, inanity, discontinuity and collage, he achieves finally an art that is deeply involved with the mystery of human gesture and response."

The first stories in this idiosyncratic form were published in such small magazines as *Contact, First Person,* and *New World Writing,* and over the months as they appeared, Don would send them to me at Little, Brown. In one of his letters, he said, "This job at the museum is sapping my will to live, never great to begin with," and challenged me to summon up the courage to publish "the most brilliant work of our time," adding that a contract would inspire him to write enough new material for a substantial collection. I was awed by the controlled madness of these wildly innovative fictions, by their exuberant quirkiness, by their comic flair. Most of all, I think, I marveled at the unforced precision of the language, the seemingly effortless colloquial tone, traceable I felt to Don's newspaper days.

Finally, I showed the stories to my boss, Ned Bradford, the shrewd, dapper, silver-haired editor in chief, a midwesterner and a graduate of Depauw, which made us the only two non–Ivy Leaguers in the editorial department. For the next hour or so I could hear him roaring with laughter in his office as he read the Barthelme oeuvre. Emerging at last, he said, "This bastard is either crazy or a genius. Probably both. Story collections don't exactly fly off the shelves, even when they're not this esoteric, but we can't pass up a chance to publish someone who might turn out to be an American Kafka or Joyce. And one of these days he might write a novel that more than ten people want to read. Sign him up."

I told Don the amazing news, and it instantly galvanized him into action. He wrote two stories in three days—"Marie, Marie, Hold on Tight" and "A Shower of Gold," which Roger Angell bought for the *New Yorker* and which were part of the fourteen that made up Don's first collection, *Come Back, Dr. Caligari,* published in 1964. The critics hailed it, and it sold well enough to earn out its modest advance. By then, Don had separated from Helen and accepted a job in New York as managing editor of *Location,* an art–literary review. Yet another Young Man from the Provinces saga in the making.

When I left Little, Brown to become an editor at Atheneum Publishers in New York City, Ned agreed to let Don follow me to the new house. He'd decided to expand one of his latest stories, "Indian Uprising," into a novel.

Time passed. Don was now divorced from Helen and from his editorship of *Location.* He seemed unable to get a handle on the novel. He longed to absent himself from the clatter and pressure and distractions of Manhattan. He needed to get out of town—way out of town. Denmark, in fact. Could it have been the Hamlet in him, crying out to return to Elsinore? Off he went to Copenhagen. A year later he returned with a fiancée, Birgit, and the manuscript of his novel. "You'll see that it's not *Indian Uprising,*" he announced. "But I don't think you'll hate it." It turned out to be *Snow White,* a zany version of the old fairy tale, set in New York City. The dwarfs earn a living by washing skyscraper windows and manufacturing Chinese baby food. Snow White is a neurotic, promiscuous woman who sleeps with all seven of them. I didn't hate it. I marveled at it, and laughed myself sick. The *New Yorker* published the entire manuscript, and we brought it out a couple of months later, to critical acclaim and a respectable sale.

In the wake of *Snow White*'s publication, Don and his agent, Lynn Nesbit, who'd been representing him from the start (they'd met at a writers' conference on Staten Island), at first complained of what they considered Atheneum's niggardly advertising campaign, and then demanded an extravagant advance, or so I saw it, for Don's next book. Waiting in the wings to snatch up the new manuscript if we failed to make a deal was Henry Robbins, editor in chief of Farrar, Straus & Giroux and long an ardent devotee of Don's. In a phone conversation with Lynn, I exploded, accusing her of using Henry to extort an outrageous sum from us. Very unprofessional of me, that little tantrum. I had taken the matter personally, looking upon it not in the spirit of honest competition but as the betrayal of a friendship.

Lynn moved Don to Farrar, Straus, and for weeks I refused to take his calls and returned his letters unopened. Then at 3:00 one morning my phone rang. It was Don: "I'm not mad at you for not giving me the fucking money. Why are you pissed off because I asked for it?" End of quarrel. In fact, he dedicated that new book, a collection of stories titled *Unspeakable Practices, Unnatural Acts,* to me.

"That was an unspeakable and unnatural thing for you to do," I told him.

"You mean it made you feel guilty? Good!" he replied. "That means you still retain a spark of Hebraism. Soon you'll join the Lubavitchers."

Years flew off the calendar, as they did in those movie montages of yore. Don divorced Birgit and married Marian, an editor at *Time.* His career continued to flourish, and he was celebrated as one of the world's supremely gifted writers of fiction, a literary icon. Ironically, this man who'd never earned a degree from the University of Houston eventually returned there to head its creative writing department.

In 1989, at the age of fifty-eight, Donald Barthelme died of throat cancer.

A few weeks before Don's death, I phoned him in Houston. His voice was ominously husky. "You sound as sexy as Lizabeth Scott did in *Dead Reckoning,*" I said, citing one of our favorite noir flicks of the fifties. "Have you turned to female impersonating in your dotage?"

"Please," he rasped, "it only hurts when I laugh."

During the memorial service at the American Place, I'd sat with Joe Moranto, another of Don's old Houston chums, a public relations consultant in Connecticut. We noted that we'd known Don longer than anyone else in attendance, and were the only representatives from his Texas past. I thought I could hear Don saying, "Don't just sit there. Take center stage and chant Kaddish for me in your Texas accent."

On that day in 1998, I had not come to the American Place Theatre to memorialize Don Barthelme. I had come to participate in a sad story of the death of kings, one killed sleeping, the other slain in battle. I hadn't seen a Shakespearean drama staged since my Elderhostel summer three years previously, and I found every moment of this production charged with visual and aural power, and a relentless emotional intensity. Some remain vivid even in recollection:

- Lady Macbeth (Elizabeth Marvel, aptly surnamed), gorgeous and sexy and elegant in a green hoopskirt, tight bodice, luscious shoulders (the antithesis of Judi Dench's severe, dressed-in-black matron, hair pulled back and covered by a kerchief in Trevor Nunn's version), sweeping onto the stage through the door upstage center, reading the letter from Macbeth in which he relates his encounter with the weird sisters. Ferociously jubilant, she leaped about in a pagan dance of joy, mouth agape with near-demonic laughter. Then came the messenger with news that Duncan will spend the night chez Macbeth. The good Lady threw herself to the floor, rose on all fours like a panther ready to pounce, eyes gleaming, thrilled with the prospect of the kill to come. When she stood and implored the spirits to unsex her, I said to myself, "Fat chance." It was a textbook example of acting against the lines. Elizabeth Marvel's Lady Macbeth was asking for a release not from her femininity but from her humanity; we did not see her possessed by spirits, as Judi Dench had seemed to be. Marvel was preparing us for the raw manipulative sexuality of her scenes with Macbeth.
- After the murder of Duncan, a tableau of hideous grandeur: the rear curtains opened, revealing the King and Queen of Hell, dressed in scarlet, with golden crowns, the stage diffused in scarlet light. The implacable couple stared directly, pitilessly, at the audience. It was all you needed to know about evil.
- The self-awareness without self-pity, the pathos of a man who realizes that he's truly damned, condemned to a life without honor, love, friends, the melancholic resignation conveyed so poignantly by Bill Camp in Macbeth's "My way of life is fall'n into the sere" speech. Apparently, Camp had mastered the technique, stressed by John Barton, of thinking and discovering the words in the text out of the situation and character. At one point during the speech, Camp's face actually twisted into a piteous grin, which did not seem like a rehearsed piece of business, but torn spontaneously from the experience of the pain of the moment. Here was a man who had slain his king, his close friend, and worst of all, the wife and children of a rival, and yet your heart

went out to him. Mine did, at least. If you can't identify with at least one of the Macbeths, the production, not the play, has failed.

Returning home to New Jersey on the bus, I thumbed through the program again and came upon a couple of significant items that had escaped my attention the first time around. First there were several prominent ads (one from the Shakespeare Society, an entity unfamiliar to me and, I thought, worth looking into) congratulating TFANA and its artistic director, Jeffrey Horowitz, on the organization's twentieth birthday. My my, the place had existed for twenty years without my support, without my even being aware of it. There were testimonials from *New York* magazine ("[TFANA] is providing the most enthusiastically acclaimed Shakespeare in New York City and very possibly the United States") and the *New York Times* ("TFANA's team of directors are among the most imaginative working today"). And there was a brief description of TFANA's American Directors Project, "a mentoring program for early and mid-career directors of Shakespeare led by Cicely Berry, Director of Voice, Royal Shakespeare Company." Cicely Berry, whose book *The Actor and the Text* had made such an impact on me in the early stages of my Bardomania.

TFANA had my complete attention now. I wanted to know what had led Jeffrey Horowitz to create his remarkable theatre, how he'd managed to keep it not only viable for twenty years but prestigious enough to attract the likes of Cicely Berry as the teacher of a master class. So I wrote him a note, describing my background and my newly acquired addiction to Shakespeare and its pedagogical consequences, and asking if I could meet with him and learn the secrets of his success. Ultimately, I had in mind arranging a way to attend the Cicely Berry classes as an observer, but that would have to wait until I'd had a chance to show Mr. Horowitz that I wasn't actually a senescent backstage groupie desperate to rub elbows with a legend. Or was I? Within days I had a call from his assistant, Benjamin Krevorin, who said that Jeffrey would be delighted to see me in his office at three o'clock two weeks hence.

On the appointed day, I showed up for my appointment with Jeffrey Horowitz at the TFANA offices on Christopher Street in Greenwich Village. Nothing glitzy/showbiz about the premises. The building could have been a converted warehouse. Jeffrey met me in the foyer of the third-floor suite and led me into his small, modest office, cement block walls painted light yellow, lined with bookshelves and a couple of obligatory posters from TFANA productions. Horowitz was a man perhaps in his mid-forties, tall, with shaggy gray-brown hair and a close-cropped salt-and-pepper beard, wearing a gray herringbone sport coat, light gray cords, a white pullover, loafers. Soft-spoken, effortlessly cordial, erudite without a whiff of pedantry.

A graduate of UCLA, he'd spent three years at the London Academy of Music and Dramatic Arts, then returned to New York and managed to get some acting jobs, working on Broadway and in regional theatre. Finally, he realized he was limited as an actor. "What truly fascinated me," he told me, "was how plays were done, and why they were done a certain way. I felt I had a contribution to make as a director and producer."

How did he come up with Theatre for a New Audience? " 'New' is about discovery and freshness—it refers to the theatre and to the experience an audience has. I wanted a theatre in which Shakespeare's poetic language would be spoken naturally and expressively. I wanted an audience to connect its own feelings, its own sense of truth, with the form of that language. In the beginning, there were four actors, including me. We had met in an acting class. We had a director, we rehearsed, we were paid with an Equity contract. I got bookings for us, and for four years we toured the Northeast, the provinces, community centers, schools, doing collages of Shakespeare scenes, soliloquies, songs."

Then, in 1983, Jeff went to see a production of *The Haggadah,* the saga of the Jewish Passover, that a young director named Elizabeth Swados had put together with a then unknown young artist named Julie Taymor. "I had this idea of doing *Midsummer Night's Dream* in masks," he continued, "and I looked up Julie in the phone book and called her. And that was the beginning of her relationship with TFANA.

"Joe Papp auditioned us and gave us space to produce *Dream* at the New York Shakespeare Festival's Public Theatre. The production was a success. Then in 1986, Julie directed *The Tempest* for us, and it made a huge impact off-Broadway. That was our turning point. People were definitely aware of us. We were a classical theatre, with an audience socially, ethnically, racially diverse. And diverse in age: young people are a considerable part of our audience."

Jeff learned that to include that audience, he had to build an educational program with the New York public schools as part of TFANA's component.

"In the beginning, everyone had told me, 'You have to cut Shakespeare for children. You should do a forty-five-minute version for the classroom.' But we said, 'No, they have to come to the theatre and see the same play that adults see, the real thing. Why would we want children to have a lesser experience than adults?' "

What about the language? I asked. Can children comprehend it sufficiently to grasp what's happening onstage? "The way we dealt with that was by never insisting that students read the play. In addition to providing teachers with study guides, we have teaching artists—young people, directors and actors, just entering the profession or still in college—who visit the classrooms. And they'll say to the kids, 'We want to tell you the story and the theme of this play.' And we'd work with teachers and, taking *The Tempest* as an example, we'd ask, 'What is the theme that goes through the entire play, a theme we can work on?' We chose Usurpation—it happens to Prospero, who does it to Caliban and Ariel, and Caliban in turn tries to do it to Prospero. Then we'd tell the story to the kids in our own words: once upon a time there was a duke who came from Milan, and whose brother was very jealous of him, and put him in a boat with his daughter . . .'"

TFANA has a short season, two or three months a year, January to late March or early April. "We're concerned with quality, not quantity," Jeff remarked. "The question I ask colleagues and directors before choosing a play is, 'What is there in this play that's going to touch us all?' If you really get to that and make it vivid, it's exciting."

I asked if he'd chosen the next production. "Yes, *King John*. Rehearsals begin in December, and we'll open in January. The director is Karin Coonrod, who did a splendid production of *Henry VI* at the Public Theatre last year. And Cicely Berry will be here in the fall for the American Directors Project." There was my opening. "Yeah, that squib about her in the program grabbed my attention. I've been a fanatical

Berryite ever since I read *The Actor and the Text* a couple of years ago, and I wondered, how the hell did this bunch at TFANA manage to hook up with her?"

He laughed. "Well, let me tell you a story. Once upon a time, in 1993, I heard her lecture at the Stella Adler School. Afterwards, I introduced myself, we had coffee, and talked about how challenged American actors felt when faced with Shakespeare's text. I invited her to do a workshop here for actors, and she accepted. Finally, she and I created the American Directors Project to support American directors in their efforts to work with actors on Shakespeare's text. The ADP is not a series of master classes. It's a process of exercises which can lead to rehearsal techniques aimed at helping the director and actor enter the world of Shakespeare through the language. And consequently it will be primarily the text, not some ingenious 'high concept,' leading the audience into Shakespeare."

"I'd love to be a fly on the wall at one of those sessions." Nothing ventured, nothing gained. "I'm afraid this will sound presumptuous, but could you fix it for me to watch the group for an hour or so? The more I can learn about making Shakespeare's language come alive from watching theatre professionals at work, the better teacher I'll be." Hey, Horowitz, I'm no backstage voyeur, I'm doing this for my students.

"I don't see why not, as long as Ciss agrees," he said without a pause. "Check with me around October and I'll let you know."

11.

Shortly after visiting Jeffrey Horowitz, I joined the Shakespeare Society, which held out the promise of a constructive and dynamic experience—unusual, I imagined, in the realm of literary societies and reading groups. It had been founded in 1997 by a pair of savvy, high-powered entrepreneurs and cultural activists: Adriana Mnuchin, who had established and sold two successful retail businesses and was a member of the board of trustees at the Whitney Museum, and Nancy Becker, a former high school English teacher who, with her husband, had founded the Beethoven Society and had served as a member of the Carnegie Hall Special Events Committee. Its academic advisers included such noted professors as David Scott Kastan (Columbia) and Stephen Greenblatt (Harvard), and among its artistic advisers were Claire Bloom, Judi Dench, Ralph Fiennes, and Derek Jacobi. I hardly envisioned all these eminences convening regularly to cook up intellectual and theatrical adventures for me, but neither did I imagine they'd lent their distinguished names to the organization simply as stationery adornments to entice the credulous.

And the membership benefits offered were considerable: five Monday evening programs (most recently, a panel discussion of "Shakespeare's Villains," moderated by Professor Kastan, who was joined by Tony Randall, and an evening in which Professor James Shapiro, author of *Shakespeare and the Jews,* hosted a discussion of *The Merchant of Venice);* an annual subscription to the *Shakespeare Newsletter,* a quarterly published by the department of English at Iona College; and an opportunity to participate in seminars at the Society's East Seventy-eighth Street offices under the leadership of a scholar not specified in the brochure.

An unexpected consequence of joining the Shakespeare Society was my discovery of one of our great national treasures, one that in fact is internationally prized. In early May I received a flyer from the society offering a private tour of the Folger Shakespeare Library in Washington, D.C. Until then I'd mainly associated the Folger with the paperback editions of Shakespeare published under its editorship by Simon and Schuster's Washington Square Press. Its larger purposes and functions escaped me. Now the Shakespeare Society flyer had piqued my curiosity, and scanning the Folger's website, I discovered that among other things it was a major center for scholarly research, a museum devoted to Shakespeare's legacy and a repository for the world's largest collection of Shakespeare's printed works. Also, it published a renowned literary journal, the *Shakespeare Quarterly,* and it offered Shakespearean productions in an intimate Elizabethan theatre. All of this not across the Atlantic but a mere two hundred miles from my home.

Yes, an exploration of the Folger was long overdue, but I was reluctant to join a touring expedition. I'd learned on the web that the reading room and the collection are open only to Ph.D.'s and above (i.e., professional scholars and teachers), and graduate students writing dissertations; the public, including private tours, is excluded. To me, the whole point of going to the Folger was precisely to see the collection and spend time in the reading room, so I dropped a note to the Folger librarian, Richard Kuhta, first citing my background in publishing and my present situation at Caldwell College, as I'd done with Jeff Horowitz, and then saying that although I was aware that access to the collection and reading room is limited to academicians, in the light of the newfound direction my life had taken I hoped he might consider waiving the rule and allowing me at least a brief period to observe the work being done on the premises. Eureka! A few days later I had a call from Mr. Kuhta: come on down. I could be admitted for a day or two under the category of Special Permission. And he'd be glad to chat with me for a while and brief me on the Folger operation.

So I found myself on a pristine spring day about to enter one of the world's preeminent specialized research libraries, a neoclassic marble building with art deco grillwork, dominating a block on East Capitol Street, across the street from the Library of Congress and the Supreme Court, and only a couple of blocks from the Capitol. In this setting, and not all that far from the memorials to Washington and Lincoln and Jefferson and FDR and to those who fell in the Korean and Vietnam Wars, the building seemed to imply that if you want to know about war and peace, politics and power, the strengths and weaknesses of great men, the struggle for a just society, come inside and learn from the man who saw life and saw it whole, the man who like God created a world and all its creatures with his word.

Decorating the outside of the building are bas-reliefs depicting scenes from *Midsummer Night's Dream, Romeo and Juliet, The Merchant of Venice, Julius Caesar, King Lear, Richard III, Hamlet,* and *Henry VI, Part 1.* And inscriptions: "For wisdom's sake, A word that all men love"—*Love's Labour's Lost.* "This therefore is the praise of Shakespeare, that his drama is the mirror of life"—Samuel Johnson. "Thou art a monument without a tomb, and art alive still, while thy booke doth live, and we have wits to read and praise to give"—Ben Jonson.

The Folger appeared to me neither monument nor tomb nor mere library but holy temple of Herodian grandeur erected to the world's supreme literary deity, a shrine in which sacred writings were preserved and where study was the form of worship by priests and scribes who labored over learned and sometimes arcane exegeses. What manner of man was Henry Folger? What had led him to create this splendid edifice?

That was the first question I intended to put to Richard Kuhta, the Folger's librarian, who greeted me at the door and ushered me into his office. Trim and precise, infinitely courteous, and probably in his mid-forties, he looked a bit like the actor Roddy McDowall and came across as a man aware that his was not a job but a higher calling, a man who had taken holy orders. He had fallen under the Shakespearean spell during a senior seminar at Swarthmore, and then, at his professor's recommendation, enrolled in an M.A. program in Shakespeare studies at the Shakespeare Institute, which was then affiliated with the University of Birmingham, in England. After graduating, he returned to America and worked for a time in the antiquarian book trade before entering Columbia University and getting a master of library sciences degree. He'd been university librarian at St. Lawrence University in Canton, New York, for eight years when he was nominated for the position of librarian at Folger, where he was hired in February 1994.

No sooner had we sat down to have coffee, the obligatory rite of hospitality, than I asked him to tell me about Henry Folger, and as if on cue—

obviously he was accustomed to the public's curiosity on the subject—he launched into a succinct biographical sketch with the warm familiarity of those museum docents who give the impression they actually knew the people they're describing:

"Henry Clay Folger's passion for Shakespeare was ignited during his senior year at Amherst College when he paid twenty-five cents for a ticket to a lecture on Shakespeare by Ralph Waldo Emerson—we have that ticket in the collection. This lecture persuaded him to study the plays, and he bought an edition of Shakespeare, his first Shakespeare purchase. After graduating from Amherst, he took a job as clerk in the Standard Oil organization, and also began to study law at Columbia, where he received his LL.B. cum laude and was admitted to the bar. Four years later he married Emily Jordan, who had been educated at Vassar. Henry rose through the ranks at Standard Oil, ultimately becoming president and then chairman of the board."

But Henry Clay Folger, I discovered, was not a typical self-made man. He was a corporate bigwig with a difference, an idiosyncratic American character who, I'm confident, would have gladdened the heart of a William Dean Howells. Richard continued the Folger saga, glancing occasionally at notes he'd placed on the coffee table in front of us: "All along he'd been adding to his growing collection of books, and he and Emily continued to familiarize themselves with all the major scholarly works on Shakespeare." So the Folgers were a power couple, I learned, united by their shared monomania. In fact, Richard explained that it was not until their marriage—which, as it turned out, was childless—that Shakespeare became the main focus of their lives. "Eleven years after her marriage," Richard said, "Emily received an M.A. degree from Vassar. The title of her thesis was 'The True Text of Shakespeare.' Henry pursued a great variety of source material, works of scholarship, theatrical relics, playbills, portraits, all sorts of Shakespeare memorabilia, but this never distracted him from the principal objective of his collecting: the Folio editions of Shakespeare, especially the First."

In my first lecture at the LLI, I'd discussed the First Folio, with which no one in the class had been familiar. In 1623, seven years after Shakespeare's death, two of his former theatrical colleagues, John Heminges and Henry Condell, had edited a collection of thirty-six of Shakespeare's plays

in folio format, with pages about as wide as those of a modern encyclopedia, but two or three inches taller. It was the first collected edition of
Shakespeare.

"During his lifetime, Henry managed to collect seventy-nine copies
of the First Folio, almost one-third of the surviving copies, and more
copies of each of the subsequent Folio editions than had ever been as-
sembled in one place since each was first published." Why, I asked, had
Folger been so obsessed with acquiring as many First Folios as possible?
"Good question. We don't know for certain, but apparently he believed
that it was important to collate large numbers of copies so that all the variants could be found. Back in 1991, Peter Blayney, currently one of our
Long Term Fellows, was the curator of an original and compelling exhibition of twenty-four of our seventy-nine First Folios—before you leave
I'll get you a copy of the brochure he wrote for it. Peter says that the Folgers believed that a study of the variants would help to establish 'the True
Text'—but only in the sense that it would establish the text of the Folio
itself.

"Henry retired in 1928 and spent the last two years of his life building what he called the Shakespeare Memorial to house a collection of
some 93,000 volumes packed in more than two thousand cartons stored
in several warehouses. I should emphasize now that this material was
wide-ranging in scope and included literature from and about the Tudor
and Stuart periods. In fact, our collection today is so strong that it supports research on early music, the history of science, religion, the Reformation, British political thought, astrology, astronomy. From Caxton to
Dryden, 1475 to 1700, if you're working in any of these disciplines in that
period of time, the Folger is the library to come to. For the period from
1475 to 1640, Early English Printed Books, the Folger is the largest collection outside Britain, the third largest in the world—the Bodleian at
Oxford, the British Library, and the Folger.

"Henry and Emily engaged Paul Philippe Cret as architect for this
building. They designed the plans, bought the property, and made this library a gift to the nation. Stratford-on-Avon had been considered as one
of the sites, but Henry said, 'I'm an American, I want the library to be
here.' " I found myself wishing that old Howells had been alive to write
a novel based on the Folgers, if only for me to have read the scene in

which he describes Henry resisting the plans of cultural snobs and Anglophiles to establish the collection across the Atlantic. "The Folgers lost a considerable sum in the Crash of '29, but enough remained to construct the building. Two weeks after the cornerstone was laid in 1930, Henry died"—yet another episode that Howells would have dramatized, I know, with a note of poignance and irony. "The building opened in 1932, but there was not a lot of money to set up an endowment for programs or acquisitions. Mrs. Folger died in 1936 and left the estate to the library, but of course it wasn't as formidable as it had been in the late twenties. It took a number of years before the endowment could really grow. Fourteen years ago it stood at around twenty-two million. Today, 1999, it's one hundred and ten million."

Richard had mentioned that Peter Blayney was a Long Term Fellow, and I asked him if he'd mind elaborating on the fellowship program. Mind? His face lit up. "This program is the catalyst in the life of the Folger. It's one of the things that keep the Folger so dynamic, so alive, so much at the center of international Shakespeare scholarship. Long Term Fellows are the stars in the field, people who have made substantial contributions, who have published at least one book in their specialty. Short Term Fellows are postdoctoral scholars. Once a scholar is out of the university environment, free of campus politics and committees, he or she has more time and opportunity for exchange, for sharing with colleagues."

Richard took a sip of coffee and looked at his watch. "In just a few minutes, Georgianna Ziegler, our reference librarian, will be coming by to show you around the reading room and the collection. I've arranged for you to spend the day in the reading room tomorrow, by the way. Let me explain something quickly about the collection. We're still acquiring material aggressively. Sixty percent of the budget goes for rare books; the rest is spent on new material, work that's being produced now. We feel the need to collect works of modern scholarship, the work that's going on in our reading room and ends up in print. Publishers' print runs are shorter and shorter these days because of economics, and if we let the material go out of print, we'll never be able to obtain it, or we'll have to acquire it later on at great expense. We at the Folger are responsible for a legacy of literature that needs to be available for all time to all people.

We're an institution which creates access to the ineffable." Access to the ineffable. Quite a stirring turn of phrase. And what a grabber of a slogan it would make for a commercial, right in there with G.E.'s "We bring good things to life."

It turned out to be Richard's curtain line, too, because knocking politely at the office doorway was Georgianna Ziegler, the reference librarian. After making introductions, Richard said, "Georgianna, make certain to show Herman the Fuseli paintings." Then, to me: "The Folger has the largest collection of paintings on Shakespearean themes in the world. I've written extensively on the Swiss artist Henry Fuseli. He went to England and painted Shakespearean scenes for fifty years. He was a contemporary of David Garrick's, and was at Covent Garden and Drury Lane for decades, recording what he saw when he attended Garrick's performances. We have six Fuseli paintings—*Macbeth Consulting the Vision of the Armed Head, Two Murderers of the Duke of Clarence, Romeo Stabs Paris at the Bier of Juliet, Puck, Ariel,* and one non–Shakespearean painting which Mr. Folger purchased believing it was Shakespeare's Mab, although it turned out to be Milton's Mab from *L'Allegro.*" Fuseli. That was the surname of one of the most compelling characters in Clifford Odets's *Golden Boy,* sinister Eddie Fuseli. I wondered if this had been a show-off allusion aimed at the cognoscenti or at his cultivated associates, Clurman and Strasberg.

Georgianna turned out to be a delightful and ebullient young woman, given to wry grins and a relaxed just-folks style that tempered the sense of awe generated in the temple. She led me first into the oak-paneled chandeliered reading room, modeled along the lines of an Oxford library/hall. At one end was a stained-glass window showing the "Seven Ages of Man" as described by Jaques in *As You Like It.* At the other, over a recess, was a replica of the bust of Shakespeare in Stratford's Trinity Church. Pointing to the recessed space, Georgianna whispered, "The Folgers' ashes repose in there. Behind the brass plaque, and under the Shakespeare bust." Even in death, the Folgers were still very much with us, resting under the watchful eye of their deity. No wonder whispering was de rigueur in the reading room, lending it an aura of sanctity. Judging from the reactions of the handful of people at work in the room, even a whisper here grated on the nerves.

We proceeded into the adjacent new reading room, designed for those who use personal computers—not a breed, I imagine, that the Folgers would snuggle up to. No sense of awe in that brightly lit space, but the code of *omerta* was still in force—silence reigned. The walls, however, shouted with dramatic power. As soon as I entered I came upon Fuseli's *Macbeth Consulting the Vision of the Armed Head,* and realized why Richard was so taken with this artist. The painting smote me as forcefully as some of the performances I'd seen on stage and screen. Occasionally, the force of Shakespeare translated into other forms has moved me as much as if not more than any movie or stage version of the play: Verdi's *Otello,* for instance, and the Stuttgart Ballet's production of Prokofiev's *Romeo and Juliet,* choreographed by John Cranko.

Finally, with barely contained eagerness, her step quickening, Georgianna took me through a door and down a flight of steps into . . . The Collection. Among the riches: 229 quartos of the plays and poems, the 79 copies of the First Folio, over 1,000 promptbooks of Shakespeare's plays (copies of the plays with marginal notations on stage business, actors' movements, etc.) dating from the late seventeenth through the mid-twentieth centuries (with the strongest in the nineteenth century), and fifteenth- through eighteenth-century rare books. I was anxious to see some of the promptbooks, and Georgianna obliged by showing me those from Charles Kean and Edwin Forrest productions. She opened a large box, revealing *The Holie Bible,* printed in London, 1568. Velvet binding over oak boards decorated with silver clasps and bosses bearing the Tudor rose, the monogram and coat of arms of . . . Elizabeth I, Queen of England and Ireland. Good grief, this was Queen Bess's very own Bible, kept in her chapel. It's not unlikely that she held it in her hands after the executions of Essex and Mary, Queen of Scots, searching for consolation in the Psalms.

Then Georgianna plucked from a shelf a volume of Cicero, *Commentu in Ciceronis Officia,* and seemingly at random opened it to a particular page. What struck me at first was that the format was identical to that of the Talmud: a block of text in the middle of the page, surrounded by commentary, with a marginal gloss at the left. Georgianna could not explain the format. The book was printed in Lyon in 1502. Could the printer have been a Jew, secret or otherwise, who was having a little joke at the expense of the goyim? Georgianna called my attention to the interlinear notes which the owner had written in tiny Latin script, and she then pointed to a note written in the bottom margin of the page: "Thys boke is Myne Prynce henry." Henry VIII. Since Henry didn't succeed to the throne until shortly before his eighteenth birthday, he was a teenager when he penned this declaration of ownership, an adolescent struggling with Cicero when he probably wished he could be falconing or tilting. Was this inscription a warning by a serious student and heir to the throne that whoever had dared to take the volume without permission and read thus far was in deep trouble if found out?

Before leaving this treasure trove, Georgianna showed me one last item: a handwritten manuscript draft of an article by Walt Whitman that appeared in the *Critic, 1884,* advancing a provocative theory about Shakespeare's history plays. This was news to me; for all I knew, Justin Kaplan or Jerome Loving had mentioned it in their Whitman biographies (I'd read Kaplan's book almost thirty years earlier, Loving's more recently), but if so, it hadn't made enough of an impact on me to remain in my memory after all this time. "If you'd like to take the time to read this carefully," Georgianna offered, "I'll leave it at the desk in the reading room and you can pick it up when you come tomorrow." So now I wouldn't be simply a browser in Fellowland, I had a scholarly mission to perform, a piece of research that might come in handy the next time I taught the history cycle.

Before breaking for lunch, Georgianna walked me through the great hall—a high-ceilinged space with oak-paneled walls, a tile floor with insets of the masks of Comedy and Tragedy, and a scrapwork ceiling bearing motifs seen throughout the building (Shakespeare's coat of arms, the Tudor rose and fleur-de-lis)—to the Folger Theatre. Here was an intimate Elizabethan theatre with a three-tiered gallery, carved oak columns, inner and outer stages, a balcony, a sky canopy, and walls of timber and plaster.

At the security desk, which was down the corridor from the theatre lobby, Georgianna told me that Richard had arranged an appointment for me in the afternoon with Janet Field-Pickering, the Folger's head of education. And off I went for a solo lunch at a neighboring coffee shop; Richard and Georgianna had meetings outside the office.

Ms. Field-Pickering, I discovered upon meeting her after lunch, had succeeded the legendary Peggy O'Brien, who left the Folger to join the Corporation for Public Broadcasting. Ms. O'Brien had created, among other things, the Shakespeare Set Free series, a three-volume series for which she was the general editor and which combines scholarship with practical approaches for engaging students with Shakespeare.

A large, pretty, vivacious former schoolteacher, a person who comes across as a pragmatic idealist, Janet was no slouch herself. I'd noticed in the reception area gift shop *Discovering Shakespeare's Language,* a ring-bound collection of activity sheets for student work which she coauthored with Rex Gibson, director of Shakespeare and Schools Project at Cambridge University. Also on display was O'Brien's Shakespeare Set Free series.

Janet began our conversation by telling me about the Folger's Teaching Shakespeare website, which provides teachers with lesson plans, illustrations from the Folger collection, etc. "The website plans are free—we're trying to help teachers and students find Shakespeare more accessible. This isn't simply altruistic—the mission of the Folger is to preserve the collection, to spread the word about Shakespeare." It was clear to me that those who make Shakespeare a life's work are indeed on a mission, dedicated to preserving the sacred texts, spreading the gospel. Richard had said that the Folger offers an access to the ineffable. Wasn't that what religion was all about?

I mentioned to Janet that I'd seen her book in the gift shop, and I asked her the same question I'd put to Jeff Horowitz about how to make Shakespeare's language less forbidding for students. Her approach to the challenge differed markedly from Jeff's. "Of course the language can be intimidating to them," she replied, "but not if you use techniques that break it down. One of the techniques we use is called Finding the Voices in a Soliloquy. For example, in Macbeth's 'If 'twere done when 'tis done' soliloquy, if you can identify what Macbeth goes through in terms of pros and cons—why should he kill Duncan, why shouldn't he—then a horrendously dense passage such as 'heaven's cherubim, horsed upon the sightless couriers of the air' will stop causing them to go bonkers. You can say, if you have to make a movie of what Macbeth is imagining, cherubim horsed upon sightless couriers, what kind of an image would you show? In *Discovering Shakespeare's Language,* Rex and I created lesson plans that will help students see that Shakespeare's language is the heart of his plays."

By "students" she obviously meant those in middle and upper schools, but it occurred to me that the methods she and Gibson had developed could probably be used just as effectively in teaching adults, who at the beginning of their studies are as likely as teenagers to find themselves more bothered and bewildered than bewitched by Shakespeare's luxuriant imagery. I'd have to buy a copy of the book before leaving.

Richard had asked me to stop by his office as soon as my meeting with Janet was over. When I arrived, Georgianna was there, and we went downstairs to the tea room for the daily thirty-minute tea ritual. The room was half-filled, the atmosphere quietly congenial, no raucous laughter, no vehement discussions. Observing the vows of silence or whispers during the day, readers probably considered anything above a soft conversational tone a breach of etiquette. Richard pointed out Peter Blayney, Mr. First Folio himself, seated at a nearby table with several others. Bald, with a fringe of white hair, and middle-aged, wearing a short-sleeve white sport shirt and dark slacks, he had the abstracted mien of someone lost in contemplating the urgencies of a century long past, while pretending to listen to what his table companions were saying.

Richard told me that a reader's card would be waiting for me the next morning at the visitor's desk and that he'd arranged for the Whitman article and a commentary on an exhibition titled "Shakespeare in the Worlds of Communism," put together in 1996 by Carol Brobeck, the fellowships coordinator, to be at the circulation desk. He and Georgianna then let me in on a significant discovery recently made at the Folger. A variorum editor for *Hamlet* had spotted in an otherwise undistinguished edition of Shakespeare's works bought by Henry and Emily Folger in 1912 penciled annotations that heretofore had been attributed tenuously to Thomas Carlyle. The quality of these notes prompted the editor to bring the volume to the attention of two fellow scholars, one of whom confirmed that the annotator was none other than George Eliot, and that additional notes had been written by George Henry Lewes, the celebrated man of letters who had lived with the novelist from 1854 until his death in 1878 (his inability to divorce his wife had made it impossible for him to marry his paramour). Sensing what I was about to ask, Richard quickly added, "It won't be possible for you to see this edition while you're here. Maybe at a later time." So I would have to make do with Whitman.

On the subject of *Hamlet,* Richard asked me if I was familiar with Stephen Dedalus's ingenious fantasia about Shakespeare and Hamlet and Hamlet's father in the library episode in *Ulysses.* I'd read *Ulysses* but hadn't the faintest recollection of this episode. Richard, as it turned out, had studied Joyce and Yeats in a postgrad program at Trinity College in Dublin. "You should go back and take another look at it," Richard urged. "Dedalus claims that Shakespeare was not Hamlet but Hamlet's father, which is strange, since Dedalus resembles Hamlet and thinks of himself as Shakespeare. But to appreciate the richness of Joyce's thinking about Shakespeare as a creative force, part of a Trinity—God, Shakespeare, Dedalus—you'll have to reread that episode and you should, now that you're so involved in things Shakespearean." As one who'd been mulling the godlike qualities of Shakespeare, I needed no convincing, and I made a mental note to crack open my copy of *Ulysses* again (or at least Stuart Gilbert's classic exegesis) in the near future and try to figure out exactly what Joyce was getting at. But for now, my heart belonged to Walt Whitman, and I was eager to read what he had to say about the history plays.

The next morning I got my reader's card from the guard at the security desk and proceeded to the portals of the reading room. I felt like the reporter in *Citizen Kane* about to enter the hallowed, hushed Kane Memorial Library in search of a solution to the mystery of "Rosebud." Andrew, the sober young man in attendance at the registrar's desk, examined my card, good for the day only—I was the shortest of the Short Term Fellows—and asked me to sign in. Thence into the sanctum, where two people were already at solemn labor, one of them Peter Blayney, sitting erect at one of the tables, taking notes in what was surely a meticulous script. I went to the circulation desk and whispered my name to the fragile young Indian woman who responded in an even lower, virtually inaudible whisper. Perhaps she's made no sound at all, I thought, and I'm required to read her lips. When I asked her to repeat what she'd said, she smiled painfully and without uttering a word handed over the goodies that Richard had left for me.

I took my seat at a table, Fellow for a Day. I felt somewhat the impostor, the role player, as I settled in, adjusting the lamp, taking off my jacket and unbuttoning my collar as if raring to come to grips with some whip-ass scholarship. Surely someone was bound to find me out, smell my rank presumptuousness, recognizing a layman posturing as a priest. Like Aaron's sons, I'd brought unholy fire into the temple and would pay the awful price. Any moment I would be accosted by Mr. Blayney, or by the grim matron seated a table away in front of a pile of what I imagined to be sixteenth-century arcana involving the prevalence of moon-goddess symbols in Elizabethan drama, and asked to show my credentials. The little tan reader's card would not suffice, I feared.

To hell with them, I thought, with a surge of bravado. Why should I feel insecure? I should be relishing my privileged status, no matter how short-lived. I should savor these hours in the cloister to the fullest. Any longer than a day in the reading room and I might have started to have visions, or long for the company of hard hats grousing about the Jets at a neighborhood bar in Queens. So I relaxed into the seductive spell of intellectual solitude, academic isolation. I was beginning to feel the role, not affect it; I'd started to take on the character of a tenured professor, indeed a Long Term Fellow. In acting, the mise-en-scène—set, props, costumes—can do as much, if not more, to generate truth in characterization as any amount of psychological exploration.

I withdrew my legal-size yellow pad from the folder I'd brought and opened the Whitman file. The manuscript, protected by some sort of glassine wrappers and written in longhand with a pen, bore Whitman's instructions to the printer. Accompanying it was a typed version, although I found the handwriting quite legible. A note on the transcript revealed that the manuscript comes from the collection of G. W. Gilder, editor of the *Critic,* which published the essay in 1884, and adds that in this piece Whitman suggests an interpretation of Shakespeare's plays never before advanced. In the historical dramas, which he considers Shakespeare's masterpieces, he found "the inauguration of modern democracy." I read the manuscript, then copied what I considered the crucial parts on my yellow pad, occasionally glancing up to see if Mr. Blayney and the stern-visaged scholaress were impressed by my relentless professionalism. They pretended not to notice me.

Here's what I extracted from Whitman:

What lurks behind Shakespeare's historical plays? We all know how much mythos there is in the Shakespeare Question as it stands today. Beneath a few foundations of proved facts are certainly engulfed far more dim and elusive ones, of deepest importance—tantalizing and half-suspected—suffering explanations that one dare not put in plain statements. But coming at once to the point, the English historical plays are to me the most eminent as literary and dramatic performances (my maturest judgement confirming the impressions of my early years, that the distinctiveness and glory of the Poet reside not in his vaunted dramas of the passions . . . but those founded on the contests of English dynasties and the French wars) and form, as we get it all, the chief in a complexity of puzzles conceived out of the fullest heat and pulse of European feudalism—personifying in unparalleled ways the medieval aristocracy, its towering spirit of ruthless and gigantic caste, with its own peculiar air and arrogance—only one of the "wolfish earls so plenteous" in the plays themselves, or some born descendant and knower might seem to be the true author of these amazing works—works in some respects greater than anything else recorded in literature [was Whitman, I noted, suggesting that someone such as Bacon had written the plays?] . . . for it is impossible to grasp the whole cluster of those plays, however wide the intervals, and different circumstances of their composition, without thinking of them as, in a free sense, the result of an essentially controlling plan. What was that plan? Or rather, what was veiled behind it? For to me there was certainly something so veiled.

Whitman then credits his friend William O'Connor with inspiring this interpretation by saying that Shakespeare couldn't have been trying to promote a love for feudalism, since the atmosphere of the plays is one of barbarous and tumultuous gloom. And Whitman continues with his theory:

The summary of my suggestions would be, therefore, that . . . it is possible a future age of criticism, diving deeper, mapping the land and the lines freer, completer than hitherto, may discover in the plays named the scientific (Baconian?) [aha, I jotted down, this seems to be more than a hint of the "true" author of the plays] inauguration of modern democracy—furnishing realistic and first-class artistic portraitures of the medieval world . . . and may penetrate to that hard pan, far down and back of the ostent of today, on which (and on which only) the progression of the last 2 centuries has built this democracy which now holds secure lodgement over the whole civilized world.

A bit convoluted, almost in the Jamesian mode, with all those parenthetical qualifiers, but old Walt might have been onto something, I thought, even if he was straining to discern a democratic vista in the Man from Stratford's perspective. I put away my pad and pencil, repacked the manuscript in its protective case, and for a few brief moments actually convinced myself that I'd made a discovery that would astonish the Halls of Academe all over the world. I was the one who'd dredged up from obscurity the key that would unlock the mystery of a vital part of the canon. I would be the lone member of that future age of criticism envisioned as a possibility by Whitman. I would be the one to dive deeper, map the land and the lines freer. For the first time I appreciated just how it might feel to uncover an earthshaking cultural relic. I was tempted to rush over and pat old Blayney on the back and exclaim, "Look what I've found, Pete! And you think those First Folios are a big goddamned deal!" But the moment passed, the fantasy ended, the role playing was over. I was content to have been guided by Richard to this unorthodox and, as far as I could tell, almost unknown exegesis of Shakespeare's histories by our American bardic giant. When I got back home, I'd check the Kaplan and Loving biographies and see if they came to grips with this essay.

I then turned to the material from Carol Brobeck's exhibition, "Shakespeare in the Worlds of Communism." Two items enticed me. First, it seems that Karl Marx cited Shakespeare as one of his favorite authors and quoted *Timon of Athens* when describing the merciless power of money, further proof to my mind that this play is moralizing rant. Second, in the East German director Heiner Muller's adaptation of *Macbeth,* the protagonist's ambitions result in the onstage slaughter of peasants who, of course, are not in Shakespeare's text. To a Marxist, I supposed, you can't be truly evil simply by knocking off a few kings and thanes; you have to wipe out a herd of serfs.

Thinking about *Macbeth* as I sat in a building that on first sight yesterday had brought to mind visions of Herod's temple, I found myself making a connection between Macbeth and Herod, two complex, contradictory, power-mad rulers, valiant warriors, violent men whose ambitions drove them to barbarous acts. Herod seems tailor-made as the subject of a Shakespearean tragedy. Born to Idumaean Arabs and forced to convert to Judaism by Hasmonaean conquerors, he became Herod the Great, King of the Jews, a towering figure, a friend or enemy of Antony, of Cleopatra, of Augustus, a psychological enigma, a loving husband and father capable of executing wife and sons who were proved conspirators, a divided man, good warring with evil inside his soul, a much-maligned historical figure, a character well deserving of Shakespearean ambiguity and irony. Now, that would be a find: the foul papers of *Herod,* a tragedy by W. Shakespeare, stored all these centuries in a trunk recently exhumed from a site uncovered during the construction of an office complex in Southwark.

I could have lingered much longer over such reveries in the reading room, basking in its reverential serenity, its aura of eternal wisdom, and the comforting presence of the remains of the Folgers, but it was one o'clock and I had an afternoon train to catch. So I returned the material to the circulation desk, picked up my exit card, which certifies you have been on the premises legally and without which you cannot leave the room, and handed it to Andrew as I signed out. I said my good-byes to Richard and Georgianna, vowed to send them my ten-volume study on the democratic meaning of Shakespeare's history plays, bought copies of *Discovering Shakespeare's Language* and *Shakespeare Set Free: Teaching "Twelfth Night," "Othello,"* and prepared to leave the building.

The enchantment had ended. Once again I was an unaccommodated man, a mere mortal, shorn of privileges. I didn't want to go. I remembered a time, back in the fifties, when I'd returned to Texas A&M to pick up a couple of letters of recommendation from former professors to accompany my application to the Pasadena Playhouse. One of these professors was Tom Mayo, a Rhodes Scholar before arriving at Aggieland, where he'd become librarian, English professor, and ultimately chairman of the department. He had a wizardlike, owlish aspect, chain-smoked Lucky Strikes, and loved movies (in fact, he died of a heart attack in a movie theatre that was probably showing a western, his favorite genre). He was appalled by my decision to pursue a career in drama. "You can't do that, young sprout. You're a scholar." His declaration shocked me. Yes, I'd been an English major and excelled academically, but I'd never intended to pursue graduate studies. As I left the Folger, I began to wonder about that road not taken. And I realized that Dr. Mayo was wrong. I had not been cut out for a scholarly career. My ambitions, my capacities, had led me down other roads until I was fortunate enough to be directed to the right one. My reluctance to leave the Folger had nothing to do with fantasies of a life that could have been, and everything to do with the tantalizing and all-too-brief experience of the pursuit of scholarship in ideal surroundings. That was heady stuff. It could spoil a fellow.

Part Two

To Oxford
and Back

12.

In the latter part of June 1999, I found myself touchy, melancholic, edgy, even panicky. And for good reason: a dream I'd long harbored was about to come true. I was about to leave for Oxford.

For years I'd been tantalized by the Oxford/Berkeley Program, which offers three-week courses in a variety of the liberal arts. Oxford had been for me the symbol of the ideal classic education; lacking an Oxford degree, I'd felt intellectually and culturally underprivileged, and envious in particular of Rhodes Scholars such as Willie Morris. Attending Oxford in the summer would be the academic equivalent of those baseball fantasy camps at which the American male gets a chance to take the field with bona fide pros and pretend he's a major leaguer. It would also provide yet another opportunity for pursuing scholarship in ideal surroundings—I *had* been spoiled—and enlarging my understanding of Shakespeare. I enrolled in the course in Shakespearean tragedies, beginning in late June. Given my desire to brush up on the comedies, I'd have preferred the course in that genre, but it fell in the next session, starting in early August, and that created a domestic problem. Barbara was eager to sign up for the course on Roman Britain, allegedly to enhance her capabilities as a Latin teacher, but actually to make certain I behaved myself, and it was available only in the first session. So for the sake of marital harmony I made the great sacrifice, and my suitemate at Worcester College, Oxford, would be Barbara Gollob. I could do worse.

Several weeks previously the orientation brochure arrived, pregnant with information about the course, about preparations for going to Oxford and living and studying there. Exhilarating stuff to me, generating anticipatory thrills, an excited impatience to begin the adventure. At first.

Then, inevitably, the weeds of anxiety began to sprout in the enchanted garden of my imagination. I was going to be a student again. In fact, a freshman at a centuries-old citadel of learning. One of our species' recurring nightmares is finding ourselves back in college, uncertain where or how to register, fumbling around for directions to the dorm, wondering why we were so foolish ever to have longed so desperately to leave the security of home and confront the hazards of the unknown. I was about to find myself in a group where the achievements of a career were meaningless; all of us were starting from scratch, and would be defined only by the intelligence and wisdom and humanity and humor with which we responded—in seminar discussions, in a written essay and an oral presentation (both were required)—to the works we'd be studying. The compulsion to prove myself in competition, to excel, began to dominate my thoughts. Or, to put it less aggressively and more insecurely, I was determined to make certain I didn't wind up the class idiot. So for the past few weeks I'd been cramming. The brochure recommended that we read the Oxford editions (naturally) of *Macbeth, Hamlet, King Lear,* and *Antony and Cleopatra.* Likewise, Andrew Gurr's *The Shakespearean Stage* and Michael Mangan's *A Preface to Shakespeare's Tragedies.* I owned the Oxfords and the Gurr, and, always the one to do as authorities instructed, I added the Mangan to my library. Reading through the latter, one of the things I learned and that I'd failed to discover in the analyses of my favorite scholars and critics was that act 1, scene 2, which is initially dominated by Claudius, "both announces and enacts one of the major themes not only of *Hamlet* but of all the major tragedies: the point at which public and private identities interact. . . . These twin themes of the tensions and contradictions within the court, and the relationship between public and private identities are given an emblematic stage presence in the figure of Hamlet himself. . . . He has . . . split himself into two parts: there is the outer self, for public consumption . . . and some deeply subjective area of his character which is not for public consumption at all."

Gorging on Mangan, rereading the tragedies, and poring over the introductions were not enough to allay my fear of failure, my dread of not performing with distinction. The specter of The Paper had begun to obsess me. Should I pick a subject now and get a head start? Or would the tutor assign a topic, thus rendering these feverish preparations futile? My tutor, the brochure revealed, would be Emma Smith, M.A., D.Phil., Fellow of Hertford College and Lecturer in English Literature at the University of Oxford.

I realized I'd have access to the Bodleian Library, which has been one of the world's premier scholarly institutions for more than four hundred years, but what if the books I needed were not available when I required them or would take too long to retrieve? I needed backup. Off I rushed to Mail Box, madly xeroxing pages from Maynard Mack and Samuel Schoenbaum and Caroline Spurgeon and Helen Luke, and from more recently perused volumes—Charles Nicholls's *Chemical Theatre,* a study of the alchemical patterns in *King Lear;* Robert Speaight's *Shakespeare: The Man and His Achievement* (Speaight had been an actor with the Old Vic); C. S. Lewis's *Reflections on the Psalms*—and essays by Hazlitt, Dr. Johnson, and Lionel Trilling.

I'd been mulling the idea of trying to develop a paper by amplifying, elaborating on, and enriching the notes I'd made for my LLI lecture about the Judaic, or Hebraic, nature of *King Lear.* But perhaps I wouldn't write a paper at all. I'd relax, join in class discussions, disgorge a little pedantry on my classmates, soak up the wisdom of Emma Smith, and glide through the three weeks as a carefree dilettante, with an Elderhostler's merry I'm-getting-culture-through-osmosis smile on my face. What could the college officials do to me? Write my parents? I'd hit the pubs vigorously and go on long serene walks with Barbara, who, need I add, was not plagued with the doubts that beset me. For her, the unknown holds no terrors. Quite the contrary, her curiosity about life makes her crave the unexpected and the unpredictable. That's what I like about her. That's also what I don't like about her. I am not one of those Spontaneous Me, Whitmanesque types decried by William Strunk and E. B. White in *The Elements of Style.* I do not loaf and invite my soul. I'm the stereotypical Control Freak. It's one of the qualities that, I think, made me a good editor. The manuscript of an out-of-control writer is not a pretty thing to behold: sloppy, confused, slapdash, disjointed. Out of this chaos the editor must bring order—structure, organization, coherence. So there are times when being "into control" is not only permissible but essential. But it definitely threatened to defeat the vital purposes of the trip, which were to participate in the rigors and enjoy the rewards of an Oxford education, to undergo what the program described as a "brief, but serious, encounter with the Oxford method of teaching—the result of centuries-old traditions that make it one of the greatest universities in the world," to open myself to new ways of thinking about Shakespeare and new approaches to making his work come to life for students. I might find it difficult to loaf, but I'd damned well be prepared to invite my soul.

Two weeks before leaving I received my class roster. Nine of us were enrolled in the course—seven women, two men. Did that ratio, plus the female tutor, foretell an emphasis on gender issues, a study of Ophelia and Cordelia as victims of male hegemony?

At last came the time for departure. I'd intended to bring along Michael Mangan's book on Shakespeare's tragedies for last-minute cramming to nourish me through the first hours of the course. But Barbara suggested that might be overkill, and I opted instead for escapism. After we'd settled into our seats, I checked the British Air magazine for the movie listing. The news was not good. Ominously, the film on our flight to London was *Shakespeare in Love.*

The two people I was aware of in the English-speaking world who had proved immune to the charms of this production when it was released the previous winter were myself and a former publishing colleague, Jackie Everly, a hugely talented and funny marketing executive. Both of us considered the movie's romance tiresome (Gywneth Paltrow vapid as ever), its backstage comedy arch. What truly irked me was that for all the surface authenticity of the period detail, the essentials were dead wrong, because the authors of the script, Tom Stoppard and Marc Norman, too often tried to be Mel Brooks and Woody Allen, stooping to heavy-handed burlesque and coy anachronisms to draw the 'twas-ever-thus parallels between showbiz then and now. Shakespeare borrowed the story of *Romeo and Juliet* from a poem by Arthur Brooke, *The Tragical History of Romeus and Juliet,* but Norman and Stoppard thought it was hilarious to have young Will laboring away at a story handed to him by the entrepreneur Philip Henslowe—*Romeo and Ethel, the Pirate's Daughter.* Later, to get across the fact that theatre was, and always will be, a collaborative venture, Norman and Stoppard had an oh-so-cute little scene in which the rival young playwrights, Shakespeare and Marlowe, encounter one another in a tavern, and Marlowe gives Shakespeare some ideas for what actually winds up in *R&J* (e.g., Mercutio). And the most annoying conceit of all: Norman and Stoppard would have us believe, as the story unfolded, that *R&J* was autobiographical, based on Shakespeare's own ill-fated romance with a wealthy young woman affianced to a cruel Tybalt-like aristocrat, and that the newfound depth in his work (the hack script now abandoned) could be traced to the pain of this episode. Another phony touch was the characterization of Henslowe. In reality a shrewd, pragmatic raffish sort, a dyer by profession, also a slum landlord, pawnbroker, and brothel keeper, who, as described by Russell A. Fraser in *Young Shakespeare,* had "a skin like a rhino's," he was merely a caricature in the hands of Norman and Stoppard and Geoffrey Rush, who portrayed him, a buffoon wide-eyed with fear and desperation as he tried to elude his creditor, Mr. Pennyman, a ruthless moneybags whose character was actually more in keeping with that of the real-life Henslowe. ("How can I pay my actors?" Henslowe asks Pennyman. "Give them a share of the profits." "But there will be no profits." "Exactly," says Pennyman. And we, the audience, are supposed to get a bang out of this reference to the way movie studios pad their overhead to make profit sharing academic.) And another arch touch: Shakespeare visiting a psychiatrist to help cure his writer's block. I hated the goddamned thing. But perhaps I'm just an old stick-in-the-mud: around me on Flight 184, passengers, many, I assumed, watching it for at least the second time (Barbara included), were laughing and crying, leaving me to nurse some vague misgivings that my failure to savor this phenomenally successful movie might be a symptom of some calcification of the sensibilities.

At Heathrow, we boarded a bus to Oxford and were off to the city of dreams. It was drizzling when we pulled into town, and the driver let us off a block from the hotel, the Eastgate, across the street from Merton College. Registration at Worcester College would be on Monday afternoon at two, but we'd decided to arrive a day earlier to allow time for jet-lag recovery and a civilized unhurried transition to the medieval world. As we registered at the hotel, a middle-aged American approached the desk clerk and asked, "Where's the pub where Inspector Morse drinks?" Once we were unpacked, we ambled down (or up?) the High, past Magdalen College, and over the bridge, rhapsodizing over the exalted cathedral/castle aspect of the milieu, the towers, turrets, spires, the parks and gardens, the flowerpots hanging from streetlamps. The day before had been the completion of exam week at Oxford, and we passed clusters of students still attired in their college gowns. For a moment, I envied them the privilege they'd enjoyed of being a part of this rarefied culture, and their youth, but what the hell, I was about to become Herm, a Yank (or Reb, or Rebbe) at Oxford, and who knew where that might lead? I might have been finishing my sixth decade, but luckily, I hadn't yet grown up. At Magdalen Bridge, I stood and gazed into the Thames, trying to picture Samuel Johnson standing here in 1729, wondering how long he could remain at Oxford. I knew he'd been at Pembroke College, but surely he wandered here occasionally. And I thought of Thomas Hardy's Jude, the stonemason whose consuming ambition to enter Oxford was thwarted by poverty and the indifference of college authorities. Back in our post–Korean War days in Houston, Barthelme and I would occasionally razz each other with literary monikers alluding to our little weaknesses and frustrations: aware of my quixotic notions about an Oxford education, he tabbed me Jude the Obscure Jew; zeroing in on his aloofness, his tendency to say I Prefer Not To, I labeled him Bartleby the Scrivener. We were a couple of bright boys, yes we were.

Monday afternoon we took a cab to Worcester College, most of which is walled off, not visible from Worcester Street. What we saw through an iron gate was an eighteenth-century dark gray limestone two-and-a-half-story building of classical design. We walked a few feet up the sidewalk to a covered archway, where several women were milling about while porters were loading baggage onto carriers. To our right was the Porter's Lodge, repository of room keys, mailboxes, bulletin boards. A cheery, brisk, bespectacled youth named Paul, who turned out to be one of the three "deans"—young social and administrative assistants in charge of shepherding the flock of students from the moment of arrival to the hour of departure—directed us to the porter's desk, where the attendant handed us our room keys and a key to the gate, which is locked at night, and diagrammed for us on a map of the college the way to our residence hall, Linbury. We emerged from the lodge and to our right came upon a colonnaded terrace called the Cloisters, overlooking the Main Quad, a breathtaking expanse of green more dazzling than the field at Boston's Fenway Park. To the left was a row of cottages built in the thirteenth century by various monasteries of the Benedictine Order. This row became an Oxford college in 1714. In 1789, a building of classical design was constructed on the opposite side of the main quadrangle, and at its far end were the imposing Provost's Lodgings. Running the length of each building was a luxuriant flower bed in full polychromatic blossom. Beyond the Quad were hedges that screened the Provost's Garden, and beyond that were trees shading playing fields, more gardens, and a lake.

Beguiled by the surroundings, Barbara and I felt more like gawking, gleeful sightseers than anxious students as we went down a flight of stairs leading from the Cloisters to the Quad, walked to our left through a stone archway topped by a red lion's head, and proceeded to Linbury, a fairly modern dormitory built around the late 1970s and set in the midst of gravel paths winding through the garden. We had spacious quarters, twin beds, a pair of comfortable old armchairs, two desks, two swivel fluorescent lamps, quirkily positioned so that only one of them illuminated a desk and an armchair, the other attached to the wall over one of the twin beds. The large bathroom had only a tub, no shower.

We checked in for tea at the junior common room, located in that row of thirteenth-century buildings, and were handed orientation folders crammed with an assortment of visitor's guides to Oxford, maps, information on libraries (notably the Bodleian) and on living in Oxford and on the archaeology and history of Oxford. As I read through the material, trying to get my bearings, I was suddenly beset by a sense of uneasiness; soon I was swarmed by an overpowering melancholia. Good God, it couldn't be: I was homesick! I'd regressed. I was a freshman again, alone and afraid in a world I never made. I didn't know the drill. I was lost. This was Oxford, its medieval spell irresistible, its very air electrically charged with the accumulated cerebrations of five centuries of scholarship, and I was about to immerse myself, if only briefly, in this heady atmosphere. Yet I found myself feeling as forlorn and displaced as I had more than fifty years ago when I first glimpsed what was to be my home for my first year at Texas A&M—the black tar-paper shacks of what had been, during World War II, Bryan Army Air Field, and what was now called the A&M Annex. This was to be home to the Class of 1951, isolated several miles from the main campus to protect us from the depradations of upperclassmen whose overzealous hazing of freshmen the previous year had forced a huge percentage of students to drop out, thus creating a statewide scandal. Ensconced in an overstuffed sofa in the junior common room, sipping coffee and devouring chocolate cookies, I was no happier than I'd been one rainy evening in 1947, clad in olive-drab fatigues, hair cut close to the scalp, hunched over a table in the mess hall as I tried to gag down a mysterious chunk of meat which one of my roommates described as "something cut out of the crotch of a billy goat that died of clap."

At seven-fifteen, we had dinner in Hall. Dinner was a formal meal. Students were asked to be punctual. Men were requested to wear a jacket and tie, women a dress, suit, skirt, and blouse, or pantsuit. Hall was imposing—windows rising from midwall to the high ceiling, portraits of former Worcester luminaries along one wall, two long rows of tables stretching to High Table, which ran along the width of the rear wall and literally was raised several inches from the floor. Members of the staff dined at High Table, and we'd been informed that each evening they would invite a few students to join them and to have sherry with them in one of the college sitting rooms beforehand. At some time during the three weeks, each of us would receive such an invitation. The pre-dining ritual our first night, as it would be every night: once the students had gathered in Hall, the doors were closed; we all stood for a few moments until someone knocked on the doors; they were opened, and in filed the staff, who proceeded to High Table; the person who was to recite the benediction pounded the gavel, gave the blessing in Latin, and we took our seats. At dinner, we were served by waiters and waitresses. (Lunch and breakfast were informal self-service affairs.)

My spirits began to lift, and spirits had something to do with my mood change—the wine, complimentary that night, flowed freely. Seated next to me was a sprightly, voluble retiree from Los Angeles who had owned a company that represented the manufacturers of executive gifts. He was taking a course in philosophy. His wife, who was just as lively, would be studying modern art. Looking around the room, I noticed that the enrollment was not exclusively geriatric; at least a dozen young people, mostly female, were among us, university students from the States taking courses for college credit. After dinner, coffee and tea were served in the Cloisters, the colonnaded terrace, and next we adjourned to our respective classrooms to meet our tutors.

My class was in the sitting room of a residential suite three flights up an ancient wooden staircase in the eighteenth-century building opposite the row of monks' cottages. The room contained a breakfront, a fireplace, two relatively comfortable armchairs, and an assortment of uninviting table chairs. I was the last to arrive. My classmates were Don, fortyish, medium height, dark-haired and swarthy, his brown eyes glinting with humor and affability; Marie, probably in her mid-seventies, thin, with a severe narrow face, thin lips, and shrewd blue eyes behind wire-rimmed glasses, her black hair pulled back in a knot; Gillian, early sixties, short gray hair, pug-nosed, exuding an air of confidence and directness; Maury, at least seventy, brown-haired, deep circles under her hazel eyes, which seemed to signal earnestness; Lou Ann, late forties, large, robust, a headful of long blond curls; May, late seventies, with heavy, masculine, George Eliot features, long dark gray hair reaching almost to her waist and pale blue eyes magnified by thick glasses; Kate, late fifties, attractive, short brown hair, slender figure, the image of a suburban wife and mother; and Sally, the youngest, late twenties, blond and fragile.

Emma Smith, the tutor, was an ample, fresh-faced young woman with straight brown hair that reached midneck. She went around the room asking us how we'd like to be called. Then she repeated our names, correctly—nice little memory there. She distributed a Draft Programme of the course: FIRST WEEK: What Is Tragedy? Introduction to Elizabethan Theatre. Shakespeare's Life and Works. *Hamlet*—plot, themes, characters. *King Lear, Macbeth, Antony and Cleopatra,* ditto. SECOND WEEK: Tragic Structure, Beginnings—*Macbeth* and *Hamlet.* Endings—*King Lear* and *A&C.* Public vs. Private—the Politics of Tragedy. Individual tutorial meetings if required. Shakespeare's Use of His Sources in *Hamlet* and *King Lear.* Double Trouble—Shakespeare's Love Tragedies, *A&C.* Witchcraft and Belief—*Macbeth.* Gender in the Tragedies. THIRD WEEK: Clash of the Titans: *Hamlet* vs. *Lear.* Individual presentations.

Then came the inevitable question, posed by Maury but expressing a group uneasiness: how long does our paper have to be? All of us were grown-ups, most of us had been involved, or were still involved, in careers that had required no little amount of writing, and yet there, in a classroom situation, each of us had become that ageless entity, The Student, fraught with fear and trembling over the dread prospect of THE

205

PAPER! Emma, benign and patient, had her ready response: "As long as you wish—three pages, ten pages, whatever it takes to get over your ideas." She then explained that the Programme was indeed a "Draft," which could be modified to suit our needs. If we were bored with one topic, we could move to another; we could raise subjects for discussion not on the sheet, explore other areas. Our individual oral presentations could relate to our essay or not, as we chose. Emma would suggest a range of topics, from which we could select one that struck our fancy, or, after consultation with her, pick our own topic. You could have cut with a knife the thick sense of relief that began to pervade the room, but I had misgivings. My temperament was authoritarian. I preferred a structured format in which a charismatic lecturer dispensed knowledge and wisdom. I liked the Draft Programme just fine. I didn't want it altered to suit the whims of consensus.

On that note, we adjourned to Linbury Building, adjacent to the dorm where Barbara and I were quartered, for a get-acquainted wine-and-champagne reception. Don and I walked over together, and on the way I learned that he was a former policeman and attorney who currently owned a private school in southern California and was in the midst of a divorce. "I can't wait to start," he said. "I don't know much about Shakespeare. I'm sort of a blank page, and I want to cram it full." For all his experience with the underbelly of life as a police officer and a lawyer, he radiated an innocence, a goodness actually, that was infectious. In the Linbury, we spotted Lou Ann gabbing away with Kate, and we joined them. A few glasses of champagne later I had a dossier on the two women. Lou Ann, divorced with a couple of grown children, was a community college teacher in Alabama; Kate, a Chicagoan, had indeed led the kind of domestic life I'd imagined for her for thirty-five years, until her husband, a successful cardiologist, left her for a much younger woman. And from Lou Ann I got the dope on Maury, who'd sat across the table from her at dinner. "She's a widow from Philadelphia, and not what you'd call a welfare case. Very hoity-toity, a culture vulture. Symphony subscription, many, many trips to New York to see operas and ballets and plays. She can't wait to share ideas with such a diverse group. She made 'diverse' sound like a low rung on the social scale. Maybe I can persuade her to write my paper for me."

Finally, I excused myself to go in search of Barbara, who I assumed was mingling with her Roman Britain group, but she was nowhere in sight. I found her back in our room, just getting into bed. "I'd have let you know I was leaving, but you seemed deep into the getting-acquainted mode, and I didn't want to tear you away." Barbara had found a soulmate in her class, an unmarried woman in her early sixties who taught high school Latin and English in Oregon and had been coming to Worcester for the past twelve years. When I told her about my conversation with Don and Kate and Lou Ann, she said, "Do you realize that almost everyone here is divorced, widowed, or single? Underneath all the glad-hand merriment tonight I could almost hear Sinatra singing 'Only the Lonely.' "

And then it was lights-out for the Gollobs. A big day loomed tomorrow: our enrollment in the Bodleian Library, my class's trip scheduled for the morning, Barbara's in the afternoon.

Tuesday. A chilly fifty degrees and a steady rain falling, an oppression to the soul. My identity crisis was resurgent as I'd regressed again, this time to an even earlier stage of personal development than before. Standing at the Porter's Gate with a forlorn little group which included Don, Kate, and Lou Ann, waiting for our dean, Chara, a serene olive-skinned young woman of Greek descent, to take us to the Bodleian, I felt like the main character in Barthelme's short story "Me and Miss Mandible," who discovers one day that he's back in grade school because he's made such a botch out of his life that now he's required to start from the beginning and see if he can get it right this time. Out of my controlled environment I was utterly lost, adrift, despondent. Off we went under our umbrellas, stepping lively to Chara's brisk pace, a procession right out of *Make Way for Ducklings*. After a ten-minute hike we arrived at our destination, which was not, as it turned out, the Bodleian, but a part of the Bodleian system, the Rhodes House Library, several blocks from the central Bodleian site.

We were ushered into a spacious book-lined room and took our seats in rows of folding chairs which faced a long table at which stood a Rhodes House functionary, middle-aged, balding, with a close-cropped sandy gray-flecked beard. He recited a brief history of the Bodleian, which began, he said, as a library room over the University of Oxford's new Divinity School. Over the years the library endowment proved inadequate, and the university found itself without a library until 1598, when along came Sir Thomas Bodley, who had abandoned a distinguished academic career for diplomacy, retired from public life, and decided to devote himself to restoring the old university library. (I thought to myself, this Bodley sounds like old Henry Folger, whose eminent professional career was overshadowed by his obsession for preserving our cultural heritage.) By the mid-seventeenth century, a series of extensions, which included the Old Schools Quadrangle (the schools of the liberal arts), had been completed. And by 1860, space problems had led to the Bodleian's taking over the adjacent Radcliffe Camera, an eighteenth-century building. Later the Bodleian absorbed the Radcliffe Science Library, the Indian Institute Library, and Rhodes House Library, and in 1939, the New Bodleian Library was built, separated from the Old Library by a main road and a quadrangle. And more than four hundred years of history, I thought.

When the lecture was over, we were called up to the table individually, where we were issued our Bodleian reader's cards and were required to read aloud, then sign, a declaration promising to obey all the library rules. This requirement was instituted by Sir Thomas himself when he refounded the library. The oath: "I hereby undertake not to remove from the Library, or to mark, deface or injure in any way, any volume, document, or other object belonging to it or in its custody; not to bring into the Library or kindle therein any fire or flame, and not to smoke in the Library; and I promise to obey all the rules of the Library." This swearing-in ceremony was for me a morale booster. Rules. Regulations. Procedures. Just tell me the drill and I'll hop to it.

Life was beginning to take shape, I was getting my bearings. I was part of a privileged elite, a sacred order of scholars. A Bodleian reader. Fond memories of the Folger reading room surfaced. In the bowels of the Bodleian, would I come across a treasure such as the Whitman essay on Shakespeare's history plays (which, as it turned out, had gone unmentioned by Kaplan and Loving)? A heretofore undiscovered, unexamined note, stuck between the pages of an obscure early-seventeenth-century book of medical advice, from Dick Burbage to Will S., "I think I'll play RIII with a slight lisp. Just a notion. Your thoughts?"

We left the Rhodes, and Don, Sally, and I wandered in the rain to

Cornmarket Street, one of the tackier areas of Oxford, a pedestrian mall with the standard emblems of urban blight—McDonald's, Kentucky Fried Chicken, discount shops. Along the way, Sally told me she was from Michigan and was preparing to go to New York to study fashion design. "Who knows, maybe someday I'll design costumes for a Shakespearean production," she laughed. At W. H. Smith's, we bought school supplies— paper, ballpoints, notebooks—and readied ourselves for our first full class in the afternoon.

At the start, Emma handed out a sheet with definitions of tragedy from the Renaissance and asked us for comments. The strongest reactions were provoked by Sir Philip Sidney's definition: "Tragedy, that openeth the greatest wounds and showeth forth the ulcers that are covered with tissue . . . ; that, with stirring the effects of admiration and commiseration, teacheth the uncertainty of this world and upon what weak foundations gilden roofs are builded." Marie commented that Sidney's remark about ulcers covered by tissue showed a concern with the question of appearance versus reality. A retired insurance claims investigator from the San Francisco Bay area, Marie was all too aware of how appearance often belied reality. Kate picked up on Sidney's idea that tragedy underlines life's uncertainty. "Yes," I said, "and that's what Ophelia means in one of my favorite lines from Shakespeare, 'We know what we are, but know not what we may be.'"

Wednesday. Sunny, balmy, a perfect spring day in late June. Emma devoted the morning session to an introduction to the Elizabethan theatre. She first discussed a development that brought changes to the theatre— the Act of Vagabondage, 1572. Respectable people feared the rise of the underclass, beggars, criminals, "masterless men." From now on, actors would be considered the latter unless they acquired a patron. The lord mayor of London and the aldermen to the Privy Council, puritanically opposed to the theatre, urged the suppression of stage plays at which "masterless men . . . and thieves, horse-stealers, whoremongers . . . contrivers of treason . . . were known to come together and to recreate themselves." Then she filled us in on the Burbages—James, the former actor and carpenter who built the first theatre, called the Theatre, and his son Richard, the most famous actor of his day—and such items as the Elizabethan concept of *theatrum mundi,* "all the world's a stage." End of morning session, and to me it hadn't been particularly satisfying. Too sketchy, fragmentary, nothing about the companies, the players, the staging. True, I'd read Gurr and Mangan, but at least Emma could have distilled this material, recapped it. And why hadn't she taken us through Shakespeare's life, his education, his father's ambitions and reversals, which may have fueled his own yearning for fame, fortune, and status? Emma's approach was casual, almost offhand. Obviously, she knew the subject in depth, she was articulate and clever and amusing, but she definitely was not in The Lecturer mold, if the morning had been any example. She didn't seem inclined to stand before us and give us the benefit of her vast erudition, except ad hoc. Whereas I, from the Old Fart School, in my introductory class at the LLI, had devoted two full hours to Shakespeare's life and career, to the thought of the Elizabethan era, to the plays and the players and playhouses and theatrical conventions of the time, and had even screened the first five minutes of the video of Olivier's *Henry V,* which showed the play as it was being performed at the Globe.

I'd told none of my classmates or Emma that I lectured on Shakespeare at the LLI. It was my dirty little secret. I wanted to avoid even the faintest chance of seeming like some kind of tin-pot expert, presuming to be an authority on a subject I'd only recently begun to explore in any depth, or perhaps even worse, embarrassing myself by a display of ignorance which would draw expressions of amused contempt. And I didn't want Emma to look at me and see a Pompous Old Fart second-guessing her classroom technique. Which is exactly what I, a Pompous Old Fart, was doing.

In the afternoon, Emma showed a videotape of the opening moments of Olivier's 1948 movie version of *Hamlet,* with his ridiculous, oversimplified voice-over summing up the "theme": "This is the story of a man who could not make up his mind." You might imagine that would have put off an audience: who wants to see a flick about an indecisive Dane? What's tragic about indecision? But the movie was a box-office smash, the cultural event of the year. Emma reminded us that Olivier cut about 40 percent of the play—for example, Rosencrantz and Guildenstern are gone, ditto Fortinbras. Then she asked us what we thought *Hamlet* was about. Me: coming of age, end of innocence, change. The others: idealism, justice, revenge, judgment, betrayal, intrigue, vacillation, family, recklessness, appearance vs. reality. Following this was the kind of freewheeling, disconnected bull session that had become routine to this class. Finally, Emma broke away to screen Olivier's soliloquy "Oh that this too too solid flesh." It was done voice-over, Olivier's vocal tones and facial expressions projecting a monotonous neurasthenia. Emma followed this with Branagh's version, which seemed to me just right, infinitely more dramatic. Branagh uses his entire body, he paces the room agitatedly, thinking out loud, not in voice-over, displaying a variety of emotions—rage, pain, despair—which up to then he may have been suppressing but which, after the public head-to-head with Claudius and the sight of his mother reveling in her new marriage, he now unleashes. But I was alone in my admiration. Everyone else thought that Branagh was "over the top." What we didn't do was look at the text—read the soliloquy and discover the clues as to how Shakespeare intended the soliloquy to be acted.

But Michael Mangan did, and his analysis bears out Branagh's approach: "The first few lines . . . had been rational, reflective, eloquent. But as it progresses . . . the speech begins to verge on incoherence . . . Hamlet's [subordinate clauses] are simply a series of interruptions, which break up his line of thought and show a mind overwhelmed by ideas which it cannot control . . . his syntax shows itself incapable of organizing his emotions into an orderly passion." Amen.

Before class began on Thursday, I asked Emma to recommend some of her favorite pubs in the area. "Well, you might try Jude the Obscure—several blocks left down Walton Street." Jude the Obscure. If only Barthelme hadn't died before I could tell him about this discovery. I confessed to Emma my passion for Hardy's novel, and how torn I was by the scene in which Jude discovers that his son has killed himself and his siblings to lighten the load on his parents, leaving behind that wrenching suicide note, "Done because we are too menny." Emma said, "I don't know—I really can't stand that novel. And when I get to that scene, I feel the way Oscar Wilde did when he said of *The Old Curiosity Shop*, 'One must have a heart of stone to read the death of Little Nell without laughing.' It's just too much." No sloppy sentimentalist, Miss Emma Smith. Much as I cherish the novel, intensely as I may have disagreed with her, how could I not laugh? Her remark was so effortlessly contrarian, unexpected, un-smart-alecky, I found it endearing.

Our class on *King Lear* began. Right off, Emma asked for comments about her approach thus far. Sally said, "I'd prefer a mixture of lecture and discussions." Marie: "But we get insights from each other." To which Emma responded, "I learned from one of my tutors that someone who's read a poem, or book, or whatever, for the first time, could have insights just as valid as those of a scholar who'd studied the work for decades." Correct. Let's not be literary snobs, I thought to myself. I've always treasured Dr. Johnson's salute to the Common Reader: ". . . for by the common sense of readers, uncorrupted by literary prejudices, after all the refinements of subtilty [*sic*] and the dogmatism of learning, must be finally decided all claim to poetical honours." Still, group discussions generally produce more heat than light, more opinions than insights, and can ramble on incoherently. We were only into the third day, and I could see that happening already. It was one of the pitfalls of the uncontrolled participative method. And Emma's graciousness and courtesy and good humor were not exactly deterrents to the terminally loquacious and those who seemed to be at Worcester for group therapy. I abandoned hope of linear, organized instruction and decided to go with the flow. As hard as that would be for me.

Today Emma identified the sources of *King Lear,* among them Holinshed's *Chronicles,* which, as I'd discovered earlier, gave biblical parallels for the time frame in *Lear.* Then she asked us to read Lear's opening words. We were going to read the text! "Meantime we shall express our darker purpose." Why "darker," Emma asked, instead of "secret"? They're both trochees—strong/weak beat. Is Shakespeare using it ironically, to foreshadow the grim events that lie in store? We voted yes. Ultimately, we got around to Cordelia's truth-telling "Nothing, my Lord" response to Lear's "what can you say to draw / A third more opulent than your sisters?" And I discovered that Emma shares my assessment of Cordelia as something of a self-righteous prig. "Her response," said Emma, "is rational, logical, but impersonal."

Before we broke, Gillian, a retired G.E. product development executive (and also a divorcée with married children) sensitive to issues of stolen ideas, expressed shock at discovering that Shakespeare derived all his plays from other sources, that none of his stories were original, and Emma responded that Shakespeare had to turn to material readily available to satisfy the audience's hunger for fresh material. Don warmed to the subject of Shakespeare's sources; in fact, he seemed avid to the point of obsession, prompting Emma to recommend Geoffrey Bullough's eight-volume *Narrative and Dramatic Sources of Shakespeare,* which was in the Bodleian. After class, Don asked me if I'd dipped into Bullough and I confessed I'd been ignorant of this work until Emma enlightened us. I felt I'd somehow been cheating my students the past three semesters. How could I have overlooked so crucial a reference work? Well, that's what my self-styled sabbatical was all about, filling in the gaps. Don and I arranged to make our initial visit to the Bodleian the next afternoon, our first free period of the week.

But this afternoon, Emma continued with *Macbeth.* Before class, I was relaxing on the steps overlooking the Quad and marveling at its dazzling manicured greenery and riotous bursts of flora, when along came Don to break the mood with a provocative question: "Emma hasn't said anything about that visit to the Globe, has she, the one that's described in our course booklet? Do you think she's made arrangements, or is it a scratch?" I hoped to hell it was still in the works. All this talk about Shakespeare's theatre and we wouldn't get to see it? So right off, Don put the question to Emma, and she blithely replied no, the Globe junket was off. It seemed that last year's trip was a fiasco—terrible seats, bus an hour late leaving London for Oxford, etc. So, no Globe for us. We took the news unhappily but without protest. No one bothered to ask Emma why she assumed the fiasco was destined to be repeated and why, instead of canceling the event, she and/or whoever planned the expedition hadn't decided to take a bit more care in selecting proper seats and a reliable bus company this time around. The readiness is all, don't you know?

In the afternoon, we viewed the opening scenes of two movie versions of *Macbeth.* First, Orson Welles's 1948 movie. Emma pointed out that in the text, the scene in which Duncan learns of Macbeth's valor and Cawdor's treachery precedes the scene in which Macbeth and Banquo come upon the witches and hear the prophecies; the witches tell us what we already know. In Welles's adaptation, Macbeth and Banquo encounter the witches, whom we've first seen plucking a slimy gobbet from a pot and molding it into a sort of midget Macbeth, and hear the prophecies before Ross and Angus and the gang show up and break the news that Macbeth is the new Thane of Cawdor. Welles's transposition of the scene, along with the shaping of the voodoo doll, implies that the witches were shaping events, not simply foretelling them. The second *Macbeth* was the opening scene of Roman Polanski's adaptation. Battle noises sound over credits, and then follows a scene of carnage, Macbeth and Banquo hacking away at the enemy in the last stages of their victorious battle. Emma reflected that this effectively conveys the idea of a bloody society and noted that Macbeth is praised for his butchery, that this is a fierce, brutal culture. Is Duncan a good king, she asked, or are all these warriors violent men? A predictable discussion ensued: was Macbeth a good man destroyed by his vicious mole of nature, ambition, incited to murder by a ruthless domineering bitch of a wife, or was he equally bad, simply using his wife as a sounding board?

One amusing moment: when Maury, ever so sensitive and humane, spoke of the exceptional vileness of Macbeth's ordering the slaughter of Macduff's wife and children, Emma said, "Oh, I don't know, the woman seemed a bit of a shrew," and I picked up on it: "And that little boy was a wiseass—nobody loves a wiseass."

Emma laughed. "Exactly."

I continued, "As Richard III once said, 'So wise, so young, they say, do never live long.' "

Emma parried, "One must have a heart of stone to fail to laugh at this scene." Our private joke.

That night, after dinner, I started to outline in some detail my concept for the paper. I'd decided to develop my ideas of the Judaic, or Hebraic, quality of *King Lear*, which I'd fashioned into the lecture at the LLI. At the time, I'd fixed on the apparent influence on Shakespeare's imagination of the Book of Genesis and the Prophets, and I'd proposed the theory that *King Lear* is an allegory of the evolution of religion from paganism to ethical monotheism. But subsequent reading had broadened my perspective, which I hoped would be enlarged even more by what I might unearth at the Bodleian and the Radcliffe Camera.

In the paper I would challenge—and perhaps refute—what I considered the parochial obtuseness of the scholarly community, which as far as I could tell unanimously agreed that *King Lear*, being devoid of any transcendent Christian ideology, is, as A. C. Bradley asserted in *Shakespearean Tragedy*, resistant to the idea of "any theological interpretation of the world on the author's part." That is, since the tragedy is without *Christian* significance, it has no religious significance at all.

R. A. Foakes, professor emeritus at UCLA and editor of the Arden edition of *King Lear,* is another of these skeptical academicians who dismiss the theological essence of the play. As evidence, first of all he cites the fact that neither quarto nor Folio has an apostrophe after "God" in "God's spies," leaving us to assume that Shakespeare intended the use of the plural "Gods" to signify polytheism. How, then, to account for the capital *G* in both quarto and Folio? Furthermore, "Gods" doesn't make sense in the context of the speech, and it's clumsy, not a quality ordinarily associated with Shakespeare's language. Second, Professor Foakes declares that "the play nowhere else directly refers to the Christian God." In a play featuring blindness as a metaphor, I found ironic Professor Foakes's blindness to the pervasive Jewishness of the tragedy, given away in his speaking thusly of "the Christian God," not "the *Judeo*-Christian God." The irony was heightened by the frequent notes pointing out biblical allusions in the text. In fact, Professor Foakes commits allusion in his comments on Lear's very next speech: to Lear's "bring a brand from heaven and fire hence like foxes," he adds a note, "the word *brand* also recalls the story of Samson punishing the Philistines"; "The good years shall devour them," he explains, "is an echo from Genesis, where Pharaoh dreams of seven good years"; and strikingly, referring to "Upon such sacrifices, my Cordelia, / The gods themselves throw incense," which might indeed make the case for a godless *Lear,* he suggests that "the idea of doing good as a sacrifice may echo Hebrews, 13.16, 'To do good, and to distribute, forget not, for with such sacrifice God is well pleased.' " The clues were right in front of him, but he simply couldn't, or wouldn't, recognize them for what they were.

I began to write the opening of the paper:

"The early sixteenth century produced two enduring classics of Western culture: the collected works of Shakespeare and the King James translation of the Bible. Over the centuries we've come to read Shakespeare as we read the Bible, that is, in studying these works, we try to search out— in the stories of flawed, conflicted mortals wrestling with the meaning of good and evil, life and death, love and hate, the sacred and the profane (or holiness and unholiness)—some clearer sense of our own selves, of how to live our lives with integrity and decency and, dare I utter the word, spirituality. And we discover how subject the Bible and Shakespeare are to multiple interpretations, how prominently the narratives and the verse are marked by irony and ambiguity, paradox and antithesis, how impossible it is to perceive *the* truth in what we read, no matter how often and how profoundly we explore the text."

Then, after describing Keats's concept of "negative capability," I continued: "No one system can explain everything, Keats is saying. The creative artist needs an imaginative openness of mind and heightened receptivity to reality, qualities which might compel their possessor to transform straightforward source material into something more complex and cryptic, and which Caroline Spurgeon discerns in 'Shakespeare the Man,' the section from her *Shakespeare's Imagery* in which, on the basis of thousands of images she'd collected and examined during nine or ten years, she comes up with (among other things) a physical and psychological portrait of the Man from Stratford."

As a springboard into the subject, I pointed out how curious it was of Ms. Spurgeon to conclude that Shakespeare apparently hadn't derived any consolation from "the forms and promises" of conventional religion and then to emphasize a recurring thought in his work—the primacy of one's obligation to befriend, help, cheer, and illuminate our fellowmen, which is the gist of the Torah, *v'ahavta l'rahcha k'moka,* Love your neighbor as yourself.

"Further," I went on, "the Ten Commandments were given to ensure, by divine sanction, that we befriend, support, help our fellow human beings—to build and preserve a secure, humane, just society. And additional commandments direct the Israelites to share their crops with the needy, protect the orphaned and widowed, be generous to strangers, remembering that the Jews were strangers in the land of Egypt. 'Justice, justice shalt thou follow,' God declaims in Deuteronomy, the repetition emphasizing the significance of this concept. As J. H. Hertz explains in *The Pentateuch and Haftorahs,* justice in Hebrew thought required that a human being must be treated as a personality, and as such, has the right to life, honor, and the fruits of his labor.

"So, by Ms. Spurgeon's own description, Shakespeare was a religious man, and *King Lear* is his most religious play, religious in a way not recognized or acknowledged, as far as I could determine, by scholars and critics."

I then described the attitudes of Bradley and Foakes and, regretfully, Maynard Mack, whom I generally revere but who in this instance takes his place among the scholars unaware of the Judaic themes being sounded in *Lear:* "In his *Everybody's Shakespeare* essay on the play, 'We Came Crying Hither,' referring to one of the play's central meanings, Mack says: 'Existence is inseparable from relation; we are born from it and to it; it envelops our lives as parents, children, sisters, brothers, husbands, wives, servants, master, rulers, subjects—the web is seamless and unending. When we talk of virtue, courage, joy, we talk of what supports it. When we talk of tyranny, lust, pride, treason, we talk of what destroys it.' Mack is talking about the binding together of a community, and that's exactly what the term 'religion' means in Latin—a binding together. But Mack did not recognize the connection he was making to the crux of the Torah, the establishing of a protective, nurturing relatedness at the command of God. In *King Lear,* Shakespeare dramatizes the chaos engendered when that social bond is broken."

I'd been printing all this on a yellow legal pad. And that was the way I'd be writing the paper—by hand, in block letters to make it at least semilegible. Those old monks who haunted the premises must have been smiling at me. Only five computers were available for the entire enrollment, and I didn't want to get caught in the crush. Barbara, on the other hand, would take her chances—she's far more comfortable in the cybernetic world than I. (Her tutor's pedagogical method was the opposite of Emma's, probably because the subject, archaeology and history of Roman Britain, did not lend itself to animated bull sessions replete with opinions and feelings; most of the day Barbara sat in a classroom and listened to a lecture accompanied by slides and the distribution of copious supplementary reading.)

Was I onto something original, I wondered? Lurking in the Bodleian and the Radcliffe Camera, or rolling off the presses at that very moment, was there a work that had beaten me to the punch?

I looked at my watch. It was eleven-thirty. Barbara had been asleep for over an hour. No television in the room at Worcester; anyway, we'd decided to go on a media fast during our three weeks in residence. We were maintaining the cloistered tradition with which my regression to hand-printing a manuscript was also in keeping.

I realized, with relief, that my "Can I make a case for my thesis?" angst was fading, dispelled by an adrenaline rush as the paper began to take shape. It was rejuvenating. Messrs. Browning and Tennyson had it right. Grow old along with me, the best is yet to be. A man's reach should exceed his grasp, or what's a heaven for? Strive, seek, find, never yield. In fact, that's what this Oxford/Berkeley program was all about, to say nothing of the LLI at Caldwell College, and I vowed to curb my impatience in class at Worcester.

On Friday morning came *Antony and Cleopatra*. Emma wrote "Head versus Heart" on the board, Antony torn by duty to Rome and craving for Cleopatra. Well, that was more like it. She asked us to call out what came to mind when we thought of Antony, and wrote down the responses: a man's man; duty; honor; Rome; soldier leaving battle; bungles suicide; lacks fidelity; respects his men; in love, obsessed. Then she asked for antitheses, and wrote: love-war; country-self; man-woman; Egypt-Rome; luxury-austerity. She screened scenes from Trevor Nunn's 1972 adaptation and the BBC version done in the eighties in which Colin Blakely as Antony (he'd have been more credible as Enobarbus) prepares to kill himself. Blakely was far too hysterical, seemed on the verge of a crack-up, hardly a Roman doing the honorable thing. The only fresh insight of the morning was offered by Gillian: "The tragic thing about this play is the mess that the two lovers make not just of their own lives but of the lives of those around them. Like Enobarbus." I suppose this holds true for most of the tragedies—for example, just total up the corpses and the agonies that can be attributed to the actions of Hamlet and Lear.

After class, Don and I headed for our first experience of the Bodleian, joined by Lou Ann. "You know," Lou Ann said as we proceeded down Beaumont Street, "I teach a class in film history at Morris Community College and I love watching all these videos, even the ones I've already seen like Olivier's *Hamlet,* especially the one in which Gertrude, wearing that low-cut gown with her boobs hanging out, plants a kiss on sonny boy's lips. But wouldn't it be nice to read the scripts once in a while?" Ummm, yes. We were passing the august Ashmolean Museum and the staid Victorian grande dame, the Randolph Hotel, through the windows of which I could see what seemed to be statues of ancient Britons taking tea in one of the parlors. On Broad Street, we turned left and passed a marker in the pavement indicating where Thomas Cranmer, the first Protestant Archbishop of Canterbury, had been burned at the stake by Henry VIII's ferociously Catholic daughter and heir, Queen Mary.

And then there we were. The Bodleian. The Old Library. A cathedral of knowledge and learning, and its very aspect induced in the beholder a sense of the numinous—indeed, an aerial view gives it the aspect of the Vatican. The idea of the holy was intensified by our first entering the Divinity School, with its magnificent fan-vaulted, elaborately decorated ceiling. Then we emerged into the quadrangle and mingled with the tourists who were photographing the Latin inscriptions over the doors of what were originally lecture rooms and schools of the seven liberal arts (the trivium, the three elementary subjects of grammar, rhetoric, logic; and the quadrivium, the more advanced course of arithmetic, geometry, music, and astronomy) and the three philosophies (natural, moral, and metaphysical).

"Does this remind you of Texas A&M?" Don asked me.

"At A&M," Lou Ann chimed in, "they thought the trivium and quadrivium were events at a track meet, right, Herm?"

"No," I said, "but we did assume that iambic pentameter was part of the decathlon."

Banter ceased abruptly as we stepped into the library and its reading room, where none but privileged bearers of the Bodleian reader's card may enter. The virus of elitism lies dormant in all our miserable little souls, waiting to erupt into a flourishing disease under the right, or wrong, circumstances. Don, Lou Ann, and I could scarcely contain our glee as the guard examined our cards and admitted us into the holy of holies, where only the priests of culture may tread, separating us from the unpurified. We headed for the upper reading room, reaching out to touch the ancient stone walls along the wooden staircase, as if this gesture were part of some genetically ingrained rite or worship. On this visit, Don and I decided to browse the books kept on open access on the shelves. Lou Ann, more ambitious, launched the process for ordering volumes from the book stack—checking the on-line catalog, filling out a green slip, the whole schmeer, aware that the book might not be delivered for a day or longer.

I quickly located Geoffrey Bullough's eight-volume *Narrative and Dramatic Sources of Shakespeare,* plucked the volume dealing with *King Lear,* and excitedly discovered a meaningful passage: "We cannot be sure why Shakespeare altered the Leir play in the way he did. . . . His imagination immersed itself in the emotional and ethical implications of the story and initially with the obvious themes embodied there, e.g. ingratitude, discord in the family, parent against child, child against parent, greed, questioning of divine justice—the ethical themes are stated more explicitly in this play than in any previous one . . . Shakespeare wished to lend the domestic events a . . . cosmic significance and to project questions about ultimate causes." This was astonishing. Bullough, the authority par excellence on Shakespeare's sources, was also a member, along with R. A. Foakes, A. C. Bradley, and Maynard Mack, of the Blindness Club. He'd failed to make the obvious—to me—connections of the ethical themes in *Lear* to the stories in Genesis of Cain and Abel, Ishmael and Isaac, Jacob and Esau, Joseph and his brothers. He was uncertain of Shakespeare's reason for altering the sources, unable to grasp the Judaic influence behind this alteration, unaware that the significance he lent to domestic events was specifically Judaic, not generally "cosmic." This would strengthen my case against the Blind Old Farts.

That morning at breakfast, I'd learned from the tutor of a class in philosophy that almost four centuries earlier, in this very library, Robert Burton, the clergyman and savant, had for years researched *The Anatomy of Melancholy,* a work of bewitching eccentricity, distinguished by its prodigious use of quotations and citations, and as I pored over Bullough, I longed for more time at Oxford, at least enough to allow me to read through all seven volumes of his work.

Don approached me, pointing to his watch: time to break for lunch. We spotted Lou Ann at one of the inquiry counters, where a staff member, a shaggy-haired young scholar gypsy wearing the obligatory earring, was lecturing her with grave severity on what for all we knew might be a useful piece of Bodleian arcana. "This guy says there's a terrific pub near here called the Turf," she greeted us. "Been around even before the time

they charbroiled poor old Cranmer. Why don't we have lunch there?"
Spoken like a genuine scholar.

Following Lou Ann's directions, we walked a few blocks to where the
Bridge of Sighs (yes, a replica of the one in Venice) forms an arch over
the street and saw a signboard menu for the Turf on the sidewalk next to
an alley. Through the labyrinthine way we went, and I beheld the pub of
my dreams. Several rooms, two of which were rather small bars, oak
beams, shellacked plank tables, wooden benches, and an outside beer garden with unvarnished picnic tables. I selected what turned out to be the
richest ale I'd ever swilled: Old Speckled Hen. It sounded unappetizing,
and I didn't want to know the origin of its name. All I knew was that I
wanted to die in that place, drowning myself in barrels of Old Speckled
Hen, like Richard III's unfortunate brother Clarence, murdered in the
Tower by two thugs who plunged him headfirst into a cask of wine. A
consummation devoutly to be wished.

My companions, my dearest friends in all the world, joined me in that
potation, and we all ordered the same meal—steak and ale pie. Was that
the happiest moment of my life or what? First the Bodleian and the Bullough. Now the Turf and the Hen. Don said he had no idea what he
wanted to write about, he simply intended to read all seven volumes of
Bullough cover-to-cover. Lou Ann complained that the book she ordered
up might not surface for a week. "It's about folktales that might relate to
Lear." "Jewish folktales?" I asked, scarcely able to hide the tremor of apprehension in my voice. Could she and I by some satanic coincidence be
following the same line? *"Jewish?"* she responded, as if I had exceeded my
limit of the Hen Nonpareil. We finished up, weaved our way back
through the maze of the alley, and strolled glowingly back to the
Bodleian—rather, to the Radcliffe Camera, directly behind it.

The Camera, a large circular building topped with a lofty dome, was
completed in 1749, built with money bequeathed by John Radcliffe, an
illustrious physician. And I'd been mistaken: the Camera, not the Old Library, is the holy of holies. Whereas tourists may clutter up the Divinity
School, the quadrangle, etc., no part of the Camera is open to visitors. As
the three of us approached, we noticed groups of the unanointed gazing
wistfully through the iron gate that protects the premises; and speaking a
trifle too animatedly about our adventures in the temple of scholarship,

we ostentatiously made our way past them and up the long walk to the entrance. Inside the Camera, high arched windows soared up to the dome, the Duomo. Yes, a cathedral. We spent the next several hours in the lower Camera reading room. I found a book that made my pulse quicken: *Shakespeare's Biblical Knowledge,* by Richmond Noble, published by Macmillan in 1935. Had Mr. Noble been the first to discern the traces of Judaism in *King Lear?* False alarm. Mr. Noble was alert to the biblical allusions in *Lear,* but did not speculate on Shakespeare's possible motives in their use. For instance, Gloucester's lines in act 1, "brothers divide . . . and the bond cracked 'twixt son and father," he compares to a phrase in Mark, "brother shall betray brother," but fails to detect the influence of Genesis. It's as if the Pentateuch never existed. As I read and made notes and comments, I was aware that gone was the sense of being an impos-tor, a poseur, a dilettante, that nagged me while I was at the Folger. True enough, "discovering" the Whitman article was a kick, and I'd undoubt-edly be able to use it when I took up the history plays again at the LLI. But the research I was doing now was for a specific academic purpose— writing the course paper. I was not posturing as a scholar; for the mo-ment, I *was* a scholar. It felt good. After three semesters in front of a class at the LLI, and only a few days exploring the process of research, I felt myself building up a head of steam that might propel me toward some as yet uncharted territory in the universe of teaching.

That night Barbara and I took our place at High Table. First we joined the other Chosen and the tutors and administrators for wine and sherry in one of the residential suites, and then walked to Hall, where we en-tered in procession. Grace was brief that evening: *Benedicte, benedicte.* No *patris, filii, et spiritus sancti,* and I was sort of relieved. I felt no sense of spir-itual violation at standing for Christian prayers, but that night happened to be Friday, Shabbat eve, and invoking the Holy Trinity on that occa-sion might have caused me a twinge of discomfort. As the waiter poured the wine, I said the blessing in Hebrew to myself: *Baruch atah adonai, elo-henu melech ha olam, borai pri hagafen*—Praised be Thou, O Lord our God, King of the Universe, Who has created the fruit of the vine. And of course, Old Speckled Hen.

After dinner, Barbara and I walked through the park and the gardens and along the treelined canal. One of the trees was a glorious aberration, a majestic freak of nature, its giant trunk parallel to the ground, extending over the water, the tips of its huge thick branches submerged in the canal. I thought of the willow over the river in which Ophelia drowned, and in the dusk I can almost make her out, her saturated gown growing heavy, pulling her under. We know what we are, but know not what we may be. In my case, the uncertainty was both thrilling and not a little scary.

The next evening, Don and I finally paid a visit to Jude the Obscure, which proved to be a disappointment, less a pub than a neighborhood bar. But they did have the Hen. Don and I discovered that we'd been blessed with close relationships with our fathers. Don's old man was an electrician, who'd been determined that his son would get the education he'd missed. Don told me that when he'd read Polonius's advice to Laertes for the first time two days previously, he thought of his father. "It's something he would say, in fact something he's actually said, only not in blank verse. Finding what our own self is and then being faithful to it—that's what makes us human beings."

"Right, Don. Know thyself. No problem, right? Listen, if Shakespeare tells us nothing else, it's that the human animal is a crazy patchwork of contradictions. And he probably got the idea from Montaigne, the sixteenth-century French aristocrat who invented the essay. Montaigne said that it's hard to know who we really are, since like everything else in the world, we're constantly changing, and we carry inside us the entire human constitution. Realizing this is probably what made Shakespeare a hell of an actor, and not too shabby a writer."

"Hell, this is turning into a big-time boozy college-type bull session," said Don, just as the bartender was announcing last call. "Lucky it's almost closing time, or before you know it we'd be arguing politics and religion and whacking away at each other."

Later that night as I lay in bed I continued thinking about the difficulty of achieving self-knowledge, which seemed to be occasioned not only by our complex and contradictory nature but also by our expertise at the art of self-deception. I looked at Barbara asleep beside me, even in slumber an influential presence. The closeness of this rare spirit, one of life's precious truth-tellers, incapable of lying to herself or anyone else, prompted me to acknowledge in a short burst of self-honesty one of my abiding flaws, which I called the only-child syndrome. I recalled that when I played Richard III at the Pasadena Playhouse, I was perhaps most convincing in the scene in which the Duke of Buckingham persists in reminding Richard of his promise to grant him an estate, and Richard cuts him off with "I am not in the giving vein today." Those words connected to something deep inside me that has remained virtually unchanged all this time, the only child's resentment at being asked to do or to give, a trait that has triggered many of the quarrels between Barbara and me during our thirty-eight years of marriage. On my own I'll do and give with alacrity, I'll be generous and helpful to a fault. But don't impose on me, don't push me. Don't ask. Wonderful quality for a husband, father, son, friend, citizen, teacher. I'd have to keep working on that weakness. And time was not on my side: in just a few days I'd turn sixty-nine. The geriatric maxim, "Grow old if you must, but don't grow up," arch at best, now seemed—well, dangerous.

On Monday, Emma posed the question, if Shakespeare intended *Hamlet* in part to dramatize the relationship between the political and the personal, how can directors justify cutting Fortinbras, Prince of Norway and a daring man of action considered a threat to Denmark, thus eliminating the public and political? A meandering discussion followed, with some of the class (not me) arguing that only the psychological aspects should be emphasized. Tuesday, Emma recommended Michael Neill's *Issues of Death: Mortality and Identity in English Renaissance Tragedy.* She said that Neill declares that in Greek tragedies, heroes aren't required to die, whereas in English Renaissance tragedies they are. The Elizabethans (if I correctly grasped Emma's take on Neill) were trying to come to terms with death, assailed as they were with plague, war, infant mortality. So Renaissance tragedy is all about control: nobody just dies, they're killed. God doesn't kill, humans do.

On Wednesday, Emma handed out excerpts from Shakespeare's sources for *King Lear,* including one possible source, "Cordell Annesley Defends Her Father's Sanity and Property," in which a young woman pleads with Lord Cecil and the Privy Council to thwart the attempts of her sister and brother-in-law to have her father declared insane and to assume control of his property. It's uncertain whether Shakespeare was aware of this case, and if it was the trigger that prompted him to search out other sources. I suggested, and Emma concurred, that Shakespeare being a man of property and a man who was prone to litigation, it was not unlikely that he was familiar with the Annesley case, and that it made an impression. And that as the father of daughters, he might have been concerned with how his property would be disposed of. And I mused to myself that the case might have reminded Shakespeare of the timelessness and universality of Genesis, of its knowledge of the tensions inherent in family life and the ugly conflicts they could produce.

That night, the student body traveled to Stratford to see the RSC production of *Antony and Cleopatra* starring Alan Bates and Frances de la Tour. According to reports, the opening scene had created quite a buzz among audiences: when we first glimpse Antony, he's performing cunnilingus on Cleopatra. One wag, David Grylls, a university lecturer at Oxford's Kellogg College, had quipped, "I suppose it could be considered a tongue-in-cheek interpretation of the scene." Barbara was staying behind, not out of a prudish disinclination to watch Mr. Bates have at Ms. de la Tour, but because she had a field trip to Wales the next day and wanted to get to bed early. Before I left, she surprised me with birthday gifts—a Worcester College lapel pin and a navy-blue sport shirt bearing the Worcester coat of arms. Did this mean she wanted me to junk all my Aggie paraphernalia—the sweatshirt, the baseball cap, the beer mugs—and assume a classier identity?

As for the production: Alan Bates seemed tubby and scruffy, more a debauched Falstaff than a ruined Antony, and Frances de la Tour looked and acted like Carol Burnett on a bad day, Doll Tearsheet to Bates's Falstaff. The evening was almost redeemed by Malcolm Storry's Enobarbus, the best Enobarbus I'd ever seen, including Patrick Stewart's. The cast must have hated him: tall, strapping, craggy-faced, with a stunning emotional range and a voice to match it, he dominated every moment he was onstage. And his death was inventively staged by Stephen Pimlott, who had him commit suicide by pounding himself on the chest, each blow increasingly more violent, as he spoke the lines in 4.10 beginning with "O sovereign mistress of true melancholy" and ending with "But let the world rank me in register / A master-leaver and a fugitive. / O Antony! O Antony!" Heretofore, in the productions I'd seen it was evident that Enobarbus died of a broken heart, emotionally stricken. But in Pimlott's production, Enobarbus broke his heart physically. The only tragic moment in the production.

I spent Thursday and Friday afternoons in the Bodleian and the Camera working on the *Lear* paper, referring to the excerpts I'd brought from home and the material I'd been culling from the library, printing as quickly as I could and at the same time trying to be legible. In Bullough, I found an observation that, along with an excerpt I'd xeroxed from C. S. Lewis's *Reflections on the Psalms,* strengthened my contention that in moving from Edmund's "Now, gods, stand up for bastards!" to Lear's "God's spies," Shakespeare was implying mankind's evolution from polytheism to monotheism. Lear has followed the tragic hero's cycle of change, described by Maynard Mack. He has become his own antithesis, his journey from his court to the heath the manifestation of his inward change, from pagan king to Judaized prophet. Bullough says that "Edmund worships nature as opposed to any divinity *above* [italics mine] nature. As well as being a Machiavellian and a supreme egoist . . . he is also [a] seventeenth century atheist." Lewis notes, "In the [Judaic] theology of creation, a . . . timeless unconditioned God is above and outside all that he makes. . . . This is an amazing leap by an overwhelming theological genius; it is not ordinary pagan religion. To say that God created nature empties nature of divinity."

My hand was beginning to cramp from that feverish and painstaking monk-work. I feared that even in block letters, the manuscript might present a certain legibility challenge. And I wasn't certain I was going to have the stamina to make extensive revisions.

On Saturday morning, Barbara and I decided to walk several miles along the river to a country pub, the Perch, where she and her class had stopped a few days previously on their way back from a field trip. Cloudless sky, temperature a very dry eighty degrees, God was in his heaven. At the Perch, Barbara and I had lunch and ale outdoors in a picnic area near the river. It was a family hangout, with a miniature playground where the kids could frolic while Mom and Dad threw back a few pints. Only in England. I talked of how I'd come to think of Don as a true friend, not simply a drinking buddy, and I said that what I really liked about him was his inherent impulse to do good. When and why had it become fashionable to mock do-gooding, do-gooders? Whence the cynicism? Why was it assumed that a do-gooder is either a hypocrite or a humorless prig? Was selflessness that suspect? Barbara said, "Well, rest easy. Until very recently no one would have accused you of being selfless. Even your bar mitzvah was as much about you, your moment to shine, your moment in the sun, as it was about any spiritual regeneration, any humble turning away from the self and towards God. But I could see something in you start to change when you became a hospice volunteer. I remember at the time you said, 'I'm doing this because I think I ought to. I'm a hypochondriac, I hate being around the sick, but I owe something to the community. All this talk in the Torah about loving your neighbor, helping the needy, it's getting to me.' Maybe the impulse isn't natural, but the idea in Judaism is that performing good deeds long enough will improve your character. Doing good will make you good."

On Monday, the final week at Worcester began. Emma began by reading us James Thurber's *The Macbeth Murder Mystery,* in which Thurber and an American woman who bought *Macbeth* under the misapprehension that it was a detective story discuss who really killed Duncan, and after eliminating Macduff and one of the weird sisters, hit upon Lady Macbeth's father as the true culprit. From this we saw the ridiculous extremes to which overinterpretation could lead us. Next, she screened a video of Peter Brooks's black-and-white movie version of *King Lear.* I found the opening scenes of the movie stultifying—Eisenstein crossed with Bergman. Ostentatiously grim with a soporific monotony of pace (slow) and tone (somber). Paul Scofield looked and talked as if he were on a life-support system, so weak he could barely utter his lines. Then came a joltingly theatrical moment: enraged by Cordelia and Ken, Lear suddenly rose, swathed in fur and skins, huge and terrible, every inch a king, in fact a king of beasts. Emma related that Brooks was influenced by Jan Kott's interpretation of *King Lear* as an example of theatre of the absurd, a la Samuel Beckett. I hadn't read Kott's *Shakespeare Our Contemporary;* a friend had warned me off by telling me that Kott's unrelieved existentialism tended to warp Shakespeare's intent, but now I thought I ought to take a crack at it before tackling the last section of my paper.

So off I went to the Camera after class and read Kott's chapter on *Lear,* titled, in deference to Beckett, "*King Lear,* or Endgame." To Kott, *Lear* was not devoid of theological import; it was in fact antibiblical, God-denying. "In Shakespeare's play," he alleged, "there is neither Christian heaven, nor the heaven predicted and believed in by humanists. *King Lear* makes a tragic mockery of all eschatologies: of the heaven promised on earth, and the Heaven promised after death; in fact—of both Christian and secular theodicies; of cosmogony and the rational view of history; of the gods and the good nature, of man made in 'image and likeness.' " I found this a perversely wrongheaded interpretation, and I had an excellent rebuttal from no less a figure than Lionel Trilling. When I'd xeroxed the excerpt from Trilling's essay on *Lear* before leaving for Oxford, I wasn't certain whether I'd be able to use it, or how. But it so happened that in the material I'd brought, Trilling takes on Kott's cynically existential vision of the play. When I read Trilling's essay, I hadn't bothered to read Kott to find out exactly what Trilling was refuting. Some kind of scholar, I.

By now I was nearing the conclusion of the paper, and I would use Trilling's refutation of Kott to make my final argument about the Judaic import of Lear's ordeal. Out came the yellow pad and the ballpoint pen.

I described the terrible cost that Lear had had to pay, most grievously the death of Cordelia, for turning order into chaos. He has divided his kingdom, distributing his possessions in his lifetime and sowing discord among his children by discriminating between them. And perhaps Cordelia, too, had been judged, I speculated, for refusing to honor her father. "But what are the consequences of Lear's actions," I asked, "beyond divine punishment, divine retribution, divine justice? And Shakespeare, I'm convinced, means for us to see this as *divine* judgment: in the source, Leir and Cordella are spared, but Shakespeare's transformation of the story demonstrates not a denial of theodicy, as one noted scholar has claimed, but an affirmation of its purifying grandeur." Among the citations I used to make my case was a quote from Dostoyevsky's masterpiece, in which Alyosha Karamazov cries out, "God, make me worthy of my suffering!" "It is suffering," I said, "that prompts Lear, at last, to recognize the 'poor naked wretches' of the world. Suffering has led him to self-discovery, self-knowledge. It has led him from egotism to altruism. Lear himself realizes that 'the art of our necessities is strange, / That can make vile things precious.' Or as God thunders in the Bible, 'I will test them and try them in a crucible of affliction.'

"Not everyone, of course, agrees that suffering ennobled Lear and restored his tragic greatness. Notable among these deniers is the Polish critic Jan Kott, who in his influential book *Shakespeare Our Contemporary* equates *King Lear* with today's theatre of the absurd, the school of modern drama dedicated to representing the metaphysical pointlessness of human life. Kott stresses the meaningless cruelty of Shakespeare's world. In the manner of R. A. Foakes and his ilk, Kott misses the Judaic note in *Lear;* correctly noting the absence of 'Christian and secular theodicies' in the tragedy, he doesn't comprehend the Jewish theodicy. But apparently Lionel Trilling does, as he pointedly implies in 'The Tragedy of *King Lear,*' from his *Preface to the Experience of Literature,* where he takes issue with Kott's notion that Shakespeare's vision is nihilistic. Trilling, until his death in 1973 a revered professor of literature at Columbia University and a world-renowned literary critic, argues that 'the incompatibility between rational man and an absurd universe is only one of the two explanations of human suffering suggested in *King Lear.* The other holds man himself accountable for his pain. . . . When it is said that Lear is "regenerated" and "redeemed," the change that is being remarked upon in the aged king is his new consciousness of man's inhumanity to man ["You must love your neighbor as yourself"—H.G.], of the general failure of justice. . . . and with the new consciousness of justice goes a new sense of the need for . . . the solicitude of human kindness [here Trilling quotes the "Poor naked wretches" speech]. . . . The object of his new consciousness is . . . man's falling short of what is required of him in doing justice and loving mercy.' Surely Trilling intends us to detect here the echoes of the prophet Micah, but he will not admit that this new consciousness is a religious consciousness, that Lear's obsession with justice is the kind of justice demanded by Yahweh in Leviticus: 'Justice, justice shall you follow' (The irony here is that Trilling was Jewish, and the only critic and scholar I've read who as much as implied a Jewish context to *Lear.* Perhaps his reluctance to make this explicit derived from his being the first Jew hired as a professor in Columbia's department of English. Heretofore, Jews had been considered racially ill equipped to interpret the classics of English literature. Thus it's understandable that even late in his distinguished career he recoiled from offering a provocative, singularly Jewish reading of *Lear* which might prompt nasty I-told-you-so comments from the Old Guard in the department.) For Trilling, moral virtue is implied by a human normative principle. Our society is committed, he says, to the idea of the normative virtue of man, which depends on belief in transcendent *reason,* a belief derided by the likes of Jan Kott. 'The dramatist of the absurd,' he continues, 'takes for granted a metaphysical negation which has the effect of destroying the old human meanings and of making human life grotesque, whereas such a causal sequence was not conceived by Shakespeare. He took for granted a rational and moralized universe but proposed the idea the universal order might be reduced to chaos by human evil.'

"But I would say that Shakespeare believed in a moralized universe fashioned by a transcendent God who created mankind, as the Bible reveals, with impulses good and evil, impulses at war in the psyches of all Shakespearean tragic figures, and in those of all of us as well. He believed, too, that the ultimate good is to love thy neighbor as thyself—the wisdom of the heart—and that the ultimate evil is, in the manner of Shakespeare's villains, to love thyself alone—the cunning of the egotistical mind.

"In *King Lear,* therefore, it was not traditional Christian theology but the precepts of the Torah and the Prophets and the Psalmists which were determinative to Shakespeare's moral vision. John Keats once declared that his credo was the 'holiness of the heart's affections,' and so, too, could it have been the credo of Shakespeare, the man who, as Helen Luke contends in *Old Age,* 'penetrates into the hidden mysteries, who sees at the heart of every manifestation of life, even behind the trivial talk of "poor rogues," the *mysterium tremendum* that is God, who knows that the true mystery is the eternal paradox at the root of life itself.'

"André Gide once said that Shakespeare was not quite God. But he is, to my mind, God's spy."

Done. I gathered my papers, stuffed them into the manila envelope that served as my briefcase, and then, as an afterthought, pulled out the legal pad and wrote across the middle of the page, "God's Spy: The Judaic Quality of *King Lear.*"

Barbara was off on another field trip, so after dinner I rounded up Don and Lou Ann for one of our last pub crawls. First the White Horse, a cozy pub across Broad Street from the Bodleian, and then our favorite, the Turf, where it was last call and a throng was shoving up to both bars, desperate for that final pint. With all the jostling and pushing, there was not a trace of bellicosity or rudeness; quite the opposite, the mood was festive and affable, everyone grinning and laughing at the shared determination to have one more for the road. In America, especially Texas, fists would have been flying at the merest hint of body contact. And when at the witching hour the pubs empty, the same boozy geniality fills the streets—nothing raucous or rowdy in the processions home, just youthful exuberance. Yes, most of the crowd was young, students and townies, rarely anyone who appeared past thirty. No, I was not Prince Hamlet, nor was meant to be; rather I was Falstaff, hearing those chimes at midnight, with my good companions Prince Hal and Doll Tearsheet. Don and Lou Ann were singing a rock ditty unfamiliar to me, and their harmonizing rang pleasantly in my ears. Then Don broke off to tell me he wasn't going to give an oral presentation; instead, he intended to read Polonius's advice to Laertes. I drank to that.

On Wednesday, though, only three of us gave presentations: Marie, Gillian, myself. Don failed to show up—a problem, he told me later, with the divorce proceedings in California had kept him on the phone all morning. The others had decided to let the written word suffice. Marie read her "Dialogue Between Shakespeare and Freud," the former speaking words of wisdom about the human condition culled from his plays, the latter clinically reducing human behavior to neurotic complexes. Imaginative, clever, perceptive. "Very fine work," Emma said. "A delightful concept." Gillian paraphrased her paper, "Energies in Shakespeare," and even displayed a chart illustrating some of the points, as if Shakespeare's plays were an ingenious new G.E. product she was explaining to the marketing mavens. Chart or no, I didn't understand a word of it, and I'm not certain Emma did, either. "A complex analysis, very stimulating," she commented. And then it was time for my discourse on *Lear*.

Emma had limited our time to fifteen minutes, a restriction that Marie and Gillian had observed. But rehearsing aloud in my room for the past few days, I'd found that even by making a few cuts I couldn't talk fast enough to keep my presentation under thirty minutes and still be comprehensible. And I saw no way to condense the paper radically without ruining what I liked to think of as its cumulative impact. I doubted that Emma would keep a little hourglass timer on her desk and cut me off before I'd finished, but now that I'd seen Marie and Gillian stick to the rules,

I was uneasy at the prospect of coming across as Mr. Hotshot, flouter of restrictions. And I was not a little intimidated by the presence of Emma. To test a provocative concept on fellow students was one thing; to expose it to the critical scrutiny of an Oxford scholar steeped in Shakespearean and Elizabethan studies was something a bit more daunting. Taking a seat facing the class, I sensed how it would feel to defend a doctoral thesis. I looked around the room for encouraging smiles, but the faces bore the impassive expressions of jurors and judge. As I read my paper, I was aware of complete silence and stillness—not a whisper, not a cough, no restless shifting in chairs. The moment I'd finished, Emma whooped and clapped her hands. "Super! Just super, Herman! I thought about stopping you at the fifteen-minute mark just to see how you'd handle it, but that would have been too nasty a trick. And the fact is, I was hooked. And I speak for the class, right?" she said. The group nodded and grinned and gave thumbs-up and—the ultimate accolade—asked for copies to take home. Lou Ann laid an arm on my shoulder and said, "I guess you're a guy who knows his triviums, after all. But how are you coming along with the quadriviums?"

After lunch, I phoned Anthony Branch, cofounder and director of the British American Drama Academy (BADA), which was in residence at Balliol College. A few weeks before leaving for Oxford, I'd seen a BADA ad in the Sunday *New York Times* announcing dates for auditions, and I'd written Branch a letter, asking if the BADA curriculum included courses on Shakespearean acting, and if so, might I sit in on one of them. He'd responded that he wasn't certain that he could make such an arrangement, and suggested I call him when I was in Oxford. He answered the phone himself, and as soon as I introduced myself he said heartily, "When are we going to see you?"

"How about right now?"

"No, sorry, that won't work. I'm off to London shortly for the next few days. And I have to put the final touch on arrangements for John Barton's arrival. He's doing a master class here tonight on Shakespeare's sonnets."

Tonight?! Be still, my heart. Could my timing actually have been that perfect? John Barton, Shakespeare's prophet, would be there, and perhaps

I could watch him preach the gospel and perform miracles of instruction. Trying not to come on too strong, I asked, "Any chance of my sitting in on that class?"

"Well, you know," he said, "it's really not for the general public. John sometimes does open these sessions to outsiders, but this one is for sixteen students only. And one or two of the faculty." I said nothing, and after a long pause he finally said, "But I suppose we can make an exception this time, given that you teach a course yourself and you've been studying these past weeks at Worcester. John will be here at five, and stays until nine. A short break for sandwiches. Why don't you plan to come at five-thirty or so and slip into a seat at the rear. Since I won't be there, I'll tell my assistant to let you in, so there won't be a fuss."

Late that afternoon in the room, Barbara was assembling the pages of her formidable-looking, computer-typed thesis, complete with footnotes and bibliography, fresh from the college's sole printer. On my desk was the sheaf of yellow legal pages bearing my profundities in the block letters of a third grader, marred in more than a few places with words scratched out and interlinear additions. It was still not what I'd consider a final draft—it cried out for reorganization and amplification—but that hand-printing stint already had my right hand feeling as if it belonged to Richard III, and I lacked the fortitude to continue the process. Looking at my paper reminded me of a moment in one of Stanley Elkin's novels, *Boswell,* in which the main character attends a science exhibition of his underachieving son's sixth-grade class and observes, among such creations as a model spaceship, a miniature water-processing plant, and a robot, his son's contribution: a couple of raisins, a bent paper clip, a wad of toilet paper, a dead fly, and a scrap of paper on which the boy had scrawled, "grbge dunpf." My paper looked like the academic equivalent of a grbge dunpf. To hell with it—I'd simply attach a disarming note to Emma, begging her indulgence.

As I waited around for time to pass until I could leave for Balliol, I started to grow edgy about showing up there after class had begun. Few things panic me as much as the prospect of arriving late to a meeting or a class and being the object of attention. I confessed my anxieties to Barbara. "Just go there at five. Don't make such a big deal out of it. What will they do—bar your entrance? Flash them your Bodley reader's card. Don't be such a whiner." Thank you, Lady Macbeth.

I screwed my courage to the sticking place (as S. J. Perelman might have said, I always bring along a sticking place just in case), and at five sharp I arrived at Balliol, which was on Broad Street, down the block from the White Horse and diagonally across from the Bodleian. I joined a group of students making their way into the Balliol lecture room and, unchallenged and unnoticed, took a seat in the rear. Barton stood at the front of the room, looking drawn, noticeably more fragile than when he appeared on the *Playing Shakespeare* tapes. But that, of course, had been twenty years earlier. He had the same rumpled, disheveled aspect, though. Olive-drab cardigan sweater, yellow shirt scarcely tucked into brown slacks, and that bush of curly, semi-unkempt graying brown hair. Each of the students had been assigned a sonnet in advance to memorize for presentation that afternoon. I wondered how many of them spent sleepless nights at the prospect of performing before John Barton, and I remembered the hysteria that had unmanned me the day before I had to do my first Sense Memory exercise in Lee Strasberg's class back in the fifties. Barton began to speak:

"The most important thing about Shakespeare is how his mind works. The best way to determine the workings of his mind is to pay close attention to his words. What you want to do is make Shakespeare's words and thoughts your own. And with the sonnets, you must ask yourself, 'What is the argument I need to share with the people I'm talking to?'"

A woman who looked to be in her middle thirties stood and delivered Sonnet 29, "When in disgrace with fortune and men's eyes." Barton walked to the back of the room, listening intently, folding his arms and cupping his chin in his hand—he would do this during each delivery. When the woman finished, Barton returned to the front of the room and told her she had to be more aware of the metaphorical leap that Shakespeare makes in line 11, when he likens his state to a lark. He asked her what she considered the key word in the sonnet. She was at a loss, and he said, " 'State.' First he beweeps his outcast state, then when he thinks of the object of the sonnet, his state changes, becomes like to the lark at break of day. Keep in mind those changes of state." Not only was she unflustered, she repeated the sonnet in a way that dramatically incorporated Barton's suggestions of only moments before. The ability to think on your feet, to absorb direction quickly and transform it imaginatively, and under the pressure of a master's attention, was no mean feat.

Sonnet 17, "Who will believe my verse in time to come," was grappled with by a swarthy young guy who strove to make it sound like everyday conversation. Barton jumped right on the problem: "You're being artificially naturalistic. You're taking too many pauses, you're being too 'reflective.' Let the words do the work, don't force yourself. You must journey with the words. An actor must always ask the question 'Who am I talking to?' You don't seem to be sharing a feeling, you're acting an emotion, you're performing all sorts of tricks." The young man struggled with the sonnet at least a half dozen times—Barton was exceptionally patient—with scarcely any improvement.

An attractive young woman, a slender brunet, tried Sonnet 116, "Let me not to the marriage of true minds / admit impediments," and elicited a familiar critique from Barton: "You seem to be making a presentation. You must actively imagine the situation. You're answering someone who's claimed that love should alter when it alteration finds. You're arguing, rebutting." She did it again, with noticeable improvement.

On his feet for Sonnet 18—"Shall I compare thee to a summer's day?"—was a balding man in his forties. Barton: "You're much too soppy here. You fell into the classic trap of this sonnet—you think Shakespeare is being sentimental. That's exactly why I chose it, to see who would fall into the trap." Unlucky fellow, the balding chap; he was fool enough to take the bait. "This sonnet is antipoetry, antisoppy—simply notice how Shakespeare uses paradox here. The lines stress counterpoint: rough winds shake darling buds, summer's all too short, the sun's too damned hot—so why would I want to compare my love to a summer's day? You have to look for the *story*—these sonnets are telling stories. You've just heard someone making such a soppy comparison, and you're having none of it." Twice more, with scant improvement.

Time for a sandwich break. Barton sat alone at a raised table. No one approached him. Had the students been warned in advance that Mr. Barton did not do buddy-buddy during these sessions? Or was his stature sufficient to promote an awed distancing among the class? It certainly kept me from moseying up to him and saying howdy; I feared I'd be tongue-tied, or that he'd recognize me as an intruder and demand my expulsion. But could he actually have been aching for someone bold enough to come forward and ask a question, even a stupid one? His presence was not at all intimidating. His comments during class were candid and firm, pointed and illuminating, but given without a trace of condescension or contempt, qualities that came quite naturally to Lee Strasberg.

Class resumed with a tall comely blonde doing Sonnet 94, "They that have pow'r to hurt and will do none . . . rightly do inherit Heaven's Graces." When she finished, Barton asked the class, "Did she take you with her?" Alas, she hadn't. "You were making a statement, as if you'd already reasoned this out and wanted to explain it. That's not what this is all about. Remember: you don't know what Shakespeare is getting at until the end. The last two lines are always the most important. You need to create suspense as you move towards those lines, 'For sweetest things turn sourest by their deeds; / Lilies that fester smell far worse than weeds.' You acted it, you were more concerned with your performance than with taking the audience with you. Much of Shakespeare has to do with irony—this sonnet is a classic example. Look at the last line, 'Lilies that fester smell far worse than weeds.' Speech is about the effect of words on the audience, not about your emotions and feelings. The kick here is that the words are deadly; they don't need to be acted. The best way to act is not to act—then you're *acting* not acting."

A few more sonnets followed, with critiques in a similar vein, then Barton took his leave. He would be back for another session the following week. I, though, would be in New Jersey by then, considerably more enlightened about the sonnets after just a few hours in Barton's spellbinding presence.

Thursday was the next-to-last day of classes, and finally, we were doing scansion! We were actually doing a close reading of the text. By some eerie coincidence, this came directly on the heels of Barton's precise analyses of Shakespeare's technique. Even better, Emma referred to Cicely Berry's *The Actor and the Text*. Why had she waited so long? Was it deliberate, a part of her teaching method, or was it a happy afterthought? I recalled that I hadn't gotten around to talking about scansion until halfway through the course on the history plays, but I was new at the game, not an Oxford professor. "Berry tells you that you have to pay close attention to stress in the verse—it tells you what the speech is about. Study the end words of lines and you'll see the meaning of the speech. The actor must have a sense of lines and line endings." She also cited Berry's advice on how to get a sense of tempo, and of the emotional quality of the lines: speak the lines as you walk, and every time there's a piece of punctuation, turn around.

In the afternoon, first we reviewed the intersection of the public and the private, the domestic and the political, in the tragedies. Hamlet is the Prince of Denmark, and the son of a murdered father and an adulterous mother. Lear is king and father. Macbeth is feudal baron and husband. Antony and Cleopatra are rulers and lovers.

Then it was video time again: the opening scene from Arnold Schwarzenegger's monumental flop, *Last Action Hero,* which I, along with millions of others, had avoided. A kid who's a rabid fan of action flicks starring an Arnoldesque hero played by none other than Arnold is bored with school until one morning when his teacher, played by Olivier's widow, Joan Plowright (the movie, Emma related, was ever so self-referential, produced by Arnold himself, his way of coping with the monster he's created), shows the class Olivier's *Hamlet* and refers to the prince as "the first action hero." The kid then fantasizes Hamlet, played by Arnold (carrying an Uzi and chewing on a cigar), blowing away Claudius and all his adversaries, in a scene reminiscent of Arnold's previous movies. It seemed to be a species of pop culture destined to incite hermeneutic frenzies in academia, and I imagined it wouldn't be long before the scholarly journals were swamped with articles deconstructing its text.

After dinner, Barbara and I took a last walk in the gardens and then sat on a bench overlooking the lake. Behind us was the wall, and just beyond that the canal, lined with houseboats, many of them garishly painted and not a few in a state of dilapidation. It was silent, except for the wind in the trees. The weather remained idyllic, cool and dry after that first day of gloom, the air restorative, the sky at dusk a blue that almost exactly matches the color of my wife's eyes. I recalled the opening lines of Karl Shapiro's poem "V-Letter": "I love you first because your face is fair, / Because your eyes Jewish and blue, / Set sweetly with the touch of foreignness / Above the cheekbones, stare rather than dream." Barbara is a realist who can sniff out the faintest reek of phoniness a mile away. She had come to Oxford with no illusions, no fantasies, and had wound up loving her course. Her tutor had been exacting, precise, and, it turned out, whimsically amusing as well. Now she asked me, "Has this been all you dreamed it would be?" I'm the dreamer of the two. I think it was Mencken who concluded that in general women are practical, men are romanticists. If I hadn't been a dreamer, I'd have remained in Houston, Texas, doing God only knows what. Perhaps managing a branch of Barnes & Noble and participating in community theatricals. Oh my.

"Oxford itself was all that I imagined it to be," I said, "and more, as we say in our postcards to family and friends. The Bod, the Camera, the Turf, the White Horse, Old Speckled Hen, simply wandering the streets and going medieval. And Worcester—these walks, the friends, High Table, the gardens, tea in the Cloisters, our room with those crazy goddamned lamps. But I expected more from the course. Maybe I should say I expected a different kind of course. One that wasn't so fragmented. And a tutor who would say, 'Here's what we're going to do today,' not ask, 'What would you like to do today?' Emma loved us not wisely but too well. Maybe because she's young and the class, with one exception, was older. She's obviously a brilliant scholar, but she didn't share enough of that brilliance with us. It wasn't until yesterday that she talked about scansion. I learned as much by listening to Barton last night as I have in three weeks of classes with Emma. Early on, when Sally expressed a preference for more lecturing, Emma said that a person didn't need to be a scholar to come up with valuable perceptions about Shakespearean plays. Which may be fine when applied to insights into character and about Shakespeare's moral vision, but who else besides a scholar with specialized training can educate us to the fine points of Shakespeare's techniques? Sure, we could get it out of books, but we paid our tuition to drink from your cup of knowledge. It's frustrating. The only challenge was writing the paper."

"But that's what Oxford's all about," Barbara said. "The paper is what's important. What you're actually telling me is that you wish you'd had Big Herm as the teacher, right? Someone who'd do it your way." She gave me one of her wry who-do-you-think-you're-kidding looks, and I knew it was useless to remonstrate with her. With a "guilty as charged" smile, I put my arm around her and we stayed a while longer, silent for the most part, storing up memories of this entrancing place.

Friday was the finale. We had come full circle. Emma handed out a different set of definitions of tragedy, completing those she distributed at our first meeting. Lou Ann, who was sitting next to me, leaned over and pointed to one of the entries, a letter of Lord Byron's. "I bet this was a favorite at Texas A&M, right?" It read: "When Voltaire was asked why no woman has ever written a tolerable tragedy, 'Ah (said the Patriarch), the composition of a tragedy requires *testicles.*' "

Emma handed us back our papers. To mine she affixed these comments: "This is a revelation. Thank you. All this learning and scholarship! I'd always thought of *Lear* as a bleak, unChristian play—what you've brought out is its deep indebtedness to the language and tone of the Old Testament. And your title is inspired. Well done. PS It's interesting how many illustrations of Lear make him look like God, or an OT prophet." The paper was ungraded. I kicked myself for my weak-kneed decision to opt for pass/fail rather than risk the trauma of discovering a C emblazoned humiliatingly on my grbge dunpf of a manuscript.

After that last session, we headed for the Pump Quad, where we were giving Emma a going-away lunch, al fresco. Don, in an urgent aside, told me to give a toast. My old Unspontaneous Me dread at being asked to make impromptu remarks kicked in, but I was trapped. "Emma," I said, "our revels now are ended, and we thank you profoundly for your gentle magic, and your wicked humor, which have made these three weeks of learning so damned much fun." Emma laughed and raised her glass in appreciation. She had the kind of wholesome, healthy handsomeness that made me think of those farm lasses victimized by lecherous young nobs in a Thomas Hardy novel. No wonder she didn't like *Jude the Obscure,* although I didn't recall any young nobs figuring in the plot. Loosened by the wine and the knowledge that we were civilians again, we pried into Emma's background. As Lou Ann said, "Now it's time for you to mix the public and the private, Emma."

We learned that she was from Yorkshire, that her parents taught at a state high school, that she graduated from Somerville College, Oxford. She had a fellowship to All Souls, where she received a doctorate, and later a lectureship at New Hall, Cambridge. Now she was at Hertford College, teaching Shakespeare and Renaissance literature, 1590–1642. And also the university Anglo-American film course. No slouch, our Emma. And that wasn't all. She'd recently edited and written the introduction to the Penguin edition of Thomas Kyd's *The Spanish Tragedy,* the revenge play that was one of the precursors of *Hamlet.* Someone asked, "How big are your classes at Hertford?" "Most students I teach either one to one, or one to two. They write a paper each week, and that's the agenda for the discussion. I don't lecture—they've done their work before we meet, and they ask questions about things that have come up in their reading. Students have the opportunity to pretty much teach themselves."

During the lunch, I reflected on Emma's characteristic graciousness and generosity and naturalness and easy humor. And I mulled what she told us about tutorials, in which she dealt with two students at most, and about her nonlecture approach, which encouraged students to teach themselves and think for themselves. Perhaps for the Oxford/Berkeley course she had devised a technique that combined the intimate tutorial with a process that reached the "middle-range" students, and counted on the initiative of those who wanted to dig deeper into certain aspects of the plays. From the start, she'd made it clear that she was available for individual tutorial sessions beyond the two that were scheduled. And I hadn't troubled to arrange more than one tutorial, which I zipped through quickly, mentioning only that I was coming at *Lear* from what I felt was a unique perspective. All along I could have availed myself of her formidable knowledge, scheduling individual meetings or maybe getting together with Don and Lou Ann to come up with a topic we might discuss with Emma in a three-to-one tutorial, or, since Emma was amenable to our own ideas, I could in private have asked her to spend more time on scansion and dramaturgy. I bemoaned these lost opportunities and my pigheadedness and lack of resourcefulness in failing to adjust to the situation.

And finally it was time to bid Emma good-bye and all that. Hugs, a few tears, the traditional promises to keep in touch. Before leaving, Emma managed to amplify my already considerable pain of regret and guilt when she grasped my hands firmly and said, "It's been such a pleasure to have a kindred spirit in class. I expect to read your paper, or a ver-

sion of it, in a learned journal one of these days. Good luck. And remember, one must have a heart of stone to fail to laugh at Cordelia's
death."

After the party, I paid a last visit to my favorite haunts. We were leaving early the next morning. I recalled a scene from one of the funniest
movies ever made, *A New Leaf,* written and directed by Elaine May, who
costarred with Walter Matthau. Matthau's character, a debauched playboy
who's squandered the family fortune and has to sell off his treasured possessions to pay his debts, visits each of them to say farewell—his Ferrari,
his penthouse, his beach mansion, his private plane. My first stop: the
Bodleian and the Camera. I'd decided to say good-bye from the outside,
on the cobblestone area between the two buildings; going in would have
been too painful a reminder of the wealth of material I'd been unable to
examine, and of the interior atmospherics so conducive not only to study
but to fostering dreams of scholarship that was attainable to the persever-
ing. A more pleasurable reflection was the knowledge that the complete
works of Clavell and Barthelme were part of the Bodleian treasures. A
few days earlier, I'd asked one of the assistant research librarians to see if
these titles were available, and by God they were.

I sensed a presence beside me on the cobblestones and turned to find
an awkward, lumpish young man costumed in the garb of a bygone age.
He, too, seemed gripped by an agony of regret. Hey, Jude! But no, it
wasn't Jude Fawley, Hardy's stonemason. This chap's clothes were shabby,
and his shoes so worn that his feet showed through. Something was
wrong with his eyes—he could have been blind in one of them, and from
the look of the other, it was defective, too. Face scarred, probably from
smallpox. He turned out to be the son of a penniless Lichfield bookseller,
and his disease had not been smallpox but scrofula, a form of tuberculosis that damaged the eyes and ravaged the skin. Like me, he was saying
good-bye to Oxford. With only a small legacy left to his mother by a
cousin, and a gift from a friend, he'd been unable to last a year at Pembroke College. He'd come here a Young Man from the Provinces filled
with the romance of the Oxford tradition, ambitious for renown. But
now the funds were exhausted. He must leave. Name was Johnson.
Samuel Johnson. I should have tried to cheer him up, maybe ask him to

join me in an Old Speckled Hen at the Turf, but his aspect was too grim. Well, I thought, don't take it so hard, Sam. You'll have your fame soon enough. Perhaps someday you'll even edit an edition of Shakespeare's works and write a preface that will be studied until Dead White European Males are expunged from the curricula. He disappeared.

And so did I: Finis!

13.

When Emma screened a segment of Schwarze-
negger's movie *Last Action Hero* for us at Worcester, I speculated that
someday it would prove fertile exegetic ground for academicians eager to
connect the equally valid (so they say) "texts" of pop culture and classic
literature. I hadn't realized the day would come so soon. In late August,
just over a month after we'd returned from England, the cover article in
the summer 1999 issue of *Shakespeare Quarterly* was "You Kilt My Fod-
dah; or, Arnold, Prince of Denmark," by Eric S. Mallin, a professor at the
University of Texas. The movie, asserts Mallin, "slyly appropriates and interprets Shakespeare. And it introduces Arnold Schwarzenegger as a self-
conscious yet unconscious 'paratext'—a version located 'beyond, or
contrary to' (from the Greek *para*) the originary text while remaining
broadly referential to it." Paratext: that tips Professor Mallin's hand, warns
us of the jargon-burdened flights of hermeneutical ingenuity that are to
follow. One brief sample should suffice:

"Jack Slater [the police detective played by Arnold in the movie] is
not, he discovers, a person at all. He is, instead, a Ghost: an identity without a reality to attach itself to. In this sense he bears similarities to King
Hamlet, who shuttles between his purgatorial holding cell and Elsinore,
and, curiously, to Schwarzenegger himself, a 'star' in a fictive and unstable firmament."

Happily, this sort of near-parodistic explication was atypical of the
Shakespeare Quarterly. Most of the articles in the eight issues I'd read thus
far in my subscription cycle were, if not exactly riveting, at least straightforward, unfussy, thoughtful, and illuminating. The book and performance reviews, however, were a pleasure, penned with verve and humor
and erudition.

And for over a year I'd been receiving, every three months, the *Shakespeare Newsletter,* a thirty-to-thirty-five-page collection of scholarly arti-

243

cles, minutes of seminars and meetings and conferences, seminar abstracts, reviews, announcements. The contents of one representative issue included an unenthusiastic cover review of Harold Bloom's *Shakespeare: The Invention of the Human* by the *SNL*'s coeditor Thomas A. Pendleton, and minutes of the Columbia University Seminar on Shakespeare, where a panel discussed "Competing Editions of the Complete Work (Bevington, Norton, Riverside)." I noted among the participants in the Columbia panel none other than the Anti–Old Fart from my neck of the woods, who had good things to say about the three editions, probably because the editors—Bevington, Greenblatt, Evans, respectively—were not among the ancien régime.

Reading *SQ* and *SNL* gave me the sense of living vicariously in the community of scholars and allowed me to keep up with the goings-on in academia, familiarize myself with the best and worst of Shakespeare scholarship. And scholarship, at least my layman's version of it, was precisely what occupied me at the moment.

I had begun preparing lectures for the LLI course I'd arranged to teach in the fall. I'd decided not to build it around the comedies. Instead, I'd be offering a medley, an olio from the Folio as it were: two of the darker comedies, *Twelfth Night* and *Love's Labour's Lost,* both of which deal to a large extent with the ill uses to which language can be put; *The Winter's Tale,* a tragicomedy, or as Polonius might have defined it, a tragical-romantic-comedy-fantasy of redemption and reconciliation; and two historical dramas, *King John* and *Henry VIII,* the former sounding those familiar Shakespearean themes of usurpation, legitimacy, unholy alliances, and wars, foreign and domestic, the latter partly an almost fawning tribute to Henry VIII, partly a devastating tragedy of the fall of the monumentally hubristic Cardinal Wolsey. In all the plays, women had much to teach men about morals, ethics, humaneness, and good old-fashioned honest love. I liked the blending of the genres, the variety, and I thought the mixture achieved certain harmony that would appeal to the class, as would the fact that all but *Twelfth Night* would probably be new to them. Roxanne had agreed, and the course was scheduled for five weeks in November.

But a sense of frustration started to nag at me with the realization that given the LLI time limitation—slightly less than two hours for each play, including at least a half hour for video excerpts—I could put to use only a fraction of this rich material. And I thought about expanding my horizons as a teacher. It seemed unlikely that the LLI could absorb more than one Shakespeare course a semester, unless offered sequentially, and that would hardly be a solution to the problem of time. Perhaps one play a semester was the answer, or even two, anywhere from ten to sixteen weeks devoted to each work. And why not investigate the possibility of an adjunct professorship at Caldwell College, in addition to teaching at the LLI, thus working both ends of the age spectrum? Teaching undergraduates would challenge me to develop and broaden my pedagogical capacities. And it could be exciting to influence the formative minds of late adolescents, to make Shakespeare's plays sing in their heads and hearts. Adjunct professorships, I'd learned from a friend who teaches at the CUNY Graduate Center, were essentially part-time positions on a faculty; an adjunct professor could be hired at the last minute to handle the overflow from a particular course or to teach a course for a semester or two in his/her area of special expertise. I'd run this idea past Roxanne in November. When I mentioned it to Barbara, she said, "I know you'll find it deeply gratifying and richly rewarding to read student papers on why *Hamlet* is no better than a Bugs Bunny cartoon or how Mercutio is a real cool dude."

In the midst of this planning and deliberating came a Shabbat during which we read chapters XXI, 10–XXV of Deuteronomy, and as the cantor was chanting the Torah portion, one of the footnotes in my Chumash caught my eye. To line 16, "then it shall be, in the day that he causeth his sons to inherit that which he hath, that he may not make the son of the beloved the first-born before the son of the hated, who is the first-born," the editor, J. H. Hertz, had added this commentary: "Not necessarily at the approach of death, but at any time when he announces what the division of his property is to be at *his death*. The Rabbis forbid a man to distribute his possessions, Lear-like, in his lifetime; and they also warn a man against any discrimination between his children, aside from the privileges of the first-born." I regretted that I hadn't been aware of that passage and the Hertz elucidation when I was writing the *Lear* paper. The line itself had also escaped Richmond Noble's attention in his *Shakespeare's Biblical Knowledge,* which I'd come across in the Bodleian the past summer, and for good reason: without the rabbinic interpretation, nothing really ties it specifically to *Lear.* Now there was something to investigate: the influence of the Talmud on Shakespeare. Had he befriended a secret Jew, supposedly a *converso*—convert—but surreptitiously practicing the faith of his fathers, living and working as a goldsmith in Southwark, who instructed him in Mishnah and Gemara, and served as a model for Shylock? According to James Shapiro in *Shakespeare and the Jews,* "Perhaps the largest surviving body of evidence of the presence of Jews in Shakespeare's England concerns those Jews living in London in the last decade of the sixteenth century and the first of the seventeenth." And Park Honan, in his *Shakespeare: A Life,* reports that these *conversos,* or Marranos, Spanish and Portuguese Jews, also supplied intelligence to the crown before and after the war with Spain began in 1585. He also mentions a second small community of Jews, sixty or a hundred, descended from musicians recruited in Venice by Henry VIII; "some descendants," says Honan, "included royal musicians, a few of whom were likely to be known later to the author of *The Merchant of Venice.*" Perhaps this Southwark Jew was the actual playwright, slipping old Will the manuscripts in return for not revealing his identity to the authorities. Perhaps it was time for me to join the anti-Stratfordians with my stunning unmasking of the Bard's true identity: *Shakespeare and His Jew.*

At the Kiddush following Saturday morning services, the rabbi, Michael Monson, a stout, bearded dynamo, whose love for teaching, matched by his wide-ranging erudition, had energized our congregation since his arrival the previous year, approached me with his characteristic ebullience. "I know you have a passion for Shakespeare, and I think you might be interested in a book which landed on my desk the other day. It's about the Victorian attitude toward Shakespeare. The Jewish Book Council sent it to me but I won't have time to look at it for a while. Maybe you'd like to borrow it." Certainly I would. I'd briefly mentioned to him my ideas about the Jewishness of *King Lear,* but I'd yet to show him the paper. Exposing it to Emma Smith's inspection had made me jittery enough, and I wasn't quite prepared to suffer the judgment of a rabbinic scholar likelier to have found my speculations presumptuous, if not elementary.

On Monday morning, I picked up the book at the rabbi's office: *Shakespeare and the Politics of Culture in Late Victorian England,* by Linda Rozmovits, a lecturer in the departments of history and cultural studies at the University of East London. I wouldn't be able to read it until I'd finished polishing and rehearsing my lectures for the November course at the LLI. But I couldn't help browsing through the opening chapter, and it was a dismaying interlude.

In the first fourteen pages, Professor Rozmovits cited six books of which I'd been unaware and which might have made a difference in my conclusions about the Judaic influence on *King Lear: Shakespeare's Knowledge and Use of the Bible,* by Charles Wordsworth, Bishop of St. Andrews and nephew of the poet; *Biblical and Shakespearean Characters Compared,* by James Bell; *Shakespeare's Debt to the Bible,* by T. R. Eaton; *Sacred and Shakespearean Affinities,* by Charles Swinburne; *God in Shakespeare* and *The Messiahship of Shakespeare,* by Charles Downing. Surely these books were in the Bodleian Collection, but I hadn't bothered to check the card catalog for books relating to Shakespeare and the Bible. Some kind of scholar.

My performance, with its smug lack of initiative, its intellectual laziness, its dopey failure to grasp the basic processes of research, had actually been sub-dilettante. What a waste of an opportunity and a resource. And speaking of wasted opportunities, why hadn't I specified to Emma exactly what avenue I was pursuing in the *Lear* paper? What on earth had I thought a tutor was for? Had I feared she'd tell me the subject had already been treated, that I was reinventing the wheel? That I was another Mr. Casaubon, George Eliot's desiccated pedant, who discovered that the research he'd been doing for his book, *Key to All Mythologies,* was futile because he hadn't troubled to learn German, the language in which most of the new developments in the field were recorded? Who knew, that might be exactly what I'd find out if I could get my hands on those yet unread books. Emma probably hadn't been aware of the literature herself, or she would have called it to my attention gently in her comments on the paper, but at least she would have suggested that it might be a good idea to dig a bit deeper into the subject. You know, do a little goddamned research or something, as long as I was lounging around the Bod and Camera, waiting for Don and Lou Ann to pick me up for a trip to the Turf.

But why bother with asking my tutor for help? Who needed it? I had my sheaf of Xeroxes, I was ahead of the game.

As long as I was enjoying such a merry self-flagellation, why not look for a handful of salt to toss on the lacerations? I grabbed my copy of Schoenbaum and checked his bibliography to see how many of the Rozmovits Six he'd included. None. *None!* Thank you, God. Even more consoling, the only book he did list was none other than Noble's. But what did that prove? I'd still been guilty of shoddy, shallow, piss-poor research. And until I'd actually read the Six, I wouldn't be satisfied that my approach in "God's Spy" was unique. Me and Mr. Casaubon.

Time for a moment of truth. I checked out the Six on the Internet, to see if they were in print, or at least available from the website dealing with out-of-print books, Bibliofind. Two of the volumes turned up on Bibliofind: *Shakespeare's Knowledge and Use of the Bible* and *The Messiahship of Shakespeare.* I ordered both. And on the Net I discovered what might turn out to be an even more disturbing work, this one published only a few months previously by the Oxford University Press: *The Biblical Presence in Shakespeare, Milton, and Blake,* by Harold Fisch. Among the Shakespearean plays was *King Lear.* Not a good sign. I ordered it, too, with grave misgivings. The author was emeritus professor at Bar-Ilan University and, I assume, an Israeli, whose antennae couldn't help picking up the Judaic vibrations in *Lear.*

Coming swiftly and appropriately on the heels of my seizure of self-chastisement were the Days of Awe, the High Holy Days, Rosh ha-Shanah and Yom Kippur, for Jews a celebration of the start of a new year and an effort to atone for sins of the past year, a period of rigorous self-examination, during which we pray for forgiveness and renewal, hoping to become, as Michael Strassfeld puts it in *The Jewish Holidays,* "a new and improved version, not just the same old self one year older and deeper in debt." My attempts since retiring to evaluate what I'd done and what I wanted to do, who I really was and who I really wanted to be, had made the last several High Holy Days especially significant for me.

During his Rosh ha-Shanah sermon, Rabbi Monson reminded us that one of the Jewish sages had declared that publicly humiliating a person is the equivalent of murder. I recalled the times when, as a boss, unable to resist the bullying impulse, the urge to crush and demean, I'd rebuked employees at meetings for their inadequate job performances, and when I, in turn, had been stung by the abuse from the head of the company in the presence of colleagues. And I realized that what the rabbi had said related directly to two of the plays in my forthcoming course.

First, the scene in *Love's Labour's Lost* when the pedant Holofernes and his risible cohorts present the ridiculous Pageant of the Nine Worthies to the King of Navarre, his lords, the Princess of France and her attending ladies. It's a screamingly funny episode at first as Shakespeare mocks the ineptitude of amateur players, with the spectators interrupting the goings-on with taunting jests, and we join these aristocrats in their glee at the expense of these posturing bumblers—then, suddenly, Shakespeare shows us how cruel they (and we) have been simply by having Holofernes say, at last, after suffering the incessant japery of the lords, "This is not generous, not gentle, not humble."

I also thought of how Shakespeare makes us sympathize unwittingly with Malvolio, the prim, vain, status-seeking steward in *Twelfth Night*. Malvolio has been tricked into believing that Olivia, the rich countess whom he serves, loves him, and he consequently behaves so preposterously that he's deemed mad and for a time locked in a dark, windowless room. But his humiliation and fear have been so painful that we begin to realize the pranksters—not a lovable group to begin with—have gone too far, and when at last Malvolio confronts Olivia, who's unaware that his behavior has been the result of a practical joke, with the agonized reproach "Madam, you have done me wrong," she seeks an explanation, and at last enlightened says, along with us, "He hath been most notoriously abused."

And the Yom Kippur services brought to mind another of the plays I'd be teaching, and one I'd taught the first semester. As we stood for the Viddui, the confessional, during which some congregants gently smite their chests with closed fists in a gesture of self-condemnation, I remembered Malcolm Storry's Enobarbus beating his breast with lethal vehemence, the soldier's ultimate atonement for betraying a commander. During Neilah, the concluding service of Yom Kippur, which ends dramatically with the final blast of the shofar, the ram's horn, evoking the feeling that we've passed from sin to repentance, from death to life, an image flashed in my head from *The Winter's Tale*. Leontes, whose jealous rage has caused the death of his son and, he believes, his wife, Hermione, and their infant daughter, atones for sixteen years and then, in the concluding scene, watches as what he's been told is a statue of Hermione comes to life. Of course, she hasn't been dead at all, merely hiding in the home of her friend Paulina, awaiting the fulfillment of an oracle predicting (correctly, as it turns out) that her daughter was still alive. But this doesn't lessen the impact of the symbolic tableau of salvation, atonement, forgiveness, pardon, healing, peace, renewal, as marble is made flesh.

On the way home after services, another image came to me: the secret Jew in Southwark whom I'd envisioned, the goldsmith who's become friendly with Shakespeare and trusts him not to reveal his true identity. On this particular night, the conclusion of Yom Kippur, he shows Shakespeare the shofar and explains its significance, maybe even dares to sound it briefly. Perhaps on other occasions he's shown Will such ritual paraphernalia as tallis (prayer shawl) and tefillin (phylacteries), and demonstrated how to wrap the latter around his forehead and arm. But on this night what reaches deep into Shakespeare's soul and will haunt him forever is that piercing cry of the shofar, the single long note, the essence of which he will try to express in the conclusion to *The Winter's Tale.*

The week after the High Holy Days, as if in answer to penitential prayers, arrived the three books dealing with Shakespeare and the Bible that I'd ordered with some trepidation. I tore open the cartons immediately, dreading that I'd find evidence that what I thought was an original approach to *King Lear* had been explored by savants past and present. But the out-of-print volumes from the past blessedly yielded no long-buried mines of interpretation that would explode in my face. Bishop Wordsworth's *Shakespeare's Knowledge and Use of the Bible* contained three long chapters dealing with noticeable forms of speech and noticeable words found in the English Bible and Shakespeare, allusions in Shakespeare to the historical facts and characters in the Bible, Shakespeare's religious principles and sentiments and poetry derived from the Bible. Downing's *The Messiahship of Shakespeare* fulfilled the expectations of its bizarre title. In *God in Shakespeare,* which I'd been unable to obtain, Downing read the plays (so Linda Rozmovits tells us) as a progressive revelation of Christian doctrine. In the small volume that followed, and which I read, Downing tries to prove the idea behind his title with a brand of exegesis that combines the kooky, the convoluted, and the inscrutable. For instance: "Shakespeare, at one with the Spirit and with God, at one with Christ the Judge, in a series of great tragedies had judged the world . . . the theatre of Shakespeare becomes as sacred as the Church of Christ and one with it." Outlandish? Well, I myself was among those who mulled the supernatural qualities of Shakespeare, the mystico-religious nature of the theatre, and the religious impulse behind the construction—and the latest reconstruction—of the Globe. And as one who was suggesting that *King Lear* depicts an evolution from paganism to ethical monotheism, and that Shakespeare had the Torah in mind when he wrote the tragedy, who was I to call Mr. Downing a kook? At least he had had the decency not to intrude in my playground.

Turning to the contemporary book by Harold Fisch, I discovered, as I had suspected, that he perceives biblical patterns in *King Lear*. But scarcely anything in his essay, "King Lear: Organized Incoherence," anticipated my argument, and nothing in it invalidated my observations. What distressed me was that with more enterprising and aggressive research, I might have spotted this highflier on the radar screen and used it to enrich my paper.

Professor Fisch argues quite correctly that the Gloucester-Edgar-Edmund subplot has a moral pattern that is specifically biblical, and offers as an example Edgar, as Tom o' Bedlam, "referring the world's troubles not to a nature mythology but to the biblical code of moral judgement: 'Take heed o' th' foul fiend. Obey thy parents; keep thy word's justice; swear not; commit not with man's sworn spouse; set not thy sweet heart on proud array'" (3.4.80–83). That's a segment I'd overlooked while working on my paper; I could have used it to good effect in speculating on the paganism-to-ethical-monotheism motif.

Later in the essay, he singles out "another biblical pattern no less important for this play to which I wish to draw attention, and that is the story of Isaac's blessing of his two sons, Esau and Jacob. . . . Here is what may be termed the biblical subtext of *King Lear*. Isaac like Gloucester is blind. His two sons had been in competition for the birthright which Jacob had earlier wrested from Esau. There is a close and subtle pattern of analogy linking the biblical text with Shakespeare's play: the blind

251

Gloucester cries out to his supposedly absent son Edgar: 'Might I but live to see thee in my touch, I'd say I had eyes again' (IV.1.23–4) recalling the words of the blind Isaac to his son Jacob: 'Come near, now, that I may feel thee, my son.' " I'd found additional biblical instances of sibling rivalry, and of fathers favoring one child over another.

Significantly, Professor Fisch notes that the blessing motif seems to have been suggested to Shakespeare's mind in the first place by *The True History of King Leir*—the source of the main plot. For example, Leir at one point declares to Cordella, "The blessing which the God of Abraham gave / Unto the trybe of Juda, light on thee. . . ." Professor Fisch concludes that it's probable that this scene prompted Shakespeare "to turn the blessings in Genesis to dramatic account." But I wondered why he chose not to acknowledge any possible influence on Shakespeare (or on the author of *Leir*) of Holinshed's biblical parallels for the history of Leir.

Overall I found Professor Fisch's ideas provocative and learned and deeply meditated, and I determined to draw on them if ever I expanded my grbge dunpf.

The first week in November I returned to the teaching mode at Caldwell College's Lifelong Learning Institute, lecturing on the mixed quintet of Shakespeare for two hours on Tuesday mornings. I'd missed the classroom, missed my friends, missed the simple processes of driving to the college, browsing through the library stacks before class began or going over my notes one more time in the teachers' lounge. Reinvigorated by the visit to the Folger, the time at Oxford, and my recent studies, I was eager to apply what I'd learned in terms of teaching techniques, insights into the plays, and ways of probing character and analyzing dramatic structure and language.

Before class I dropped in on Roxanne and asked her if she thought an adjunct professorship would be out of my reach. "I don't see why. The only obstacle might be your lack of a graduate degree, but your life experience, your achievements, ought to count for something. Send your résumé with a covering letter to Sister Elizabeth Michael Boyle, the chair of the English department. And meanwhile, I'll put in a good word for you. The success of your Shakespeare course at the LLI could be another mark in your favor." She handed me the class roster for the fall. Obviously, the idea of a medley of plays hadn't been a deterrent: the enrollment to-taled twenty-five, about half of them returnees. But I noticed that Midge's name was absent from the list. I wondered if she'd tired of my routine. That would be depressing. But the reason for her nonenrollment was more than depressing. It was devastating. "Midge passed away last June," Roxanne said. "She had a heart condition." I thought of one of her fa-vorite lines from *Troilus and Cressida*: "that old common arbitrator, Time, will one day end it." Good-bye, Midge. I'm sorry you didn't get around to writing that Quartet from *T&C*.

In the classroom, my pals, feisty Bob and waggish Lou, greeted me with a present—a Shakespeare marionette, which they positioned so that it perched on the edge of my desk. "We thought of getting you a votive candle to go along with it," said Lou, "but decided it would be de trop." Also back for more were Gilda and Rose, and the sisters Madelyn and Marie, joined now by three additional members of our synagogue, Phyl-lis and Howard and Arnold. Almost a minyan.

I began by describing, with thanks to Peter Saccio's *Shakespeare's En-glish Kings*, a striking change Shakespeare makes in the source material for *King John*. He adds a character who turns out to be one of his most mem-orable creations—Philip Faulconbridge, bastard son of Richard Coeur de Lion. And in contrast to historical interpretation of John's reign, Shake-speare presents John as a flat-out usurper and makes legitimacy the central idea of the play, as it was throughout the history plays we'd studied in a previous semester. Thus Philip the Bastard, a man of dubious social status, ironically proves to be nobler than the blue bloods who surround him.

I read aloud the Bastard's irony-charged sililoquy at the end of act 2, scene 1. He has just witnessed two bitter enemies, King John and the French king, Philip Augustus, who is supporting the claim to the throne of John's young nephew, Arthur, put aside—at the suggestion of Hubert de Burgh, the canny leading official of Angier—their differences and agree to a diplomatic marriage between John's niece, Blanche, and Philip Au-gustus's son, Lewis the Dauphin. After the deal is done, the Bastard, left alone onstage, rails against "tickling Commodity, . . . the bias of the world." Commodity—self-interest, compromise, expediency, oppor-tunism. Then, in what appears to be a disarming burst of candor, he de-clares that he's indignant only because Commodity "hath not wooed me yet," and vows "Since kings break faith upon commodity / Gain, be my lord, for I will worship thee." The irony is that the Bastard is the least deceitful, least opportunistic, least Machiavellian character in the play, remaining loyal to John until the end. Why then, I asked the class, does he take the audience into his confidence and deliver such cynical pronunciamentos? These are the kinds of speeches that Shakespeare usually gives to his villains. Does he expect us to believe the Bastard? Does the Bastard himself believe what he's saying? Or is he trying to convince himself that he can be as ruthless and hypocritical as those around him? How would an actor deliver these lines, especially the final one, to convey the various interpretations? We agreed that he's trying to persuade himself, that he's talking more to himself than to us, and that the most effective emotional note would not be one of defiance, a la "Now gods, stand up for bastards," but rather one of feigned wryness, concealing a painful disillusionment.

I also read aloud the scene in which John proposed to Hubert de Burgh, the consummate politician, diplomat, and opportunist who had suggested the marriage of convenience, that de Burgh kill John's nephew, Arthur, removing a potential threat to the crown (the harmony between France and England had been brief; hostilities again erupted, the French were defeated, and Arthur was captured). At once appalling and comic, I said that it reminded me of the scene in *Richard III* in which Richard, after dropping hints to his disingenuously dense accomplice, the Duke of Buckingham, comes out bluntly with his plans for the two young princes in the Tower: "I want the bastards dead." John plays it coy at first with Hubert, who a la Buckingham, misses the point, and finally John wastes no more time in circumlocution. In a ten-word exchange, John makes himself perfectly clear, and Hubert quickly assents.

> KING JOHN: Death.
> HUBERT: My lord?
> KING JOHN: A grave.
> HUBERT: He shall not live.
> KING JOHN: Enough.

Two masterly verse lines, the first being only one word, and the second a shared verse line. I asked the class how they would direct the actors to deliver the lines. Quickly, with no pauses, each actor picking up the cue instantly, since this is a single pentameter line? A single pause somewhere? A pause after each short speech? Lou favored a lot of pauses, Phyllis and Marie voted for none. I then read to them a section in Barton's *Playing Shakespeare,* during which David Suchet and Patrick Stewart discussed their approach. Suchet said that he and an actor who played the king rehearsed the scene once with a pause after every line, and he recalled that Barton made them do it again quickly. Stewart suggested that because of the two verse lines, there was another choice—taking a pause after "Death"—that is, after the end of the very first verse line instead of running the whole thing together. Barton agreed that it was possible. "It's what I call an earned pause," he said. "If we have lots and lots of pauses, we will probably overload things. But if we have one in the right place, particularly at the end of a verse line, it can be very telling." I mentioned Cicely Berry's remarks about the reason for a short line: "a demand within the situation . . . for silence. It may be that . . . the thought needs time to settle between the characters." Which definitely justifies the pause after "Death."

Finally, we watched segments from the BBC production of *King John.* Especially moving was Claire Bloom's portrayal of Constance, Arthur's mother. This semester I wanted to make certain that performance criticism was not simply free-flowing but as often as possible related the visual to the verbal, observing how the director's and actor's interpretation relates to what Shakespeare has written. So I pointed out that in her final three lines in the play, lamenting the death of her son—"O Lord! My boy, my Arthur, my fair son! / My life, my joy, my food, my all the world! / My widow-comfort, and my sorrow's cure!"—Ms. Bloom starts to exit but at the end of each phrase turns before speaking the next, lending the words an exceptional force. In so doing, she seems to be taking a page out of Cicely Berry's *The Actor and the Text,* in which Berry, as Emma had noted in class, suggests that in order for actors to discover their feelings as they speak, it is helpful to walk on each punctuation mark in a speech.

In October, I had a call from Jeffrey Horowitz's assistant at TFANA, Benjamin Krevorin, who told me that Cicely Berry's classes would begin in November, and we agreed on a day when it would be appropriate for me to attend, which was the day after my first LLI class. I entered the Ballet Tech Studios on Broadway near Nineteenth Street, in a near-frenzy of expectation at the prospect of watching Ms. Berry at work and, knock wood, of meeting her. The building was ancient, with the bleak scruffiness unique to rehearsal studios. I rode the vintage elevator, the kind that requires an operator, to the eighth floor and was greeted in the corridor by Benjamin: "Ciss should be along shortly. The class will be doing exercises for the first ten minutes or so. Why don't you take a seat and I'll call you when we begin to present scenes." He explained that on previous days the participants, all of them working professionals, had been off in separate groups rehearsing scenes from Shakespeare, using exercises devised by Ms. Berry, and that today they'd do a "show-and-tell" for her to critique. He showed me to an alcove which served as a reception room and I plunked myself on a tattered, faded maroon sectional couch. I'd just started to relax when a diminutive white-haired woman materialized from around the corner and, approaching me and smiling radiantly, said, "Mr. Gollob?" I stood up and as we shook hands she continued, "I'm Cicely Berry. So nice to have you here. We'll be starting our exercises in a moment, and afterwards Benjamin will come fetch you."

Caught off guard, suddenly face-to-face with a legend, I was totally flustered. Not that she was an intimidating presence: she couldn't have been more than five feet tall, if that; her face, somewhat lined, glowed with warmth, and her eyes were at once merry and piercing—she would not suffer fools gladly, but she wouldn't humiliate them, either. She was dressed in a black pantsuit, the jacket open and loosely fitting, and a black pullover. Squarish and slightly on the heavy side, she was a bit stooped, but charged with vitality. I mumbled something fatuous, like "What an honor to meet you," and thought to myself, This will never do, this bashful oafish starstruck routine, for God's sake. At least let her know you're aware who Shakespeare is, but try not to show off. She was just starting to walk back to the studio when I blurted out, "Miss Berry, may I ask you a question?" She turned and peered at me intently, her smile a trifle less engaging, it seemed. I continued: "In that scene in *King John* in which John orders Hubert to murder Arthur, should there be any pauses in that shared line which follows John's 'Death'?"

Without missing a beat, she briskly replied, "Yes, you see there's a caesura there, right after John says, 'A grave.' A pause before Hubert replies, 'He shall not live.' But I call it a 'poise' on the word—the word lifts for a moment before Hubert picks up the second half." And off she went, leaving me to marvel at her exact recollection of the passage as I waited for Benjamin to fetch me, which he did a short while later.

Ms. Berry was sitting at a table, taking notes. Those not performing ranged themselves in chairs around her. I recognized several people from appearances in *Law and Order* and the TFANA's *Macbeth*. I sat behind and to the left of Ms. Berry. The director of the first segment, a young woman with very short brown hair and a café au lait complexion, explained that her group had chosen 3.2 from *As You Like It,* featuring Rosalind, disguised as the man Ganymede, and Orlando; that she'd squelched her desire to tell the actors what to do, where to move, and instead allowed them to do movement exercises to free their imaginations; and that we'd be seeing their first attempt to incorporate what they'd learned into the performance. The actor was swarthy, had a black mustache, and appeared to be in his twenties. The actress, a blonde also in her twenties, wore a baseball cap sideways on her head. They read from paperback copies of the play. Orlando was sulkily lovesick; Rosalind urged him to let her (or him—Ganymede) cure him of this madness. They did the scene three times, altering the tempo (slow and deliberate at first) and the movement and the line interpretations. When they finished, the director said, "An hour before we started this morning, we discovered this whole scene is a game—the two characters are trying to find out exactly what the game is." I had no idea what that meant. Ms. Berry said, "Each time you did the scene, you began to find the rhythm. You're getting the rhythm beautifully. The humor is in the rhythm. We must obey the unalterable laws of rhythm. Those rhythms are there in the text—we need to inhabit them." Elaborating on this, she described an experience she had when she was coaching the actress who was playing the Fool in a production of *King Lear.* It seemed that the actress's father, a stand-up comic in Scotland, happened to be at rehearsal one day and was astonished that the rhythms Shakespeare had created for the Fool were the same the comic used in his routines. Someone in the class asked the actors if the movement exercises

257

had helped them find the humor. The answer: "We were not looking for the humor." Ms. Berry commented that "we must delight in the sound of the language—don't think about it intellectually."

Next, a group, also reading from a script, showed the work it had done on the scene in *Antony and Cleopatra* in which Antony returns in disgrace from Actium and angrily confronts Cleopatra. The black actor playing Antony had been acting a feeling—he'd been concerned with the result of an action rather than the action itself. So Ms. Berry instructed the class to build a "tower of chairs" in the middle of the room; Antony would have to try to pull it down, all the while being harassed and blocked by the group, some of whom stood in his way so that he had to push them aside, others replacing the chairs as he removed them. That was the way to make the language come alive, Ms. Berry said, to create the absurdity and chaos that produce the emotions. "It's not what we feel, it's what we do. I don't want to hear about feelings." Faced with the resistance created by the tower of chairs, Antony's shame and rage were charged with conviction and immediacy. Moreover, when the actors repeated the scene, the actor playing Antony was able to apply what he'd learned from the exercise, and the scene was vastly energized. To Antony, Ms. Berry remarked, "What you've learned is that you have to discover shame and anger—discover the feelings, not merely describe them." The RSC credo.

Next, two actors with scripts in hand worked on 4.5 from *Henry IV, Part 2,* in which Prince Hal, at the bedside of his mortally ill father, mistakenly concludes that the king has died and tries on the crown himself, only to be bitterly chastised by the revived monarch. The actor playing Henry was in late middle age, robust and ruddy, with short wavy gray hair and rimless glasses. He looked like a prosperous banker, except for the corduroys and the sweater. Hal was a tall scholarly-looking young man, also bespectacled, wearing a short neatly trimmed beard. The first attempt was little more than an intelligent reading, the actors unable to bring life to this complex scene, which is tense with unresolved issues between father and son. One of the class declared, "There's actually a third character in this scene—the crown." Ms. Berry seized on this avidly: "Yes, yes, absolutely. I wish I'd thought of that. Keep that thought, and do the scene again."

As the two actors began anew, Ms. Berry whispered something to a young man in the class. A few seconds into the scene, the young man plucked the crown—a simple black circular headpiece, a rehearsal prop—from a table beside the king and handed it to someone in the audience. Moments later Hal retrieved it, only to have it wrested away by another actor. This process of "who's got the crown, who wants the crown, who needs the crown" continued to the end, forcing the two actors to focus on the essence of the scene, the changes in mood and thought, as the tower of chairs had done in the previous scene, and similarly infused it with vitality. All the while Ms. Berry leaned forward in her chair, her face clenched with an almost forbidding concentration, lips compressed, projecting a sense of determination I could only think of as Churchillian. At the finish of the scene, she said, "There's no sentiment in this scene. It's all about dying, about the need to be real, to be practical—it's the hardness of realpolitik, and that's what you're showing. That's why the emotions are real. We must find out what we're thinking before we can feel."

When the class broke for the afternoon, I thanked Ms. Berry and Benjamin for allowing me behind the scenes to watch a dedicated band of players work at developing their craft and discovering ways to achieve a sense of emotional honesty and immediacy in Shakespearean performance. "Do come again," Ms. Berry said, "and next time, perhaps you can join in our exercises before class." Right, gracious lady. Just the thing for a man whose chief desire in these situations—a stranger in a strange land—is to blend in with the scenery.

My second lecture at the LLI covered *Henry VIII*, and as I drove to Caldwell, I reflected on the time I first became aware of it: the summer of 1979, the day before my father's operation for prostate cancer. It was Sunday; I'd arrived in Houston on Friday, to bring him home from the hospital where he'd been examined and diagnosed. The operation was scheduled for Monday at M. D. Anderson Cancer Center, one of the world's leading facilities for cancer treatment.

That Sunday was aggressively hot and humid. When I'd recoiled from the first blast of dragon's breath that struck me upon opening the front door of our house, now stripped of its air conditioners, my father, unfazed by the heat, reassured me, "Son, as soon as it gets dark you'll start feeling those cool Gulf breezes." In a Houston July, Gulf breezes are rare, and never cool. Most often, a Gulf breeze was a hurricane, which flooded the streets in a matter of seconds and lifted up trees and dropped them on your car.

Right away, I noticed that the house sorely needed a fierce scouring. Debilitated by an illness that he'd too long refused to acknowledge, my father had been unable to perform even basic housekeeping. And he'd always been averse to cleaning services: "The sons of bitches will check out the house, see I'm here alone, and then come back with theft on their minds." I didn't know why that prospect disturbed him: the house was damned near burglarproof with bars over every window, and my father kept a veritable arsenal of pistols on the premises—five to be exact, one by his bedside at all times. Coupled with the heat, the grime and scum in the kitchen and bathroom made the place uninhabitable, southern gothic in fact. The thought of my father spending the past few months in this squalor was not something to dwell on. And I knew I couldn't stay there even a week unless I immediately broke into a maniacal Comet and Lysol routine. So I stripped to my shorts, and the fun began.

I attacked sinks, tub, stove, cabinets, toilet bowls with a sense of mission, a man possessed. It was an act of restoration, of reclamation. A metaphoric act of healing, a ritual that might produce a similar restoring of my father to soundness of body. Gushing sweat like a stoker on an old coal-fueled freighter, I began to experience an odd sense of euphoria; perhaps I was purging myself of all the impurities of mind and body I'd acquired in the iniquitous East—another healing process—or, to be less fanciful, perhaps it was merely the result of the glacial cans of Pearl beer I was swilling every few minutes to replenish my precious bodily fluids. My father kept the refrigerator (or icebox, as he insisted on calling it, a colloquialism I, too, retain) stocked with six-packs of Pearl, designated for my use only, during my too-infrequent visits. He'd been virtually a teetotaler all his life, with the exception of those Saturdays long ago when he brought home a pile of barbecue and unfailingly washed it down with beer, which he had poured over a juice glass filled with ice cubes. Beer on the rocks. Awful.

In the living room that Sunday, watching television while I scoured away ecstatically, my father was experiencing his own euphoric blast. He called out to me exuberantly, "Son, get in here! You've got to see this goddamned thing. They're showing Shakespeare's *Henry VIII* on TV!" From the sound of his voice, you'd never have guessed that this was a man facing surgery for prostate cancer in less than twenty-four hours, and enduring such terrible pain in his legs (the cancer had metastasized into his lower back) that he could scarcely walk. I told him I'd pop in as soon as I finished policing up the area (in my father's lexicon, the word "cleaning" did not exist; it was always "policing up"), and I asked him to turn up the sound so I could at least hear the language. I was unfamiliar with the play; not only had I never read it, I'd never heard of it.

Scraping a few inches of grease off the top of the kitchen range, reveling in the sense of accomplishment engendered by the completion of simple menial tasks, I could hear tantalizing scraps of Bardic dialogue and an occasional encomium from my father: "Son, the bastard who's playing Wolsey is as good as Paul Muni!" And a few minutes later: "Son, this Claire Bloom will make you cry. Did you know she's Jewish?" From the sound of her voice, wafting from the living room to the downstairs powder room, where I was giving the commode a Lysol gargle, Ms. Bloom, as Queen Katherine, was in the process of dying, an irony not lost on me.

By the time my domestic artistry was completed and the place gleamed like the interiors in *House Beautiful*, *Henry VIII*, too, had come to an end. And I was to see it for the first time twenty years later as I collected material for the LLI course. During the intervening years, I couldn't bring myself either to read the play or to find a videotape, reluctant to live through the memories they would arouse. But now that I'd versed myself in the play, I preferred it to some of those more favored by critics and scholars. And Kevin Billington's televised version for the BBC Shakespeare series is to me one of the most enthralling film adaptations of Shakespeare.

I arrived at Caldwell College an hour before class was to begin and spent the time browsing among the stacks in Jennings Library. And what should catch my eye but a little item titled *Biblical Influences in Shakespeare's Great Tragedies*, by Peter Milward, S.J., published by the Indiana University Press in the 1970s. Another treasure that the Bodleian undoubtedly had in its collection which I hadn't been diligent enough to ferret out. Perchance did Father Milward, with piercing Jesuitical acuity, make the Genesis connection in *King Lear;* did he discern the Jewishness of this great tragedy? Had a Mighty Hand guided me to the library that morning to teach me yet another lesson in humility? Time to find out.

In the *Lear* section, Father Milward, in his comment regarding "God's spies," did come very close to identifying Lear, as I had, with the Hebrew prophets. "These 'spies,'" he writes, "appear in the Old Testament as prophets, as in Amos iii.7, 'Surely the Lord God will do nothing but he revealeth his secret with his servants the prophets.'" If I could ever steel myself to the task of revising the work I'd done at Worcester, I'd have to cite Father Milward's observation.

At the beginning of class, I said that I wished Shakespeare (or Shakespeare and John Fletcher, since it's generally acknowledged that Fletcher collaborated on the play with Shakespeare) had written *Cardinal Wolsey* instead of *Henry VIII.* The portrait of Henry is almost ludicrously romanticized—we are shown an ideal monarch who is the very model of virtue, wisdom, benevolence, a virtual king of kings. It's Wolsey who commands our interest, seizes our imagination. Wolsey, with his towering virtues and qualities, and his classic tragic flaw—hubris. The classic overreacher. It wasn't enough that he was lord chancellor with almost all the powers of the king's council. He actually wanted to be pope, and ironically that's what brought him down; he inadvertently included in a packet of papers sent to the king an inventory of wealth he'd accumulated in order to buy the next papal election. Also included by mistake was a letter to the pope urging him not to sanction Henry's divorce from Katherine (Wolsey hated Anne Boleyn). Yes, he was greedy and arrogant and corrupt (bribe-taking and simony and the keeping of mistresses were among his myriad unsavory practices). But as Peter Saccio points out, Wolsey was the last great medieval ecclesiastical statesman of England, the man who did most of the daily work of government and the real shaping of foreign policy. And in important ways he was a man after Shakespeare's own heart: like Shakespeare, whose father was a provincial glover, Wolsey, the son of an Ipswich butcher, rose from humble origins to national renown. Both men were fueled with a passion to scale the ladder to success and status.

Again, crediting Saccio, I turned to an example of Shakespeare's dramaturgical brilliance in compressing historical events for the sake of emotional intensity and continuity: Wolsey's fall, which occurs in one long scene, 3.2., in reality took place over three years. Ed put his finger on one of the problems in characterization that result from this compression: "I thought Wolsey's repentance too quick to be for real. The lords come in and read him the riot act, and as soon as they're gone he goes into that speech full of self-awareness and regret." Excellent point. But we all agreed that abrupt though it may be, that burst of self-knowledge soars with tragic exaltation (e.g., "Vain pomp and glory of this world, I hate ye! / I feel my heart new opened").

As usual, I ended the class by showing video excerpts, in this instance the trial that questions the validity of Henry's marriage to Katherine, and the depiction of Wolsey's fall. Everyone joined me in lauding the uniformly rich performances.

I asked the class why they thought Kevin Billington had directed Timothy West, who captured all of Wolsey's meanness and greatness, to turn his back on the camera and start exiting with Cromwell when delivering his final and oft-quoted three lines, "Had I but served my God with half the zeal / I served my king, he would not in mine age / Have left me naked to mine enemies." Lou suggested that Wolsey's turning his back to us, shoulders slightly slumped, more effectively conveys a fallen titan, whereas if he'd been facing Cromwell and/or us and the camera, the lines might have sounded like a self-conscious maxim. How could I argue with performance criticism as perceptive as that?

The past May, as soon as I returned from the Folger, I'd intended to explore the Teaching Shakespeare website about which Janet Field-Pickering had waxed so enthusiastically. But to my consternation when I called it up on the Internet, the site failed to function, no matter how many times I whacked away at the icon. Having only a rudimentary grasp of computerology, I assumed that my Macintosh was congenitally incapable of connecting to this particular site and I gave up the effort. By chance I happened to bring this up in a chat with Marie and Madelyn at the end of the *Henry VIII* lecture, and Madelyn, my "technical adviser," instantly diagnosed the problem: "Your computer has insufficient memory. All you need is a new chip. Any dealer can install one in five minutes." And so he did, that very day. By evening, I'd booted up the computer and found

263

myself lost for hours in the pedagogic magic of the Folger lesson plans created by teachers around the country who are happy to share their ideas with colleagues. One striking example:

Janet herself had come up with "It's Elementary!—Stomping and Romping with Shakespeare," an approach to rhythm and meter based on her experience with Shakespeare Steps Out, the Folger's elementary outreach program in the D.C. public schools. In introducing Shakespeare to elementary students, she said, the best place to start is with the rhythm of the language in Shakespeare's songs. "Children respond to the sound and beat of Shakespeare as much as they respond to his wonderful stories and characters. Shakespeare's songs are also short, self-contained (in terms of what's going on with the rest of the play), and often include vivid images and word pictures." As an exercise, she suggested asking the children to place their hands over their hearts and feel the *da-DUM, da-DUM, da-DUM* of their own heartbeats, and then telling them that Shakespeare used the rhythm of the heart in his poems and plays. Iambic pentameter as the rhythm of the heart: I couldn't think of a more evocative definition, one that went right to the throbbing humanity of Shakespearean drama. And I couldn't think of a more dramatic method of preparing children for the experience of having Shakespeare's language pulse inside their minds and bodies. The children then form a circle and march around the room to the beat, a softly placed left foot followed by a sharply stomped right, reading aloud from Dr. Seuss's *Green Eggs and Ham,* substituting the words from "A Winter's Song" from *Love's Labour's Lost,* the play I'd be discussing during the next class.

Tom Fitzgerald, a high school teacher in Colorado, described an approach to *Othello* in "Words, Words, Words." He assigned his students words that represent the "big ideas" in the play and that recur throughout the play, and had them trace these words in the text, recording which character says the word and in what context. Students look up the meanings in the *Oxford English Dictionary* and the Early Modern English Dictionaries Database website at the University of Toronto. Fitzgerald said that a student who successfully completes this assignment will become aware of the role of diction and voice in character development.

If Emma Smith had dropped this little task in our laps at Worcester, I fear it would have sent many of us scurrying for the next bus to

Heathrow, or into cardiac arrest. How representative was Mr. Fitzgerald, I wondered, of high school English teachers across the country? And how well had the teenagers in Mr. Fitzgerald's class performed? It seemed to me that his assignment would tax the capacities of a bright university graduate student. Could undergraduates at Caldwell College be up to the challenge? Perhaps I'd be able to find out for myself as an adjunct professor of Shakespeare.

I began the lecture on *Love's Labour's Lost* by asking what key Shakespearean theme appears early in the opening moments of the play. Marie, Madelyn's sister, and the person I designated my technical adviser for her expertise with the VCR, leaped in first: "The futility of utopias, of following theories instead of listening to common sense." Then Gilda added, "I'd put it another way—the way human relations can be ruined when people follow their heads rather than their hearts." Good enough. In act 1, scene 1, we discover that the King of Navarre has established an academy, consisting of himself and three young lords who attend on him, secluded from the world and from women, for the cultivation of the intellect and the pursuit of truth for its own sake, hoping to achieve eternal fame through devotion to study. He refers to them as "brave conquerors" who "war against your own affections." One of the three, the skeptical Berowne, noticeably a spokesman for the playwright, recognizes how unnatural it is to divorce scholarship from life. "What is the end of study?" he asks the king, who responds, "Why, that to know which else we should not know," prompting from Berowne the biting rhetorical question, delivered with a straight face, "Things hid and barred, you mean, from common sense?" To which the king, not quite getting it, obtusely replies, "Ay, that is study's godlike recompense." Then Berowne bursts into an impassioned refutation of the academy's preposterous ambition, ending with "Small have continual plodders ever won / Save base authority from others' books." So much for Shakespeare's opinion of *la vie académique*.

I raised what I thought was a crucial point: Shakespeare's use of Holofernes the Pedant and his sycophantic stooge, Nathaniel the Curate, and Don Adriano de Armado, the "fantastic Spaniard" ("fantastic" because of his wild imagination and florid verbosity) as grotesque parodic mirror images of King Ferdinand and his chums. Like them, they believe that the power of words is unlimited; they think that words deftly used

265

can prove anything; and in Armado's particular case, he, too, has taken the vows to study three years as a celibate, and he, too, breaks the vow by falling in love and writing a love letter to the woman he cherishes.

Which brought us to the women. I noted that in the three plays we'd read thus far, and in the two that would follow, it struck me that the women are far superior to the men. Constance in *King John,* Katharine of Aragon in *Henry VIII,* the Princess of France and her attending ladies (especially Rosaline) in *Love's Labour's Lost,* Viola in *Twelfth Night,* and Hermione and Paulina in *The Winter's Tale.* They have achieved the Aristotelian golden mean, the balance of head and heart. In *Love's Labour's Lost,* they represent the world of reality and naturalness and common sense, in opposition to the romantic posturing and ostentatious verbal pyrotechnics of the four young men, who inevitably fall in love with them. We quickly learn that their wit is keener than that of the males, their minds more agile. Aware of the ridiculousness of the young men's conventional and artificial avowals of love, they get the best of every exchange. My favorite riposte, I told the class, was Rosaline's five-word line in her scene with Berowne in 5.2. Berowne, who is smitten with her, declares he will forswear the kind of affected language that she deplores: "Taffeta phrases, silken terms precise, / Three-piled hyperboles . . . / Figures pedantical . . . / And to begin, wench—so God help me, la!— / My love to thee is sound, sans crack or flaw." To which Rosaline replies, catching him up on this momentary lapse, "Sans 'sans,' I pray you." And a chastened Berowne admits, "Yet I have a trick / Of the old rage. Bear with me, I am sick. / I'll leave it by degrees. . . . My wit is at an end." I said that some of these battle-of-the-sexes scenes reminded me of the old Astaire-Rogers movies, with silly rich men wooing savvy beautiful women, stuff like that. And Lou chimed in, "You're right—Armado sounds like the Great Bedini, that blowhard Italian lover in *Top Hat.*"

Then Willa, a woman in her sixties who had remained silent through the course thus far, spoke up. "This play is all about self-knowledge, isn't it? Especially the knowledge that we've been acting less than human. I remember that Kurt Vonnegut said in *Slapstick,* 'Please—a little less love, and a little more common decency.' These men have to be taught common decency, human kindness, by the women. Berowne may be dead-on about the inanity of the academy, but he's not exactly Mr. Nice Guy. Rosaline says to him that he is known as 'a man replete with mocks, / Full of comparisons and wounding flouts'—he likes to make cruel jokes at the expense of men of every sort who are at his mercy. All he cares about is being amusing. He doesn't give a thought to the effect his mocking humor has on his victims. And Rosaline comes up with the perfect cure: to make himself a more considerate person, he has to spend a year visiting the sick and testing his wit out on them. If they aren't amused, he has to give up his 'idle scorns.' I guess Shakespeare leaves it up to us to decide if Berowne has enough character to pass the test. Personally, I wouldn't bet on it." I took a vote: the men in the class, myself included, thought he'd reform ("Fred Astaire would, or he'd never get Ginger," Lou declared); the women didn't.

I screened segments of the BBC production, directed by Elijah Moshinsky. The performances had verve and style and precision and, most critical of all, heart. Perhaps best of all was David Warner, a remarkably poignant and infinitely funny Armado. What impressed Phyllis about Warner and John Wells (playing Holofernes) was that they never stooped to caricature, to burlesque: "They acted as if none of this was supposed to be funny, and that made it all the funnier."

That afternoon I reached Sister Elizabeth by phone. She'd read my résumé, was impressed with my background, and thought there might be a niche for me teaching freshman comp. I demurred, gracefully I hoped ("I don't want to sound like a prima donna, but editing manuscripts for forty years was too often the equivalent of grading freshman papers"), and told her that my sights were set a bit loftier, in the exalted realm of literature. "It's just possible," she said, "that next fall we might very well need someone to handle any overflow from Sister Brigid Brady's courses in Shakespeare and creative writing—they're very popular, much sought-after. Or someone to teach a course in Romantic poetry. But we won't know until later this year, possibly this summer, if any slots will be available. Why not check with me sometime in the spring?"

Not exactly a polite dismissal, I supposed, but not all that encouraging, either. Had I alienated her by sniffing at the prospect of introducing freshmen to the wonders of grammar and syntax? Did she interpret this as hubris? Had I detected a faint chill in her tone from that point on?

The following Tuesday, I turned to *Twelfth Night,* a comedy built around gender-masquerading and mistaken identities. Viola, shipwrecked on the strange island of Illyria and mourning the death by drowning of her twin brother, disguises herself as a boy, Cesario, and joins the service of Duke Orsino, with whom she promptly falls in love. But Orsino is hopelessly smitten with a woman who spurns him, Lady Olivia, herself in mourning for a dead brother. Orsino sends Viola/Cesario to help him woo Olivia, who promptly falls in love with the messenger.

I started at the ending, by sending in, or bringing in, the clown Feste, Olivia's jester. I read his song, which concludes the play, and I asked the class to act as chorus, chiming in with the lines "With hey, ho, the wind and the rain," and "For the rain it raineth every day." The effect was quite powerful, and emphasized from the start the dark side that underlies this festive comedy. Feste has served as commentator and chorus all along, keeping us aware of—what? I asked. "The passing of time," said Frances, a cheery brown-haired woman probably in her mid to late sixties with a vibrant eagerness to learn. "Good times don't last. The wind and the rain are signs of the real world."

Her mentioning the couples led me to the subject of gender confusion and cross-dressing, and I read a section from C. L. Barber's indispensable *Shakespeare's Festive Comedy:* ". . . the disguising of a girl as a boy in *Twelfth Night* is exploited so as to renew in a special way our sense of the difference [between men and women] . . . a temporary, playful reversal of sexual roles can renew the meaning of the normal relation. . . . The effect of [Viola's] moving back and forth from woman to sprightly page is to convey how much the sexes differ yet how much they have in common, how everyone who is fully alive has qualities of both."

Next, I focused on the dialogue between Viola (as Cesario) and Feste about words (3.1). Frances and Lou volunteered to read this scene, and when they finished, I brought up the comment in the Shakespeare Set Free series that Viola and Feste "deplore, even as they playfully illustrate in their exchanges, the dangerous flexibility of language . . . Feste squeezes a single phrase to produce three different meanings: live by = support oneself, follow the doctrines of, reside near . . . Viola milks the phrases 'lies by' and 'stands by' and the two begin to explore the ethical implications of their practice, noting that . . . such clever manipulation can cause words to lose their reputation. . . . And Feste tells Cesario that he is not Olivia's fool, but her 'corrupter of words.' " I emphasized that Feste is definitely going through a career crisis, an identity crisis, a midlife crisis. As one who'd tired of a professional life devoted to words, words, words, I had no problem identifying with the jester's dilemma. Early on we learn that he's been absent for some time, much to Olivia's irritation ("Who does that remind you of?" I asked, and Gilda answered, "Lear's Fool. He came on the scene late, too"), and at one point he angrily exclaims that he does not wear motley in his brain. Willa asked, "Could you compare Feste with Berowne? Both of them realize the need to be more careful in their use of words. They see that language can be a lethal weapon." "Yes," I replied, "but Berowne still has a long way to go with his reformation."

On to the videotape, Trevor Nunn's movie adaptation with Helena Bonham Carter as Olivia and Imogen Stubbs (so perfect as Desdemona in Nunn's *Othello*) as Viola/Cesario. The majority of the class relished the production. I thought it too strenuously cinematic, too fitfully paced. And Stubbs seemed far more insolent and brash, too self-consciously "boyish," than the occasion warrants. But Marvin, a retired doctor speaking up for the first time, saw in her performance the attempt of an actress to subtly convey what it might have been like during Elizabethan times to watch a boy playing a girl masquerading as a boy.

In the final class, we considered *The Winter's Tale*. I began by asking if anyone noticed an unintentionally amusing stage direction in the play. Lou's hand shot up: " 'Exit, pursued by a bear.' " It's the most famous stage direction in Shakespeare. The vision of a character fleeing from a bear calls to mind something from a Warner Bros. animated cartoon. Perhaps it's the offhandedness of the stage direction. Here, Mr. Director, see what you can do with this one. I briefly recounted the situation: Antigonus, on instructions from Leontes, King of Sicilia, is abandoning on the seacoast of Bohemia (which has no seacoast, as scholars enjoy pointing out) the king's newborn baby, Perdita, whom Leontes is convinced is the product of what he mistakenly believes is his wife Hermione's adulterous relationship with his best friend, Polixenes, King of Bohemia. No sooner has Antigonus completed his mission, and observed how dark the day is, than he abruptly says, "A savage clamor! / Well may I get aboard! This is the chase. / I am gone forever." Then comes the exit direction. How would you stage the scene? I asked. "Use a real bear and hope for the best—or

269

worst." Lou, of course. Other ideas: let the actor flee screaming, with off-stage sounds indicating his fate; bring on an extra wearing a bear mask.

Then it was time to deal with the play's three major elements: King Leontes's jealousy, Perdita and Polixenes debating art versus nature, and the "statue" of Hermione coming to life.

First, Leontes's jealousy. Did the men in the class find Leontes's insanely jealous reaction at the sight of Hermione laughing and holding hands with Polixenes unbelievable? Not a soul. All of us admitted to experiencing jealous rage and irrational suspicion, mainly in our youth and early manhood, occasionally even in middle age, at the slightest indication that a girlfriend or wife seemed a bit too charmed by someone at a social occasion. We don't need Iagos to conjure up our green-eyed monsters; we're our own Iagos.

Then we proceeded to a depiction of a mind deranged by the certainty of a spouse's infidelity as harrowing as that in *Othello*—Leontes's speeches and asides in 1.2. I began by reading Leontes's long speech directed at first to his little son, Mamillius, but quickly turning into a virulent soliloquy:

> *Inch-thick, knee deep, o'er head and ears a forked one!*
> *Go play, boy, play: thy mother plays, and I*
> *Play too—but so disgraced a part, whose issue*
> *Will hiss me to my grave. Contempt and clamor*
> *Will be my knell . . . there have been,*
> *Or I am much deceived, cuckolds ere now;*
> *And many a man there is, even at this present,*
> *Now while I speak this, holds his wife by the arm,*
> *That little thinks she has been sluiced in 's absence*
> *And his pond fished by his next neighbor. . . .*
> *It is a bawdy planet. . . .*
> *. . . be it concluded,*
> *No barricado for a belly.*

All the speeches emphasize Leontes's intensifying incoherence as his mind darts from his son to his wife to his own misery.

Taking a cue from Field-Pickering and Gibson's *Discovering Shake-*

speare's Language, I read Leontes's "Is whispering nothing?" speech from 1.2.284–96 as an example of how Shakespeare's use of repetition invests his language with dramatic potency. Here, the repetition of "nothing" builds to a fierce crescendo: ". . . is this nothing? / Why then the world and all that's in't is nothing, / The covering sky is nothing, Bohemia nothing, / My wife is nothing, nor nothing have these nothings, / If this be nothing." When I finished, I discovered that by repeating that single word, building up to it by citing all the "evidence" (real? imaginary? or actions terribly misconstrued?) of infidelity—"leaning cheek to cheek," "meeting noses," "horsing foot on foot"—and spitting it out with irony and contempt, and almost screaming the final "nothing," I'd worked myself up into a lather, I was agitated, bellicose, ready to kick ass. "Quick, someone get a cold towel for his forehead," Lou called out. Cicely Berry and John Barton were right: don't try to "act"; let the words carry you along into the emotion.

Leontes sends minions to consult the oracle of Apollo to determine Hermione's guilt or innocence, but before they return he decides to hold a trial anyway. Hermione defends herself with dignity and pathos; I read a segment of her speech before the tribunal, and when I finished, Ruth said, "She reminds me of Katharine of Aragon. She combines pride and humility, and she's brave, she's willing to stand up to her husband, who is the king."

While the trial is progressing, messengers arrive to report that the oracle has pronounced Hermione innocent, but Leontes won't accept the verdict. And at that moment a minion rushes in to announce that Leontes's son has died of shame at the accusation of his mother. Leontes is shattered and overcome with remorse; Hermione faints and is carried off. As Leontes is vowing to make amends for his disastrous paranoia, Paulina, Hermione's closest friend—and wife of Antigonus, soon to exit chased by a bear—enters and announces that Hermione has died of grief.

The next motif: art versus nature. Sixteen years have passed. We're in Bohemia where Perdita, who was found and adopted by a shepherd and reared as his child, is presiding over a sheep-shearing festival. It's spring. What pattern is emerging here, class? "Winter, spring, death, life, tragedy, romance." Right! Among the celebrants is Florizel, Polixenes's son, disguised as a country swain. Only Perdita knows his true identity: the two are in love. And who should show up at the festival but Polixenes, disguised as a commoner—this is Shakespeare, right, appearance masking reality, the public intersecting with the private—to check out the rumor that his son is pursuing a creature from a lesser caste. Polixenes and Perdita engage in one of the highlights of the play, a debate concerning the relative values of art and nature. Perdita tells Polixenes she doesn't believe in crossbreeding flowers, because such artifice usurps the power of "great creating nature." Polixenes replies: ". . . this is an art / Which does mend nature—change it, rather—but / The art itself is nature." Improving on nature is itself natural.

I asked if anyone could think of a biblical parallel to the idea of art as a demonstration of man's hubris in challenging God, or as Perdita says, "great creating nature," in her pre-Christian lexicon. Phyllis, Howard's wife, warm, bright, generous, a gifted painter and decorator, and a superb cook whose artistry in the kitchen was legendary among her friends, said, "We may be talking about two things. There's Art, the desire to be godlike in creating a world. Shakespeare did that, he created a world. Writers and painters and musicians do that, but I see that as imitating God, not challenging Him. And there's Science, man's desire to be omniscient, to be as smart as God, the point of the Garden of Eden story and the Tower of Babel. The head prevailing over the heart. In Art, that's not the case." I added, "You might want to consider the passage in Exodus when God chooses Bezalel to design and construct the tabernacle because he's an artist who has the wisdom of the heart."

Last scene of all. By now all the principals are in Sicilia, Perdita revealed as Leontes's daughter, Leontes reconciled with Polixenes, who in turn blesses the forthcoming marriage of Perdita and Florizel (after all, Perdita's the daughter of a king!). And then we see the party at Paulina's house, ready to view a statue of Hermione carved by an Italian master. The statue scene is one of the most moving scenes in Shakespearean drama. Standing before the statue, Paulina seems almost a priestess, a magician, calling out, "Music, awake her, strike! . . . 'Tis time; descend; be stone no more, approach." And Hermione descends. A naive audience would believe at that moment that she has been resurrected. But we quickly learn that Hermione has been alive all along and has agreed to being kept hidden because the oracle had implied that her daughter would survive.

And I could think of no better way of ending the lecture, and the course, than by quoting further from Michael Goldman's *Shakespeare and the Energies of Drama* on the subject of Shakespeare's last plays: "The gestures that the play concentrates on are largely gestures of *kindness*. . . . Broadly speaking, kindness refers to all acts and states of soul that tend to establish or identify human ties . . . kindness, in this large sense, is one of Shakespeare's central subjects. . . . The climactic gestures of the four last plays re-establish important human relations, family ones particularly; they are gestures of sympathy and generosity—recognitions, reconciliations, pardons, reunions. What is restored is a harmony that involves the closest of human ties." From the time I began to teach Shakespeare, that was essentially the point I'd been trying to make by emphasizing what seemed to me Shakespeare's implicit warning about the consequences of following the head instead of the heart. And it was at the core of my paper on *Lear* in which I sought to demonstrate the influence of the Torah, with its command to love thy neighbor as thyself, on Shakespeare's vision of humanity.

And then it was time for a long good-bye. I announced I wouldn't be teaching the course in the spring. Earlier in the week, I'd told Roxanne that I wanted to keep my schedule open to capitalize on opportunities, planned and serendipitous, for priming the pump in anticipation of teaching a new series of Shakespeare courses beginning next fall. And who knew—perhaps even an adjunct professorship awaited me, although after my conversation with Sister Elizabeth, I wasn't counting on it. "Don't be discouraged," Roxanne had said, customarily upbeat. "I'll keep tabs on the situation for you, and continue to put in a good word—discreetly of course."

On the way to the parking lot with Bob and Lou, I had a seizure of the blues at the prospect of being away again for an extended period. Barbara had once told me that one of the things she loved best about teaching was explaining things to people. And I'd discovered that this was a process I deeply enjoyed, too, and one at which I considered myself more than a little adept. In fact, that's probably what to a large extent had motivated me as an editor, the need to explain to authors how a work might be improved. Before reaching our cars, Bob, with his customary postclass volubility, described a conference on Robert E. Lee at Gettysburg he'd attended at Gettysburg College and enthused about his participation in the Long Island Classic "Tour for the Cure," which raises money for prostate cancer research (he'd been operated on successfully for prostate cancer the previous year). Lou told me that he'd memorized the insulting neologisms aimed by Berowne in *Love's Labour's Lost* at the epicene and servile Boyet, attendant to the princess and her ladies, and then proceeded to rattle them off: carry-tale, please-man, slight zany, mumble-news, trencher-knight. A line from James Michener's novel *The Bridges at Toko-Ri* jumped into my head: a navy rear admiral during the Korean War, marveling at the quality of the pilots in his command, asks, "Where do we get such men?"

Part Three

Shakespeare's Jew
(and Other Notables)

14.

Of all the actors living today, I have a feeling that the only one whom my father would rank with Paul Muni is David Suchet. For one thing, Mr. Suchet is Jewish, which went a long way toward qualifying an actor for greatness in my father's eyes. Second, he is an infinitely resourceful, dynamic, and versatile character actor, and one performance in particular would have earned my father's boisterous kudos: Suchet as Shakespeare's Jew of Venice in the *Playing Shakespeare* series. Whenever I watch that segment, I imagine I can hear my father shouting, "Son, you've got to be a Jew to play Shylock. Look at Suchet—that Jew is terrific. Paul Muni couldn't have done it better."

Late one afternoon in January, I found myself having an instructive and entertaining conversation with this terrific Shakespearean Jew in his dressing room at the Music Box Theatre. He had come to New York to star as Salieri in a revised version of Peter Shaffer's *Amadeus,* directed by Sir Peter Hall, along with John Barton and Trevor Nunn a jewel in the Royal Shakespeare Company's crown. I'd written him care of the theatre, told him how much I admired his work in *Playing Shakespeare* and in a recent movie, *Sunday,* described what I'd been up to since retiring, and asked if he could spare me a few minutes to talk about the Shakespearean aspects of his career. Weeks passed without a response, then one evening he phoned to apologize for taking so long to get back to me and agreeing to have a chat with me after a Wednesday matinee.

Still in costume, which included a black wig—in life he's almost completely bald, with fugitive wisps of dark brown hair combed over his pate—he had just finished eating a garden salad when I entered, and as we talked he occasionally reached into a bowl of grapes on the coffee table in front of him. His aspect is decidedly Levantine, his manner unfailingly gracious and urbane. He projects an incisive intelligence and an ironic sense of humor which, though essentially benign, I was certain could if

provoked turn that strong mouth and those dark laser-beam eyes into expressions of contempt capable of withering the innards of an offending
party. There was almost something sinister about the way he plucked a
grape from the bowl and stared at it pensively for a moment before pop-
ping it into his mouth. I expected him to ask me if I'd come to reveal the
whereabouts of the Maltese Falcon.

Right off, in homage to my father, I brought up the Shylock tape.
"You know, Herman," he said—actually making "Herman" sound as elegant as "Nigel"—"many people seem to be taken with that episode. I
understand it's especially prized by students in university drama departments. In fact, the whole series has enjoyed remarkable success as a teaching tool. As to Shylock, John Barton first directed Patrick Stewart in the
role, then later remounted the production of *The Merchant of Venice,* and
unfortunately for him he cast me as Shylock—I wasn't going to play it like
Patrick. Patrick's stance was that it didn't matter if Shylock is Jewish or
not, he was simply an outsider. But I felt that Shylock was an outsider
precisely because he was a Jew. You'll note that during the play he's called
'Jew' more than he's called 'Shylock.' "

Next, he told me about his interpretation of Caliban, which he'd
played with distinction at the RSC. "Caliban was the role that really
launched me in a very big way, and transformed the way people saw this
character. At our first meeting, the director told me he wanted me to play
Caliban as a half-monster, sort of a fetus or something. I came out of that
meeting so distressed that I went to the Shakespeare Institute and studied
the history of the role. I always study in the Shakespeare Library at the
Shakespeare Institute. I read up on the previous productions. Then I
study all the books I can find pertinent to what Shakespeare is writing
about. I'll try to read the sources. I will always study the script in both
the text form that I have, and the quartos—if they exist—and always the
Folio. And usually I will also work from three other modern editorial
texts, because the notes and commentary vary from edition to edition. So
I get a very full idea of what people thought, then I make up my own
mind. At the institute, I discovered that Caliban had been played as a
monkey—Herbert Beerbohm-Tree swung from tree to tree onstage—
and as a turtle, turned on his back by the other characters at one point in
the action. It was terrible. Then a woman at the institute pointed out to

me that when Trinculo lifts up the blanket covering Caliban, he says Caliban is 'legged like a man, and his fins like arms.' So Caliban has legs. And arms. Not arms like fins, fins like arms. Every single thing points to Caliban having a human shape. I played him basically black, with a type of Neanderthal forehead, but when I moved I would change color. I played the Universal Native. I'm certain that Shakespeare wrote the play as a reaction to British colonization. I think he meant to use Caliban as the Universal Native, put upon, ousted by the superior white. I don't think it's an accident that 'Caliban' is an anagram of 'cannibal' and that *calibone* is Romany for 'black.' Also, we have Caliban worshiping the moon; during Shakespeare's time, the natives who worshiped the moon were the Eskimos. In those days, pictures—sketches—had been received from travelers and explorers abroad of their first contact with the natives, and because they would meet natives with ears sagging and distorted from the weight of ornaments, and with thick lips made thicker by devices inserted into the mouth, they sent back these monstrous drawings. Shakespeare hit upon this, and although he makes Caliban the villain of the piece, he gives him justification for doing what he does."

I mentioned that Shakespeare also gives Caliban one of the most beautiful, poetic speeches in the play, beginning, "The isle is full of noises, / Sounds, and sweet airs . . ."

"The remarkable thing, Herman, is that he says this after speaking the most monstrous lines in the play, when he says he wants to batter Prospero's skull, paunch him with a stake, cut his weasand with a knife. And in that speech he starts talking about Prospero's daughter, and drools over her. So just twenty or forty lines later, you've got this monster who's just spoken this horrible speech, rhapsodizing about the sweet airs that give delight and hurt not. Shakespeare is deliberately putting them in counterpoint to each other, giving us the antitheses, to show the extremity of mankind. Prospero has made Caliban his slave because Caliban attempted to rape Miranda. Although it wouldn't be rape in Caliban's terms. We bring our own sophistication to the situation, but Caliban hasn't been conditioned by the moral code of the West. He's an islander who's seen a desirable woman with whom he wanted to sleep and by whom he wanted to propagate the island with many Calibans."

He then described to me one of his unique, if not eccentric, methods of working up a part: "Rather than ask myself 'How do I play that role?,' which I find is very egocentric—you're only thinking about yourself—I take my part completely out, I read the play without me in it at all. It's as if you had a big stew and you remove some of the ingredients and then find out what you need. For instance, I read *Othello* with Iago eliminated from the script. A stormy beginning, Othello and Desdemona with her father, the duke, who finds out that Othello has married his daughter but is willing to forget that because he needs Othello to go to Cyprus. Then they sail in separate ships to Cyprus, all the enemy's been drowned in a storm, Othello and Desdemona live on the island and have a wonderful honeymoon. End of play. The thing that's missing, of course, is what the play deals with more than any other subject—jealousy. And it's only by Iago's presence that we get jealousy personified. He talks about jealousy as a disease. Everybody he touches is infected. And that's how I found out how to play Iago."

I was curious about the genesis of *Playing Shakespeare.* He told me that one day in 1982 John Barton came up to him and said, "I've been invited to do this program about Shakespeare as a result of the Southbank Show, and I'd like you to take part in it," and Suchet said, "Of course." The Southbank Show had been done a couple of years previously, with Trevor Nunn as host and participants such as Barton, Suchet, Ian McKellen, Patrick Stewart, Alan Howard, Jane Lapotaire, Michael Pennington. When it resumed in 1982, Nunn was gone, and at the helm now was John Barton, a powerful influence on Suchet.

"When I first joined the RSC, I went in as sort of a rebel. I thought I could do Shakespeare in my own way. In fact, I got the Worst Verse-Speaking Prize from John Barton in my first season there. But at the end of my first year, when I started playing real roles, I realized that I truly had to address myself to the fact that I'm either going to play Shakespeare correctly or I'm not. And I suddenly got terribly excited and that's when I began to make it my main study, one which has lasted for years and years, to master the craft of speaking verse in Shakespeare's dialogue, basically under John's tutelage, and Cicely Berry's. Practice, practice, practice. Wherever I was I would learn speeches, speak speeches, go to John and plead, 'Hear me, hear me, correct me, correct me.' Learn, learn,

learn. And now I teach it, at Stratford, at Birmingham University, drama schools all over England."

I felt it was time to let this generous and civilized man get some rest. In just two hours, he'd be taking the stage again in one of the most demanding roles ever written. It's almost a monologue, with Salieri addressing the audience frequently and at length. But Suchet didn't seem all that exhausted. Perhaps the sense of triumph after a prolonged standing ovation had his endorphins hopping. And he wouldn't let me go until he told me about the Shakespearean role he hadn't played and would love to tackle: Leontes in *The Winter's Tale*. "But it's another jealousy play [Salieri is of course insanely jealous of Mozart] and I want to give that a rest for a while. I'm all jealousied out, Herman. But Leontes is a fascinating role. I don't believe that Leontes's jealousy just happens at the moment he sees his wife and his friend laughing and holding hands. I think he comes on jealous. I think it would be a mistake to see him suddenly become jealous. When I play it, unless my research proves differently—I've not researched this play so I won't commit myself—but my gut feeling at the moment is that I'm going to walk on already completely eaten up with jealousy. You're not going to see it happen, because the fact that Leontes's wife, Hermione, and his best friend, Polixenes, take hands, that's not enough to trigger a sudden onslaught of jealousy. His friend has been there for nine months. You can't just see him and your wife holding hands and become instantly jealous, as if nothing had been going on for nine months. And that's the problem with the play, making Leontes's jealousy plausible."

In my discussion of the play at the LLI, I'd taken just the opposite view, certain that Leontes's abrupt and irrational seizure of jealousy was perfectly natural. But Suchet's insight about a long-term buildup of jealous feelings occasioned by who knows what "evidence" made sense. I'd have to take this into consideration the next time I taught *The Winter's Tale* or *Othello*. And I was aware that the fund of knowledge about the complexities of Shakespearean drama, the art of Shakespearean performance, and the creative methods of teaching Shakespeare I'd been amassing since those early visits to TFANA and Jeff Horowitz and the Folger would be something on which I could draw productively in whatever capacity I'd be serving at Caldwell College.

That evening on the bus to Montclair, I thought of David Suchet's commentary on Caliban and Prospero, dwellers on an enchanted isle, and about a bewitching isle close to my own experience, Martha's Vineyard, at a period of special enchantment, the sixties and early seventies, when Barbara and the kids would spend the summer at our shingled beach cottage and I'd fly up for the long weekends and then for the last two weeks of August. I remembered Emily and Jared rushing up to me ecstatically as I stepped off the plane, as if I'd been gone for decades, and while I hugged their tanned bodies I could smell the sun in their damp blond hair and I was regenerated, transported into another realm, a place of innocence and joy and love. My two favorite pictures of them, taken at the Vineyard, actually invoke scenes from *The Tempest*. In one, Emily, aged nine, in her nightgown, is standing on the beach in front of our house at dusk, with the sun just setting over West Chop in the background. Her expression is heart-wrenchingly serious and disillusioned, as if she were Miranda right after learning the facts of Prospero's exile. In the other, Jared and I are on the beach at Gay Head. I'm forty-two, exceedingly dark (the result of reckless overexposure to the sun that will lead to skin problems), seated on one of those legless plastic chairs, staring out to sea with a look of infinite grief, Prospero pondering his banishment. Jared is standing beside me, slightly to the left, sipping Pepsi from a paper cup, an impish gleam in his eyes, Ariel waiting for his chance to conjure up a storm that will assault the ship bearing Prospero's usurping brother and his retinue. Today my children are adults, superb professionals in the worlds of finance and medicine and endowed with a rectitude lightened by the gift of laughter. But even now, whenever I hug them, I can still smell that scent of the sun in their hair, the smell of innocence and joy and love. The smell of goodness. O, brave new world, that has such people in't!

15.

For months I'd been determined to fill in the yawning gap in my Shakespearean education created by that missed opportunity to visit Shakespeare's Globe while I was in England during the summer of 1999. So I phoned the Globe box office on February 1, the day it opened for the new season. Since the theatre's season runs only from early May to late September, tickets are at a premium, and I felt lucky to book a seat for the matinee performance of *Hamlet* on June 2.

And wouldn't you know, the ensuing Shabbat seemed designed to arouse in me, as it had less than a month ago, mystical speculation about the Globe. In his commentary on the Torah portion, God's instructions to Moses for the building of the Sanctuary, Rabbi Monson quoted from Franz Rosenzweig, the German Jewish philosopher who wrote his classic, *The Star of Redemption,* when he was a soldier in the trenches during World War I (later he would collaborate with Martin Buber on a German translation of the Hebrew Bible). Rosenzweig, said the rabbi, explained that by creating the Sanctuary, the Israelites were imitating God's creation of the world, which, I thought, is exactly what Mircea Eliade had concluded in *The Sacred and the Profane.*

In preparation for my hegira to the Globe, I'd been reading Francis Fergusson's *The Idea of a Theater* and Barry Day's *This Wooden "O": Shakespeare's Globe Reborn.*

Fergusson sees *Hamlet* as a ritual drama in which a succession of ritual scenes "focus attention on the Danish body-politic and its hidden malady: they are ceremonious invocations of the well-being of society, and secular or religious devices for securing it." He further comments that the Elizabethan theatre had a ritual aspect and that Shakespeare's audience "was prepared to accept his play not only as an exciting story but as the 'celebration of the mystery of human life.' "

Barry Day seems nonplussed by the mysteries of the Globe playhouse itself. Its basic religious symbolism eludes him. Although he recognizes that the circular shape represents the "theatre-as-universe with the actor as Man, the microcosm playing with parts within the Macrocosm," he wonders "what it is about this particular structure that continues to haunt the imagination of certain individuals in every generation. . . . There are those who feel there's something mystical about its shape—the theatrical equivalent of the Great Pyramid or Stonehenge." Nary a word from him about Eliade, or the Great Temple, either Solomon's or Herod's.

The New Globe's artistic director, Mark Rylance, who would be playing Hamlet in the forthcoming production, altogether misses the religious significance of the structure and, like Day, appears unaware of Eliade's thoughts about sacred space. Rylance sees the Globe as symbolic of that aspect of Elizabethan culture that did not draw lines between the scientific and spiritual: "Geometry was at the heart of this building. The round shape was considered the heart of a human being . . . the body and spirit coming together in the soul. . . . They were conscious of the marriage of male and female within society and within each of us." This prompts Rylance to woozily envision the Globe "as the female womb containing the square (male) tiring house out of which pour a stream of men, some of them playing women. . . . That sounds fanciful to us but it wouldn't to them." No? Perhaps not to those who'd quaffed several pots of ale.

In an increasingly *Hamlet* frame of mind, I made it a point one evening in March to attend a special event in honor of Sir Derek Jacobi arranged by the Shakespeare Society for its members. Sitting on the stage of the Danny and Sylvia Kaye Auditorium at Hunter College, Sir Derek talked with his friend, fellow actor, and—tonight—his interlocutor, Roger Rees, about his Shakespearean performances, video excerpts of which were shown on a giant screen hanging from the flies. Most of their conversation had to do with Sir Derek's experiences with various productions of Shakespeare's most famous and most problematic play.

Sir Derek played Laertes in a production of *Hamlet* directed by Olivier at the National, starring Peter O'Toole. "The critics hated it," he said. "But O'Toole had one marvelous moment. When Polonius asked him what he's reading, O'Toole's Hamlet says 'Words,' takes a long pause while Polonius stares at him, waiting for some elaboration, then repeats 'Words,' another long pause while Polonius waits, then O'Toole spells it out—'W-O-R-D-S—WORDS!' Wonderful." Now that I thought of it, when I'd spoken with Olympia Dukakis almost three years earlier, she told me Richard Burton's Hamlet had impressed her because Burton caught the humor in the role, and I imagine that O'Toole had reached for that quality as well. The Hamlets I'd seen thus far—Fiennes, Branagh, Williamson, Olivier—had struck the comic note infrequently, if at all.

Rees showed a video excerpt of Sir Derek speaking Hamlet's first soliloquy—"O that this too too solid flesh"—from the BBC's *Hamlet,* directed by Rodney Bennett, with Patrick Stewart as Claudius, Claire Bloom as Gertrude, Eric Porter as Polonius. At the conclusion, Rees wondered how Jacobi made the verse so real, how he made it sound as if he actually spoke that way. "I try to make it sound like spoken thought," Jacobi explained. "And if it's poetry, speak it as prose. If it's prose, speak it as poetry. Change the punctuation. This upsets scholars, but they're paid to be upset."

Jacobi recalled that while he was playing Hamlet at the Old Vic, Richard Burton came to see him backstage after the performance. "He asked if we could go out on the empty stage for a few minutes. He hadn't been on that stage for twenty-eight years. This was a tremendously moving occasion for me. Because Burton had been a powerful influence on me when I was young—indeed I'd seen him at the Old Vic in the 1950s. In those days he'd looked a million dollars, he'd sounded a million dollars. So there we stood, looking at the empty theatre, and he told me that during one performance Winston Churchill was seated on the front row, and Burton was disconcerted to hear Churchill softly reciting the soliloquies along with him."

On the subject of soliloquies, Sir Derek said he considered them the most taxing elements of Shakespeare for an actor. "It's just you and the audience alone. I imagine the audience as one person to whom I'm speaking." If that one person happened to be Churchill, I supposed Sir Derek would find the audience speaking back to him, making the task all the more challenging. I noticed in the video clip he indeed looked directly into the camera much of the time, personally involving the audience in his introspection. This is the technique favored by John Barton—engage the audience as you discover your thoughts, make us a part of the process.

But in one peculiar instance Sir Derek favors addressing a soliloquy to a character onstage: "I've always felt that Hamlet should speak 'To be or not to be' directly to Ophelia," he said with the slightly bellicose fervor of someone proposing a controversial idea. "She's the one person to whom he could most open his heart. I did it this way onstage, but I wasn't allowed to repeat it on television. However, when I directed Ken Branagh in the part at the Birmingham Repertory Theatre, he agreed this was the way to do it, and that's the way it was staged," he said, almost defiantly, as if Branagh's concurrence proved the point conclusively. Not to me. I thought it an arbitrary, self-conscious gimmick, a labored striving for interpretive originality. Hamlet is supposed to be opening his heart in confidence to us, the audience, not to another character in the play. Whatever would prompt him to approach Ophelia and abruptly launch into these reflections, without any preparation? The desire to further the impression of madness? Or did Sir Derek imagine them entering together, Hamlet now completing a harangue that has been going on for some time? It made no sense at all, and no one in the audience, certainly not self-conscious old me, nor Rees for that matter, asked for Sir Derek to explain himself a bit further.

Rees turned to Sir Derek's performance in another role in *Hamlet,* as Claudius in Ken Branagh's film version, marveling at how he makes us actually care for the alcoholic, adulterous, murdering usurper. Sir Derek explained: "Ken told me, 'You know, Derek, a lot of people who see this movie aren't going to know the plot of the play.' [I thought of my Aggie roommate, Sam Tom.] They won't know at first that Claudius has killed Hamlet's father and committed adultery with his mother. The people of Denmark don't know this, either. And Hamlet himself isn't entirely convinced until the play-within-the-play—he's testing the ghost's veracity, not Claudius's. So you have to show the majestic, charming, powerful Claudius, with whom Gertrude fell in love, and who commands the respect of the populace."

Finally, prompted by Rees, Sir Derek gave the following advice to any young person contemplating a career as an actor: "If you want to act," he said, "if you have the desire to act, *don't*. If you *have* to act, if you *must* act, then do it. I always knew I'd be an actor. I had the acting gene. Actors are born, not made. When I was a young boy, my parents took me to a performance of *Cinderella*. Prince Charming, played by a woman, brought some of the children in the audience onstage. I was among them, and from that point, for me it was downhill all the way."

In April, I stepped up preparations for my imminent expedition to see *Hamlet* performed at the New Globe. Subsequent to Derek Jacobi's Shakespeare Society appearance, I bought the video of the BBC's production of *Hamlet* in which the director, Rodney Bennett, had not allowed Jacobi to indulge his bizarre whim of addressing his "To be or not to be" soliloquy to the fair Ophelia. Jacobi's Hamlet turned out to be the only one I'd seen thus far that fully captured what Marvin Rosenberg has referred to as the "clashing multiplicity of human personality—imaginative, sensitive, spiritual, social . . . that Shakespeare has crammed into a single dramatic character." Branagh had come close, but Jacobi's antennae seemed more finely tuned to inner and outer worlds. Marvin Rosenberg quotes Michael Pennington on the challenge of playing the role: "Hamlet is a blank sheet—he becomes the actor that is playing him. . . . That makes it rather difficult to talk about [the role] objectively—you bring in whatever your basic personality traits are." That's precisely what Jacobi appeared to be doing, and it allowed him to evoke the polyphonic range of the character with spontaneity and immediacy.

One pertinent example: at the end of his "words, words, words" scene with Polonius (2.2), as the old man asks to take his leave, Hamlet's sardonic reply is, "You cannot, sir, take from me anything that I will more willingly part withal—except my life, except my life, except my life." Jacobi's ironic courtesy in delivering the first part of the line was hilarious. But it's when Hamlet once again speaks in threes that Jacobi's genius shone through. He delivered the first "except my life" pensively. Or was he being mock pensive? Was he affecting despair for the old man's benefit? Suddenly, speaking the phrase a second time, he pulled out his dagger and pointed it angrily at Polonius, frightening him, and then quickly, uttering the phrase a last time, he reversed the dagger toward his own stomach, offering Polonius the dagger to thrust. Was this supercharged dramatic outburst genuine? Had any of it, the despair, the violence, been real? Of course not. After Polonius had fled in terror, Jacobi instantly dropped the mask, and turning away, said with airy and cruel disdain, "These tedious old fools," foreshadowing Hamlet's brutish lack of remorse after he's unwittingly stabbed Polonius to death.

The second phase of my pre-*Hamlet* shaping-up regimen was enrolling in the Shakespeare Society's bimonthly seminar on the tragedy, an hour and a half every other Wednesday afternoon during March and April. The seminar was led by Robert Gutman, a stocky white-haired infectiously droll and jaunty academic whom I'd put in his late sixties, early seventies. He'd taught at the State University of New York, the New School, Bard, and Duchesne. His speciality was classical music: his biography of Mozart had just been published and he was the author of a highly regarded biography of Richard Wagner. His premise in the seminar was that we were there to reread the play from start to finish under his guidance, reacquainting ourselves with its power and mystery, discovering aspects of character and ingenuities of dramaturgy that had escaped us previously. His method might be described as non–Emma Smith: at each meeting he would read a section of the play aloud in his faintly British accent, occasionally stopping to analyze a passage, call attention to a footnote (we were using the Arden edition, edited by Harold Jenkins), ask for a volunteer to read a speech or soliloquy, or allow for comments or questions. All was orderly, sequential, and, happily, under Gutman's quiet courtly authority.

There were twelve of us in the class, a third of us men and most of us in our sixties or beyond, maybe one or two in middle or late fifties, the usual suspects from the Elderhostel/Lifelong Learning Institute set, undoubtedly representative of the Shakespeare Society's demographics.

By early April, the seminar was well under way. When we reached act 3, Gutman read from 3.2.289 to 3.4.160, which included Hamlet's reproof of Guildenstern for trying to "pluck out the heart of my mystery" (what, I wondered, would Shakespeare think of generations of students, we battalions of Guildensterns, trying to do the same to the prince? Was this his warning to his audience, and those of us in the future, not to try to understand Hamlet too quickly, if at all?), Claudius's commissioning of

Rosencrantz and Guildenstern to accompany Hamlet to England, the murder of Polonius, and most of Hamlet's reviling of Gertrude.

The ferocity of Hamlet's attack on his mother prompted a discussion on the source of his rage and anguish, and all of us agreed that only an adolescent could react with such horror at the thought of Mom making the beast with two backs, an image that most teenagers prefer not to dwell on. So how old is Hamlet? Thirty, as the gravedigger's calculation would have us believe? Not likely, although that has little to do with it; some of us admitted to knowing in our lifetimes more than a few thirtysomething people who suffered chronic delayed adolescence. I mentioned that A. C. Bradley figured him to be around twenty-five, using his maturity of thought as one of the bases for this calculation, although even Bradley admitted to receiving a general impression from the play that Hamlet was eighteen or twenty. I also called attention to the fact that Hamlet was an only child, a condition that, on the basis of personal experience, I could cite as something of an obstacle to emotional maturity.

At the penultimate meeting of the seminar, we continued with Hamlet's excoriation of Gertrude in 3.4, and Gutman zeroed in on Gertrude's line "O Hamlet, thou hast cleft my heart in twain": she's torn between her passion for and loyalty to Claudius, and the guilt engendered by Hamlet—guilt for remarrying, not for complicity in murder. Hamlet has never told Gertrude that Claudius murdered her husband (actually, in the bad First Quarto, he did tell her). And Gutman emphasized that Hamlet is now forcing Gertrude to play a dangerous, complicated game of deception, warning her that if she reveals to Claudius that Hamlet is not mad, her life will be in peril, the implication being that if she were to disclose that Hamlet has revealed to her he's been shamming madness, Claudius would assume that Hamlet had also confided to her his knowledge that his father was murdered. But Gutman felt, and the class agreed, that Claudius loves Gertrude too much to kill her.

Gutman moved on to the tense moment at the start of 4.1, when Claudius asks, "What, Gertrude, how does Hamlet?" A suspenseful moment, as we wonder how she'll reply. "Mad," she says, obeying Hamlet's instructions. She's indeed in a difficult situation, anxious for her son's safety, appalled at what he's done (there's considerable pathos in her straightforward heartfelt description of Polonius as "The unseen good old man") but attributing it—in Claudius's presence at least—to a "brainish apprehension," his disordered mind. And amazingly, she claims that Hamlet "weeps for what is done." Surely this is a lie; it's the way she'd like to believe he reacted. Or, as I suggested, is Shakespeare giving the actors a belated stage direction, indicating that earlier, when Hamlet delivers his callous eulogy to Polonius—"Thou wretched, rash intruding fool, farewell"—he's actually weeping as he speaks? Possibly, was the consensus.

At our final meeting two weeks later, just before the class broke I raised a question about the structure of act 5. I found it odd that Hamlet's long account of how he, with the help of "divinity," was able to thwart Claudius's scheme to have him executed in England comes at the beginning of 5.2, rather than when we first encounter Hamlet and Horatio in 5.1, as they approach the churchyard. Wouldn't Hamlet be itching to tell Horatio this story as soon as he sees him again?

"Yes, yes," Gutman replied excitedly. "I've always wondered about that, too, and so have many of my colleagues." Was he humoring me? "Why indeed does Shakespeare hold off Hamlet's long expository speech until 5.2? What did he have in mind?" But time had run out and there was no time to pursue this question.

As I left the building, I realized that over the past several weeks Robert Gutman had become my latest pedagogical role model. No matter how many times he'd read and taught and seen *Hamlet,* he still delighted in mining it for fresh discoveries; he was almost boyishly jubilant when someone in the class ventured a provocative interpretation, and unfailingly respectful of even the most outlandish hermeneutical takes. Inspired by his example, I resolved to add a Gutmanesque seminar to the LLI curriculum, and to strive for the patience and open-mindedness and craft to bring it off with distinction.

Two weeks after my exposure to the sprightly unintimidating erudition of a Robert Gutman in his seminar came a morning spent at Juilliard observing the formidable Michael Kahn, one of the world's preeminent directors and acting teachers, put the third-year students in his Shakespearean acting class through their paces.

Kahn is not only director of the Drama Division at Juilliard but also artistic director of the highly regarded Shakespeare Theatre in Washington, D.C., where his production of *Hamlet* starring Tom Hulce won a Helen Hayes Award and where he'd recently directed a modern-dress version of *Coriolanus*. For ten years, he ran the American Shakespeare Theatre in Stratford, Connecticut, and among the plays he directed there was *The Merchant of Venice* starring Morris Carnovsky.

I'd written to him a month ago, asking if I could sit in on one of his Juilliard classes, preferably one in which a scene from *Hamlet* would be performed. Two weeks passed without a response, so I followed up the letter with a phone call, and his courteous young assistant, Carlos, recognized my name right away. "Oh, yes, Michael got your letter but simply hasn't had a free moment to answer it. There should be no problem with your attending a class—people are always doing this." I reminded him that I wanted to pick a day when *Hamlet* was on the agenda. He checked the schedule and said, "It's next Thursday. Class starts at nine-thirty. Come to the office first and I'll take you to the rehearsal room."

On the chosen day, just before pushing through the revolving doors at the entrance to the Juilliard School in Lincoln Center, I caught a glimpse of the Walter Reade Theatre at the other end of the building. The Walter Reade is devoted mainly to revivals of American and foreign movies, and their programs often focus on the work of a particular actor or director. I went there for the first, and thus far the only, time five years ago to see a double feature in the John Garfield Festival series, *The Breaking Point* (a truer and more accomplished adaptation of *To Have and Have Not* than the Howard Hawks clunker which starred Humphrey Bogart and introduced Lauren Bacall) and *He Ran All the Way,* Garfield's last movie and perhaps his finest, released in 1952, less than a year before his death, in which Garfield played an ill-fated two-bit lowlife who holds a family hostage after he kills a policeman during a bungled robbery. Expecting the theatre to be deserted, I arrived a few minutes before feature time and was lucky to find a seat. The place was packed with Garfield fans, most of them my age or older. Of course. How many young Garfield devotees are you likely to find today? Coincidentally, the man sitting next to me had been in Korea, as had I, and we reminisced about how Garfield died at the age of 39 in 1952 while copulating in the

Manhattan apartment of his girlfriend, and recalled how saddened and shocked we were to hear the death announced on Armed Forces Radio. And of course we'd uttered the inevitable "What a way to go!" I think that what my generation found so appealing in Garfield was his mixture of toughness, yearning, and heartache, a combination matched most notably in Frank Sinatra, on whom Garfield was a major influence. I know this for a fact.

Thirty years ago, during a party at William Styron's house on Martha's Vineyard, I was in the kitchen talking to a friend when in came Sinatra, on the prowl for ice cubes. I knew his reputation for bellicosity when accosted by anyone outside the Rat Pack, but I'd have kicked myself if I'd let mere cowardice stand in the way of having a word with a legend. And if he punched me—well, how many people can boast of being kayoed by Ol' Blue Eyes? "Mr. Sinatra," I piped up as he was passing me on the way back to the merriment, "your performance in *The Manchurian Candidate* reminded me of John Garfield in *The Fallen Sparrow.*" The latter was a spy drama in which Garfield played a veteran of the Abraham Lincoln Brigade in the Spanish civil war being pursued by a Nazi Gestapo agent (deliciously limned by Walter Slezak) who had tortured him when he was a prisoner. Sinatra's character in *The Manchurian Candidate* had been captured while in combat during the Korean War and he, too, was haunted by his ordeal in prison.

Sinatra stopped in his tracks and looked at me in astonishment. Uh-oh. Moment of truth. Should I throw the first punch, a surprise attack, and become a legend myself, the guy who put Sinatra away with a short right uppercut? Taking a drag on his cigarette and narrowing his eyes, he said, "Julie was one of my closest pals." Garfield's real name was Jules Garfinkle. "And yeah, matter of fact, I had him in mind when I did *Candidate.* He was my model. Who the fuck are you?" Rhetorical question from the tough guy with the heart of gold. Before I could identify myself and shower him with my knowledge of all Garfield's film roles, even the obscure ones (Porfirio Diaz in *Juarez,* for example), he was gone.

Later in the evening I saw him sitting on a couch in the living room, deep in conversation with none other than Barbara. Famous for putting the make on any woman he found desirable, their marital status notwithstanding, was he trying to lure her into the bedroom? What would I do if suddenly they rose from the couch and went upstairs? Shout "You have excellent taste, sir"? Or pull a Leontes and go bonkers? Moments later Barbara got up and came over to me. "Wipe off that glare. We were only talking about how difficult it is to raise children." What's the matter, wasn't my wife good enough for him? "He's very sensitive and has a lot of common sense. I bet he's almost as good a daddy as you."

At Juilliard I was greeted by an apologetic Carlos, who had disappointing news: *Hamlet* had been advanced a day and *Othello* was on tap this morning. "Not to worry," I told him. "As the feller said, there's a divinity that shapes our ends, rough-hew them how we will. If I'm destined to see the students have a go at the Moor instead of the Dane, so be it." Carlos then guided me to a rehearsal room, where class would not begin for another fifteen minutes, and took his leave.

I sat alone for a while in the cavernous high-ceilinged fluorescent-lit windowless room, two of its walls draped in black, possibly to mitigate the glare from the overhead lights. The performing space was designated by black lines painted on the floor and by a black wood-paneled screen positioned in the center of the room and reaching less than halfway to the ceiling. A portable black wooden staircase was set up stage left. Three black wooden blocks were placed at left and right center stage. Folding chairs lined the back wall, facing, and just a few feet away from, the stage area. An atmosphere made to order for a Samuel Beckett romp.

The class, an even mix of young men and women in an assortment of jeans, slacks, T-shirts, sweatpants, and sweatshirts, began to file in, and I took a seat at the far end of the row, near the wall opposite the door. Then Kahn appeared. Dressed in a gray turtleneck and gray slacks, he was an imposing figure well over six feet tall, exuding confidence and a bristling combative intelligence, to say nothing of a Coriolanean imperiousness. Bald with a fringe of white hair, he had a strong mobile face, piercing black eyes, and the wary affability of someone who will not suffer fools gladly. He stood in front of one of the seated students and said, in mock irritation, "You're sitting in my chair. Have you eaten my porridge?" A burst of chuckling from the group. Then he signaled that the games were to begin.

Othello, 3.3. The Moor was played by a glowering young black man with shaved head; he wore a T-shirt, khakis, sneakers. Iago was a kid with dark curly hair and the preoccupied expression of a student with term finals on his mind. He was decked out in army camouflage fatigues and half-boots. As the scene began, Othello was alone onstage, observed from above by Iago, who was standing on the landing of the staircase behind the partition, only his head visible. Desdemona had just exited, and Othello delivered the short speech, "Excellent wretch! Perdition catch my soul / But I do love thee! And when I love thee not, / Chaos is come again." Next comes Iago's line "My nobel lord—," which should be spoken instantly, the cue picked up immediately, Chaos and Iago linked in a flash, perfect Shakespearean timing. But Iago paused too long before speaking, then descended the staircase, and as the scene progressed continued to take too many pauses, as did Othello. Consequently, the scene lacked dramatic tension and intensity, and the pauses tended to nullify the effect of Iago's lightning-swift cunning. And during his "Who steals my purse steals trash" speech, Iago literally takes out his wallet, riffles through the contents, and tosses it away.

Unsurprisingly, at the conclusion of the scene Kahn pounced right away on the flawed timing. "You take far too many pauses, and Shakespeare is not about long pauses. You have to pick up the cues quickly here." John Barton would have agreed. And Kahn spent the next forty-five minutes guiding the two students through a reinterpretation of the roles, which included some reblocking. For example, he felt, as did I, that Iago was placing too much stress on the "purse" element in his speech; when the student replied that he was emphasizing the metaphorical aspect, Kahn advised him, "Don't get stuck on the metaphor. That's not the crucial thing in the speech. He goes on to say that the purse is trash, it's nothing, so that's the way you treat it—you toss off that element as if it's trivial. The thing to emphasize is 'good name.' "

Kahn kept probing the students with questions, searchingly, relentlessly; he challenged them, but not cruelly; his method was not public humiliation. "What is your tactic?" he asked Iago, who answered, "To make him suspicious, jealous." "No," said Kahn, "that's your objective. Your tactic is to convince him that *you're* a jealous person, that you're talking about yourself, you're the victim of the green-eyed monster, you're full of false thoughts, jealousy, suspicions, that's the kind of person you are, and that Othello should never believe anything you tell him. Which of course is exactly the way to make him believe everything you say. So when Othello says to him that he's not worried that Desdemona is unfaithful, Iago can reply, 'Oh, good, you're not the jealous type. Now I can tell you all my stupid little suspicions.' "

That was a perspective on Iago that had never occurred to me. Kahn's close reading had caused me to see this moment in an entirely new—and funny—light. It excited me, and my first thought was, "I can't wait to teach *Othello* again, so I can relate Kahn's slant on this speech." Another deposit to make in that fund of knowledge from which I could draw when preparing future courses.

At the end of class, I went over and introduced myself to Kahn. First I thanked him for letting me sit in on the proceedings, told him how much I admired the way he worked with his students and how impressed I was with his insights into Iago's "green-eyed monster" speech. Then I asked him why he'd decided to stage *Coriolanus* in modern dress at the Shakespeare Theatre.

"First, you have to remember," he replied patiently, but with a slight edge in his voice, "in Shakespeare's day the Romans onstage were dressed like Elizabethans. And the female roles were performed by boys. Not long ago, the elocutionary manner of delivering a Shakespearean speech was considered de rigueur. We can't be arbitrary about these things. It's a matter of what a director sees in the play. Each age reflects its own character and fashions in the way it interprets Shakespeare. Shakespeare didn't use his plays to express his opinions. He let audiences come to their own conclusions, which is why they are so full of interpretive possibilities. *Coriolanus* is a play made for the primary season. In every election, we've done a Shakespeare play that deals with political issues. *Coriolanus* deals with the problem of political compromise—how does a proud man handle it? It's about a candidate's personal and family relations, the changeability of the mob and how it can be swayed—all very contemporary issues. And it's all there in the text. The text is what's important. Those words that Shakespeare wrote. Bad directors are those who choose to ignore the text, who're interested in other things—painting or video, whatever, everything except the text itself."

I said that I assumed he was referring to directors who distort the meaning and content of the plays by showing off their alleged inventiveness and ingenuity, resorting to gimmicky stylization and rendering the characters and story incomprehensible.

"Precisely. It's always about them, not about Shakespeare. It's always about 'Let's see how clever I can be.' But it should always be about 'What can I do to clarify the play for the audience, to bring it alive for them without vandalizing the text?' "

As to bad actors: "They don't study the text carefully, they don't listen carefully. They don't understand the words they're speaking, they don't get the specifics, they comprehend only the general emotional feeling—hate, love, fear."

I mentioned John Barton's insistence on how crucial it was for an actor to find out how Shakespeare's text works, to actually discover the words as he/she is uttering them, and Cicely Berry's admonition to her class that she didn't want to hear about "feelings."

"Yes. An actor has to realize that 'To be or not to be' is not an audition piece. It's not something the character has already prepared, has already worked out in his mind. He has to give the impression that he's searching for these words, these thoughts."

I couldn't resist urging him to tell me what it had been like to work with Morris Carnovsky in the American Shakespeare Theatre's production of *The Merchant of Venice*. Carnovsky, the actor whom Milton Lewis, the Paramount talent scout, had urged me to consider a role model. I saw him onstage only once, as Andrei, the young brother, in an off-Broadway production of Chekhov's *The Three Sisters* in 1956. He was too old for the role (how ironic—as a young actor he'd played old men), but his artistry was such that within minutes of walking onstage he made you believe he was in his twenties.

Kahn looked at his watch. "I have a meeting in a few minutes. So I'll give you the short version. My relationship with Morris was complicated because he had done Shylock once before at Stratford. He was a great actor, but I had some ideas about the play that varied from his. As a Jew, as an actor who had been blacklisted during the witch-hunting era, Morris felt very responsible for making Shylock sympathetic. At that time, I was interested in the complexity of Shylock as opposed to the simplification of Shylock. I had to struggle with Morris to take a more balanced approach. I remember that when he delivered the lines 'My daughter! O my ducats,' after Jessica runs off with Lorenzo, he would speak 'my daughter' loudly and painfully and then mumble 'my ducats' almost inaudibly. I thought that both daughter and ducats were important. Shylock's Venice is a world that's all about money; money is what makes people tick. The play is a biting critique of capitalism. Shylock is one of the people who are invested in capitalism. Money is important to him. But the way he's treated by other people leads him to behave the way he does. Morris thought that everyone else should be hateful, and Shylock nice. Of course they are hateful, but Shylock doesn't have to be nice.

"I did *Merchant* here recently with Hal Holbrook. I'm much older, I've done a lot more things, I have many other ideas, and I think I was able to make *Merchant* into a very tough play about prejudice everywhere. I had to make the world around Shylock the world I think Shakespeare wrote about. When I met the cast on the first day of rehearsal, I asked why the play is not titled *Shylock* or *Antonio*. There's no name in the title. There's an occupation and a city, which then together make up a definition of a person. We set the play specifically at the beginning of the sixteenth century, but we filtered it through the consciousness of our own time. *Merchant* is about how capital affects relationships, affects how people live and the way they think about each other. I'd come to realize that everybody in the play is either a merchant or merchandise, and sometimes they switch back and forth."

As we rose to leave the room, I told him I'd noticed in his curriculum vitae that in Stratford he'd directed a rock-and-roll version of *Love's Labour's Lost,* and I described my fantasy of an Astaire-Rogers version of the play. Raising his eyebrows, he said, "Ken Branagh's done just that. I read a piece in one of the papers not long ago that his new movie is a modernization of *Love's Labour's Lost,* using Cole Porter's music. So I imagine it's very much what you had in mind."

At first I felt outraged, as if Mr. Branagh was a hacker who'd invaded my computer and filched an ingenious concept. Then I complimented myself on being on the same wavelength as this aging wunderkind. I asked Kahn if he was an admirer of Branagh.

"Yes, even though I wasn't all that taken with his *Hamlet.* He's too old for the part."

I said that although I thought Branagh was ideal if Hamlet was indeed thirty, I, too, envisioned Hamlet as a late adolescent, and the play as his tragic coming-of-age.

"That's all it's about," he pronounced emphatically. "Nothing else but that."

What a pity that Gutman's *Hamlet* seminar had ended. I could have cited Kahn's remark in our discussion of the prince's age, and earned points for name-dropping: "As Michael—Michael *Kahn*—was telling me at Juilliard the other day . . ."

I'd thought to take a brief respite from Shakespeare during the short time remaining before I left for London, and turn for a change of time and place and genres to contemporary American fiction. But there was no escaping the Bard of Avon, my own hound of Heaven, which pursued me relentlessly down the nights and down the days, down the labyrinthine ways of my own mind. And I discovered in the unlikeliest, at least most unexpected, place, yet another Shakespearean teacher I yearned to emulate: Murray Ringold, one of the major characters in Philip Roth's novel *I Married a Communist.*

The publication of Roth's latest novel, *The Human Stain,* made me aware that I had yet to read his previous novel, *I Married a Communist,* published almost two years earlier. So I checked it out of the library and found myself quickly engrossed with Murray, a ninety-year-old retired high school teacher from Newark who tells much of the story in conversations with the narrator, Nathan Zuckerman, Roth's alter ego. Late in the novel, Murray is speaking about a time in the past when he was certain his wild, violent younger brother, Ira, a radio star and, as it happens, a communist, intended to murder his—Ira's—wife (I wondered if Roth was familiar with one of Irwin Shaw's lesser-known novels, *The Troubled Air,* which also featured a radio star who was a communist). And this realization triggers the memory of a prose line from the last act of

Twelfth Night, Feste the Clown to Malvolio: "And thus the whirligig of time brings in his revenges." That line had never registered with me, but it did with Murray—and how!—and from then on it would with me also.

Here's Murray explaining why he couldn't get the line out of his head: "Those cryptogrammic *g*'s, the subtlety of their deintensification—those hard *g*'s in 'whirligig' followed by the nasalized *g* of 'brings' followed by the soft *g* of 'revenges.' Those terminal *s*'s . . . 'thus brings his revenges.' The hissing surprise of the plural noun 'revenges.' Guhh. Juhh. Zuhh. Consonants sticking in me like needles. And the pulsating vowels, the rising tide of their pitch—engulfed by that. The low-pitched vowels giving way to the high-pitched vowels. The assertive lengthening of the vowel *i* just before the rhythm shifts from iambic to trochaic and the prose pounds round the turn for the stretch. Short *i*, short *i*, long *i*. Short *i*, short *i*, boom! Revenges. Brings in his revenges. *His* revenges. Sibilated. Hizzzzuh! . . . those ten words, the phonetic webbing, the blanket omniscience. . . ." In the midst of relating a dramatic moment from his past, Murray, the consummate teacher, stops to analyze the verbal magic of Shakespeare and link it meaningfully to his own experience.

Had Roth, as a high school student in Newark, actually been blessed with a teacher as magnificent as Murray Ringold? Was the Shakespearean analysis the real Murray's, or Roth's? I was willing to credit it to Roth; what the hell, he'd taught comp lit at the University of Pennsylvania and Hunter College, he'd studied at the University of Chicago, he was a smart boy, he knew his Shakespeare, more particularly he probably knew his George T. Wright, that esteemed expert on Shakespeare's metrical art.

And there was definitely a Shakespearean cast to the themes sounded in the novel: appearance versus reality (Nathan as a boy reveres the radical Ira, unaware of his flawed character), role-playing as an aspect of character ("Time to prepare a face to meet the faces that we meet," as Eliot's Mr. Prufrock puts it), the intersection of the public and the private (Murray and Ira are ruined by anticommunist witch-hunting), the menace of utopianism (Roth is merciless with ideologues of all stripes). Given the emphasis on Shakespeare in the climactic last chapter, and Roth's decision to make us consider passages in the plays not ordinarily subjected to close readings, I was inclined to believe that Roth had Shakespeare very much in mind while at work on the novel.

Something besides the references to Shakespeare spoke powerfully to me in *I Married a Communist,* spoke to me as a person who had turned in his uniform and was pursuing satisfactions to be found off the playing field. Nathan Zuckerman, who, like Roth, has moved to his home in the remoteness of rural Connecticut and who, like Roth, has been mellowed by a serious illness, reflects on the idea of the isolated shack as "the place where you are stripped back to essentials, to which you return . . . to decontaminate and absolve yourself of the striving . . . [the place] where you shed your batteredness and your resentment, your appeasement of the world and your defiance of the world, your manipulation of the world and its manhandling of you. The aging man . . . is all alone under the mountain, receding from the agitation of the autobiographical. He has entered vigorously into competition with life; now, becalmed, he enters into competition with death, drawn down into austerity, the final business."

Powerful indeed. I read it over and over, almost committing it to memory, the credo of Retired Man. And yet, and yet . . . for all its electrifying truth, it was also to a large extent the romantic vision of solitude, with a tincture of self-pity, self-dramatization, the tragic Byronic hero ready for the curtain to fall. I've fought the good fight, I've won a few and lost a few, and now silently I retire to search my soul, read the books I've saved for this special time, reread the books I've loved and forgotten, listen to music, keep a journal, etc., etc. But as I discovered, that's the life of a bubble boy, safe perhaps, but sterile. Competing with death, as Roth phrases it, really means continuing to live life to the fullest, in or out of a professional career, before cormorant, devouring Time has its way. Strive, seek, find, never yield: that's not a hermit's motto. Even Thoreau didn't stay in his Walden cabin all that long. And Montaigne, a mere three years after retiring to the tower in his château to write the *Essays,* was back in Paris exercising his gifts as a diplomat.

For me, as for most people I think, learning is almost impossible when it's done for its own sake, in a vacuum. We study with a goal in mind beyond self-enrichment: to earn a degree, to teach effectively, to research a book or an article, to share ideas with our peers in a classroom. Learning is as much a societal enterprise as it is an exercise in self-enrichment. And that is especially true for adult education, Elderhostel, everything that falls under the umbrella of lifelong learning.

Nearing the end of my self-styled sabbatical, I looked forward to getting back in harness at Caldwell College, teaching at the LLI and, who knew, maybe having a whirl as an adjunct professor. Bring on that agitation of the autobiographical! I had more chapters to write.

16.

Passover loomed, and yet another link between
Shakespeare and the Hebrew Scriptures seemed evident to me on the
Sabbath immediately preceding the holiday, the Sabbath Hagadol, the
Great Sabbath, so called because traditionally the rabbi is required to describe at length the rules governing proper observance of this festival.
Rabbi Monson departed from tradition, much to the relief of his congregation. And in his remarks prior to the chanting of the haftarah portion, Malachi III, 4–24, he singled out the final two verses as particularly
meaningful:

> *Behold, I will send you*
>> *Elijah the prophet*
> *Before the coming*
>> *Of the great and terrible day of the Lord.*
> *And he shall turn the heart of the*
> *fathers to the children,*
>> *And the heart of the children to their fathers;*
> *Lest I come and smite the land with utter destruction.*

I could imagine a time in Shakespeare's life when he came upon the
writings of Malachi, a man who, appalled by the moral degradation of his
society, foresaw redemption in the form of familial harmony and the reconciliation of parents and children, youth and elders. And that as a result
he began to write *King Lear* and just a few years after that the Late Romances *(Pericles, Cymbeline, The Winter's Tale, The Tempest)*, dramatizing
the idea of redemption as the process of reconciliation and/or reunion
between parents and children: Pericles and Marina; Cymbeline and his
daughter, Imogen, and his sons, Guiderius and Arviragus; Leontes and
Perdita; Hermione and Perdita; Prospero and Miranda (Prospero recon-

ciled to Miranda's coming-of-age, Miranda reconciled to and reunited with her past through her father's long expository speeches in 1.2); and Lear and Cordelia.

In this vein, I continued to indulge my fantasy of Shakespeare's Jew. In *Shakespeare and the Jews,* James Shapiro cites the testimony before the Inquisition of Vicente Furtado, who, on his way to Amsterdam and Hamburg, stayed in London at the home of two *conversos* during the Passover. Furtado "was able to observe the holiday there, and on the first and last two days of the holiday and on the Sabbath in between 'wore clean linen . . . and ate unleavened bread.' " I envisioned Shakespeare putting himself and his Marrano friend in grave danger by joining the Seder of the latter—a goldsmith, merchant, doctor, court musician, whatever— and also by observing the Great Sabbath in the friend's home, participating in a discussion of Malachi's prophecy of the coming of Elijah.

Shakespeare's Jew. Not a bad title for a novel. Not a bad idea for a novel. I found myself back in the publishing mode, nostalgic for those brainstorming sessions at editorial meetings. Hey, fellas, who can we get to write a novel about Shakespeare's Jew? Burgess is dead. Updike's not likely to consider another Shakespeare conceit now that his novel *Gertrude and Claudius* has bombed. What's John Fowles done lately? Or how about A. S. Byatt—she has the right combination of intellectual strength, narrative resourcefulness, and imaginative power. Who's her agent?

Come to think of it, on one occasion, and only one, I did propose a book with a Jewish theme during an editorial project meeting at Little, Brown, not a company that sprang to mind in those days when you thought about Judaica. I'd read an article in *Time* dealing with an internationally eminent Jewish rabbi, Joachim Prinz, a Berliner who'd escaped the Holocaust and was now presiding over a large congregation in South Orange, New Jersey. In the article, he was quoted as saying that the modern Jew faced the dilemma of being caught between the nightmare of the Holocaust and the dream of a better world to come. I thought that he might be able to develop a book on the subject, titled *The Dilemma of the Modern Jew: Between Nightmare and Dream,* and I'd mentioned this to the managing editor, John Cushman, a polymath. There seemed to be no subject on which he wasn't well versed, and he was ever at the ready to answer questions, to enlighten. He loved to explain things to people. Like me, he'd been a literary agent before coming to Little, Brown, and I've never met anyone more knowledgeable about the business side of publishing. He and Alan Williams, a fellow polymath, had been classmates at Exeter. Alan had gone on to Yale, John to Harvard. Working with these two Mr. Wizards, and learning all that I could from them, was my Harvard and Yale.

John was keen on the idea of a Prinz book and told me to bring it up at the next project meeting. "I'm surprised, though, that the *Time* article caught your eye," John said. "You're not a devout Jew, right?" "No, and maybe that's my dilemma. I wasn't even bar mitzvahed. I can't read a word of Hebrew. I'm one of those marginal Jews, floating between observance and assimilation."

The meeting voted unanimously in favor of my asking Prinz to write the book I had in mind. "It should be valuable in several ways," said Ned Bradford, the editor in chief. "As a statement of belief, a credo. As a prophetic call to a reawakening, a reassessment, a renewal of identity." Then with a wry smile, he looked at me and said, "What's your dilemma, Herm?" "He can't read Hebrew," Cushman answered for me. Everyone laughed, except the president of the company, Arthur Thornhill, Sr., seated at the head of the conference table, opposite Ned.

I thought of Thornhill as a sort of Harry Truman of publishing: blunt, feisty, fearless, shrewd, a self-made man who'd never finished high school and had risen from the stockroom to the presidency via a period as one of the great salesmen in the business. Cushman had told me that at a sales conference long before I joined the company, Thornhill, who at lunch habitually downed three Canadian Clubs, which made him especially pugnacious in the afternoon, once railed against "those kikes at Random House" (Bennett Cerf and Donald Klopfer, who had founded the company and served as president and chairman of the board, respectively, were Jewish). But he was always civil to me, would even drop by my cubicle on occasion to ask how I was faring or reminisce about his experiences on the road for Little, Brown way back when, carrying trunks filled with titles he was peddling to bookstores across the country. And there he was at the end of the meeting, unamused by Cushman's little jest. Why?

That afternoon I wrote Prinz and described the book I had in mind;

he phoned me shortly thereafter to say he'd be delighted to write it—in fact, felt compelled to write it (he did, the book was published under the title I'd suggested, and enjoyed, if that's an apt word, modest sales). And in the interim between my letter and Prinz's call, something quite extraordinary happened. Sitting at my desk one morning, absorbed in whatever manuscript I was editing at the time, I heard the distinctive quick-tempo clicking of heels coming down the corridor, signaling the approach of Arthur Thornhill. In the afternoons, after the Canadian Clubs, that could mean trouble, and we trembled at the thought of those clicks stopping outside our door, like the V-bomb suddenly going silent just before falling on London. The mornings were another matter, and I looked up without fear as Arthur came through the door. Before I could say hello he dropped a paperback on my desk and said, "If you're a Jew, you should know how to read Hebrew. I thought this would help." The book was *Learning Hebrew the Easy Way*. Caught off guard, I stammered out a few awkward words of thanks. He nodded curtly and strode off, leaving me just a shade nonplussed. The subtext as I imagined it was, "If I'm going to have a Jew on the premises, I want a real Jew, an honest-to-God Jew, a proud Jew with religious convictions, not some kind of namby-pamby, wishy-washy, shilly-shallying half-assed version who can't make up his mind where he belongs and has never even bothered to learn the lingo of his people. What's the matter, are you ashamed or something?" How's that for Shakespearean irony and paradox? A man who was known once to have reviled the kikes at Random House had just made me feel guilty about not being true to my Jewish identity, but instead floating in limbo between, well, nightmare and dream. Such a dilemma! What did Arthur expect me to do? Join the Lubavitcher Hasidim and start showing up at work wearing the long black coat, the broad-brimmed black hat, the tzitzits (prayer shawl fringes), the payess (side curls)? That would serve him right for assaulting my conscience. In a bad novel, this incident would have inspired me to return to the traditions of the fathers, and I'd have been bar mitzvahed with Arthur sitting proudly in the front row of the sanctuary, aware of his role in my spiritual rebirth. In real life, what happened was that I felt sheepish for the rest of the day, then put the book in my desk drawer and didn't get around to learning Hebrew until twenty years later.

Only Connect. Such was E. M. Forster's message, delivered through the character Margaret in *Howard's End:* see life whole, experience the relatedness of all its aspects, and you'll find the true meaning of integrity. That, at least, was my fix on it, enabling me to discern a pattern as I connected the dots between David Suchet and Caliban and Prospero and Emily and Jared, and between Rabbi Monson on Malachi and Shakespeare's Jew and Joachim Prinz and Arthur Thornhill. And it was very much on my mind at the conclusion of a Sabbath service in May at which the Torah portion was the Holiness Code in Leviticus.

I was struck, as I'd been last year, by how its essence resonated in Shakespeare, and how it connected to a profile of Harvard political scientist Robert D. Putnam which had appeared coincidentally (or providentially) in that morning's *New York Times* and to a section in Park Honan's *Shakespeare: A Life,* which I was still in the midst of reading. The central precept of the code, "love thy neighbor as thyself," sums up its various principles: revere your parents, show consideration for the needy, pay prompt wages for reasonable hours, deal honorably with your fellows, do not carry tales or bear malice, be magnanimous to the stranger, give equal justice to rich and poor, keep just measures and balances. Precepts and principles that establish and preserve a community, which connects its members with a communal bond.

"Connectedness really matters," Putnam had said in the *New York Times* article, which went on to describe Putnam's message about the waning of social connectedness in contemporary America: "civic engagement—the neighborhood friendships, the dinner parties, the group discussions, the club memberships, the church committees, the political participation . . . —has declined over the last 30 years. Trust and reciprocity, which Mr. Putnam calls social capital, have been damaged." Putnam was raised a Methodist but converted to Judaism, his wife's religion, thirty-seven years ago. Could that have accounted for his finely developed concern for the threat to the ties that bind us? The *Times* noted that Putnam had "reaffirmed his original conclusions and supported them with greatly expanded data, all presented in a new book, *Bowling Alone: The Collapse and Revival of American Community. . . .*" Yet another volume to put on my Required Reading list.

It was that sense of community, that sense of connectedness, that Shakespeare had acquired to such a remarkable degree. According to Park Honan, a Tudor boy "was taught 'all obeysance and courtesie,' or decorum—which turned him into a little actor at 3 or 4. Decorum meant knowing . . . how to play one's role in a deferential society . . . to discern what was proper in relation to all things, places, times, persons . . . [Shakespeare] is humane, receptive, and alert to tenderness and the public good, as if he had affinities with Warwickshire's past[,] and the Gild that linked the generations and influenced a local council in Elizabeth's day helped to form the mind of Shakespeare." As did the Hebrew Scriptures, most assuredly the Holiness Code, I would add.

Lo and behold, boning up on the circumstances of the Globe's reconstruction in the final days before my pilgrimage to that newly consecrated temple, I discovered Shakespeare's Jew, or at least a twentieth-century equivalent: Sam Wanamaker, the visionary monomaniac who for almost a half century pursued his dream of reconstructing the Globe on or near the site of the original in Bankside, Southwark, and who died as the building was in the final stages of completion.

And irony of ironies, Wanamaker was not British. He was an American Jew, an expatriate, born in Chicago to Russian Jews who'd fled the 1905 pogroms. So two of the world's most awesome memorials to Shakespeare, the New Globe and the Folger Shakespeare Library, were conceived by Americans of strikingly different backgrounds (Henry Folger, Standard Oil executive; Sam Wanamaker, actor and social activist) who died before their dreams came to complete fruition.

Wanamaker's struggle to fulfill his grand design (predictably, at the outset the British establishment suspected the project of Disneyfication) is recounted in Barry Day's *This Wooden "O,"* one of the books I'd been reading for the trip. According to Day, Wanamaker's magnificent obsession had been triggered when as a teenager he'd seen Shakespeare performed at a small replica of the Globe at the 1933–34 Chicago centenary exposition. Two years later, during a summer vacation from college, he joined the Globe Shakespearean Theatre Group, which performed thirty-minute versions of Shakespeare's plays at the 1936 Great Lakes Festival in Cleveland in a plywood replica of the Globe donated to the festival by the British government.

As a young actor Wanamaker worked in radio soap operas, which had originated in Chicago (back in my Little, Brown days, I edited a memoir, *A Corner of Chicago,* by Robert Hardy Andrews, a pioneer writer of soaps), then in Hollywood and on Broadway. His career was interrupted by World War II; he served as a marine and saw combat on Iwo Jima, not a bad testing ground for the battles he would face later in England with politicians, businesspeople, architects, philanthropists, scholars, archaeologists, actors, and directors on behalf of rebuilding the Globe.

Wanamaker's postwar career on Broadway was thriving (he played opposite Ingrid Bergman in *Joan of Lorraine,* and he directed and acted with Madeline Carroll in *Goodbye, My Fancy),* and he also continued to appear in films. While in London in 1949 to star in *Give Us This Day,* a film based on Pietro di Donato's novel about immigrant workers, *Christ in Concrete,* he made a pilgrimage to the site of Shakespeare's Globe, marked by a plaque on the wall of the Courage Brewery in Park Street, which had at one time been Maiden Lane, and was appalled that this was the only memento of the greatest playhouse in the history of the theatre.

By then Wanamaker's passionate social activism and his lifelong commitment to union causes (his father had worked in the garment trade) had caught the attention of Senator Joseph McCarthy. Although not a communist, Wanamaker realized that more than likely he faced the prospect someday of giving a command performance before the House Un-American Activities Committee, and went into self-exile in London, where he actually received—and ignored—a subpoena from the committee while he was starring in a play by another witch-hunting victim, Clifford Odets, *Winter Journey (The Country Girl* in America), which he also directed.

In 1957, with the backing of wealthy American socialite Anna Deere Wiman, Wanamaker converted a neglected Victorian theatre, the Shakespeare, into the New Shakespeare Cultural Centre, described by Barry Day as "a dress rehearsal for the project that was to haunt him for most of the rest of his life." The centre included a conventional theatre, a film society, and a restaurant-cum-social center. And there were lectures and art exhibitions.

Two years later Wanamaker returned to the theatrical mainstream, appearing for the first time in a major Shakespearean production as Iago opposite a fellow self-exile, Paul Robeson, in Tony Richardson's version of

Othello at Stratford-on-Avon. Robeson, an eminent black actor and basso-baritone, had lost popularity in America when he became a champion of communism.

In 1970, in a series of ingenious and complex real estate maneuverings, Wanamaker founded what was to become the Shakespeare Globe Trust, dedicated to the reconstruction of the theatre and the creation of an education center and permanent exhibition. Twenty-three years later, only three and a half years before the theatre's gala opening with its production of *Henry V,* Wanamaker died of cancer.

In *Shakespeare's Globe Rebuilt,* a series of articles edited by J. R. Mulryne and Margaret Shewring, Andrew Gurr mentions Studs Terkel's 1980 interview with Wanamaker in Chicago. Asked why he, an American, and not Gielgud or Olivier, should be promoting a rebuilt Globe in London, Wanamaker replied that their concern in London was with the National Theatre, "a concept which had rightly separated off from the dream of a national theatre for Shakespeare." He was taking up an old British torch because its former British holders were now carrying another one. And Wanamaker also stressed that the time was propitious for developing the borough of Southwark, which had become depressed. Gurr continues: "Everything converged: his dream of a new kind of Shakespeare which would supplant the old picture-frame traditions, his understanding of what a rebuilt Globe could do for scholars and students of Shakespeare, and his concern to help regenerate a depressed section of London which had a wonderful history, now lost in its shabby miles of decaying buildings."

As to "authenticity," Gurr emphasizes that Wanamaker was determined to produce not a Shakespeare Disneyland but "the very best guess, the most faithful reconstruction, that all the leading experts working side by side could come up with." Wanamaker gathered an unusual combination of scholars and practitioners of Shakespeare's theatre, and historians from a range of disciplines who for the first time were collaborating in this kind of analysis and reconstruction. Gurr recalls: "We had to piece all the different ideas together, cemented with expert advice from all the recent scholarship into what can be deduced from the . . . available information, from the evidence for the original stagings of the plays themselves and from the surviving buildings that testify to Tudor building techniques."

I wondered how the "authenticity" envisioned by this group could be extended to the style of acting dominant in Shakespeare's time. According to Gurr, by the beginning of the seventeenth century, exaggerated or affected acting—pantomimic action—had been rejected in favor of " 'personation,' a relatively new art of individual characterization," an art defined by Hamlet's advice to the players in which he urges them to hold the mirror up to nature. But as Gurr makes clear, the fact that natural acting was the Elizabethan norm doesn't mean that we know how the player performed his part onstage. A playing company's repertory was packed—usually a different play performed each day—allowing little time for rehearsal or for "deeply studied portrayals of emotions at work." Hence the need for "theatrical shorthand in the conventions of acting that mimed the internal passion"—for example, a thoughtful man scratching his head, an angry man making a threat by shaking a clenched fist. Further, the actor was given only his own part, which had been chopped out of the complete script and pasted together to form a roll (hence the term "role") containing only the actor's lines along with the cue lines for each speech, so the actor would have only a vague idea of the overall play. And he was playing a daily repertory of fourteen or fifteen plays at the same time; since parts were frequently doubled in production, an actor may have been playing fifty different parts a month in twenty-five different plays.

Didn't the fact that the actors at today's Globe are not operating in such a demanding repertory system eliminate one of the essential means of assuring "authenticity"? And if, as Mark Rylance, the Globe's artistic director, had opined, playing in this reconstructed theatre would help unlock new meanings in the plays, how had it been possible to evoke such subtleties in Shakespeare's time when the large and rapidly changing repertories of plays didn't allow companies to spend much time on niceties of staging, as Gurr puts it? And since Shakespeare's plays were performed in several venues in addition to the Globe—great halls of noblemen, the Royal Palace, the indoor theatre of Blackfriars—wouldn't the style of acting have been adjusted for each special circumstance?

These were questions I wished I could have put to the redoubtable Sam Wanamaker, even at the risk of incurring his wrathful impatience with the merest hint of negativity concerning his cherished objective. From what I gathered in *This Wooden "O,"* he could have stepped out of the pages of a Saul Bellow novel—Chicago-born, aggressive, abrasive, a dynamo, a whirlwind, a dreamer and schemer, a picaro of sorts, an artist and an entrepreneur, a man possessed by a sense of destiny, a wandering Jewish American persona non grata in his own country and bringing about in the nation that had once expelled all its Jews one of the monumental cultural and civic restorations of modern times. I longed for a fuller portrait of the man; pity he hadn't written his memoirs. But Barry Day briefly mentions Patrick Spottiswoode, the Globe's director of education, and figuring he was just the person to have some enlightening Wanamaker stories of his own that didn't make *This Wooden "O,"* I arranged an appointment with him at the Globe for the morning of June 1.

17.

The flight to London, unlike that of the previous summer, was free of anxiety and irritation. No pre-Oxford jitters, no paper to fret about. No *Shakespeare in Love* to suffer through.

What gripped me this time was the sheer excitement of a pilgrim anticipating the moment when he'd reach at last the shrine he'd waited so long to visit. It was akin to the way I felt in 1989 when Barbara and I were on the bus from Tel Aviv to Jerusalem, approaching the site of the Holy Temple, and I tried to imagine how it would feel to pray in Hebrew at the Kotel, the Western Wall. And once I was there, my hands pressed against those ancient stones, what flashed to mind was not the vision of Jews flocking to the Temple before its destruction by the Romans but the images of Israeli soldiers after the victorious Six-Day War of 1967 sobbing when they reached the wall to which Jews had been denied access during the nineteen years of Jordanian occupation.

By the time I checked into my hotel room the next day, it was early afternoon. Too keyed up by the prospects ahead, I'd slept fitfully on the plane and by this time I was too exhausted for more than a stroll across the Tower Bridge, which was a few yards from the hotel, and a walk around the perimeter of the Tower itself, a block away.

Standing on the bridge, gazing west at the spectacle of the busy river traffic plying the waters of the Thames, I was aware that a mile or so around a bend to the left and out of sight was the New Globe. And again I thought of Richard and Cuthbert Burbage, who on a night in late December 1598 had dismantled the theatre built by their father, James, transported it, timber by timber, across the river, and rebuilt it as the Globe.

And on my amble around the precincts of the Tower, I called to mind Sir Walter Raleigh, once imprisoned there, and of Shakespeare's Sonnet 25, which alludes to Raleigh's fall from honor and glory: "The painful warrior, famoused for might, / . . . Is from the book of honour rased. . . ."

The next morning I showed up punctually at the Globe's administrative offices, adjacent to the theatre building on New Globe Walk in Southwark, and was met by Patrick Spottiswoode's charming young associate, Deb Callan, who told me that Patrick was running a bit late and was expected any moment. She ushered me into his office, where through the windows I took in the view of the Thames and of Saint Paul's, looming across the river, and then browsed through the bookshelves of Shakespeareana arranged, I noticed, alphabetically by author. And what should I come upon but Delia Bacon's book propounding the preposterous "Francis Bacon is the real Shakespeare" theory. I glanced through it and, expecting to find the ravings of a lunatic, came upon a section on Montaigne that I found surprisingly erudite and fluent. Then I remembered that even Hawthorne had been impressed: "The woman is mad but the book is a good one," he'd said. Just as I was returning the volume to the shelf, lest I find myself seduced like Hawthorne by Miss Bacon's apparent rationality, in rushed Spottiswoode, as if he'd been poised outside, waiting to see if I took the Bacon bait. He was terribly sorry to have been a mite tardy, had to deal with an unexpected little crisis and all that. He turned out to be younger than I'd expected, and a lot more robust. I'd imagined a tall, thin, severe middle-aged academic, dressed in tweed and slightly patronizing, but Patrick seemed to be in his late thirties, sturdily built, slightly under six feet, a shock of dark brown hair loosely parted in the center, ebullient, informal, jovial, and wearing dark slacks and a navy sweatshirt from, of all places, Canisius College in New York.

"I was lecturing in the States a few weeks ago," he explained. "I come there fairly often, partly on the lecture circuit, partly setting up programs with schools in conjunction with Globe Education. We run three performance courses a semester here for liberal arts majors from Notre Dame and James Madison University. And a four-week acting and directing course for Washington University, St. Louis." He went on to say that the Southwark council was going to build the Globe an education and rehearsal center: eight workshop spaces, a little theatre seating two hundred, and on the top floor two complete Globe rehearsal stages, with columns and a gallery where students could attend rehearsals.

All very impressive indeed, but I was anxious to take him back to the beginning, and his relationship with Sam Wanamaker. Patrick, it turned out, discovered a vocation by answering a classified ad. In 1984, he was a Ph.D. candidate at Warwick University, concentrating on the ideas of justice in the works of Sidney, Spenser, and Shakespeare. "But in truth I'm not a scholar," he told me, "not a researcher, and I was primed to leave. I actually bought a newspaper to look for a job—I'd never done that. And I saw this tiny ad about a job at the Globe: come to work in an Elizabethan Museum and Art Centre, with Two Theatre Spaces, a Bookshop, a Café, and an Exhibition. The way the job was described was the expression of Sam Wanamaker's dream. It sounded like the Barbican [the Royal Shakespearean Company's London venue]. The reality was something else. I arrived at a downtrodden, Victorian/late-Georgian three-story brick building on Bear Gardens, in Southwark. The place was dusty, the bookshop was two shelves, the café literally just a bar of wood, one of the theatres sat one hundred, the other was just a cockpit with some chairs in it. That was the Bear Gardens Theatre and Art Centre."

In 1970, Wanamaker thought it might be wise to get a foothold in the community. He and a couple of businessmen bought a share of the property at Bear Gardens, a clever investment. "In those days," Patrick said, "you could pick up property in Southwark for a postage stamp— no one came over here. But Sam wanted people to know about this area—that was a great service he performed. Everyone was focusing on Shakespeare at the Barbican, the Old Vic, the National, and at Stratford, but Sam kept reminding people that this area was the true Shakespearean workplace, and we mustn't neglect it. So he bought this little bit of property, and he kept on having these exhibitions, probably for the same three people that returned every time the exhibition changed. But Sam was undaunted. He had this passion, this amazing physical and intellectual energy. He was indomitable, he would see it through, watch it grow."

Patrick went for his interview, but Wanamaker wasn't there; he happened to be acting in a film at the time. "Three people interviewed me," Patrick continued, "and I got the job, a wonderful job for someone with my background and experiences. I loved the Elizabethan theatre and the literature of the period, but up to that time only in a puritanical, purist way. This job put my knowledge to good use.

"My first responsibility was to create a mini-exhibition, with no money, in two weeks. Actually, it took seventeen, eighteen weeks, and I worked with an architect. What we produced was okay, but absolutely flat. It consisted merely of posters. The most antitheatrical exhibition possible. Lifeless. Sam returned after the exhibition opened and pronounced it disgraceful. 'We're actually paying this man to do such work?' Sam begrudged that anyone should be paid. Only two of us worked full-time at that point. Sam was leery of anyone who was paid—he himself drew no salary. He suspected that people were taking the organization for a ride, just using it, not caring, and he was particularly suspicious of anyone who'd been employed without his agreement. If he'd been here when I was interviewed for the job, I don't think I'd have been hired. I don't think I'd have been hired. I don't think anyone would have been hired. Sam wanted himself, a clone."

Soon converted by Wanamaker to the Grand Design aspect of reconstructing the Globe, Patrick eventually met the man who intensified his passion for the project—Ronald Watkins, a man now in his late nineties, who'd retired as a teacher at Harrow twenty-five years earlier. "We'd created a Shakespeare festival, and Sam asked me to invite Watkins to give a lecture. I introduced him rather perfunctorily, I'm afraid, and he stood up and gave his lecture, 'The Importance of Peter Quince'—Quince of course was the carpenter in *Midsummer Night's Dream,* one of the mechanicals who's part of Bottom's group of players. The lecture looked at the Globe and its playing conditions and playing practices, showing clear links between the plays and the playhouse for which they were written. It was like going to a chiropractor who clicked your back into position. Watkins clicked my 'Globe back' into position. It turned my relationship with the organization from a kind of affair into a marriage."

Interesting way to sum up an epiphany. I suppose John Barton was my chiropractor, clicking my "Shakespeare back" into position.

Patrick turned to the troubling and critical interim when he and his colleagues were made redundant. "Sam had entered into an agreement with the local government, the local council, and a property company from Southwark. He had the Bear Gardens, but he needed more land to bring the Globe to fruition. He didn't have any money, so he said to the Southwark council, 'Here's a bit of undeveloped Bankside land—what

can we do with it? We can turn it into an art, residential, and local housing cooperative. You give us the land, which you own, bid it to property
developers, who will build the Globe free, give it to us, and in return,
you give them the rest of the land so that they can build some commercial property and make their money.' Brilliant. And it all seemed to be
chugging along nicely. Sam got the council to agree to the scheme on the
eve of the council election. But the next day a much more left-wing
council came into power and said, 'We don't want tourism, we don't
want office development. We want this whole area developed for low-
cost council housing.' We were all made. We just had to paddle and hope
that that council would not renege, but allow us to go ahead. But they
refused."

I could see that Wanamaker was more than the protagonist of a Saul
Bellow novel. The irony and contradictoriness of Sam Wanamaker, left-
wing activist and refugee from anticommunist witch-hunting, now
turned wheeler and dealer whose high-reaching commercial venture was
about to be wrecked by leftist politicos, had a Shakespearean dimension.
And in a way his troubles seemed to mirror those of James Burbage. I
wondered if it occurred to Wanamaker at the time that he had become
the hero of a Shakespearean drama, *The Jew of Southwark.*

As Patrick related the story, Wanamaker finally prevailed, without having to go to the lengths that his predecessor Burbage did. The developer
who had the money took the council to high court and sued them for
reneging on an agreement. And at the last moment, the council withdrew.
"The developers were given seven, eight million pounds, we were given
a few thousand, which did not cover our expenses over the years. But we
were given the land. The silver lining is that the whole site is ours."

Patrick surmised that the Globe couldn't have been built in the 1980s.
"If it had opened in 1987, it wouldn't be here now. It would be a ghost
town. The time wasn't right for all sorts of reasons. Public attitudes, and
the government's, towards the past, the heritage, have changed. London
as a place to enjoy life represents a change, scholarship has changed,
there's been a resurgence of interest in Shakespeare which hasn't harmed
us. Of course, this meant that Sam wasn't alive to savor it all."

Finally, Patrick summed up the experience of working with Wanamaker. "Sam was never satisfied. He was a taskmaster. But I think that as

far as I was concerned, he realized this wasn't just a job for me, it was a vocation. And this gave him confidence in me, and allowed him to give me free rein, to develop education in a wonderful way, I think. Sometimes he'd shout, 'Why don't you do so-and-so,' and I'd say, 'Because it's not my job, Sam,' and he'd say, 'Okay.' He quite accepted your standing up to him. He hated people who'd say, 'Okay, I'll do it,' and didn't. Or who'd say, 'Oh, I'm really not sure,' because that showed weakness. But if you stood up to him and said, 'Honestly, Sam, I don't think it's the right thing,' he'd accept that.

"Another thing about Sam: if you felt really good about something—'I just got a bit of money for a project'—he'd say, 'Couldn't you get more?' But if you were really feeling down, things were going wrong, he'd say, 'Don't worry, we'll work it out.'

"We never believed Sam would die. We couldn't believe that anyone with that passion could disappear. He was clearly ill, but he never let on to us that he had cancer. We actually knew, of course—but he obviously was going to live until the Globe opened, there was no way he couldn't be there. And then he was bedridden, or homebound, and he asked to see everybody. I said, 'Tell him I can't see him. I have work to do.' Which is exactly what he would expect. So I went abroad to do some lecturing about the Globe, and I came back to find the announcement that he'd died. So I never got to see him in that final stage.

"The last time I saw him he'd come here to have a look-around. He was so frail. It was clear that this was his final visit. He was walking around the building site, and he tripped, and said, 'If only I'd tripped and died, what a press story that would have made.' Then something really impressive happened, a symbolic moment if you will. He came to the outside wall, and he crouched down—actually, he lowered himself slowly, he was very weak—and he said, 'This wall's too high. Children can't look over it.' Here he was in his pain, thinking about accessibility. And that's the key to this project—Sam's concern that this building be accessible to everyone."

I left Patrick's office around noon and set out to explore the area, especially the nearby sites of Philip Henslowe's Rose and the old Globe, and the Anchor pub, said to have been one of Dr. Johnson's favorite watering places.

First I walked a couple of blocks to the modern high-rise office building on Park Street, housing in an excavated pit on its main floor the remains of the Rose. Entering, I came upon the inevitable Gifte Shoppe and a sweet matron to whom I paid the price of admission, and just down the corridor and to the left, guarded by an iron railing, was what's left of the Rose. Or, I should say, an illuminated outline of the remnants.

In April 1989, when a thirty-year-old seven-story office building that had been constructed over the Rose site was in the process of being demolished to make way for a new ten-story building, a team of archaeologists assigned by a nongovernmental agency called English Heritage conducted an investigation on about 60 percent of the site so as to preserve the relics on the premises, and discovered the foundation walls and the yard surface of the Rose. The excavation proved that Elizabethan playhouses were not circular but polygonal. Exposed to the air, the fragile remains began to dry and crack. Under considerable pressure from theatre celebrities, politicians, and the media, the developer, Imry Merchant, changed the design of his office building at a reported cost of ten million pounds so that the building could be constructed on stilts over the excavated pit containing, now carefully re-covered, the sixteenth-century theatrical treasure, the exact location of the foundation outlined in lights, which appear at appropriate moments during a taped history of the premises narrated by Ian McKellen.

Only three of us were at the railing, listening to Sir Ian as we gazed into the rubble. After all, it was just past noon on a weekday, not a peak time, I imagine, for visiting theatrical shrines. Standing a few feet from me was a young man with long sideburns and wearing an earring. "It's just a bloody hole in the ground," he muttered bitterly. "And some bloody rocks." Then he stalked off. I wondered if he'd had the same reaction at Stonehenge. I did feel a shiver of excitement as I stared into the cool, dark, dank pit. But I resented not only the audio narration but also, and to an extreme, the video projections on screens suspended above the pit; from time to time, scenes from—you guessed it—*Shakespeare in Love* depicting performances at the Rose flashed before me. Why the need for those intrusions of someone else's re-creation on my own imagination? And I could have done without McKellen over the loudspeaker, merely repeating what was effectively displayed in text and photos on the wall to the right of the pit. Why not allow visitors the privilege of silence and a site uncontaminated with flickering images? Why not let us piece out the imperfections with our minds as we strain to envision what once was, to hear voices from the past deliver lines that still sing in our brains, to sense the spectators around us, relishing the moment?

With that grumpy reflection I left Henslowe's domain, crossed the street, and walked fifty yards or so to the site of the Rose's main competition, the first Globe. Long ago the old Anchor brewery had been constructed on the site of the remains of the Globe. In 1986, part of the brewery had been bought by a developer and knocked down; the developer, according to Barry Day, was in no hurry to build and the site was empty when, in October 1989, an archaeological team, looking not merely for the Globe but for Roman remains as well, uncovered a layer of hazelnuts that made up the flooring surface of the Globe. It was determined that 10 percent of the Globe had been destroyed by nineteenth-century construction work, 20 percent was a narrow strip of empty land, 30 percent was under Anchor Terrace, now occupied by a row of empty Georgian buildings dating back to the 1830s and protected by the English Heritage preservationists, and the rest was under the surface of the Southwark Bridge Road, built 1814–19. Further excavation was prohibited, but so, also, was construction on the site. From the small portion of the Globe that had been excavated, two important inferences were drawn: it was a twenty-sided building and had a diameter of one hundred feet. These tantalizing remains were returned to the earth, embalmed in sand and concrete, and now rest under a car park paved in brick, its surface emblazoned with "Shakespeare's Globe" in gold lettering.

I stood at the iron railing that barricades the area and in front of which has been placed the bronze plaque moved from its original site on a wall of the Anchor brewery where Sam Wanamaker had once seen it and been inspired with his dream of a new Globe. No such visions overwhelmed me as I looked around the area. Guiltily, I felt not even the tinge of awe I experienced upon first looking into the bloody hole in the ground bearing an illuminated outline of the remains of the Rose. Perhaps a cool, dark, dank pit works on the spirit far more effectively than a parking lot in the bright sunlight. Legend has it that shortly after arriving in London from Stratford, Shakespeare's first showbiz job had been to take care of the horses on which patrons had arrived at Burbage's Theatre. I suppose this made him the equivalent of a parking lot attendant, a neat tie-in to the new environs of the old Globe. Still, looking through the iron bars of a fence at a mere parking lot, for the life of me I could imagine none of the sights and smells and sounds of Shakespeare's Southwark. Nothing at all. Nothing would come of nothing, as Lear once admonished Cordelia, and I took my leave and made for the Anchor pub, an eighteenth-century weathered brick haven a few yards from the Thames and very near both Shakespeare's Globe and the site of the old Globe.

Inside, the half-timbered room was filled with cigarette smoke and the noise of a happy throng. The atmosphere of a festival prevailed, hardly surprising. Is there a more sociable institution than an English pub? I squeezed into a tiny space at the bar, between a construction worker from one of the adjacent developments-in-progress and an elderly gray-haired woman. Each of them held a lighted cigarette in nicotine-stained fingers and stared benignly into a pint of ale. I noticed among the draft ales and beer the absence of Old Speckled Hen. Just as well. That belonged to the Oxford Experience. When in London . . . Waiting for one of the young female bartenders (no Doll Tearsheets or Mistress Quicklys, they), I studied the array of brands available, trying to fix on a likely substitute for the Hen. My effort must have been reflected in my perplexed expression, for the woman next to me said, with a smile revealing teeth that suggested the excavations at the Rose, "Can't make up your mind, is it?" "Well," I replied, "I could use some help from an expert." "Ah then," she offered, "go for the Boddington's. You'll find it friendly enough." Is there such a thing as an unfriendly ale? I have yet to find one. A slender redheaded bartender appeared; she might have been a descendant of Nell Gwynn, one of England's first actresses, who before going on the stage in 1665 had sold oranges in the Theatre Royal, and became a favorite of Charles II. "A glass of Boddington's," I said, as if that was my usual. But the adviser at my side quickly interjected, "Ah, no, be a man, have a pint." I affirmed my masculinity and revised the order. "You won't be sorry, love," my new good friend assured me, snuffing out the stub of her cigarette and quickly lighting another. I imagined she was a teenager during the Blitz, and I could see her making the best of it while crowded into the Underground during a bombing, trying to cheer up her old mum, while Dad, maybe a lorry driver on duty as an air-raid warden, was risking his life on the streets above them. When bombs seemed to be falling closer, she leads the group around her in a Gracie Fields number, "We'll meet again, don't know where, don't know when."

Looking around the room, I let my imagination, fueled by the rapidly disappearing pint of Boddington's, roam further back into the past, trying to catch a glimpse of that Olympian man of letters Dr. Samuel Johnson at table with his good friend Henry Thrale, owner of the nearby brewery constructed over the site of the old Globe, and his chum David Garrick, the actor/manager celebrated for his Shakespearean productions. Young provincials, Johnson and Garrick had endured poverty and obscurity together while struggling for eminence in their fields. Thrale was born to wealth, the son of a self-made man from whom he inherited the brewery. Did I hear Garrick twitting Thrale for owning property built over sacred ground? And was that roar the intimidating growl of Johnson, berating Garrick for his ill manners in daring to suggest that Thrale could in any way be held responsible for the location of the brewery, or that the old Globe should be considered a shrine at all? Or was the subject being discussed the agreement Johnson has recently made with a group of London booksellers to edit a collection of Shakespeare's works, an enterprise that will ultimately produce Shakespearean criticism of enduring magnitude?

The apparitions receded, my glass was empty, it was time to leave. I said farewell to the Blitz survivor at my side, and before taking a cab to my hotel, I roamed awhile through Southwark. First down Bear Garden street, site of the bear-baiting arena. The term "dogs of war" used by Antony in *Julius Caesar* was not a metaphor. The dogs who demonstrated their ferocity in the bear-baiting arenas were used in combat by Roman armies, who would unleash them to attack the opposing force. Earlier, in the arena, a line would be scratched in the dirt floor, and the dogs who failed to cross that line and attack the bear would be deemed "not up to scratch"—that is, unfit for battle. Next, the site of the Clink, one of England's oldest jails, dating to the sixteenth century. Here, in Elizabethan times, public hangings were conducted. The Clink Prison Museum now occupies the space. I didn't go inside—hokey "fun house" scareathons depress me. Down a narrow street I went, stopping briefly at the ruins of the Bishop of Winchester's palace, where it's possible that Shakespeare and his company, the Lord Chamberlain's Men, subsequently the King's Men when they enjoyed the patronage of James I, performed. Thence to Southwark Cathedral, once presided over by none other than Launcelot Andrews, Bishop of Winchester, whom James commissioned to prepare a new edition of the Bible. Some people actually believe that Shakespeare rewrote—that is, wrote—Psalm 64 and provided a numerical code secretly attesting to his authorship: 46 is the reverse of 64; the 46th word from the beginning of the psalm is "spear," and the 46th word from the end is "shake." I wonder if Delia Bacon was aware of this.

The next day, shortly before two o'clock, clutching a cushion that I'd rented for a pound (a necessity when sitting on a wooden bench without a back support for the length of a Shakespearean play) and a program for which I'd paid two pounds, almost four dollars, I entered the Globe and beheld, at last, the holy of holies. I'd studied the sketches and color photographs in Mulryne and Shewring's *Shakespeare's Globe Rebuilt,* but nothing had prepared me for the multicolored ornateness, the visual splendor, of the stage and how it dominated the interior.

In the foreground, two pillars, painted to resemble marble, and ornamented with *rosso antico* work, supported the stage cover, a ceiling decorated with a celestial scene resembling a night sky. Brightly painted figures of the zodiac circled the central panel of the "heavens," which is decorated with a supernal light (I recalled the astrological symbols embedded in the mosaic floor of the ancient remains of a synagogue in Tiberias). A sun and a moon had been located at the two foremost corners of the cover. In one of the essays in *Shakespeare's Globe Rebuilt,* Siobhan Keenan and Peter Davidson speculate that seeing as how the Burbages called their new playhouse the Globe, it's not unlikely that they "commissioned a decorative scheme intended to foster an emblematic conception of the theatre as a microcosm of the real world. . . . Consequently, a simple iconographic message, elaborating upon this conceit, has underpinned the designs prepared for the reconstructed theatre . . . [where] under the starry sky . . . we can perform the mimesis of all human life." As I took in the sight before me, lines from the morning prayers that are part of the Jewish liturgy ran through my head: "Praise shall be Yours, Lord our God, for Your wondrous works, for the lights You have fashioned, the sun and the moon which reflect Your glory." And "He created the world with His word. Praise Him. . . . His word, His performance. Praise Him." This temple had been built to worship another creator, one who had created a world with words, one whose word was performance. It, too, was a sacred space.

Above the stage cover was a gabled hut with a window. And at the rear of the stage was the carved and painted tiring-house (dressing room) wall, known as the *scaenae frons,* or scenic frontispiece, with three arched openings for entrances and exits. The doors of the *frons* were plain timber. Above the *frons* were balustraded boxes called the Lords' Rooms, because in Shakespeare's day they were reserved for the privileged.

Surrounding the stage were three covered galleries of tiered wooden benches. The thatched roof of the timber and plaster theatre was permanently open, and the groundlings who packed the yard would be at the mercy of the weather, which, luckily for them, was fair and mild. I was seated at the far left of the middle gallery, close to the stage, where in a few minutes *The Tragedy of Hamlet* would unfold. I got the impression that the pillar nearest me would not seriously obscure the action. The theatre was almost full and a festive mood prevailed. Perhaps these folks had just come from the Anchor. Or the air of let-the-games-begin merriment stemmed from the sun pouring through the open roof and the excited expectant buzz and hum rising from the groundlings in the yard. My thoughts turned decidedly unreligious, and now I was reminded of the times I used to take my son to New York Knicks basketball games at Madison Square Garden.

Near me were three couples who'd brought a hamper filled with food and drink—the Globe's version of tailgate picnicking. A perky short-haired woman in the party offered me a cookie, and we struck up a conversation, during which I mentioned that I taught Shakespeare at the LLI. She turned to the oldest member of her group, a fellow with a shock of white hair and a tanned, lined face, and said, indicating me, "This gentleman teaches Shakespeare also." Seems that the tribal elder, who happened to be her father-in-law, was headmaster of a school in Cornwall, where he also taught English and directed plays. He was coming to New York in the fall, and we exchanged addresses and phone numbers. In front of me, a man wearing a paper sun visor leaned against the balustrade while his attractive blond wife massaged his back. "Is that a service provided by the management?" I asked. "If so, I'm next." The wife laughed, and the husband, also amused, turned and said, "Quote me a price." This coarse jocosity between strangers is uncommon in theatre audiences, but not at sporting events. Few people, I imagined, had come to worship the Bard, or to have an Elizabethan fling. They were truly playgoing, they were there in the spirit of play, of fun; they were out for a good time in the company of players. So what if the play was a tragedy? They wanted to be entertained, to be moved, to be—enchanted. By the end, however, they'd have undergone a far deeper experience, one that it would not be an exaggeration to term "spiritual."

At two o'clock sharp (punctuality is the motto at the Globe), two trumpeters appeared in the open windows of the gabled hut above the *frons,* and one at each end of the middle gallery. The notes they sounded were almost ominously majestic, as if they were paraphrasing Calpurnia's lines from *Julius Caesar* to read, "The heavens themselves blare [not "blaze"] forth the death of princes." The play began.

From the outset, it was obvious that lively action would be the order of the day. Lines spoken trippingly on the tongue, cues picked up quickly, few of those deadening pauses that John Barton and Michael Kahn pronounced to be the bane of contemporary Shakespearean production, the stage alive with continuous movement, something happening in all parts of the stage, sort of a three-ring circus, with overlapping entrances and exits (e.g., in 2.2, after their first meeting with Claudius and Gertrude, Rosencrantz and Guildenstern were escorted to the exit stage right by Gertrude, and the trio then pantomimed an exchange of pleasantries while Polonius told Claudius that the ambassadors of Norway had returned).

And the central dynamizing force was Mark Rylance's vigorous, youthful portrayal of Hamlet. Rylance must be in his late thirties, his hair beginning to recede on top, and yet he was every bit the young prince, restless and charged with energy, a study in perpetual—sometimes frantic—motion. He first appeared onstage not brooding and sullen, standing apart from the royal party, solitary and hostile, in the manner common to most renditions of this tragedy. Instead, he entered from the discovery space, center stage, with the entourage preceding the arrival of the king and queen, attired in a fashion befitting a Renaissance noble (thank God,

the production was Elizabethan in its costuming as well as its staging),
complete with elegant cap—the clothes were black, but ornamented in
places with gold, certainly not the mourning duds typical of the Hamlets
I've seen—and took his place at the royal table, actually genuflecting in
homage, left arm extended, hand palm-up, when Claudius and Gertrude
entered and exited. Upon the couple's exit, he remained kneeling and delivered the "O that this too too solid flesh" soliloquy in what began as a
dazed confused rush of words, his head bowed, a young man in a state of
emotional concussion from the blow delivered by his mother's marriage
to his uncle so soon after his father's death.

A rich consequence of Rylance's boyish interpretation of Hamlet was
the antic humor he, with the guidance of the director, Giles Block, was
bringing to the role. His Hamlet was actually funny (a quality that
Olympia Dukakis had admired in Richard Burton's interpretation);
"antic" in "antic disposition" came across at times simply as wildly comic,
not grotesque, certainly not a form of madness—after all, we know he's
faking it, that's why it's funny—and I, along with the audience, not infrequently roared with laughter. Hamlet was a university student, and his
clowning had a collegiate—yea, late adolescent—flavor. At one point,
Hamlet, attired in a stained nightshirt and white socks about fifty sizes too
big—clown indeed—jumped up on a table while Polonius was addressing others onstage and behind the old man's back mugged like a chimp,
playing outrageously to the audience, especially the groundlings, and of
course bringing down the house. It reminded me of Jim Dixon, the
Lucky Jim of Kingsley Amis's wicked satire, a new young college instructor who made absurd faces, mostly simian, behind the back of a
pompous old bore of a professor. I wondered if Rylance/Block had this
in mind. Again, in a risible vein, Hamlet entered in 2.2 colorfully attired
in garments that suggested a Fool's costume and carrying a little drum (a
favorite prop of Dick Tarleton, celebrated clown of Shakespeare's time;
had this been an allusion intended by Rylance/Block?) and addressed his
"speak the speech" lines as a critique-in-progress to one of the players,
who was rehearsing much to his dissatisfaction in front of him. For instance, when the player began to recite a line floridly, Rylance interrupted him with an exasperated little smile and proceeded to tell him how
offended he was to hear a "robustious periwig-pated fellow tear a passion

to tatters, to very rags, to split the ears of the groundlings"—then he turned and spoke directly to those in the yard—"who for the most part are capable of nothing but inexplicable dumbshows and noise." Spontaneous good-natured booing and protesting and here and there an obscene gesture from the groundlings. That kind of interaction with the audience would have been impossible on a proscenium stage in a darkened theatre. Here it gave the audience an emotional breather. It reminded us that we were watching and hearing players having fun at their job, that all of us were participants in a communal event. (I was reminded of the bar mitzvah, which combines solemnity with jocular reactions between those on the *bimah*—the platform where the Torah is read—and the congregation.) Later in the scene, as the king and queen and court gathered for the performance of the play-within-the-play, and Polonius told Hamlet about his enacting Julius Caesar during his university days, Block had devised a piece of stage business at once richly comic and eerily portentous: when Polonius said he was stabbed in the capital by Brutus, Hamlet mocked stabbing him with drumsticks as he said, "It was a brute part of him to kill so capital a calf there," poking fun at the old man in the manner that presages the actual murder to come.

Block's staging of the death of Polonius epitomized his directorial imaginativeness, his capacity to be original always in the context of the dramatic possibilities inherent in the scene, never out of a hey-look-at-me compulsion to astonish. Block won me over from the start by setting the scene in Gertrude's closet, her sitting or dressing room, not her bedroom, so that we were spared even the slightest Oedipal hint in Hamlet raging at Mommy. Joanna McCallum's Gertrude was a handsome matron, full of high spirits and generosity and warmth, glowing rosily with a healthy sensuousness and reveling in the ardor of her new marriage. When Hamlet grabbed her violently in front of her dressing table, her shouts of "Murder" elicit Polonius's cry for "Help" from behind the arras that covered the discovery space at the center of the *frons* and through which Hamlet stabbed the form that he believed was Claudius. At this point, Hamlet usually parts the arras to reveal Polonius's corpse. Not so at the Globe. Hamlet did draw back the arras, but discovered Polonius standing, mortally wounded and in a state of shock but still alive. Hamlet, no less shocked himself, appalled and on the verge of hysteria at the terrible mistake he made—and here we saw the young man, the university student, frantic with regret and possibly fear, who we have to imagine for the first time had stabbed a man fatally—helped Polonius to the chair beside the dressing table and desperately stroked his face, as if trying to stave off the inevitable. Polonius struggled to his feet, convulsed, and died in the arms of Hamlet, who embraced him and, grief-stricken and weeping, sobbed out the lines "Thou wretched, rash, intruding fool, farewell," now invested with poignance, not scorn and disgust, the reaction we've seen from other Hamlets. So Block obviously felt as I had that day when I suggested that Gertrude hadn't been lying when she told Claudius that Hamlet had wept at the sight of Polonius; she'd been revealing an oblique stage direction of Shakespeare's about how Hamlet should react in the earlier scene. Instead of recoiling from a callous, brutal Hamlet, we shared his feelings of pity and terror.

Hamlet's embrace of Polonius was foreshadowed, in a sense, by his scene in 1.5 with the ghost of his father. The ghost's first appearance in 1.1 was almost comic. No attempt at special effects preceded his entrance—no smoke, no mist, no ominous offstage music. And of course no lighting, except for the sunlight streaming through the open roof and illuminating the entire theatre, hardly an atmosphere evocative of the supernatural. Out of the *frons* opening stage right clomped this figure in black armor, going downstage past Marcellus and Bernardo and Horatio, then exiting through the opening upstage left. I was reminded of the Tin Man in *The Wizard of Oz*, or Sid Caesar in one of the movie parodies on *Your Show of Shows*. And sure enough, there were some muffled titters in the audience, especially among the younger groundlings. I wondered if Block had intended the spectators to be amused. Since it would be very hard to conjure up scary effects in broad daylight, why pretend—why not simply call attention to the fact that this is just a player in armor, earning his salary? The old theatrical self-reflexivity angle. But with their reactions the three players onstage actually managed to convince us that they'd witnessed something unearthly and unsettling. And there was nothing amusing about the ghost in his scene with Hamlet. Here something quite extraordinary occurred. The ghost took off one of his gloves, reached out, and grabbed Hamlet by the arm. It was a stunning moment. But why shouldn't he have made body contact? This was not an apparition. It was a creature of substance, of flesh and blood, and made a stronger emotional impact on Hamlet, and on us, than any chasing after stagy phantoms would have. Then came an even more stirring action: Hamlet and the ghost actually embraced. Hamlet's back was to the audience, and as the two men hugged each other vehemently, aware that this reuniting would soon end, the love between father and son was dramatized in a stirring tableau. Against the armored body of his father, clutched in those steel-bound arms, Hamlet seemed small and fragile, like a little boy who didn't want his daddy ever to let go. We've all had dreams of meeting loved ones and friends who have died, and it was the memory of how we felt when we thought we'd cheated death that made that dramatic picture so powerful. I couldn't help concluding that Block intended to echo it, mirror it, in Hamlet's subsequent embrace of the dead Polonius.

Rylance approached the "To be or not to be" soliloquy as if it were an essay that Hamlet was in the process of writing: he entered holding a sheet of paper to which he referred from time to time while delivering the speech. In his own essay in *Shakespeare's Globe Rebuilt,* Rylance stated that for an actor to make even a speech as familiar as "To be or not to be" seem fresh, he should not present it as something prepared offstage (" 'To be . . .' is not an audition piece," Michael Kahn had declared) but should discover with the audience the words he needs for this particular situation (undoubtedly a lesson learned from his days with Barton and Berry at the RSC). And at the Globe he achieved this by seeming to involve the audience in the act of composition, the act of thinking.

At the beginning of 4.5, as the mad Ophelia, in a piercingly effective performance by Penny Layden, was singing one of her melancholy ballads, Claudius, played with bluff, vigorous authority by Tim Woodward, entered in robust good humor, confident of Hamlet's imminent execution at the hands of the King of England, and was actually whistling the melody he'd heard offstage as he approached, unaware of Ophelia's derangement. He stopped, of course, when Gertrude addressed him with the dismayed "Alas, look here, my lord," but was still puzzled by the situation until he greeted Ophelia with "How do you, pretty lady?," heard her hauntingly gnomic response, "They say the owl was a baker's daughter. Lord we know what we are, but know not what we may be," and grasped the grim truth that she'd been "divided from herself and her fair judgement" (could that have been the first description of schizophrenia?). It sounds like a small thing, that whistling and its abrupt cessation, but for me it summed up the concept of peripeteia, the reversal of circumstances, foreshadowing Ophelia's haunting "we know what we are." I wondered if that was devised by Block, or improvised by Woodward during rehearsal and wisely retained by Block.

In the graveyard scene, Hamlet took Yorick's detached jawbone and, holding it in place against the rest of the skull, wryly used that death's-head as a ventriloquist's dummy, moving the jaw up and down so that Death himself seemed to be delivering the ironic reflection on mortality and the meaninglessness of existence in which "Imperious Caesar, dead and turned to clay, / Might stop a hole to keep the wind away." Talk about metaphorical action! And it prepared the audience for an awesome finale.

As the play ended and the audience rose and began to cheer and applaud wildly, suddenly trumpet, trombones, fiddles, and drums struck up a tune that was ominously stirring, rousingly defiant, and through the discovery space appeared the entire troupe, carrying staffs topped with death's-heads and dancing a jig. It was like *Riverdance* crossed with the sinister dance of the Capulets in Prokofiev's ballet *Romeo and Juliet*. And a jig it was, in the Elizabethan meaning of the term, an end piece, a revival of, and variation on, that bygone custom of offering bawdy song-and-dance farces after the plays were finished. Frequently, these were commentaries on political, religious, or personal matters; the *Hamlet* jig, though, was a danse macabre, an electrifying dance of death by the characters returning from the grave, a sardonic reflection on the tragedy itself. It was not a curtain call—that would come later. After a few moments the characters made way for a dancer/jester wearing a voluminous gray robe and a death's-head mask, capering with mocking glee for the benefit of the audience. Then from beneath its robe emerged a smaller dancer, dressed in tights and death's-head mask, prancing and gamboling with grim humor, then, at the jig's conclusion, wiggling his/her ass obscenely at the audience while following the troupe offstage. Far from being a mere "end piece," the jig, resounding as it did to key motifs, had reinforced the pity and terror of the play. I had a hunch that the concept for the jig had been inspired by Michael Neill's chapter "Tragedy and Macabre Art" in his superlative book *Issues of Death: Mortality and Identity in English Renaissance Tragedy,* which Emma Smith had praised during our classes at Worcester College and which I'd bought upon returning home. The *Hamlet* jig prompted me to recall one of Neill's surmises in particular: he suggests that when Fortinbras orders a soldier's music to be played for the dead Hamlet, it is likely an echo of a passage in an Elizabethan prayer book talking of drums that call soldiers to doomsday. The brass and drums in the jig that day, following instantly the funeral procession ordered by Fortinbras, did have a martial ring.

Five years earlier, in a Broadway theatre, the spirited and ingenious production of *Hamlet* starring Ralph Fiennes had galvanized me into a life-changing exploration of the planet Shakespeare. But the staging I'd just witnessed in an Elizabethan playhouse, Shakespeare's Globe rebuilt, struck me as even more resourceful, dynamic, and profound. Emerging from the theatre, I felt maniacally exhilarated, and could scarcely restrain myself from shouting, "I have seen the past, and it works!"

On the return flight to Newark, I read with fascination *The Byrom Collection and the Globe Theatre Mystery,* by Joy Hancox, which I'd bought at the Globe gift shop after the performance of *Hamlet.* The book deals with Ms. Hancox's discovery of 516 drawings in the original manuscripts of John Byrom's private journal, an edited version of which had been published in the 1850s. Byrom was an eighteenth-century scientist and mathematician whose interests, like those of his contemporary Newton and of John Dee, combined the occult and the scientific: he was a freemason and a Cabalist and had formed his own Cabala Club in London. (The Cabala was a mystical movement in Judaism that flourished throughout Jewish communities of Europe during the Middle Ages; Cabalists sought hidden meanings in every word and letter of the Hebrew Bible.)

Among the drawings in the Byrom papers are those that have been identified as the setting-out plans for the original Globe and the Rose. According to Ms. Hancox, the concept behind these designs, which she terms "sacred geometry," is shared with the Temple of Solomon, the round churches of the Templars, the Church of the Holy Sepulchre in

Jerusalem, the mosques of Islam, and the open-air theatres of ancient Greece and Rome. In an appendix, Leon Crickmore, whose credentials are unspecified, describes the essential patterns underlying the sacred geometry in the collection's enormous variety of drawings, including those of the Globe: a square containing a circle, a square contained within a circle, a square and a circle of equal perimeters. "A circle," he goes on to explain, "is a symbol of eternity, the 'spiritual world'; in various mystical traditions it represents God or the Self. The square, on the other hand, symbolises the 'material' world. In a number of Renaissance drawings, a male figure is placed within the cosmos represented by a circle or a square, to show man as a 'microcosm' within the 'macrocosm' and at the same time a mirror of it. . . . Such geometry expresses the harmony which was traditionally perceived between human and cosmic proportions."

And that was the harmony I'd sensed at the Globe, that balance of the numinous and the earthly. And the communal sense, the feeling of belonging to a community bound together (religion—a binding together) by its participation in an age-old ceremony. Hadn't there been a religious note in the catharsis we'd undergone during the dance of death jig at the end of *Hamlet?* Couldn't all that clapping and shouting by the spectators while it was in progress be compared to the evangelical fervor inspired by gospel choirs? And at the conclusion hadn't I experienced a sense not of exhilaration but of exaltation, of transcendence? I recalled, as I had when I first glimpsed the Globe from the Thames, that Elizabethan drama was indebted in part to those medieval religious works, the Corpus Christi mystery plays, which celebrated the entire history of the world from the Creation and the Fall to the eventual Day of Doom, restating eternal truths and allowing the whole community to share in the rituals of a common faith.

Referring to the "profoundly human mixture of the high and low, sublime and trivial, tragic and comic" in Shakespeare's work, Erich Auerbach defines it as the conception of "a basic fabric of the world, perpetually weaving itself, renewing itself, and connected in all its parts." Tragic characters, he continues, "are all connected as players in a play written by the unknown and unfathomable Cosmic Poet; a play on which He is still at work, and the meaning and reality of which is an unknown to them as it is to us." And what was it that the Jesuit Jean-Pierre de Caussade had proposed in *Abandonment to Divine Providence:* "The darker the mystery, the more we are illumined by it."

Thirty thousand feet above the Atlantic, with cloud puffs, burnished by the sun, drifting in the vivid blue sky, the world indeed charged with the grandeur of God, an old man's fancy dwelled on the Globe as a temple, sacred geometry in a sacred space. The Globe, a minicosmos, a representation of the creation itself, wherein was enacted the Cosmic Poet's version of Holy Scripture, his retelling as sacred myths the stories from his sources, refashioning them as metaphorical dramas reflecting humanity's relationship with God.

Shakespeare. The Cabala. Sacred geometry. The Globe. Only Connect. And a few days after returning home I came upon a stunning passage in James Carroll's *Constantine's Sword,* a history of the Catholic Church's anti-Semitism over the centuries since its founding. Discussing Isaac Luria, the sixteenth-century prophet of Cabala, he writes, "In Luria's view, as Harold Bloom summarizes it in *Kabbala and Criticism,* creation itself is 'God's catharsis of Himself, a vast sublimation in which his terrible rigor might find some peace.' Luria posited a primordial catastrophe in which elements of the Divine Being were splintered into an infinity of broken pieces. . . . The purpose of creation, this splintering of God, was seen as nothing less than, in Neil Asher Silverman's words, 'Destroying the principle of evil within.' " Amazingly, this sounded practically identical to A. C. Bradley's definition of Shakespeare's presentation of evil in the tragedies as "something alien to the order of the world, which order, nevertheless, seems first to produce it, then to struggle with it, and finally, with great loss and waste to itself, to expel it." Unknowingly, Bradley had added a significant element connecting Shakespeare to the friend and mentor I'd created for him.

Shakespeare's Jew, now in my mind assuredly a Cabalist, had taught him well.

Epilogue

Late one stormy afternoon in July I poured my-
self a Scotch (no ice, splash of soda) and sat at the kitchen table, watching
the torrential rain cascade off the gutters, remembering those sudden
summer thunderstorms in Houston which would turn streets into rivers
within minutes, bringing the ferocious winds that were always "cool Gulf
breezes" in my father's estimation. And I thought of that day at the LLI
when we were discussing *Twelfth Night* and I had the class chant Feste's
rueful final song in unison, and how poignant it had sounded. "The rain
it raineth every day." As we recited each verse, the meaning was in-
escapable: long ago we'd put away our toys and come to man's estate.
We'd married, raised families, we'd pursued careers. And along the way
we'd come to terms with reality: the rain that raineth every day, sweeping away illusions, strengths, skills, friends and loved ones, youth (in an
earlier song, Feste had plaintively declared, "Youth's a stuff will not endure"), and, most recently for me, a home, my parents' house in Houston: 2331 Wordsworth. Named after the poet. The entire neighborhood
was a Westminster Abbey poets' corner, from its name, Windermere, the
Lake District in which Wordsworth lived, to the streets: Goldsmith, Dryden, Sheridan, Swift, Addison, and, yes, Shakespeare. The city planner
who laid out that area must have been an English major.

I'd sold it, on the recommendation of Hank Gavens, the Realtor
who'd been managing the property for me since my father's death in
1982. The tenants, the nurse and her two children, had decided to move.
Once they were gone, Hank told me, considerable repairs and repainting
would be in order, new appliances would be needed, pest infestation
would have to be eliminated. Time to take advantage of a seller's market,
Hank advised. Decent and dependable, cheerful and conscientious, he'd
done well by me for almost twenty years and I trusted his judgment. The
deal was done and I signed the papers the week I got back from London.

Almost immediately I felt desolate, as if only now had the impact of my parents' death truly hit me. No longer could I think of the house as theirs; that no matter who the tenants were, the essence of my parents still inhabited the place. I remembered a similar feeling of loss that swarmed me the day I was clearing out the house right after my father died, preparatory to putting it up for rent, and discovered that he had kept my mother's clothes in a closet all those years since her death. "Miss Rubye" he had called her in the southern fashion, through the good times and the bad, and in my mind there was nothing ghoulish in his wanting to preserve the reminders of her elegance and beauty and, I supposed, to soften somehow the memory of the terrible mental anguish he'd watched her endure.

And no longer the owner of a piece of Texas real estate, I had the sensation of being cut adrift. The house on Wordsworth may not have been a House of Mirth but neither was it the House of Usher. It was there that I'd watched my father tend luxuriant rosebushes and grow lemons as big as a baby's head. It was there that he taught me how to box, and where at dusk on summer evenings we'd toss around a softball, the sound of crickets accompanying the whack of the ball as it struck our leather mitts. It was there that I practiced the accordion every afternoon, my mother calling in an occasional request from the kitchen where she was drinking her tenth cup of coffee and smoking her fiftieth cigarette of the day— "Play 'More Than You Know,' baby, it's my favorite," every song she asked for being her favorite. It was there where I played six-man tackle football in the backyard with my buddies, afterward slaking our thirst from the garden hose, spraying each other with water and then lolling on the thick Saint Augustine grass, yakking about the girls we were dating and the girls we yearned to date, the girls who were putting out and the girls who were holding out, fretting about the clusters of acne that never seemed to disappear, even after drinking quantities of loathsome Fleischmann's yeast mashed up into tomato juice. It was there one miraculous afternoon that I discovered that the key to the ignition of my parents' '38 red Chevrolet fit the ignition to the '38 black Chevrolet of my best friend, Ed Lasof, but that his key didn't fit ours, and delighted in the look of horror on his face when he realized that for months to come, wherever he parked his car while out on a date, more than likely it would have been moved elsewhere by the time he and his girl returned from the movies or from dinner at Bill Williams's Chicken Shack.

One of the reasons I'd never felt the pull of my native soil, the urge to return to my roots, was that by owning a home in Houston I still in a way belonged there. But now, after forty years in the East, almost thirty-five of them in the same house in Montclair, with a wife and two grown children, in a community filled with friends, somewhere deep inside I would, for a time, consider myself alone and afraid in a world I never made.

I'd asked Hank to send me as a memento the mezuzah I'd seen nailed to the door the last time I visited the house, and within days it arrived. Hank had removed as much of the paint from the brass as he could, but traces remained in some of the crevices. It was a small box, 3″x1″, but as I held it in the palm of my hand it seemed to possess the magical power of an amulet. Inside the box was a small scroll containing the first and second paragraphs of the Shema prayer, the closest thing to Judaism's credo: *Sh'ma Yisra'el, Adonai Eloheinu, Adonai Ekhad*—Hear, O Israel, the Lord is Our God, the Lord is One (Deuteronomy 6:4)—followed by three additional paragraphs, including "You shall love the Lord your God with all your heart, with all your soul, and with all your might."

Squeezing the mezuzah tightly, I summoned up the memory of a steamy Saturday afternoon in the summer of 1944. I'd returned home from the movies and went to the kitchen for an RC cola. In the backyard my father was cultivating his garden and a short, squat, frog-faced black yardman named Thomas was mowing the lawn. Thomas happened to be one of my father's clients, paying his fee in trade. Some weeks earlier, Thomas had come to blows in a restaurant with a bully who had made derogatory remarks about his looks and beat the fellow, as the saying goes, within an inch of his life. The police were called, Thomas was charged with assault and battery, and with my father as his attorney was given three months' probation without a fine. So there he was that Saturday, working off my father's fee. My father used the barter system with any client, black or white, low in funds, one of the reasons we ourselves were often financially strapped. My mother was off visiting one of her sisters. She always tried to be out of the house when Thomas was around. Like the bully, she found something disturbing about his appearance. "That little schvatza scares me," was the way she put it. "Schvatza" was Texas Yiddish for "schwartzer," black. In my mother's eyes, blacks were either lovable or menacing. She was, after all, Miss Rubye, at heart a Jewish southern belle. Yet she was also the Miss Rubye who, as a juror during the trial of a young baby-faced black man accused of robbery, was the lone holdout against conviction because notwithstanding the testimony of eyewitnesses, she saw in him a quality of childlike innocence.

One Jew never heard to say "schvatza" was Abe Gollob, champion of the underdog, the underprivileged. To him, it was at best patronizing, at worst bigoted. How Jews could be prejudiced against blacks amazed and appalled him. Jews, of all people, should know better. Jews, who had been slaves in the land of Egypt. Jews, victims of discrimination for centuries. And my father would never allow the word "nigger" to be uttered in his presence. When I was about nine or ten, we were listening to Amos and Andy on the radio—yes, my father thought their ethnic humor funny and endearing, no more racist than the Goldbergs were anti-Semitic and *Life with Luigi* anti-Italian—and during a commercial I said something like, "The Kingfish is a funny nigger." My father quietly rose from his chair, went upstairs, and came down with a white sheet. "Here, son, cut some holes in this and go join the other white trash and find yourselves a nigger to lynch. Because that's what you're doing when you say 'nigger.' You're lynching a Negro with your mouth." That, as my father would say, got the job done. From that moment, "nigger" was gone from my lexicon.

My father was not a "civil rights activist." He didn't join organizations and protests and marches. He was content to lead his life decently and honorably, and in his own personal and professional life treat people with kindness and respect, and to see that every person got a fair shake from the law. Bad laws would change with time. Meanwhile, if you were a Jew or a Negro, you had to work harder, study harder, make something out of yourself. You'd be noticed, and your example would help bring better days to come. Look at Paul Robeson, Marian Anderson, George Washington Carver. Look at Justices Brandeis and Frankfurter, Hank Greenberg, and Paul Muni. Politically, he was a devout Roosevelt Democrat who once lost a valuable client whom he denounced for joining the

Dixiecrats, the ultra-right-wing race-mongering splinter group that broke off from the Democratic Party in the election of 1948. My father believed the Democrats were champions of the downtrodden, the tired and the poor, the huddled masses yearning to be free; Republicans, on the other hand, were plutocratic anti-Semitic immigrant-hating Sons and Daughters of the American Revolution, to whom nothing alien was human. When Martin Luther King appeared on the scene, my father said, "They're going to kill him. Sooner or later. But he's the one who'll shame us all into becoming human beings. He's right. His people have waited too goddamned long. He's not just a preacher man. He's not some kind of Holy Roller. He's a goddamned prophet. And they'll kill him."

That Saturday afternoon in 1944, my father and Thomas took a short break and came into the kitchen for a glass of iced tea. My mother had left a pitcher in the refrigerator. Entering the room, Thomas happened to spot the mezuzah on the doorpost. "What is that, Mr. Abe?"

"Well, Thomas, that happens to be a Jewish prayer box. It reminds Jewish people of the one God Who created us, and of how important it is to love Him."

"But Jewish folks don't think Jesus is God's son, do they, Mr. Abe? Why is that?"

"Listen here, Thomas, all I'm going to say about Jesus is this. He was a fine young Jewish man who worshiped the one God of the Jews. And he believed that the way you showed you loved God was to do the right thing. To see that justice is done. That no one mistreats orphans and widow women. Now let's go on outside and get the job done."

I put the mezuzah away in a drawer in a dining room cabinet. I thought about attaching it to a doorpost in my home, but decided that I'd give it to whichever of my children was the first to buy a house. I didn't think it belonged in an apartment. It should have a more permanent domicile.

Now, sitting at the kitchen table, sipping at the remains of the Scotch, I regarded the once grand but now declining magnolia tree in the backyard. It had been the glory of the premises until assaulted three years previously by ravenging wood borers. Each succeeding spring branches withered and died, and desperately I tried to keep it alive, pounding into

337

the ground at its perimeter dozens of fertilizer stakes manufactured in, of all places, Waco, my birthplace, thus lending this nourishment a mystical dimension. And indeed, the remaining branches seemed slightly revitalized, their leaves larger and thicker.

But suddenly I thought I saw Feste walk across the yard and lean against the tree. Oblivious of the downpour, he smiled waggishly, pointed to the dead branches that had yet to be removed, and began to sing the last line of an earlier song from the play: "Youth's a stuff will not endure." Feste, you smart-ass little joker, you got the point, didn't you? I identified with that tree. And hey, thanks a bunch for reminding me that in a few days I'd turn seventy. None of the previous on-to-the-next-decade watershed birthdays had provoked so much as a faint shiver at the voraciousness of coromorant, devouring Time, but the prospect of this one had a certain eschatological zing. Would the curtain be rising on the last act of the comedy drama known as *My Life,* in which I've played many parts, the final role, or so it would seem to be, lay teacher of Shakespeare to the Elderhostel set? That was fine by me.

Just the other day I'd driven out to Caldwell College to talk with Roxanne about my plans for the coming LLI year. Earlier, on the phone, she'd told me that I couldn't count on an adjunct professorship. The student overflows in the courses of my choice seemed unlikely to materialize. Which was just as well; at least I'd be spared the challenge of grading papers or confronting undergraduates impatient to get to the mall. Roxanne had suggested that if I aspired perhaps to make myself a more valuable academic commodity, I might want to enroll in the graduate program at Caldwell College and get an M.A. in liberal studies, which is precisely what she was doing. She'd been public relations director for Bloomingdale's at Short Hills and regional director of Lord & Taylor, and was currently academic adviser to adult undergraduates at Caldwell College and to the LLI, yet she talked about her master's studies as if she'd found her true faith. She was perfectly attuned to the needs and yearnings of grown-ups in whom intellectual curiosity continued to exert its potent spell.

In Roxanne's office, I'd told her that as I'd once mentioned, I planned to teach the sonnets for the fall semester, and after that perhaps a seminar devoted to one play, in the manner of Robert Gutman's at the Shakespeare Society, with one difference—I'd use video excerpts of crucial scenes and soliloquies. That seemed just swell to her. As I was leaving, she'd again brought up the subject of studying for an M.A., her large expressive eyes glistening as she cited with near-mystical rapture the courses she was taking.

Meditating in my kitchen and sipping Scotch, I suddenly found the prospect of graduate studies glimmering with possibilities. Why shouldn't I, why couldn't I, enlarge my field of vision before the screen went blank? Get that goddamned M.A., write a thesis developing that theory of Shakespeare the Midrashist, inspired by the Jewish Cabalist, shove my way at the very least into an adjunct professorship without giving up my courses at the LLI, teach those callow unmotivated collegians, strike terror in their self-absorbed little hearts, as I'd once done when for six weeks at Kelly Air Force Base, San Antonio, I was a basic training officer for air force reservists who'd never been through the process, whip them into intellectual shape, instill them with respect for literature and pride in their cultural heritage?

Up I rose from the kitchen table and went outside. The apparition under the tree had vanished, but the storm continued unabated, and so did my elation. I stood in the middle of the yard, an old man made mad by a love of Shakespeare, a merry old King Lear in an upbeat happy-ending version, a la Nahum Tate's 1681 adaptation in which Cordelia actually survived. Drenched, I turned my face to the sky and felt like shouting out, "Blow, winds, and crack your cheeks," but not defiantly, not invoking nature to strike flat the thick rotundity o' the world. Rather, exultantly. I could feel bursting inside me, still there with a vengeance, the feeling that I'd come to count on all these years, that heightened sensitivity to the promise of life. And a whole bunch of chutzpah.

Yes! Herr Professor Doktor Gollob it would be. And at the LLI, why not teach the sonnets and the seminar during the same semester? What else did I have to do? And the next semester add a course based on the Folgerian methods, concentrating on Shakespeare in performance, using Shakespeare Set Free as texts, with my own adjustments and adaptations? And while at it, why couldn't I create Folgeresque lesson plans of my own for plays not in the Set Free series? I'd build a Shakespearean empire at the LLI, a full-scale Shakespeare Program, all the while enchanting the undergrads.

Some noble work of note was yet to be done. Bring on the seventies. You're dead wrong, Mr. Yeats, an aged man is not a paltry thing. The best is yet to be.

Acknowledgments

For their advice and encouragement, I thank two old friends and former associates at Doubleday: Bill Thomas, editor in chief, and Stephen Rubin, president.

I benefited also from the savvy and support of Toby Stein, Christian Ely, Tom Mescal, Mark and Aileen Grossberg, Marcia Dubrow, David Rosenberg, Richard and Joan Weller, William Colville, Clayton and Patricia Selph, Richard and Susan Reiter, John Jakes, Jim Volz, Noah Gordon, Fred Kaplan, and Philip and Patricia McFarland.

I owe a tip of the hat to Jeffrey Horowitz, Cicely Berry, Michael Kahn, Nancy Becker, Richard Kuhta, Georgianna Ziegler, Janet Field-Pickering, Olympia Dukakis, David Suchet, Patrick Spottiswoode, and Anthony Branch for their hospitality and generosity during extended interviews.

My literary agent, David Gernert, another onetime colleague from publishing days, was the first to see possibilities in the idea for this book. I've profited immensely from his counsel, and I'm grateful for his camaraderie and his unfailing confidence in what I was attempting. I owe thanks also to his associates—Matt Williams, Amy Williams, and Erin Hosier—for their gracious ministrations on my behalf.

I'm indebted most of all to the exemplary Gerald Howard, whose editorial artistry, tough-minded humaneness, graceful erudition, and antic wit guided and sustained me throughout the writing of this book, and whose bold vision lighted the way to a more personal work than I'd intended. And a salute is in order to Gerry's assistant, Jay Crosby, for his dependability, unfailing courtesy, and good humor.

Permissions

HERMAN GOLLOB is a graduate of Texas A&M University. After serving in the U.S. Air Force in Korea, he worked as a literary agent for the MCA Artists Agency and the William Morris Agency before finding his calling as an editor with Little, Brown. He has been editor in chief of Atheneum, Harper's Magazine Press, the Literary Guild, and Doubleday, and a senior editor at Simon & Schuster. He lives in Montclair, New Jersey, with his wife, Barbara, and teaches Shakespeare at the Lifelong Learning Institute of Caldwell College.

ML   4/02